The IBM Century

IEEE

IEEE **computer society**

CSPress

Press Operating Committee

Chair

James W. Cortada
IBM Institute for Business Value

Members

Mark J. Christensen, Independent Consultant
Richard E. (Dick) Fairley, Founder and Principal Associate, Software Engineering Management Associates (SEMA)
Cecilia Metra, Associate Professor of Electronics, University of Bologna
Linda Shafer, former Director, Software Quality Institute, The University of Texas at Austin
Evan Butterfield, Director of Products and Services
Kate Guillemette, Product Development Editor, CS Press

IEEE Computer Society Products and Services

The world-renowned IEEE Computer Society publishes, promotes, and distributes a wide variety of authoritative computer science and engineering books, e-books, journals, magazines, conference proceedings, and professional education products. Visit the CS Store at www.computer.org/store to see the current catalog.

To submit questions about the books and e-books program, or to propose a new title, please e-mail books@computer.org or write to Books, IEEE Computer Society, 10662 Los Vaqueros Circle, Los Alamitos, CA 90720-1314. Telephone +1-714-816-2169.

Additional information regarding the IEEE Computer Society Press program can also be accessed from our web site at http://computer.org/cspress.

The IBM Century

Creating the IT Revolution

Edited by Jeffrey R. Yost

IEEE Φ computer society

Φ CSPress

Page design by Monette Velasco.

ISBN-10: 0-7695-4611-0
ISBN-13: 978-0-7695-4611-7
IEEE Computer Society Order Number: P4611

For the Friends of CBI

Contents

Acknowledgements

First and foremost, I would like to thank the authors of this volume, all of whom wrote fascinating memoirs about pivotal moments in IBM's history. In serving as Editor-in-Chief of *IEEE Annals of the History of Computing* over the past four years, I have been fortunate to interact with many important computer and software pioneers writing memoirs and remembrances, as well as many talented historians. While only William McGee's article was originally published during my tenure leading the *Annals*, I have had the distinct pleasure of meeting Watts Humphrey at a CBI conference, and chatting on the phone on several occasions with Jim Birkenstock. Sadly, Watts, Jim, and many other authors have passed on—their legacy lives on in their important memoirs. Robert V. Head and William McGee are still with us.

Shortly after conceiving the idea for this book project in early 2011, I ran it by two computer historian colleagues, Charles Babbage Institute (CBI) Director Tom Misa and IBM executive Jim Cortada (who is also Chair of the IEEE Computer Society Press committee). Both offered encouragement from the start and have provided extremely helpful suggestions. Two other CBI colleagues, Katie Charlet and Stephanie Crowe, also have provided very helpful assistance—with the proofing and photographs respectively. I am grateful to CBI and University Libraries for permission to use the images contained in the introductory essay and on the book's cover.

In addition to Tom Misa and Jim Cortada, a number of other computer historian colleagues have influenced my thinking on IBM and its history through comments on my conference papers, informal discussions, and their scholarship. These scholars include Janet Abbate, Atushi Akera, Bill Aspray, David Brock, Martin Campbell-Kelly, Nathan Ensmenger, Thomas Haigh, Christophe Lécuyer, Mike Mahoney, Eden Medina, Arthur Norberg, Emerson Pugh, Dag Spicer, and Steve Usselman. Industry veterans and computer history promoters Burt Grad and Luanne Johnson have also influenced my thinking on IBM—and have invited me to numerous, valuable history workshops they have organized at the Computer History Museum on software history (with many sessions related to IBM).

At the Computer Society, I would like to offer special thanks to Product Development Editor Kate Guillemette, and Director of Products and Services Evan Butterfield. Both received the project enthusiastically from the beginning. In particular, Kate saw it through each step along the way. While not directly involved with this book, I would also like to thank incoming Computer Society President David Grier and Editorial Business Operations Manager Robin Baldwin. David immediately preceded me as editor of the *Annals* and has always been gracious with his time and insights. Robin has been helpful at every turn, made my job as editor far easier, and been a great pleasure to work with on the *Annals*.

Last but not least, I would like thank IBM's Regional Manager for Corporate Citizenship Valerie Pace and IBM Corporate Archivist Paul Lasewicz. Valerie oversaw the first project I did specifically on IBM history—a project in which founding CBI Director Arthur Norberg and I researched and wrote a short book on the history of IBM Rochester. Paul, who has masterful knowledge of IBM's history and the corporation's extensive archival holdings he manages, has been extremely helpful on numerous research projects I have completed, including the IBM Rochester study and a book I wrote on the history of the US computer industry.

Introduction: IBM's 100 Years of Leadership in Information Technology

All corporations impact various stakeholders, but few truly change the world—broadly influence modes of operation, methods of production, frames of reference, forms of thought, patterns of consumption, levels of understanding, and the scope of future possibilities. Some of the most influential companies produced transformative technologies between the late 19th and early 20th centuries—such as the Ford Motor Company, Sears Roebuck, and Eastman Kodak. Ford not only changed production techniques (innovations in mass production), but also working class wage structures (turning workers into consumers), the way people traveled, their sense of geography, and social mores. The Sears catalog and associated mail order system revolutionized standard national retail pricing and methods of browsing and purchasing goods. Handheld Kodak cameras virtually created the field of amateur photography, altering conceptions of personal privacy and transforming the way we graphically recorded the present and remembered the past.[1]

While Ford, Sears, and Kodak clearly changed the world, International Business Machines' impact arguably has been even greater—it completely transformed how information is collected, stored, processed, and used. This feat is not limited to a particular domain such as retail, manufacturing, transportation, national defense, science, or medicine; instead it has deeply influenced all of these areas and many more. From calculating census data, processing and communicating critical air defense information, putting a man on the moon, and beating a chess grandmaster to advanced weather modeling, natural language processing, and understanding the workings of the human genome, International Business Machines' information technology unequivocally has changed the world.

International Business Machines (IBM) celebrates its 100th anniversary in 2011—a milestone many corporations, large and small, never reach. Hitting such a milestone is even less common in high-technology industries where the innovator's ideal of creative destruction often succumbs to engineers, managers, and executives who cling too long to the technologies, products, and proven revenue streams of the past. While this collection of memoirs looks to the past—detailing the history of IBM's people, businesses, and technologies—it has much that speaks to the present and future. Unlike some firms that coast to the century mark in a state of decline, IBM is continually hitting new peaks. IBM is currently the global leader in the $790 billion information technology (IT) services industry[2]—a field in which it has long had strong capabilities, but one that was hardly a business for the company a quarter century ago. In many diverse and profound ways, IBM continues to change our world.

As a growing chorus of business journalists and industry prognosticators write of the imminent death of the personal computer in an era of pervasive mobile devices—posing longer term threats to information technology giants producing PCs, such as Hewlett-Packard,[3] or still tethered to the PC by supplying its software and hardware, such as Microsoft and Intel—personal computers represent a business IBM entered, quickly led for a time (1980s), but exited more than a half-decade ago.[4] IBM's history is rich with creative destruction and transitioning to new businesses—from mechanical and electro-mechanical tabulators to mainframe digital computers, from midrange systems to powerful servers, from stand-alone computer systems to engineering embedded computing devices, and from a business focus on hardware to one on software and services. At the same time, there also are the remarkable legacies of elegant IBM technologies of the distant past. Among others, these include FOR-TRAN, a programming language still in use more than a half-century after IBM first developed it, and Information Management System (IMS), an IBM transaction processing database management tool used in manufacturing, banking, finance, and other industries. IMS contributes an estimated $1 billion in annual revenue to the firm more than four decades after its original creation.[5]

This collection of memoirs begins by exploring the businesses, technologies, and processes of IBM in the pre-computer punch card tabulator era, before concentrating on the golden age of mainframe computers. It provides many insights into the engineering, management, sales, and service of IBM technologies. The volume's ten memoirs were written by IBM insiders who were witnesses to, and for the most part leaders of, the technologies and events they discuss.[6] In addition to FORTRAN and IMS, they write about early punch card tabulators, the Selective Sequence Electronic Calculator, the IBM Defense Calculator, IBM 650, IBM's SAGE AN/FSQ-7 systems, IBM 1401, IBM Stretch (arguably the first supercomputer), the IBM System/360 series, SABRE, and IBM's "unbundling" of software. The memoirs also richly convey the personalities and relationships that helped shape and define the firm and its culture.

Needless to say, these technologies and topics do not span the entire IBM century. While the memoirs in this volume address many of the most important people, technologies, and developments in the company's first seven decades, not every significant IBM machine, programming effort, or business over these decades is discussed. For instance, none of the memoirs examine IBM's typewriter business or its major advances in storage systems.

Accounts and memoirs of IBM's major developments of the past three decades—most notably the IBM PC, IBM's re-emergence as a powerhouse in supercomputing, and its major shift toward the software and services businesses—are also absent. These memoirs have yet to be written. We can only hope that senior engineers and managers centrally involved in these developments will compose and publish memoirs, that such reflection and writing is not a product of an earlier time with relatively smaller corporations, greater ties to place, more stable employment, and different work cultures. While book-length memoirs from chief executive officers continue to be published and can be informative and enjoyable to read, the carefully calculated and presented view from 30,000 feet will never replace the vivid recounting by the project leaders and engineers on the ground, and the benefits of having multiple perspectives on key developments.

The memoirs and accounts of IBM's history in this collection were all written by highly distinguished IBM technical and managerial leaders—John Backus, James Birkenstock, Bob Evans, Frank Hamilton, Robert Head, Watts Humphrey, Cuthbert Hurd, Walter Jones, William McGee, John McPherson, Robert Seeber, and George Trimble—and published originally in *IEEE Annals of the History of Computing*. They are quite simply a treasure.

Secondary Literature on IBM

A number of important books and articles have been published on IBM's history and its technical and business contexts. By far the best book on the US office machine industry from the late 19th century through the first half of the 20th century is James W. Cortada's *Before the Computer*.[7] The highest quality biographical treatment of punch card tabulator pioneer Herman Hollerith is Geoffrey Austrian's *Herman Hollerith*.[8] The leading survey on information processing technology of different types and eras is Martin Campbell-Kelly and William Aspray's *Computer*.[9] The top analysis of scientific computing history is Atsushi Akera's *Calculating a Natural World*.[10] The best general survey of IBM's history is Emerson Pugh's *Building IBM*, and the finest article-length treatment of IBM's early history in computing is Steven Usselman's "IBM and Its Imitators."[11] Surveys on the computer industry include Kenneth Flamm's *Creating the Computer* and Jeffrey R. Yost's *The Computer Industry*.[12] While all these secondary works are meaningful explorations of IBM's history, they lack the immediacy and interest that can only come from personal accounts of major developments in IBM's past. The remaining sections of this essay survey IBM's 100-year history, providing a thematic framework to understand the IBM century and to contextualize the chapters of this book. For additional resources, the annotated bibliography at the rear of this volume contains more than 170 secondary and primary sources on IBM history.

IBM's Origins

IBM originated from the technological ingenuity and entrepreneurial skill of Herman Hollerith, an inventor of punch card tabulation machines in the mid 1880s. Soon after developing the technology, Hollerith started a business that became the Tabulating Machine Company. Hollerith's success in supplying the machines to calculate the 1890 US Census, the largest information processing task of its day, provided the capital and track record that allowed him to sell his punch card tabulation machines for many other censuses, both in the US and overseas, as well as for applications across a number of industries.

In 1911 Hollerith sold the Tabulating Machine Company to businessman Charles Flint. Flint combined this company with two other firms he had recently acquired, the Computing Scale Company and the International Time Recording Company, to form the Computing-Tabulating-Recording Corporation (C-T-R). Hollerith stayed on as an advisor and member of the C-T-R board of directors for several years before resigning and retiring at the end of 1914.[13] Punch card tabulation machines and the punch cards they used became the dominant business, but C-T-R was also successful at designing and manufacturing a number of other technologies, from time recording equipment

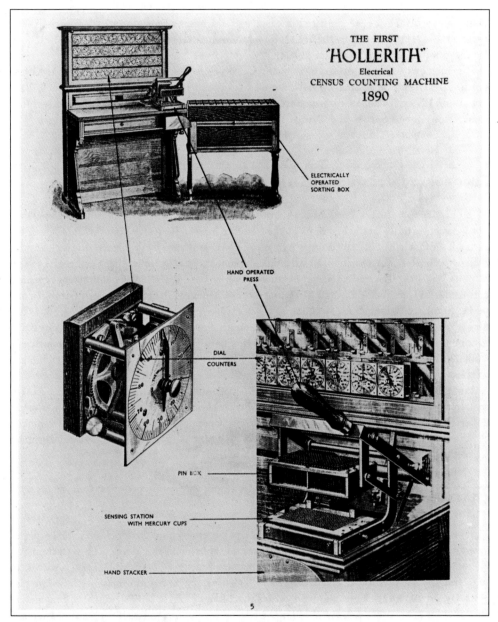

Herman Hollerith's Census Counting Machine, 1890 US Census
(courtesy of Charles Babbage Institute)

and automatic meat slicers to industrial scales. The formation of C-T-R justifiably is the recognized starting point of IBM.[14] The rapid growth of the punch card tabulation business, with its many applications for industry and government, coupled with the firm's growing international sales, led C-T-R's management to rename the company International Business Machines, or IBM, in 1924.

The success of C-T-R/IBM in the teens and twenties resulted from Hollerith's strong underlying technology and the talented leadership of Thomas J. Watson, Sr. Watson joined the firm in 1914 as the general manager and became president the following year. He came to C-T-R after a highly successful but turbulent time at National Cash Register (NCR), where he learned the art of sales from NCR's leader, John Patterson.[15] Watson, often portrayed as a strict, paternalistic figure who instituted the famed dress code, company songs, and IBM alcohol prohibition, was also remarkably adaptable to changing economic and industry conditions in fast-moving technical fields.

In the first decade of the 20th century, James Powers' tabulating machine enterprise was the primary competitor to Hollerith's firm in punch card tabulation equipment. In 1907 the US Bureau of the Census contracted with Powers to avoid what it saw as Hollerith's excessive pricing. In 1911 Powers established the Powers Accounting Machine Company, which competed against C-T-R. In 1927 Powers Accounting Machine merged with Remington Typewriter and Rand Kardex to form Remington Rand. Remington Rand was IBM's primary competitor in the punch card tabulation equipment field throughout the 1930s, 1940s, and 1950s.

To a lesser degree, IBM also competed against the other two major US office machine firms of the first half of the 20th century, companies that rounded out the big four: NCR and Burroughs. Remington Rand, Burroughs, and NCR were all hit particularly hard during the Depression years as corporate capital expenditures for office machines fell sharply and only gradually rebounded. Early Depression-era private sector declines in demand, however, contrasted sharply with public sector spending on such machines. With the Social Security Administration (launched with the Social Security Act in 1935) and other New Deal programs of President Franklin Delano Roosevelt, government spending on information processing technology rose significantly in the 1930s. IBM was the prime beneficiary of this government spending on punch card tabulation machines and the punch cards that held the data.

Watson daringly invested in expanding his firm during the Depression, while the three other office machine giants retrenched. In 1928 IBM had revenue of $19.7 million and net income of $5.3 million; both figures were the lowest among the big four. In 1939 IBM had revenue of $39.5 million and net income of $9.1 million.[16] IBM's net income that year was three times that of NCR and Burroughs and more than 5 times that of Remington Rand. By the mid to late 1930s IBM had over 87 percent market share for punch card tabulation machines.[17] In addition to its success with government contracts, IBM also leveraged its punch card tabulation lead by creating a standard 80-column card in 1928. Customer organizations invested in placing their data on such cards and faced substantial switching costs if they chose to move to a different type of card produced and sold by IBM's competitors. The cards not only tied customers to the hardware, but also were an important source of stable revenue for IBM. The IBM 80-column card became a standard in business, government, and science, as well as a cultural icon.[18]

IBM continued to thrive during World War II, and its punch card tabulation machine business was roughly ten times larger than its only serious competitor, Remington Rand. All four office machine giants would enter and become significant players in the computer industry during the 1950s.

Selling IBM Punch Card Tabulation Machines

In 1909 Walter Jones was a chief clerk with American Steel and Wire Company in Cleveland, Ohio, a constituent company of United States Steel Corporation. That year he had the opportunity to see the Tabulating Machine Company's (TMC) Hollerith machines in action at Carnegie Steel Company.

He quickly recognized the benefit these tabulators could have for his firm and ordered some through TMC salesman Phillip Merrill. A mere two years later Jones became a salesman for the Tabulating Machine division of C-T-R—joining the company two years prior to the arrival of Thomas J. Watson, Sr. In 1944 he wrote about his experiences and IBM's history over the previous 32 years, a fascinating memoir that is the first chapter of this volume. Jones presents what the company was like in the beginning, how he and other salesman went about "prospecting" for customers, and the company's commitment to providing excellent service. By 1915 he had become the top salesman for C-T-R. He discusses the education programs Thomas Watson, Sr., brought to the C-T-R sales force and the value of a well-trained technical sales staff to the success of the enterprise. Like many hardworking talented sales staff members, Jones moved through the ranks and became a manager. He ran C-T-R's Cleveland regional sales office by the early 1920s. By the late 1920s and early 1930s he was an IBM executive on assignment with IBM's European subsidiaries. His discussion of this activity provides a valuable look at the understudied European operations in the interwar years. Overall this rare gem of a memoir, which begins at the very start of IBM's century-long history, conveys the sales-orientation of the firm and the unique culture that Thomas Watson, Sr., created and fostered.

Applied Science Computing

Scientific computation was the basis for the origin of digital computers, as well as the key early market for the machines after World War II. IBM's dominance in business data processing in the second half of the 1950s and throughout the 1960s has sometimes obscured the true importance of IBM's scientific computing and its role in the firm's development of critical technical capabilities. A notable volume on the IBM Automatic Sequence Controlled Calculator, edited by famed historian of science I. Bernard Cohen (along with Gregory Welch and Robert Campbell), concentrates far more on the vision of physicist and computer pioneer Howard Aiken at Harvard University than on IBM's considerable role in funding, designing, and building this giant electromechanical scientific computer.[19]

Thomas Watson, Sr., was infuriated by the failure of Aiken to properly credit IBM engineers on the ASCC at the time of the dedication in 1944—an anger further fueled by the fact that Aiken succeeded in his effort to popularize the machine exclusively as the "Harvard Mark I." This parting of ways contributed to Watson's authorization to move forward with a large-scale electromechanical computer project all of its own, the Selective Sequence Electronic Calculator (SSEC).[20]

In this collection, Frank E. Hamilton, John C. McPherson, and Robert R. Seeber, Jr.'s, 1948 paper on the SSEC outlines the design objectives, specifications, and operations of this influential and powerful electromechanical scientific computer. Hamilton came to IBM in 1923 as a draftsman and participated in developing many punch card tabulator products prior to becoming one of the principal engineers (along with Clair Lake) in the design and construction of the ASCC/Harvard Mark I. Hamilton managed the development of the SSEC. McPherson, who joined IBM in 1930, helped establish a punch card tabulation operation at the Ballistic Research Laboratory at Aberdeen Proving Ground during World War II, was named IBM director of engineering in 1943, and became an IBM vice president in 1948. Seeber was hired by IBM in 1945 and was a senior member of Watson Scientific Computing Laboratory at Columbia University.

Given the conflict with Aiken and Harvard University, Watson looked to extend IBM's relationship with Columbia University astronomer Wallace Eckert to establish a major Columbia University/IBM partnership for a large-scale scientific computing laboratory that resulted in the formation of Watson Scientific Computing Laboratory in 1945. This relationship had begun 17 years earlier when

Thomas Watson, Sr., responded to Columbia University's head of Collegiate Educational Research Benjamin Wood's request for tabulation equipment for statistical calculations. In addition to supplying existing tabulation equipment, IBM developed a special tabulator in 1930 (delivered in 1931) specifically designed for rapid calculation—known as the "Ben Wood Machine" or "Ben Wood Calculator."[21] This is arguably the origin of IBM's involvement in scientific computing. The cooperative relationship between the company and university was extended when Columbia and IBM established the Thomas J. Watson Astronomical Computing Bureau in 1937, run by Wallace Eckert. Eckert, a key contributor to the design specifications for the SSEC, is a true scientific computing pioneer who has yet to receive proper attention from historians.[22]

**Wallace Eckert
(courtesy of Charles Babbage Institute)**

The SSEC was a leading scientific computation machine when it was dedicated in January 1948, standing out for its ability to perform arithmetic on and subsequently edit stored instructions.[23] It also became a highly visible symbol of the corporation, placed behind glass on the ground floor of its New York City headquarters. Pedestrians walking along Madison Avenue could see the dawning of the computer age.

From Capabilities to Computer Products

IBM was not the first firm to enter the electronic digital computer field—that distinction lies with the Eckert-Mauchly Computer Corporation in Philadelphia and Engineering Research Associates (ERA) in St. Paul, Minnesota.[24] Both of these companies were founded in 1946 and grew out of wartime computer and electrical engineering work. J. Presper Eckert and John Mauchly started their firm shortly after leading a project that resulted in the first meaningful electronic digital computer in the United States, the US Army-funded Electronic Numerical Integrator and Computer (ENIAC) at the University of Pennsylvania's Moore School of Electrical Engineering. ERA was formed by a group of former US Navy code breakers who convinced the Navy of the need for a digital computer to continue code breaking efforts. ERA developed a classified digital computer, Atlas, in the late 1940s and announced a modified unclassified version in 1951, the ERA 1101.

Remington Rand acquired both Eckert-Mauchly Computer Corporation and Engineering Research Associates during the first half of the 1950s. Remington Rand, which became Sperry Rand after a 1955 merger with Sperry Corporation, was the first to come out with a large-scale mainframe commercial computer, Universal Automatic Computer (UNIVAC). On the market in 1951, UNIVAC was marketed for both scientific and business computing. UNIVAC installations differed in cost based on configurations, and most of the several dozen systems sold went for between $1 million and $1.5 million. Following the first UNIVAC installation, at the US Census Bureau in 1951, through the end of 1953, most sales were to the Department of Defense or Atomic Energy Commission laboratories. In 1954 Remington Rand sold its first UNIVAC for business data processing to General Electric (GE).[25] The system was used for automating payroll, logistics, and other functions at GE's Appliance Park plant in Louisville, Kentucky. Sales to other large corporations occurred later that year, including to US Steel, Westinghouse, and Consolidated Edison.

Much has been made of IBM's late (relative to Remington Rand and a few other firms) entry into electronic digital computing with the IBM 701 in 1952 and IBM 650 in 1954. In terms of underlying organizational capabilities in electronics, punch card tabulation, sales and service network, and base of data processing customers, IBM was always far ahead of Remington Rand.[26] IBM had significantly more capital, and invested aggressively in electronics research in the late 1940s and beyond. By the early 1950s, Thomas J. Watson, Jr., was becoming the heir apparent to run the firm. In 1952 Thomas Watson, Jr., became president, but his father retained the title of Chief Executive Officer until he passed it to his son in 1956—Thomas Watson, Sr., died weeks later at the age of 82. Both Watsons were centrally involved in leading the firm in the first half of the 1950s. At the start of the 1950s Thomas Watson, Sr., was reluctant to enter the computer business. He saw little potential in the corporate market for these highly expensive machines compared to the electromechanical tabulating products that had been so successful for his firm for decades. Thomas Watson, Jr., was more open to the possibility of computers and strongly backed funds for electronics research but showed some initial reluctance and great caution in contemplating such an expensive new product line.

Several trusted senior managers, scientists, and engineers at IBM swayed the Watsons to authorize moving forward with the Defense Calculator/IBM 701 to enter the computer business. Of these individuals, none were more important than Cuthbert Hurd and James Birkenstock. In their articles in this volume, both discuss the underlying context for IBM's entry into the computer industry. Hurd's engrossing article is edited testimony from a US Department of Justice antitrust trial against IBM from 1979. It discusses his work history prior to joining IBM in March 1949, before recounting key IBM developments from his arrival through the late 1960s. Birkenstock's fascinating and lengthy memoir briefly addresses his boyhood years and education prior to concentrating on his time at IBM—from his first days at IBM sales training school in Endicott, New York, in 1935, through his work as a sales engineer, sales manager, and IBM vice president, to his retirement from the company in 1973. Birkenstock rose through the ranks quickly, interacted with Thomas Watson, Sr., frequently, and became one of the closest confidants and advisors of Thomas Watson, Jr. More personal than Hurd's article, Birkenstock's memoir provides a sense of what it was like to work for the Watsons and the underlying culture they established for the firm.

Hurd held a doctorate in mathematics and worked as an academic prior to joining Union Carbide and working at Oak Ridge National Laboratory in 1947. It was there he requested use of IBM's SSEC in New York and first developed close relationships with top leaders at IBM. In 1949 he left Union Carbide and Oak Ridge to become part of the management team of IBM and to launch its Applied Science Department.

Hurd's court testimony recounts the different perspectives in IBM's management circle on the project that became the IBM 701 and weighs the factors that led an open-minded but quite cautious Thomas Watson, Jr., to move forward with the project on which Hurd was the principal technical leader. In addition to relating the internal discussion, he provides a list of the 19 IBM 701 installations, including dates. In 1954 the company came out with the IBM 704, a machine with significant improvements upon the IBM 701, such as its more advanced architecture and use of core

Engineering Research Associates ERA 1101 (courtesy of Charles Babbage Institute)

memory rather than Williams tubes. The IBM 704 had more than 100 installations in the second half of the 1950s.

Birkenstock's memoir provides complementary insight into the Watsons' decision to enter into the computing field. Birkenstock was crucial to pushing Thomas Watson, Jr., for investment in research and development to support its move into computers. In the memoir, Birkenstock recounts the 1950 trip he and Hurd took to 22 government agencies and government contractors before coming to the conclusion that an IBM digital computer could meet 80 percent of all the government and contractor market requirements. At the end of that year he wrote to Thomas Watson, Jr., encouraging

James Birkenstock
(courtesy of Charles Babbage Institute)

him to authorize $3 million to start a computer department, and to build 20 electronic digital computers leased at $8,000/month. In 1951 Birkenstock and Hurd returned to the government agencies and contractors and secured 18 letters of intent on that basis. As Birkenstock explains, many at IBM thought the computing proposition would be dead when IBM managers determined early in the project they would have to raise the monthly rental rate by 50 to 100 percent. Birkenstock and Hurd succeeded in convincing most of the original 18 to sign on for the higher rates and found replacements for the customer organizations that cancelled. IBM almost certainly would have entered the computer industry without Hurd and Birkenstock, but it would have been later without them.

In addition to the inside perspective Birkenstock gives on IBM's entry into the computer industry, he also provides important discussion and commentary on many other significant IBM projects. These include the IBM 650 and IBM's role in becoming the principal computer contractor to deliver AN/FSQ-7 computer systems for the Semi-Automatic Ground Environment (SAGE) air defense system.[27] The IBM 650 represented the first successful attempt to build a digital computer system at a price point where it could capture significant corporate purchases/leases and usher in the business data processing market.[28] The SAGE contract was an enormous financial boon and technical opportunity that allowed IBM to greatly extend its computer system design and development capabilities. IBM delivered 52 of the AN/FSQ-7 systems, computers that were by far the largest ever built (each having more than 50,000 vacuum tubes, weighing over 250 tons, and covering roughly a half-acre of floor space).[29] The SAGE contract brought in more than 80 percent of IBM's computer system revenue in the mid 1950s—at a time when its traditional punch card tabulation machines were still by far the firm's primary product line.

Hurd's testimony provides another valuable perspective on IBM's SAGE computer project that began in 1953, including discussion of IBM's advances in manufacturing techniques for core memory and the SAGE project's technical contributions to subsequent IBM systems.[30] One further legacy of the SAGE project that Hurd mentions but does not discuss is the Semi-Automatic Business Research Environment (SABRE).[31]

SABRE was a partnership between American Airlines and IBM to develop a real-time airline reservation system. The project began right on the heels of SAGE AN/FSQ-7 production efforts in 1957, with the first experimental system going online four years later.[32] Unlike SAGE, where hardware-focused IBM showed no interest in the air defense system's programming contract (which went to RAND spin-off System Development Corporation, or SDC), IBM took on its first major programming services effort with SABRE.[33] IBM's involvement with SDC on SAGE probably had an influence on its willingness to undertake a real-time software application project in the commercial sector. SABRE was a fully operational system for American Airlines' bookings by the mid 1960s.[34] IBM contracted with other airlines and in 1968 came out with Programmed Airline Reservation System (PARS), a generalized system that worked on any of the System/360 series of computers.

Robert V. Head, who had worked for General Electric on the pioneering Bank of America Electronic Recording Machine Accounting (ERMA) system, joined IBM and the SABRE project in October 1959. By 1961 he was splitting time between the SABRE project and a spin-off system that IBM was trying to sell to Eastern Airlines. His colorful account in this volume is particularly valuable for highlighting the organizational and technical challenges with the largest and most complex commercial programming project in the late 1950s to mid 1960s. It details the uncertainties in the

IBM's George Brown at General Electric's IBM 701 installation (courtesy of Charles Babbage Institute)

new field of developing major software applications and the uneasiness this caused between IBM's sales staff, who were making many of the promises to American Airlines, and the technical staff who had to overcome unprecedented challenges to deliver.

The IBM 650, which was first delivered in 1954, was the computer that changed the industry and quickly solidified IBM's leadership position in it. IBM's management recognized that giant million dollar computers, like UNIVAC, would never capture significant volume in the business data processing market. While IBM was continuing to innovate and produce traditional punch card tabulation systems, the IBM 650 was a bold attempt to create a type of system it could offer at a lease rate that would eventually cannibalize its pre-digital computer data processing products. Unlike its competitors, IBM's leaders, in moving forward with the 650, adopted a product plan more akin to Ransom Olds' "Curved Dash" (an inexpensive basic car on the market in 1901—several years after the start of the industry— that was the first auto to be mass produced on an assembly line and to sell in the thousands of units) or Ford's Model T (on the market in 1908, the first automobile to broadly capture the mass market). While Packard, Peerless, and other early automakers built far more luxurious and expensive cars, Olds, and later Ford, captured major market share.

Digital computers, unlike cars, would not become common products for individual consumers for more than two decades, with the advent of the personal computer segment of the industry.[35]

IBM 650 (courtesy of Charles Babbage Institute)

Nevertheless, mass production entered computing with the IBM 650, which soon had more than 2,000 installations, and the IBM 1401, a system released in 1960 that had over 12,000 installations.[36] The IBM 1401 could be leased for a mere $2,500/month and allowed many smaller corporations to enter the computer era. This system further solidified IBM's leadership in computing. Hurd relates how some skeptical IBM engineers and managers argued that systems renting for more than $1,000/month could never capture much market share for business data processing—an idea proven wrong by the IBM 650 installations and shot down completely with the great success of the IBM 1401.

While Hurd gives an important high-level overview of the IBM 650 and its key features, George R. Trimble's article in this volume provides a rich discussion of its technical details. As head of the Applied Science Department, Hurd assigned two talented engineers and programmers, George Trimble and Elmer Kubie, to the project. These two were the first members of IBM's Mathematical Planning Group within the Applied Science Department at IBM's Endicott facility. In addition to outlining the hardware innovations, much of Trimble's article focuses on the programming of the IBM 650 and on how ease of programming was a critical element of the system's design.[37]

The IBM 650 established IBM's lead in the business computing market because of its low cost, ease of programming, and the firm's dominant existing base of pre-computing data processing customers.[38] IBM's unrivaled sales engineers were particularly skillful at account control—migrating existing tabulating machine customers to the IBM 650 and subsequent systems.

IBM's remarkable success in (and in many respects creation of) the business market for digital computing has sometimes obscured the fact that the IBM 650 grew out of pioneering work in the Applied Science Department and was deeply meaningful to and appreciated by scientists. Few universities could afford a UNIVAC or other million dollar systems. The IBM 650 was the first computer for many colleges and universities and the first computer used by many scientists and engineers in the 1950s. Famous computer scientist Donald Knuth was a 19-year-old student worker in the 1956–1957 academic year at Case Institute of Technology when he was introduced to computing with the IBM 650. He quickly proceeded to write his first computer program for the machine. Knuth later wrote a reminiscence of his early experience with the IBM 650 for the *Annals of the History of Comput-*

IBM 1401 (courtesy of Charles Babbage Institute)

ing—adding, in a side note to Cuthbert Hurd, that tears ran from his eyes as he wrote the following conclusion:

> ...it is impossible for me to write about this machine without writing about myself. We were very close....The 650 provided me with a solid foundation in the art of programming. It was directly related to the topics of my first two technical articles...Therefore it's not at all surprising I decided in 1967 to dedicate my books on computer programming, '....to the Type 650 computer once installed at Case Institute of Technology, in remembrance of many pleasant evenings.'[39]

FORTRAN

Programming the earliest digital computers was a particularly arduous task. With the ENIAC and other mainframes in the mid to late 1940s, this was accomplished through plug-board programming—painstakingly plugging many dozens of patch cords into control panels in a carefully planned configuration.[40]

Mathematician John von Neumann, who served as a consultant on the ENIAC project in its latter stages, outlined the logical design for a stored program computer in 1945 in a soon to be famous document, *First Draft of a Report on the EDVAC*.[41] This logical design became known as the Von Neumann architecture.[42] The Von Neumann architecture—consisting of a central processing unit (CPU) and single storage memory structure holding both instructions and data—quickly became standard. Stored program computers, first developed in the late 1940s and common by the early to mid 1950s, opened the door for developing translators between machine language and other notation. In the early 1950s Grace Murray Hopper pioneered this technology for Eckert-Mauchly Computer Corporation and, later, Remington Rand with the A-0 and A-2 compilers. Similar types of efforts to build early programming tools were made at Los Alamos Scientific Laboratory and several other organizations.[43] Though Hopper's and other early programming tool efforts were major accomplishments, "lower-level" languages (like A-2) had little abstraction from machine code and were difficult for non-experts to use.

From IBM's decision to produce the IBM 701 and onward, making programming easier for itself and its customers was a fundamental goal and major concern. The cost of programming early digital computers was immense given the amount of time and expertise needed to develop programs, debug/fix problems with programs, and other maintenance. Such costs limited the adoption of early computer systems. The IBM 701 was a digital computer targeted exclusively for the existing scientific market of the early 1950s—primarily government laboratories and major defense contractors. Its successor, the IBM 704, was primarily aimed at this same market.

Mathematician John Backus, who joined IBM in September 1950, began working on astronomical calculating programs for the SSEC before turning his attention to developing a high-level language for the IBM 701, called the Speedcoding System, for calculating with floating point numbers.[44] The Speedcoding System, completed in 1953, increased processing time marginally but decreased programming and testing time substantially and could thus speed up the overall time to calculate mathematical problems. In January 1954 Backus published an article announcing Speedcoding in the very first issue of *Communications of the ACM*.[45]

At the end of 1953, Backus proposed a plan to his supervisor, Cuthbert Hurd, for a higher-level algebraic programming language for the IBM 704. Hurd quickly approved the plan for the IBM Mathematical FORmula TRANslating System, or the FORTRAN compiler. Backus led a team that included Irving Ziller, Harlan Herrick, and, on loan from United Aircraft, Roy Nutt.[46] By late 1954, they had set the general features and visited several customers outlining their work, which was received favorably. Between 1955 and early 1957 the FORTRAN team, which had grown to over a dozen, completed and tested the program under Backus's direction.[47] In early 1957 Backus and his team presented a paper on FORTRAN at the Western Joint Computer Conference.[48] By April IBM first began to ship free copies of FORTRAN to IBM 704 customers on reels of magnetic tape. The popularity of the language rapidly grew and it became the dominant programming language for scientific computing.

In this collection, Backus provides a history of FORTRAN, FORTRAN II, and FORTRAN III. He sets the stage by outlining the context of prevailing attitudes toward automatic programming and describes some of the available coding tools in the first years of the 1950s. Backus highlights the economic motivation for higher-level programming languages, describing how the combined salaries of programmers at computer centers could often equal or even exceed the rental cost of IBM digital computer systems. He discusses how the goals of the original FORTRAN project were to develop a language that would make it possible for engineers and scientists to write their own programs on the IBM 704 and to reduce the bookkeeping and repetitive planning involved with hand-coding—saving time and money. Backus's article yields insight into this pioneering group's work on each of the sections of the original compiler, some that were planned and others that arose from the evolving project. He describes how team members would often get a few hours of sleep at a nearby hotel during the day so they could work on debugging uninterrupted all night on the IBM 704 in the company's headquarter annex on 57th Street in Manhattan.

Following his longer history of FORTRAN, and much shorter histories of FORTRAN II and FORTRAN III, he discusses his "generally…not popular" opinion on the downside of "increasingly complex elaborations" dictated by von Neumann architecture, writing:

> These 'von Neumann languages' create enormous unnecessary roadblocks in thinking about programs and in creating the higher-level combining forms required in a powerful programming methodology. The von Neumann languages constantly keep our noses pressed in the dirt of address computation and the separate computation of single words, whereas we should be focusing on the form and content of the overall result of what we are trying to produce.[49]

Backus viewed the enormous size of more recent languages as proof of the constraints dictated by programming on von Neumann architecture computers. In 1977 Backus won the Association for Computing Machinery's A.M. Turing Award for his achievement with FORTRAN and other contributions to the broader field of programming languages. Backus had contributed to international efforts in the late 1950s to create ALGOL 58 and ALGOL 60 and developed the influential Backus-Naur Form (BNF) of notation for context-free grammars to describe syntax of programming languages.[50] His relatively technical Turing Award paper, "Can Programming Be Liberated From the von Neumann Style? A Functional Style and Its Algebra of Programs,"[51] has educated many on concepts of functional programming. Meanwhile, FORTRAN is still commonly used in some areas of science such as computational chemistry and physics, and is often the favored language in supercomputing.

FORTRAN was an important tool IBM provided to its customers that helped advance scientific computing and the adoption of the IBM 704 and many later systems. By 1961 IBM had created versions of FORTRAN for the IBM 709, IBM 650, IBM 1620, and IBM Stretch. Many of IBM's competitors also created versions of FORTRAN. Beyond this, Backus and IBM demonstrated the value of higher-level programming languages, spawning the development of many other languages and having a deep impact on the emerging discipline of computer science.

In addition to programming tools that IBM provided free to customers, such as the FORTRAN programming language, customer organizations in the mid 1950s also banded together to address programming challenges. One important development in early digital computer history was the emergence of user groups—volunteer organizations to help one another with programming efforts by sharing experiences, techniques, expertise, and even libraries of code. The first such user group was formed in Los Angeles in 1955 by IBM 701 users—all initial members were aerospace and defense contractors. IBM leaders recognized the substantial benefits of Share, as it communicated critical market information on customer wants and needs back to IBM. User groups also formed among Remington Rand/Sperry Rand users and IBM's other competitors in the computer industry. With the advent of the IBM 650, IBM 1401, and subsequent systems that sold in high volume, IBM customers came from many different industries and geographies, and Share grew rapidly in membership.[52]

Stretch, SPREAD, and System/360

Despite IBM's position at the forefront of the computer industry by the mid 1950s, Remington Rand/ Sperry Rand's UNIVAC had captured public imagination. In 1952 UNIVAC was used to predict the outcome of the presidential election on national television. By being the first large-scale computer on the market, and with high-profile applications like the US Census and 1952 election forecasting, UNIVAC had become a term synonymous with computers for Americans.[53]

At the start of 1955, when the University of California's Radiation Laboratory in Livermore, California issued a request for proposals for a "superspeed computer," IBM leaders saw this as the perfect follow-on to the SAGE contract. Cuthbert Hurd was in charge of seeking the contract for the Livermore Automatic Research Computer (LARC), while the physicist who had led the US project to build a hydrogen bomb, Edward Teller, was the chief negotiator for the laboratory. Teller wanted to complete contracting by May and secure delivery of the computer rapidly—less than three years—at a cost of around $2.5 million.[54]

There was division about how to approach the contracting between Thomas Watson, Jr., and Hurd on one side and the leader of the computer group at IBM Poughkeepsie, Ralph Palmer, and IBM director of engineering Wallace McDowell on the other. Watson and Hurd favored getting the contract by offering the laboratory just what it wanted: the fastest computer based on existing component technology. Palmer and McDowell wanted to make it IBM's first solid-state computer, built using transistors, a technology that had been invented by scientists at Bell Laboratories in 1947. Transistors were incorporated into a few one-of-a-kind computers in the first half of the 1950s, but had yet to become common components for digital computers. In the end, IBM created a compromise proposal, putting in a bid to deliver a tube-based system in 42 months, but encouraging renegotiations for a more powerful solid-state machine.[55] Remington Rand put in a bid offering 29-month delivery and won the contract.[56]

Losing the LARC negotiations to Remington Rand was a major blow to Thomas Watson, Jr. Coupled with the public's identification of computers with UNIVAC, he was all the more determined to get the next pioneering scientific computer contract. This opportunity arose later that year when IBM proposed a 42-month multi-million dollar project to build the fastest computer in the world for Los Alamos Scientific Laboratory. The goal of IBM's leaders was a system that would "stretch" all areas of computing technology—the project was aptly called Project Stretch.[57] The risk was that Los Alamos would seek just another version of LARC. Because of the unparalleled computational speed and value IBM offered, it received the contract, built Stretch, and delivered it to Los Alamos Scientific Laboratory in April 1961 (at a sales price far less than development cost). IBM hoped to recover its costs by selling multiple units of Stretch systems in the coming years as the IBM 7030.

Stretch was the fastest computer in the world, 200 times faster than the IBM 701 and significantly faster than LARC.[58] However, it was delivered behind schedule and its performance met only about half what was originally proposed. This angered Thomas Watson, Jr., and he felt obligated to lower the price from $13.5 million to $7.8 million based on the lower performance. IBM produced the other eight IBM 7030 systems that were promised to customers, losing money on each one. Thomas Watson, Jr., particularly upset for not being fully informed of shortcomings in performance along the way, took years before he forgave Steve Dunwell, Project Stretch's leader, and recognized him for his significant accomplishments with what was easily the fastest computer in the world, and justifiably considered to be the world's first supercomputer.[59] The true importance of Stretch was the technical capabilities IBM built on the project. These would benefit the corporation enormously in the systems it built later in the 1960s, particularly on the IBM System/360 series of computers. The technical ad-

IBM Stretch (courtesy of Charles Babbage Institute)

vances of Stretch included multiprogramming, memory protect, generalized interrupt, interleaving of memories, and standard input-output interfaces.[60]

IBM had a far more serious problem in the early 1960s than the perception problem that wore on Thomas Watson, Jr. The company had developed many different computers that were not compatible. Customers spent large sums of money renting these systems and expected backward compatibility with upgrades to new systems. Programming applications to use early digital computers was extremely time-consuming and expensive. Some customers did applications programming internally; many others turned to the newly emerged programming services segment of the computer services industry to contract out programming jobs. Either way, a large programming investment stood to be lost with upgrades to new IBM computers. This made IBM's "selling up" efforts more difficult and opened the door for these customers to switch to a competitor's product.[61]

In 1961 a senior IBM executive and head of the Electronic Data Processing Machines division for the firm, T. Vincent Learson (who succeeded Watson, Jr., as CEO in 1971), established a task force, Systems Programming, Research, Engineering and Development (SPREAD), to study and strategize to correct this problem. John Haanstra, an executive in charge of IBM 1401 deployment, chaired the SPREAD group, and Bob Evans served as vice chair.

The final SPREAD report, which was delivered at the end of 1961, ultimately resulted in a compatible family of computers, the IBM System/360 series, named for its full circle of products from smaller business-oriented computers, System/360-30, to powerful "superspeed" computers, System/360-70.[62] One of the SPREAD members, Frederick Brooks, later led the effort to create the compatible operating system for System/360 computers, OS/360. He subsequently documented the

IBM System/360 Model 40 (courtesy of Charles Babbage Institute)

challenges of the OS/360 programming effort in his book, *The Mythical Man-Month*, which became a classic in software engineering.[63] Drawing extensively on System/360 as a case study, Brooks offered many insights, including understanding the problems caused by division of labor on large-scale programming projects.

On April 7, 1964, CEO Thomas Watson, Jr., announced System/360 in Poughkeepsie at a press conference where IBM brought in 200 reporters by train. On that day Watson stated:

> System/360 represents a sharp departure from concepts of the past in designing and building computers. It is a product of an international effort in IBM's laboratories and plants...the beginning of a new generation—not only of computers—but their application in business, science and government.[64]

System/360 was an expensive and risky proposition. *Fortune* dubbed it at the time as "IBM's $5 billion gamble." IBM's leaders bet the firm on this project that would cost more in total than the company's annual revenue at the time. While unquestionably System/360 was risky from both a business and a technological standpoint, it was a desirable move to ensure IBM's dominance in computing over the next decade. The prior lack of compatibility with systems software would have led to declining market share in computing for years to come without System/360 or another rationalized set of compatible product offerings. In addition to the large revenue streams System/360 delivered, it also introduced modularity throughout the hardware that contributed substantially to reducing costs over the long term.[65]

Bob Evans was in charge of the overall System/360 project. With a background in mathematics and electrical engineering, Evans joined IBM as a junior engineer in 1951 and worked on the IBM 701. In 1962 he was named vice-president of development for the Data Systems Division, under which System/360 was developed. In this collection, Evans provides an important look back at the history of System/360. He begins by giving an overview of IBM's longer history to contextualize the project. This includes discussion on the rivalry in computing between IBM Endicott and IBM Poughkeepsie, the "transistorization" of IBM machines, and the technical contributions of various earlier systems to System/360. Evans thoughtfully outlines the technical aspects that Stretch contributed and also the organizational ones. As he relates, this high profile project brought in many talented engineers and programmers who contributed substantially to the System/360 and associated OS/360 projects. Evans discusses and analyzes the organizational changes that Thomas Watson, Jr., made in the second half of the 1950s to restructure the firm under smaller functional groups and to delegate more of the decision-making authority.[66] This is something his father always resisted when he was in charge, but was critical to the company moving forward as it continued to grow. Evans also provides a figure that outlines the plethora of different programming systems that plagued IBM prior to System/360.

Given that some of the core elements of System/360 were first outlined in basic form in the SPREAD task force report, many historical studies have portrayed or at least implied a relatively smooth and continuous progression from planning group to successful project. Evans's article offers meaningful insight into the continuing battles and disagreements that were evident as System/360 took shape. He details how the Strategy Planning Group argued a single family was too risky, that it put all the eggs in one basket. Evans indicates that there was not a general coming together on ideas of the different groups in IBM but rather an urgency to move forward given the December 1963 announcement of the Honeywell H200 with a software product, the Liberator, which would allow for application software compatibility with the IBM 1401. This competitive threat created the imperative to solidify plans, make key decisions, and come out with a product announcement for System/360.

Additionally, Evans provides perspective on the critiques posed by MIT's computer scientists who had pioneered the field of time-sharing, Fernando Corbató and Robert Fano. Time-sharing allowed computer users on terminals to share rapidly rotating split seconds of processing time on a mainframe computer—offering efficiencies and creating the user experience of having their own mainframe. Corbató and Fano believed the System/360 design was not suitable for time-sharing environments due to System/360's lack of dynamic address translation. As Evans relates, IBM planners subsequently forecast that time-sharing might be considered essential in as many as 75 percent of all systems installed between 1964 and 1966. IBM immediately launched a time-sharing programming project for the System/360 that became Time-Sharing Option (TSO) and a parallel project to develop a time-sharing operating system, TSS, a project led by Watts Humphrey. TSO became the dominant time-sharing product and generally worked out well, but the time-sharing challenge highlighted the vulnerability to having one family of systems in a fast-moving high-technology field.

Time-sharing was one of the many challenges IBM overcame in the early years of System/360. Another significant issue was the circuits that IBM used for the system—though this turned out to be more of a problem with perceptions than with the technology itself. IBM developed Solid Logic Technology (SLT) for System/360. SLT was a hybrid integrated circuit technology developed at a time when monolithic integrated circuits were becoming the state-of-the-art. Government agencies that helped fund monolithic integrated circuit technology criticized IBM for being behind the curve.

IBM System/360 Model 90 (courtesy of Charles Babbage Institute)

IBM was taking many technological chances with incorporating modular hardware in System/360 and also developing compatible operating systems for the whole family of computers. Thus, IBM leaders chose a less risky path with its circuits. In the end, SLT performed well and saved the company money.[67] Nevertheless, the high-profile critiques were difficult for engineers and executives to endure—especially knowing the company's future depended on the success of System/360.

Finally, Evans recounts the legacy of System/360. The integrated family of computers was a substantial success. The system's models generally shipped on time or were only modestly late. While software fixes were needed in the months and years after the launch, in time they were generally successful. IBM more than doubled both its revenue and its net earnings in the half-decade following the launch of System/360. In the end, Evans states the most severe problem was antitrust litigation brought about in part by the success of System/360 and its impact on certain competitors. The standardization and modularity of System/360 had a significant impact on the industry as it spawned a successful plug-compatible market. While plug-compatible competitors remained thorns in Big Blue's side for years, these producers never seriously threatened IBM's dominant lead in the computer industry. IBM's market share was more than two-thirds throughout the late 1950s into the 1970s.

During the 1960s the computer industry came to be known as IBM and the seven dwarfs. Control Data, Burroughs, National Cash Register, and the computer divisions of Sperry Rand (Sperry Univac), General Electric, RCA, and Honeywell were never tiny, but they were dwarfs compared to IBM. General Electric and RCA likely had the greatest opportunity to challenge IBM's leadership given their capabilities in electronics and substantial financial resources, but the leaders of these two firms never focused corporate resources on the computer division. Both exited the computer business in the 1970s, and the industry then became known as IBM and the BUNCH—after the first letter of each of the remaining five major firms.[68] IBM also achieved a dominant position in Europe and elsewhere around the world, particularly in the business data processing computer market. Its substantial overseas facilities, coupled with its existing data processing base from tabulation machines, facilitated strong success for IBM's worldwide operations.

Longtime rival Sperry Univac ceased to be IBM's most formidable competitor by the mid 1960s, as a 1957 start-up formed by former Sperry Univac engineers in Minneapolis, Control Data Corporation, dominated the supercomputer market with its CDC 6600. Like the disappointment with Stretch, this was a bitter pill for Thomas Watson, Jr., but he could take solace in the fact that the very top end of the scientific computing market was much smaller than the vast majority of the business

IBM System/370 (courtesy of Charles Babbage Institute)

data processing computer market that IBM controlled.

System/360 was extended with new models in the second half of the 1960s and was followed by System/370 at the start of the 1970s. System/360 and System/370 were extremely important to the firm and have been a topic of greater study than any other. By far the most detailed analysis of these systems is Emerson Pugh, Lyle Johnson, and John Palmer's *IBM's 360 and Early 370 Systems*.[69]

Antitrust and "Unbundling" Software

In the early 1930s IBM sought to formally require customers leasing IBM tabulating machines to only use IBM punch cards and formed an agreement with Remington Rand not to sell cards to each others' customers. In 1936 the US Department of Justice found IBM guilty of illegal product ties (using dominance in one field to create dominance in another) under the Sherman Antitrust Act. IBM leaders claimed that the firm had to ensure proper quality cards for its leased tabulation machines, but the Justice Department responded that IBM could help others produce sufficient quality cards by publishing material specifications and techniques for production. The Justice Department required IBM to ensure that it sold less than 50 percent of all cards used on IBM machines in the future.[70] IBM would face government and competitors' charges of antitrust violations repeatedly in the post-World War II computer era.

In 1952, just as IBM was readying to ship its first electronic digital computer, the IBM 701, its tabulating machine business was the target of a Department of Justice suit alleging illegal practices by the corporation to maintain its 90 percent market share of that trade. IBM's defense was it only had a one-quarter share of the office machine industry (it competed with Burroughs, NCR, and others in accounting machines). Ultimately the suit resulted in a 1956 consent decree that forced IBM to offer to sell its equipment on terms no less favorable than leases. It also required IBM to sever close ties between its service bureau division (which sold information processing services using IBM equipment)—Service Bureau Corporation—and the rest of the business. Finally, it stipulated that IBM had to separately price its hardware maintenance services and spare parts.[71]

Unease of potential government lawsuits grew as System/360 continued to further IBM's substantial industry lead in the late 1960s. It was in this environment that IBM's leadership decided it was wise to "unbundle" its software.

In the early to mid 1960s the first software products were being created by pioneering computer services firms—including Applied Data Research and Informatics, Inc. These companies were looking to refine custom program code they had previously created into standard off-the-shelf products.[72] Since entering the computer industry, IBM frequently bundled "free" software tools in with hardware to make its systems more useful and attractive to customers. As software products emerged as an industry, IBM not only faced potential litigation from the Justice Department and computer firms that claimed that IBM was using software to unfairly dominate the hardware market, but also that it was preventing fair competition and retarding the newly established software products industry. In 1967 ADR and several other firms brought complaints to the Justice Department that IBM was using pre-announcements and free (bundled) software to unfairly dominate the industry. At roughly the same time, one of IBM's formidable competitors in the scientific computing market, Control Data Corporation, also filed suit against IBM.[73]

In this collection, Watts Humphrey's short memoir on IBM's unbundling of software offers critical perspective on this important event with regard to the company, the computer industry, and the software products industry. Humphrey joined IBM in 1959 as a senior engineer in the Advanced System Development Division. In 1963 he became the director of systems and application engineering on the corporate staff. In this capacity, Humphrey was to oversee software development for the corporation.

In the mid 1960s, several years before IBM plug-compatible equipment became widespread (generally peripheral equipment rather than complete systems), RCA announced the Spectra 70 series. RCA's plan with the Spectra 70 was to develop systems fully compatible with IBM System/360. As Humphrey points out, this posed a potentially serious challenge to IBM. If RCA succeeded with computers compatible with System/360 models, then RCA could have a free ride on IBM software development costs. RCA hardware, unlike IBM's, would not be burdened with high software development costs. IBM could not prevent RCA customers from using IBM software—and if IBM wanted to protect itself and sell software to RCA customers, IBM would have to price it separately (unbundle it) for its own customers.

Humphrey states that industry dynamics, with the announcement of the RCA Spectra 70, as well as worries of a government antitrust suit led IBM to unbundle its software. His memoir provides important context to the two successive IBM committees that he served on that studied the advisability of unbundling and the pricing of software. Humphrey begins by discussing the work of the first IBM unbundling task force (in 1966) that was led by IBM director of policy development Howard Figueroa.[74] The committee ruled out the possibility of protecting software through trade secrets and patents. Trade secrets would be difficult to keep for software, and patenting would quickly become overwhelming given the amount of software and different iterations of it. The group endorsed a copyright and license strategy instead.

In summer 1968 Humphrey participated in an "unbundling" panel discussion at the American Federation of Information Processing Societies (AFIPS) meeting. The possibility of IBM unbundling was rumored, and speculation was growing day by day. IBM customers thought unbundling might result in a major reduction in the cost of hardware—perhaps a 25 percent reduction. Humphrey stated that IBM had not decided to unbundle (it was still a controversial topic at the firm).

He dispelled notions of 25 percent hardware price reductions, telling the group that IBM had only 4,000 programmers on its roughly 130,000 member staff—that would suggest reductions closer to 3 percent if IBM unbundled software. When the press questioned the corporation about Humphrey's comments, IBM leaders were irate—but Humphrey had cleared his remarks with the policy office, so he got off "with a slap on the wrist." [75]

The second unbundling task force was formed early in 1968 and was led by IBM senior vice president Spike Beitzel. Following its recommendation IBM decided to unbundle its software. The announcement was made in December 1968, with first implementation occurring in the succeeding six to twelve months. This announcement did not deter the government. In January 1969, the Department of Justice filed an antitrust lawsuit against IBM. A number of its competitors also filed suits against IBM for "monopolistic practices." The next dozen years IBM's team of lawyers were busy with this litigation. The Justice Department's suit against IBM was dismissed in 1982.[76]

Back in the early 1950s IBM's leaders held preliminary discussions with J. Presper Eckert and John Mauchly about the possibility of acquiring Eckert-Mauchly Computer Corporation (soon thereafter it was acquired by Remington Rand). Discussions with IBM's lawyers and Justice Department officials quickly led IBM's leaders to abandon the possible acquisition, and the company instead poured additional resources into furthering its electronics capabilities and internally developing and launching electronic digital computer systems.[77] This, like the 1956 consent decree, was just one of many instances where antitrust laws, suits, potential suits, and settlements influenced the strategic discussions and paths of IBM. As historian Steven Usselman insightfully points out, IBM's decades of interactions with the Justice Department were not entirely combative and contentious, but also filled with constructive negotiation and dialogue.[78] Like IBM, the Justice Department was seeking to define proper paths to foster innovation and growth in the often hard to understand and constantly evolving high-technology industries of computers, software, and information technology services.

Database Systems

The strong possibility of IBM unbundling software in the late 1960s provided both an opportunity and, in many senses, an imperative for IBM to rationalize its Data Base/Data Communication (DB/DC) offerings. This was its single most important category of software applications. As IBM System/360 delivery dates for the different models approached, there were many challenges to overcome. System software was behind schedule and well over cost estimates, a fix with TSO was rapidly being developed to address the firm's early neglect of the technological and market momentum of time-sharing, and IBM had been severely criticized for using SLT rather than monolithic integrated circuits. These problems and public critiques created unease among a number of IBM top executives, managers, and engineers, and also made them all the more determined to do everything they could to create demand for System/360. Sometimes well-meaning efforts were haphazard. To attract customers IBM had 15 different development groups working on DB/DC systems. This led to inefficient redundancies and confusion among potential and existing System/360 customers. As IBM leaders contemplated a future of software products and projected what revenue streams to expect, they sought to better organize software production efforts and product and marketing strategies.

This planning resulted in three systems becoming the foundation for IBM's DB/DC by mid 1969: Generalized Information System (GIS), Customer Information Control System (CICS), and Information Management System (IMS). GIS was used for a while but was withdrawn when usage declined. CICS and IMS were rapidly adopted, have been highly influential for decades, and continue to bring in substantial revenue for IBM. CICS, which was initially called Public Utility Customer Information Control System, was first offered in 1968 as a free product. It quickly took off in the utility industry, where it facilitated rapid access to customer accounts. Over time CICS has grown into a broad-based family of applications servers that facilitate online transaction management for the banking, finance, insurance, utilities, and many other industries. Originally created at an IBM Development Center in Des Plaines, Illinois in 1966, CICS responsibility has rested since 1974 with IBM's Hursley Laboratory in the United Kingdom. Despite the immense impact of CICS and IMS—for IBM and the millions of customers worldwide—they have received relatively little attention in the existing historical literature.[79]

In this collection, William McGee's memoir provides a detailed history of IMS. McGee came to IBM in 1964 to work on physics and graphics applications at the company's Palo Alto Scientific Center. In 1970 he began work for the IBM DB/DC Systems Department group in Palo Alto, and later at IBM San Jose, where he continued work on DB/DC requirements and strategy, including on IMS. McGee's valuable account discusses the origins of IMS in a joint project between IBM and North American Rockwell Space Division for Rockwell's Apollo mission contract. He recounts how IMS was refined by IBM and launched as a product in September 1969, IMS/360 version 1 with a license fee of $600/month. It was targeted at large manufacturing enterprises and among the first 30 customers were Hughes Aircraft, Caterpillar, and Boeing Aircraft. As McGee writes, a key to IBM's sustained success with IMS—which continues today on IBM z servers in the z/OS environment—is attention to customers. He details how IBM Share and IBM Guide user groups have been critical forums to transmit customer needs on IMS back to IBM. He also outlines fundamental contributions IMS had for database technology in the areas of data consistency, data integrity, continuous availability, and queued transaction processing.

New Facilities and New Technologies

As IBM tabulation machines and punch cards took off in the interwar years, IBM established subsidiaries and facilities around the world. In the computer field, the earliest contributions came from IBM Endicott and IBM Poughkeepsie. Over time, the corporation launched or expanded facilities in the US and overseas that joined these and other New York state IBM operations to make important contributions to the company. These facilities included research laboratories, development laboratories, and manufacturing plants.

On September 10, 1943, Thomas Watson, Sr., dedicated the company's first West Coast manufacturing facility, a card plant in San Jose, California. Initially, it was a modest operation employing fewer than 120 people, but it grew steadily. As IBM geared up its electronics capabilities and engineering work force at the end of the 1940s and start of the 1950s, IBM leaders considered adding a new research facility. Many qualified engineers in California and elsewhere on the West Coast were reluctant to move to Endicott or Poughkeepsie. Seeing an opportunity, in 1951 IBM leaders chose San Jose as the home for its new research laboratory. Reynold Johnson, who Thomas Watson, Sr., had hired in 1934 to develop the first test scoring machine, was selected to run the operation. By June 1952 thirty engineers and scientists had been hired, a number of research efforts were launched, and personnel and the number and types of projects steadily expanded.[80]

IBM's investment did not take long to pay off. In September 1952 Arthur Crichlow began a project to study how information was organized, stored, formatted, and processed on punch card tabulation equipment and to develop a better method. Late in the year he came across an engineering journal article published months earlier on "notched disk memory" using magnetic-coated disks. The configuration for how this would work, outlined by the researcher at the National Bureau of Standards (NBS) who authored the article, was off, but the idea stuck with Crichlow. He and his team developed and successfully tested the first magnetic disk storage device in the middle of 1955. A key element of the technology was quickly gaining access to memory regardless of where it was stored on the disk. To achieve this random access (and in contrast to the technology described by the NBS researcher) Crichlow used continuously rotating sets of 50 large disks. In 1956 IBM came out with the IBM 305 RAMAC (Random Access Memory Accounting Machine) based on this technology. This was the start of disk drive technology and the disk drive industry—an industry that had grown beyond $12 billion in annual revenue by the early 1980s.[81]

Pioneering disk storage was a tough first act to follow, but IBM San Jose continued to produce transformative new technologies. Of its many achievements, likely none is more impressive than the work of IBM San Jose mathematician Edgar Codd. In 1970 Codd published "A Relational Model of Data for Large Shared Data Banks."[82] This article outlined how relationships between pieces of data should rest on the data's values rather than separately established nesting or linking. This opened the door for query languages (such as SQL) that can be used to do queries of data sets with unprecedented flexibility. Codd's ideas established the basis for relational databases, relational database management systems, and the dominant model for databases of the past three decades.

Much like IBM San Jose, IBM Rochester quickly grew beyond its origins as a manufacturing plant. At mid century, IBM's tabulation equipment business was still growing and it needed to add manufacturing capacity. Labor costs on the two coasts were significantly more than in Middle America, and IBM leaders launched a site study of 80 Midwestern cities. It evaluated them on quality of labor force, schools, taxes, transportation, utilities, and even morals and manners. The two finalists were Madison, Wisconsin and Rochester, Minnesota. Both scored high across the board, but Rochester had the benefit of less labor organization than Madison and was the selected city for a new manufacturing facility in 1956. Of the 174 employees who began work at IBM Rochester in mid 1956, 121 were from the area and 53 from other IBM facilities. Charles Lawson, the assistant general manager of IBM Poughkeepsie, became the first general manager to lead IBM Rochester.[83]

In its first five years IBM Rochester was strictly a manufacturing operation. In 1961, the facility's responsibilities expanded when a development laboratory was added. In the late 1960s, computing technology was well on its way to displacing tabulator machine equipment for business applications. Many large corporations had entered the computer age with the IBM 650, IBM 1401, or with IBM System/360. Shortly after launching System/360, the Model 20 was added, a smaller less expensive system. Even the System/360-20, however, was too expensive for some small businesses and organizations. With this in mind, IBM leaders sought to add a series of less expensive machines outside of System/360 that would run on a different, non-compatible operating system. IBM Rochester was given responsibility for the design of what became IBM's midrange series. The first series was System/3, developed and manufactured by IBM Rochester and on the market in the second half of 1969.[84] There were synergies to having development and manufacturing operations side-by-side, as longtime IBM Rochester employee Tom Paske noted:

> The manufacturing arm and the engineering arm worked very closely together. The facilities…were joined together with a hallway, so all you had to do was walk down the hallway and you could talk to the person who was in charge of a part. It made things easier for the manufacturing engineers and the development engineers…[85]

Rochester continued to be the home of IBM's midrange series with System/32 (1975), System/34 (1977), System/38 (1978), and System/36 (1983). IBM had success with each of these midrange series, but by the 1980s the upper end of the midrange series and lower end of System/370 series were beginning to overlap—causing confusion among customers and inefficiencies for IBM. IBM leaders in the mid 1980s began a project for a new series to be designed and built at Rochester that would cut out the overlapping products. Codenamed "Silverlake," the project resulted in the AS/400 family of computers that debuted in 1988. IBM Rochester won the Malcolm Baldrige National Quality Award in 1990 for the AS/400. In July 1991 *Datamation* reported AS/400 revenue was approximately $14 billion, more than the entire revenue of minicomputer giant Digital Equipment Corporation, the computer firm second to IBM. The AS/400 evolved into the i series line of powerful servers and, subsequently, System i. IBM Rochester also played a central role in the design, development, and manufacturing of the supercomputer Blue Gene—the first one, Blue Gene/L was shipped to Lawrence Livermore National Laboratory in 2004. At the time, it was the fastest supercomputer in the world.[86]

Roy A. Bauer, Emilio Collar, Victor Tang, and Jerry Wind wrote a book on the AS/400 and how it transformed IBM called *The Silverlake Project*, and Arthur L. Norberg and Jeffrey R. Yost wrote a short book on the 50-year history of IBM Rochester, *IBM Rochester: A Half-Century of Innovation*.[87]

Unlike some technology companies that have cut back substantially on research, IBM has remained committed to research laboratories ever since launching Watson Scientific Laboratory at Columbia University in 1945. In the 1980s and beyond, IBM has followed the trend of other major industrial research organizations (including AT&T, Bell Laboratories, General Electric Global Research, and Xerox PARC) to commit fewer resources to basic research and to focus more on applied research and connecting activities to potential product and services revenue streams. In the case of IBM, this has not resulted in a decline in research but an expansion as the company has redirected efforts and connected research to new business opportunities.

IBM built four new laboratories in the past two decades. The company now has nine research laboratories worldwide: Almaden (San Jose, California, established 1955), Zurich (1956), Watson (New York and Maine, 1961), Haifa (1972), Tokyo (1982), Austin (1995), China (Beijing, 1995), India (Delhi and Bangalore, 1998), and Brazil (Sao Paulo and Rio de Janeiro, 2010).[88] In addition to Codd's invention of relational databases, other highlights of the many important contributions of IBM's research to science and technology include Benoit Mandelbrot's development of the field of fractal geometry,[89] creating the Data Encryption Standard (DES),[90] major contributions to high-temperature conductivity, and the grandmaster-level chess computer Deep Blue.[91]

The IBM PC

The first personal computers were crude devices that did not begin to approximate the functionality of IBM's lower-end models of its midrange series computers or those of its minicomputer competitors. They were built upon semiconductor company Intel's invention of the microprocessor and lacked the software, memory capacity, processing power, and input-output technology that we now associate with personal computers. On the market by the mid 1970s, many of these machines, such as Micro Instrumentation Telemetry System's pioneering Altair 8800, were sold unassembled in kits and appealed primarily to electronic hobbyists.[92]

The personal computer market began to expand rapidly (beyond its hobbyist origins) when Apple Computer, a Cupertino, California personal computer manufacturer founded in 1976, came out with its second computer, the Apple II, in 1977. This $1,300 machine had a full-size keyboard and was expandable to 48K RAM. In the following two years several "killer apps," from independent software vendors—game-changing software applications driving demand for the Apple II, Radio Shack TRS-80, and other personal computers—hit the market, including the spreadsheet program VisiCalc and MicroPro's WordStar word processing program. This software boosted demand for home machines, while also opening the door for educational, business, and other markets.

At the start of the mainframe digital computer industry, IBM had built internal capabilities for entering the computing field but waited to launch products until there was a recognizable potential market. Likewise, Digital Equipment Corporation demonstrated the viability of minicomputing prior to IBM's launching of its midrange series. Given IBM's considerable experience in semiconductors, the firm's leaders knew that the prediction of Fairchild Semiconductor engineer and later Intel founder Gordon Moore (in the journal *Electronics* in 1965) on the doubling of circuits on a chip every year or two would mean ever faster and cheaper computers.[93]

Based on the threat and opportunity of personal computers, in 1980 IBM's Corporate Management Committee decided IBM should enter the personal computer business. In the past, IBM had followed the practice of internally building and extending capabilities for new businesses. Acquisitions and integration issues at IBM's competitors, such as Remington Rand/Sperry Rand, had often led to internal conflicts and inefficiencies. The still pending Justice Department antitrust suit also posed challenges to an acquisition strategy. At the same time, IBM product development cycles tended to be at least twenty-four months and could be considerably longer when entering an entirely new arena like personal computers. A further challenge to IBM's typical practice for internal development of new businesses was pricing. IBM's management team recognized the difficulties of getting a good personal computer product out quickly and at a competitive price.

Given all these considerations, the Corporate Management Committee made a complete break with the past and authorized establishment of an independent business unit (IBU) at the IBM Boca Raton, Florida facility. The project team would be relieved of many of the regular restrictions within the corporation, including those for sourcing and sales channels. The IBM PC was developed and on the market in 1981, just a year after the project team's formation. It achieved this by outsourcing the operating system—to a young company run by William Gates and Paul Allen called Microsoft—as well as much of the hardware. Unlike other IBM computers, it had an open architecture. IBM believed publishing and obtaining a copyright for its ROM-BIOS (Read Only Memory-Basic Input-Output) system code would provide legal barriers against imitators. Gates had insisted on retaining rights to the DOS operating system—licensing it to IBM as PC-DOS.

The IBM PC was priced at just under $3,000, more expensive than most of its competitors, but for a more powerful machine and one that carried the IBM brand. Its launch came just as businesses were beginning to make personal computers standard equipment to replace typewriters or dedicated word processing equipment. Coupled with a brilliant marketing campaign using Charlie Chaplin's Little Tramp, IBM very quickly emerged as the leading personal computer maker in the world—the machine was successfully marketed to business and personal users alike, without relying on IBM's talented but expensive technical sales force.

IBM's clear leadership in personal computing was short-lived. Its copyright on ROM-BIOS was useless after Compaq and other personal computer firms reverse engineered compatible but different code. The early lead of the IBM PC set the standard for PC-DOS. Microsoft's compatible MS-DOS became standard for Compaq and the many other PC clones that generally sold for less than IBM personal computers. Apple was the only major computer manufacturer that used a different, internally developed platform. When Apple, drawing on Xerox PARC and SRI's pioneering work on graphical user interfaces (GUI) and the computer mouse, launched its Macintosh with user-friendly desktop-

IBM PC (courtesy of Charles Babbage Institute)

based GUI and mouse, it became a quick success. Microsoft soon developed a similar user-friendly GUI called Windows. Microsoft also succeeded in developing the leading personal computer applications software and became the leading software company in the world. Meanwhile, Intel became the primary microprocessor supplier for all PC/Windows platform personal computers. IBM, Compaq, and later Dell (through pioneering with direct marketing of personal computers) all had their day in the sun, but Microsoft and Intel, or Wintel, became the big winners in personal computers by supplying the principal software and semiconductor hardware for the machines. IBM, which had a bit of a personal computer resurgence with its successful ThinkPad line of laptops in the 1990s, sold its personal computer business to leading Chinese personal computer firm Lenovo in 2004.

Ironically, IBM's strategic misstep in outsourcing the IBM PC operating system and allowing Microsoft to retain rights to the code (DOS), gave rise to the company that would displace IBM as the focus of the Justice Department's antitrust efforts in the IT industry. Among other impacts, the diminished risk of antitrust lawsuits has freed IBM up to open to the possibility of acquisitions—for decades IBM had focused almost entirely on internal growth, which served it well in the golden age of mainframes but became more limiting as the IT industry expanded and diversified. Not only was IBM hurt by a trend toward personal computers—a market IBM only controlled a small fraction of compared to mainframes—but also the early-1990s move toward a client-server model. To address the latter, IBM acquired software products firm Lotus Development Corporation in 1995 for $3.5 billion—primarily to gain its Lotus Notes, an integrated workstation/client software product to collaborate and share information (business emails, calendars, etc.) in an office environment. Further, the crisis IBM faced in the late 1980s and early 1990s—as low-margin PC/Windows platform personal computers became an ever-greater part of the computer industry—helped to precipitate its fortuitous path to focus on the IT services business.

IBM's Emergence as an IT Services Industry Leader

From the time Thomas J. Watson, Sr., arrived to manage C-T-R forward, excellence in sales and service has been central to C-T-R/IBM. Thomas Watson, Sr., placed great emphasis on technically trained sales and service workforces that could effectively market the machines, maintain the (often leased) machines, and provide assistance in using them. In the 1930s IBM established a service bureau that concentrated on the latter activity. The 1956 consent required IBM to run the Service Bureau Corporation as an independent entity that did not share workforces with IBM and that did not work exclusively on IBM systems. The consent decree was instituted just as IBM was securing its dominant position in computing, and IBM's Service Bureau Corporation was focused primarily on computer services by the early 1960s. The Service Bureau Corporation would assist clients with programming needs, sell computer time, and later in the decade provide time-sharing services. In the early 1970s, IBM sold the Service Bureau Corporation to Control Data Corporation at a fraction of its worth as part of a settlement for a CDC lawsuit against IBM for anti-competitive practices.[94] While both the Service Bureau Corporation business and many of its employees became part of CDC, some of the organizational know-how and routines, first built in punch card services and later in computer services, remained with IBM. IBM continued to provide service to customers, some of it bundled as part of hardware sales and some consulting-based work—but it was not a central business for the hardware giant.

Throughout the entire post-World War II era until 1979, IBM had grown its earnings every year, much of the time doubling earnings every five to seven years. IBM barely missed its 1978 earnings in 1979, and in the 1980 to 1984 period it resumed its phenomenal growth, jumping from roughly $3.40 billion in earnings in 1980 to $6.58 billion in 1984. In 1985 IBM's earnings fell a fraction of a percent, and in 1986 earnings fell by 27 percent. The remainder of the decade was rough for IBM, and 1989 earnings were more than 43% off the 1984 peak. In 1991 through 1993 the unthinkable occurred: IBM lost billions for three consecutive years, including losing $8.1 billion in 1993, far more than it had ever earned in a year.[95]

Many factors were at play, including broader economic conditions, but the depth of decline was astounding. IBM was facing a crisis. Following the general trajectory of Moore's law, computing memory and processing power were becoming far cheaper each passing year. Inexpensive personal computers were doing much of the work that had previously been done on minicomputers or even mainframes—and IBM had only a small share of the personal computer market. The corporation's leaders frantically began to search for new revenue streams to replace diminishing ones. The services business was a tiny portion of IBM's overall revenue in the 1980s. In 1989 IBM completed a deal for its first large-scale commercial IT services project, to build and run a major data center—for Eastman

Kodak in Rochester, New York. Following the same facilities-management strategy that had made Electronic Data Systems an industry leader, and its founder H. Ross Perot a billionaire, IBM sought additional clients to utilize excess system and labor resources. In 1991 IBM leaders became increasingly committed to making IBM a powerhouse in computing and related services.

In 1993 Louis Gerstner, Jr., became CEO of IBM. He saw many disparate businesses, unrecognized opportunities, and a general lack of rationalization. With the severe losses, IBM faced a crossroads. It could sell off some of its businesses and re-focus as a much smaller company, sell off all its assets and disband, or seek to rationalize assets in a way that took advantage of the range, depth, and knowledge its workforce possessed—turning its resources more effectively into steady revenue streams. It took the latter path, and services became the focal point of this strategy. It was a way to integrate the vast stores of knowledge, skills, and capabilities of its workforce into a coherent business plan.[96] In 1995 IBM launched its Global Services Division. In the early 1990s services represented less than 10 percent of IBM's revenue; by 2001 it was a more than $30 billion a year business that was easily IBM's largest division at more than 40 percent of the company.

In 2002 IBM acquired PricewaterhouseCoopers's (PwC) consulting business for $3.5 billion. While maintaining a core focus on traditional computer services, where it competed against Electronic Data Systems, Computer Sciences Corporation, and other longtime giants in computer services, IBM's acquisition of PwC consulting demonstrated its commitment to also concentrate on certain areas of management consulting.

In many respects IBM looks far different from the start of its journey a century ago or when Thomas J. Watson, Sr., took the reins three years later. In 1914 IBM had 1,217 employees in the US and 129 more overseas. It produced mechanical tabulation machines, employee time clocks, and industrial scales.[97] It now has more than 420,000 employees spread throughout the world, and its primary business is selling services not machines. The company, once focused almost exclusively on internal growth rather than acquisitions, started a buying spree in the mid 1990s that continues to the present. Between 1911 and 1994, IBM acquired 14 relatively small companies. Between 1995 and 2010 it acquired more than 120 companies, mainly in software and services—including multibillion dollar acquisitions of Lotus Development and PwC. IBM also has become increasingly dependent on managing a valuable intellectual property portfolio and has led the world in new US patents often in recent decades. There are meaningful continuities as well. Excellence in service by a technically trained workforce was central to Thomas Watson, Sr., Thomas Watson, Jr., and subsequent leaders, and IBM staff have long provided "solutions"—this work was just bundled into a hardware contract in the more distant past, or at least tied to IBM hardware. While the businesses are different, IBM has been a leader in information technology for its entire 100-year history. The memoirs that follow provide rich glimpses into the people who made the IBM century.

Endnotes

1. R. Mensel, "'Kodakers Lying in Wait' Amateur Photography and the Right of Privacy in New York, 1885–1915," *American Quarterly*, vol. 43, no. 1, 1991, pp. 24–45.

2. Worldwide global IT services industry figure for 2010 from Gartner Newsroom, www.gartner.com. IBM is also the leader of the more than $230 billion (2010) US IT consulting industry. IBISWorld, *IT Consulting, US Industry Report*, 11 May 2011, www.ibisworld.com. Accessed summary of report on www.ibisworld.com on May 16, 2011.

3. Hewlett-Packard has gone on an acquisition spree over the past decade. By acquiring Electronic Data Systems (EDS) in 2008 for $13.9 billion, Hewlett-Packard became a major player in IT services (second in the industry to IBM). Nearly a decade ago, Hewlett-Packard acquired Compaq for nearly twice that amount, $25 billion. Hewlett-Packard is the largest personal computer firm, and despite its diversification to develop a major IT services business, it remains fundamentally vulnerable to declines in the personal computer market.

4. IBM quickly gained the lead in the personal computer market behind its IBM PC, which was introduced in 1981. Clone producers such as Compaq and Dell cut substantially into IBM's market share later in the 1980s and 1990s. IBM reinvigorated its personal computer business with its popular Thinkpad laptop series beginning in the early 1990s. Despite the IBM Thinkpad series and Sony Vaio series, Apple has been the only personal computer firm that has maintained, and continues to maintain, substantial pricing power in this largely commodity business. IBM retained a modest ownership stake when it sold its personal computer business to Lenovo in December 2004.

5. W.C. McGee, "The Information Management Systems (IMS) Program Product," *IEEE Annals of the History of Computing*, vol. 31, no. 4, 2009, pp. 66–75.

6. Cuthbert Hurd's article is, strictly speaking, edited court testimony—though it takes the form of a memoir.

7. J.W. Cortada, *Before the Computer: IBM, NCR, Burroughs, and Remington Rand and the Industry They Created, 1865–1956*, Princeton University Press, 1993.

8. G. Austrian, *Herman Hollerith, Forgotten Giant of Information Processing*, Columbia University Press, 1982.

9. M. Campbell-Kelly and W. Aspray, *Computer: A History of the Information Machine*, 2nd edition, Westview Press, 2004.

10. A. Akera, *Calculating a Natural World: Scientists, Engineers, and Computers During the Rise of US Cold War Research*, MIT Press, 2007.

11. E. Pugh, *Building IBM: Shaping an Industry and Its Technology*, MIT Press, 1995; S.W. Usselman, "IBM and Its Imitators: Organizational Capabilities and the Emergence of the International Computer Industry," *Business and Economic History*, vol. 22, no. 2, 1993, pp. 1–35.

12. K. Flamm, *Creating the Computer: Government, Industry, and High Technology*, Brookings Institution, 1988; J.R. Yost, *The Computer Industry*, Greenwood Press, 2005.

13. Pugh, *Building IBM*, p. 39.

14. The corporation itself recognizes 1911 as IBM's start, and the vast majority of computer historians do as well.

15. Watson moved up through NCR quickly but, along with Patterson and others at the company, was found guilty of anti-competitive practices in a case brought by the US Justice Department for NCR's role in funding and running seemingly independent used dealerships of accounting machines in order to undersell and later buy out the competition. Watson appealed his original sentence, which included a fine and a year in prison, and the government chose not to pursue the matter. It was Watson's first introduction to antitrust, an issue that was prominent at IBM from the 1930s through the early 1980s.

16. Cortada, *Before the Computer*.

17. Ibid.

18. S. Lubar, "'Do Not Fold, Spindle or Mutilate': A Cultural History of the Punch Card," *Journal of American Culture*, vol. 15, Winter 1992, pp. 42–55.

19. I.B. Cohen, G.W. Welch, and R.V.D. Campbell, eds., *Makin' Numbers: Howard Aiken and the Computer*, MIT Press, 1999. Of the more than a dozen chapters, only one significantly addresses IBM's technical contributions. Cohen also came out with a biography on Aiken that same year that also gives relatively little attention to IBM's engineering accomplishments on the Mark I computer. I.B. Cohen, *Howard Aiken, Portrait of a Computer Pioneer*, MIT Press, 1999.

20. Following Thomas Watson, Sr.'s, preference, IBM's electromechanical computers were called "calculators." Electromechanical computers were never significant in the computer industry—these were generally one-of-a-kind scientific calculating machines. Even IBM's first fully electronic computer (marking IBM entrance into the computer industry), the IBM 701, was called the Defense Calculator. Subsequent machines—after Thomas Watson, Jr., had taken over the company—were referred to internally and externally as "computers."

21. J.F Brennan, *The IBM Watson Laboratory at Columbia University: A History*, International Business Machines, 1971, pp. 1-5.

22. Wallace Eckert's co-authored book (with IBM's John C. McPherson) from 1940 was republished in a Charles Babbage Institute reprint series (with a new introduction by McPherson), *Punched Card Methods in Scientific Computation*, MIT Press, 1984, and he appears briefly, in connection to the IBM-supported Columbia University laboratory, in a number of IBM histories, but his pioneering scientific computing work has yet to be analyzed in any depth. The Charles Babbage Institute (CBI) has a small collection of Wallace Eckert's papers.

23. B. Randell, ed., *The Origin of Digital Computers*, Springer, 1973.

24. Eckert-Mauchly Computer Corporation was initially called Electronic Control Company, but the founders soon changed the name (at the time of incorporation) to take advantage of their name recognition as the designers of ENIAC.

25. R.F. Osborn, "GE and UNIVAC: Harnessing the High Speed Computer," *Harvard Business Review*, vol. 32, no. 4, July-Aug. 1954, pp. 99–107.

26. Yost, *The Computer Industry*; Usselman, "IBM and Its Imitators." IBM's core organizational capabilities, particularly its technically trained sales force, are examined and emphasized in Stephen W. Usselman's excellent article on IBM and its competitors in the computer field.

27. SAGE was a radar and computer system with more than two-dozen remote locations in North America that was designed to detect and communicate information about a bomber attack. The hardware was developed between 1953 and 1956 and the software in the succeeding half-decade. By the time the system was fully operable in the 1960s, it, practically speaking, was obsolete—threats of intercontinental ballistic missiles far outweighed threats from bomber attacks in the 1960s and beyond.

28. IBM had more capital than its competitors and was able to offer leases to its early computer customers. Leases became the dominant model by which IBM placed its digital computers in order to make them more affordable. Leasing also produced steadier revenue streams. IBM's greater capital relative to its competitors allowed it to produce in greater volume than competitors, reduce per-unit costs, and create a virtuous cycle. IBM's practice of preferring leases to sales followed the company's proven practice of favoring lease structures with pre-computer punch card tabulation equipment.

29. Pugh, *Building IBM*, p. 215.

30. Usselman, "IBM and Its Imitators." This article makes the important point that efforts to transfer technology from scientific computing (centered in Poughkeepsie) to the data processing computing (Endicott facility) market seldom worked "as well as planned" for geographic, technical, and other reasons. But

without question IBM's scientific computing efforts, and particularly capabilities built on the SAGE project, had some positive impacts on subsequent commercial computers. As Usselman points out, the scientific-oriented IBM 701 and the soon-to-follow business-oriented 702 shared some technical staff. Also, the technical contributions of the scientific computer IBM Stretch, were quite significant to the monumentally important System/360 series—a series with many commercial and scientific computing customers. See F. Brooks, "Stretch-ing is Good Exercise—It Gets You in Shape to Win," *IEEE Annals of the History of Computing*, vol. 32, no. 1, 2010, pp. 4–9.

31. Originally the system was called SABER, but this was soon changed to SABRE.

32. Discussions between IBM salesman Blair Smith and American Airlines president C.R. Smith about the possibility of a real-time airline reservations system had begun several years earlier—a contract was signed in 1957 for IBM to build the system.

33. RAND initially formed System Development as an independent division, but several years later spun it off as a separate non-profit research and development corporation.

34. R.V. Head, "Getting Sabre off the Ground," *IEEE Annals of the History of Computing*, vol. 24, no. 4, 2002, pp. 32–39.

35. Virtually all mainframes and the vast majority of minicomputer installations were for institutions, not individuals.

36. History of manufacturing computers has focused primarily on designing and manufacturing the electronic components of computers and strategies for ensuring supply. Three of the four articles for a recent *History and Technology* special issue on the history of high-technology manufacturing are focused on such themes. D. Holbrook, "Controlling Contamination: The Origins of Clean Room Technology," *History and Technology*, vol. 25, no. 3, 2009, pp. 173–192; C. Lécuyer and D.C. Brock, "From Nuclear Physics to Semiconductor Manufacturing: The Making of Ion Implantation," *History and Technology*, vol. 25, no. 3, 2009, pp. 193–218; J.R. Yost, "Manufacturing Mainframes: Component Fabrication and Component Procurement at IBM and Sperry Univac, 1960-1975," *History and Technology*, vol. 25, no. 3, 2009, pp. 219–236. One other important article on manufacturing computer components is Stuart W. Leslie, "Blue Collar Science: Bringing the Transistor to Life in the Lehigh Valley," *Historical Studies in the Physical and Biological Sciences*, vol. 32, no. 2, 2001, pp. 71–113. The history of assembling computers has yet to be written. There is a small literature by economists and management scholars on certain aspects of assembling personal computers, but almost nothing on mainframes and minicomputers.

37. Kubie would leave IBM to co-found the Computer Usage Company in 1955, and Trimble quickly signed on as the corporation's technical director. Computer Usage was the first computer services firm offering programming services, rented computer time, and other services to customers. Kubie and Trimble illustrate the tremendous impact of ex-IBM employees in IT industries. Among other influential ex-IBM employees, Gene Amdahl (engineer on the IBM 704 and other systems), with Amdahl Corporation, would dominate the "plug-compatible" market, underselling IBM on some systems in the 1970s, and Gideon Gartner (IBM's Market Information Manager in its Data Processing Division) later founded Gartner Group, a premier IT market research and advisory firm that broadly served the IT and IT investment communities. CBI recently acquired the Gideon Gartner papers.

38. IBM's dominant lead in punch card tabulation was all the more important as punch cards became the primary input/output technology for early digital computers.

39. D.E. Knuth, "The IBM 650: An Appreciation from the Field," *IEEE Annals of the History of Computing*, vol. 18, no. 3, 1996, 50–55.

40. The story of the six women who initially programmed the ENIAC is discussed and analyzed in the following two articles. W.B. Fritz, "The Women of the ENIAC," *IEEE Annals of the History of Computing*, vol. 18, no. 3, 1996, pp. 13-28; J. Light, "When Computers Were Women," *Technology and Culture*, vol. 40, no.

3, 1999, pp. 455–483.

41. J. von Neumann, "First Draft of a Report on the EDVAC," *IEEE Annals of the History of Computing*, vol. 15, no. 4, 1993, pp. 27–43. [Republished with new introduction by Michael D. Godfrey.] By far the best biographical treatment of J. von Neumann and his fundamental contributions to computer history is William Aspray's *John von Neumann and the Origins of Modern Computing*, MIT Press, 1990.

42. What were original ideas of von Neumann's in the report and what ideas were being discussed by J. Presper Eckert, John Mauchly, and other members of the Moore School ENIAC team is subject to controversy.

43. The fullest biographical treatment of the pioneering programming work of Grace Murray Hopper is Kurt W. Beyer, *Grace Hopper and the Invention of the Information Age*, MIT Press, 2009.

44. Pugh, *Building IBM*, pp. 190–195.

45. J.W. Backus, "The IBM Speedcoding System," *Communications of the ACM*, vol. 1, no. 1, Jan. 1954, pp. 4–6.

46. Pugh, *Building IBM*, pp. 190–195.

47. Ibid.

48. J.W. Backus, et al., "The FORTRAN Automatic Coding System," *Proceedings of the Western Joint Computer Conference*, Feb. 1957, pp. 188–198.

49. J. Backus, "The History of Fortran I, II, III," *IEEE Annals of the History of Computing*, vol. 20, no. 4, 1999, pp. 68–78.

50. In 1959, when Backus introduced the technique to describe ALGOL 58 (1959), it did not have this name yet. In 1963 it became known as the Backus Normal Form when computer scientist Peter Naur offered some modifications/enhancements. Computer scientist Donald Knuth, in a 1964 letter to *Communications of the ACM* (7:12 pp. 735–736), suggested Backus-Naur Form would be more appropriate based on the different criteria of the term "normal" used by top linguists and also to recognize Naur 's contributions. Today, BNF commonly stands for Backus-Naur Form.

51. J. Backus, "Can Programming Be Liberated from the von Neumann Style? A Functional Style and Its Algebra of Programs," *Communications of the ACM*, vol. 21, no. 8, 1978, pp. 613–641.

52. A. Akera, "Voluntarism and the Fruits of Collaboration: The IBM User Group, Share," *Technology and Culture*, vol. 42, no. 4, 2011, pp. 710–736. CBI has the Share, Inc. organizational records.

53. Campbell-Kelly and Aspray, *Computer*.

54. Pugh, *Building IBM*, pp. 230–232.

55. In addition to pushing for renegotiation, the "42 months" also appear in line with what would be needed for a more powerful (solid-state) machine.

56. Pugh, *Building IBM*, pp. 230–232

57. The computer system produced by the project was known as "Stretch."

58. Pugh, *Building IBM*, pp. 233–237.

59. Ibid. There is controversy whether Stretch should be considered the first supercomputer, or the Control Data Corporation 6600. The CDC 6600 was significantly faster and first delivered roughly three years after Stretch, but Stretch was easily the most powerful computer when it was delivered. With virtually all of the fastest supercomputers, there was a faster system on the market within several years.

60. Ibid.

61. If an IBM system was not back-compatible, switching costs to a new computer supplier might not be any more than switching to a different IBM system.

62. IBM would later name additional model series to the System/360 group, including the low-end Model 20 and the high-end Model 90—the latter of which was a supercomputer.

63. F.P. Brooks, Jr., *The Mythical Man-Month: Essays on Software Engineering*, Addison-Wesley Publishing Company, 1974.

64. Pugh, *Building IBM*, p. 275. Quoted from Pugh, originally from *IBM News*, Apr. 7, 1964.

65. System/360 became the inspiration and focus of study for leading management scholars C.Y. Baldwin and K.B. Clark's *Design Rules*, MIT Press, 2000, a study on the power and economic benefits of modularity in engineering. Certain aspects of IBM's modularity approach to System/360 were developed earlier with Solid Logic Technology and Standard Modular System (for circuit boards).

66. There were many restructurings initiated by Thomas Watson, Jr., between the mid 1950s and early 1970s. In general, the trend was to delegate more authority and reduce the hierarchical structure that existed under his father's tenure. In part this was a difference in managerial philosophy, but it also was a response to an increasingly large and complex corporation.

67. Yost, "Manufacturing Mainframes."

68. Digital Equipment Corporation (DEC) was founded in 1957 and pioneered the field of minicomputing. It became a major computer corporation by the late 1960s. By leaving DEC out, the "BUNCH" characterization was not reflective of all the major players in the industry.

69. E. Pugh, L. Johnson, and J. Palmer, *IBM's 360 and Early 370 Systems*, MIT Press, 1991.

70. Pugh, *Building IBM*, p. 247.

71. Pugh, *Building IBM*, pp. 250–259.

72. Considerable support was necessary with most early software products.

73. Yost, *The Computer Industry*, p. 119.

74. Humphrey's article is the best existing publicly available documentation of who was on this committee and what they discussed.

75. When IBM implemented the unbundling of some of its software in 1970, the hardware price reduction was exactly 3 percent. Humphrey's quick calculation and IBM leaders' ultimate decision likely underestimated the true cost of software. The percentage of employees argument assumes that the other 126,000 employees devoted all their time to hardware design, development, manufacturing, and service—which obviously was not the case—and that programmers' and software executives' average compensation was the average for the entire company.

76. Pugh, *Building IBM*, p. 310.

77. Pugh, *Building IBM*, pp. 250–259.

78. S.W. Usselman, "Unbundling IBM: Antitrust and the Incentives to Innovation in American Computing," *The Challenge of Remaining Innovative: Insights from Twentieth-Century American Business*, S. Clarke, N. Lamoreaux, and S. Usselman, eds., Stanford Business School Books, 2009, pp. 249–279.

79. M. Campbell-Kelly, *From Airline Reservations to Sonic the Hedgehog: A History of Software Industry*, MIT Press, 2003, pp. 149–152. This source emphasizes the importance of CICS and IMS, both technically and financially. It surveys the history of each over several pages. Campbell-Kelly makes the important point that if CICS were an independent company it would be in the top 10 in the software products industry. Many histories of IBM fail to even mention CICS or IMS—showing the clear bias toward focusing on IBM's hardware.

80. Pugh, *Building IBM*, pp. 223–226.

81. Ibid.

82. E.F. Codd, "A Relational Model of Data for Large Shared Data Banks," *Communications of the ACM*, vol. 13, no. 6, 1970, pp. 377–387.

83. A.L. Norberg and J.R. Yost, *IBM Rochester: A Half Century of Innovation*, IBM, 2005.

84. Ibid.

85. Norberg and Yost, *IBM Rochester*, p. 17.

86. Norberg and Yost, *IBM Rochester*.

87. Norberg and Yost, *IBM Rochester*; R. A. Bauer et al., *The Silverlake Project: Transformation of IBM*, Oxford University Press, 1992.

88. <www.research.ibm.com/worldwide/>

89. Fractal geometry has had many applications in the sciences following Mandelbrot's pioneering paper published in 1975 while he was a scientist for IBM Research. He followed this with a classic and more accessible book on fractal theory and its application in understanding nature: B.B. Mandelbrot, *The Fractal Geometry of Nature*, W.H. Freeman, 1982.

90. J.R. Yost, "History of Computer Security Standards," *History of Information Security*, K. de Leeuw and J. Bergstra, eds., Elsevier Science, 2007, pp. 595–621.

91. F. Hsu, *Behind Deep Blue: Building the Computer that Defeated the World Chess Champion*, Princeton University Press, 2004.

92. Software hit the market at different months or years for different systems, and not all software was available on all the major systems of the time. VisiCalc was only available for the Apple II in its first year.

93. Moore's original prediction of 12-month doubling cycles was altered to 24 months and then 18 months to correspond with actual practice. As a leader of the largest microprocessor firm in the world, Intel Corporation, his company and the semiconductor trade associations set technological roadmaps for semiconductor innovation that Intel and competitors could then deploy resources (as appropriate) to try to meet.

94. This portion of CDC lives on as the Ceridian Corporation, a company formed when CDC was dismantled in the early 1990s.

95. Pugh, *Building IBM*, p. 324.

96. L.V. Gerstner, Jr., *Who Says Elephants Can't Dance: Leading a Great Enterprise Through Dramatic Change*, HarperBusiness, 2002.

97. Pugh, *Building IBM*, p. 323.

Watson and Me:
A Life at IBM

Watson and Me: A Life at IBM

Memoirs of Walter D. Jones
Edited by Don Black

Preface

All persons interested in the early history of IBM are indebted to Don Black for finding, editing, and annotating the memoirs of Walter D. Jones, who became an employee in 1911 and rose rapidly through the ranks of what he calls "The Company."

The memoirs are particularly interesting because Jones was a customer of "The Company" before he joined it and because his career provided a broad vista of company activities. Furthermore, he became an employee at a critical time. It was only one year after Herman Hollerith had sold his Tabulating Machine Company in a merger with the Computing Scale Company and the International Time Recording Company to create the Computing-Tabulating-Recording Company (CTR). It was also less than two years before Thomas J. Watson was hired in 1914 to manage CTR, which 10 years later changed its name to IBM.

The almost instant impact Watson had on the company's sales force and products is revealed in the early pages. We learn that Watson's relationship with Hollerith was not easy. We learn how Jones's career progressed through assignments with ever increasing responsibilities in the US, Europe, and Canada. We are treated to first-hand stories dealing with manager–employee relationships, product improvements, competitive products and companies, patents, graft and bribery, taxes in foreign countries, tardy bill payers, and Watson's quiet philanthropy. We also get a good view of the adoration employees had (and were expected to show) for Watson.

The memoirs are well annotated, but because of the breadth of coverage of long-ago events, one may still encounter difficulty in understanding the context or references in some of the text. The reader who works through these occasional difficulties will be well rewarded with new insights and understanding of IBM's history and culture of more than half a century ago.

—Emerson Pugh
28 December 2002

Editor's Note

Walter Dickson Jones worked for IBM for more than 40 years. He began as a Tabulating Machine Company salesman in Cleveland, Ohio, in 1912 and ended his career as chairman of the board of IBM Canada. He was the European general manager from 1930 to early 1934 when IBM Europe was headquartered in Paris. Jones was my grandfather, and my mother sometimes shared stories of the Parisian lifestyle enjoyed by her family during the early 1930s. Beyond that, what my grandfather actually did for IBM was a matter of some speculation. Various biographies and anecdotes filled in few of the details.

I contacted the IBM Corporate Archives in New York with a broad request for information that might help me round out the story of my grandfather's working life. They sent this article, written by him in 1944 when he was near the end of his career with IBM. The article aroused my curiosity about the relationship between IBM founder Herman Hollerith and James Powers (Powers was an early competitor of Hollerith). I did a Google search on "Powers-Hollerith" and arrived at an article by a Professor T.L. Bergin. Out of the blue, I emailed Bergin. He graciously answered my questions, and after a few more emails back and forth, my grandfather's article was proposed for publication in *Annals*.

To prepare the article for publication, I put it into the first person and edited for clarity. The article did contain a section on Hollerith and the very early days of the company—I've omitted this because it did not seem to add to what is already known about those days. A section on the origins of IBM in Canada has also been omitted. Explanatory comments and "nuggets" from the IBM Archives are included as sidebars. At the suggestion of *Annals* reviewers, I rearranged the various stories more or less chronologically. In cases where my grandfather is a year or two out in dates, or appears to have a somewhat selective memory of events, I have retained the original—it's what he believed when he wrote it. I've also preserved most of his somewhat reverential writing style: It's always "Mr. Watson," "Dr. Hollerith," or "The Company." When he says, "The Company is no place for the bounder or the philanderer. We have had some in the business, but they don't stick," we can see just what kind of a man would belong in IBM and what kind of a man wouldn't.

A day at the IBM Corporate Archives, ably assisted by my cousin Nick Hare, and guided by IBM reference archivist Dawn Stanford and IBM corporate archivist Paul Lasewicz rounded out the information, set the corporate context, and resulted in the discovery of many wonderful photographs. I'd like to thank each of them for their help, and to thank *Annals* editor in chief Tim Bergin and the (anonymous) *Annals* reviewers.

—Don Black
Regina, Canada, January 2003

Personal Observations and Comments Concerning the History and Development of IBM: The Perspective of Walter D. Jones

Walter D. Jones
An IBM customer, salesman, and executive
Toronto, August 1944

My first contacts with The Company were in 1909. I was chief clerk, Journal and Statistical Division, American Steel and Wire Company in Cleveland, Ohio (see Figure 1). American Steel and Wire was a constituent company of the United States Steel Corporation. I made a trip to Pittsburgh to study the application of the Hollerith machines at the Carnegie Steel Company. I decided that the machines could be useful at the American Steel and Wire Company.

I ordered the machines through Phillip P. Merrill, who was a combination salesman and repairman at the Tabulating Machine Company (TMC). TMC was one of the three constituent companies of the Computing-Tabulating-Recording Company (CTR), formed in 1911; the other two were the International Time Recording (ITR) Company and the Computing Scale Company. CTR became IBM in 1924. Merrill was in charge of the lakeshore installation of the New York Central Railroad.

Figure 1. An early photo of Jones, c. 1910. (Courtesy of Don Black.)

Figure 2. Walter Jones (front left), about 1922, with other International Time Recording (ITR) Company sales executives. (Courtesy of IBM Corporate Archives.)

As I recall, ours was the only installation in Cleveland at this time. After considerable delay, the machines arrived in the summer of 1910. When the crates arrived, Merrill was notified. He connected the machines to an electrical current, came over to my desk, and shook hands. Before he could get out of the office, I asked him what help might be given in regard to starting the work. He replied that he was only required to connect the machine to a suitable source of electrical energy. He assumed no further responsibility, except to repair the machine, if it got out of order. That was the established policy of The Company at that time, in contrast to The Company's current policy of offering assistance and help to customers. However, the machines were successfully installed and proved to be a more efficient way of handling the statistical and accounting work.

Two years later, at Merrill's solicitation, I entered the employment of the TMC as a salesman. Shortly thereafter, I offered a suggestion regarding a backstop on the punching machine. Information received from the head office in Washington, D.C., however, was to the effect that this young man "should confine himself to selling, not inventing," with the customary sarcastic reference that the idea was as "useful as a button on a shirt-tail."

At about the time I joined The Company in 1912, a decision had been made to divide the US into districts. District managers were appointed in Philadelphia (T.J. Wilson), New York (Hyde), Boston (Sayles), Cleveland (Merrill), Chicago (Hayes), and Denver (Stoddart). The district managers attended the annual meetings, either in Washington or New York. Information regarding the activities at the conferences was not divulged to salesmen. At that time it was a small, but close, corporation (see Figure 2).

Figure 3. An ITR sales meeting, c. 1922. Watson addresses the Field Force (as it was called). Jones is third from right. Among the posted exhortations: "THINK!", "Be a self starter," "Never feel satisfied," "Plan your work, work your plan," and "Time is money." (Photo courtesy IBM Corporate Archives.)

The first convention of the TMC Division was held at the Vanderbilt Hotel in New York in December of 1915. Much to the surprise of the district managers, and even more so to the salesmen, a telegram was received from Mr. [Thomas J.] Watson notifying district managers that they were to bring the salesmen to New York to the annual convention. This was the first mark of progress in The Company's affairs, since my connection with it (see Figure 3). This action brought the salesmen together as a team for the first time. Mr. Watson will never realize the uplift and inspiration that he imparted to the salesmen of that day as a result of his conduct at the meetings.

Prospecting for customers

Embarrassing incidents occurred from time to time while prospecting for customers in the Cleveland area. One such incident was to have the general manager or the president of a company reach into his desk during a sales call and pull out a four- or five-line letter from Dr. Hollerith. The letter would say something to the effect that

In answer to your letter of today, relative to the use of our tabulating machines for your business: I can say only that your company's scope and activity is not sufficiently large enough to warrant an installation of our machines.

This usually proved a hard one to hurdle!

The remarkable growth of The Company following the radical departure from the nonlister to the printer justified the time, effort, and expense that Mr. Watson incurred in making this change. The printer made complete reports without transcription, which was not the case with the nonlister. Thus, hand printing and transcribing was eliminated. Mr. Watson engineered this change in spite of the hostile and sarcastic criticism of Hollerith who was opposed to a printing tabulator.

The thought that the nonlister was superior to the printer was so ingrained into the minds of the salesmen that it took quite a period of time before the printer's obvious superiority was acknowledged. The printer then became an integral part of the accounting system, rather than a machine to grind out statistics.

In 1914, the Vacuum Oil Company of Rochester, New York, one of the Standard subsidiaries, discontinued its contract with us. The reason for this discontinuance was that the salesman who took the order had designed a faulty product code. After the monthly sorting of the cards, the product groups would have to be rearranged by hand before tabulating. The Company found that the work involved was greater than if they had just posted the information by hand in the first place. Not surprisingly, the machines were thrown out.

I had been working on Standard Oil Company of Ohio and had almost got an order when news came of Vacuum's discontinuance. I found out the facts about the faulty Vacuum code and then went to see the president of Standard Oil, Mr. Coombs. I explained the situation to him, and he agreed that I could work with the company controller, Mr. Connelly, to determine a more logical product code arrangement. I worked with Connelly for three solid weeks and coded every one of their products in the natural and proper arrangement. I got the order and installed the machines. Thereafter, Connelly was considered the product coding authority among the various Standard Oil companies.

Jones was top salesman for the Computing-Tabulating-Recording Company in 1915. The employee newsletter of the time describes his accomplishment:

"The Tabulator" (March 1916)
His Record Speaks: Leading Salesman For 1915
W.D. Jones, Cleveland, Ohio

"Your achievements have been to us an inspiration, you have glorified hard work and proven again to us the relationship of effort to accomplishment. We are glad, sir, here upon these pages, in the company of your friends and business associates, to do you this honor. To you, Mr. W.D. Jones of Cleveland, we give [this award] in recognition for having led the field force in new business received during the year nineteen hundred fifteen."

One of the toughest pieces of prospecting that I encountered had to do with a steel company in Youngstown, Ohio. After having called numerous times and been turned down by a number of top officials, I finally got a response from the assistant treasurer. He set a time for a meeting when we would discuss my proposition. Imagine my surprise when I arrived at his office for the meeting and discovered that the sales representative for our chief competitor was also on hand for the same meeting. Mr. X, the assistant treasurer, said:

Now, I have called you men in to give both of you a chance to explain what your respective machines can do for me. Now Mr. Jones, you tell us what your tabulating machine will do. When you finish your story, then Mr. Doe will explain his proposition. I will then decide which is the better of the two proposals.

This sales call was made at a time when The Company's stock was pretty active on the market and the assistant treasurer telephoned to one of his officials to see if they had the latest quotation. Apparently the stockbroker's offices were pretty busy and he couldn't get the information.

After he had asked me to start my talk, I got up and said that we could not get anywhere with two salesmen wrangling over the respective merits of their machine, and that I was willing to let my competitor have his say first.

I took the elevator to the ground floor, just at the time when the 3 o'clock edition of the paper was being brought in. I quickly got one of the paperboys, gave him a quarter, and told him to take a paper up to Mr. X right away and to tell him that Mr. Jones had sent it up to him. After about an hour, I was invited into Mr. X's office. He was cordial indeed and thanked me for the newspaper. This little incident paved the way for very cordial relations with Mr. X. I finally had the satisfaction of taking his order.

New ideas

In 1912, a limited and small commission plan was introduced to supplement the salesmen's earnings. This scheme continued until sometime in 1914. Speaking from a salesman's point of view in the Cleveland district, I never knew the basis for the payment of the commissions. It did not concern me as most, if not all, of the commission went to the district manager. It was discontinued because it was not a well-thought-out plan.

It might be of interest to record how it came to pass that Gershom Smith, comptroller of the Pennsylvania Steel Company, Steelton, Pennsylvania, came to be appointed general manager of the Tabulating Division of the newly formed Computing-Tabulating-Recording Corporation (CTR). Smith, although a good accountant and user of tabulating machines, was quite unfitted by experience and training to head this division. The facts as related to me by a friend to whom Hollerith had told the incident, are as follows.

Charles R. Flint (the trust specialist who set up the CTR in 1911) and a director visited Hollerith in Washington, to get his recommendations in regard to someone to operate the Tabulating Division. It happened that a short time before, Smith had presented Hollerith with a large framed photograph of himself. In Hollerith's words,

As I raised my eyes to Mr. Flint, they happened to rest on the photograph of Gershom Smith. I thought to save myself a lot of bother, I might as well recommend him, for I fully expect to buy this division back from CTR before my retainer expires. In the meantime, Mr. Smith could not do much harm to the business, even if he could not do much good, and I will be kept in touch with developments.

The young men (some of whom became district managers) whom Hollerith had trained in Washington to repair the machines adopted his views. This was at a time when the doctor was making his first inroads with the railways and the insurance companies. The doctor looked upon and considered his customers to be clients, in a true professional sense, rather than in a commercial sense. Hence, it was the rule to speak of customers as clients. Another deeply rooted idea which came from Hollerith was that the machines were to be used solely for statistical purposes, and they had no place in the accounting field.

At the time when Mr. Watson took over the management of CTR in 1914, it is safe to say that every member of the sales force of the CTR thought that The Company was on the upswing of an unending period of growth, and the equipment—consisting of the no. 15 key punch, hard punch, vertical sorter, and the nonautomatic, nonlister tabulator—would do the trick.

As a matter of fact, the initial impetus given to the business occurred when Hollerith installed the large machines when the railway and insurance companies were petering out and The Company was running into shallow waters. The progress made in the bookkeeping, adding, and listing machines, and the improvements made by a competitor with a similar machine, was bidding fair to eliminate us as a serious competitor in the office specialty field. The company was going downhill instead of up, and if it had not been for the new machines that the engineering and research departments had developed under Mr. Watson, The Company would have been limited to certain kinds of statistical work. These new machines such as the horizontal high-speed sorter, printing tabulator with automatic group control, electric key punches, and many other devices, have made possible the growth of The Company.

Concurrently with the improved machines, the sales department was increased. All salesmen participated in a comprehensive educational system on our products. A refresher course for the older salesmen was also developed. The Company had a new birth and was ready for larger service to the business world, beyond the dreams of the original founders.

None of the young men who had been trained by Hollerith had much, if any, accounting experience, and it was therefore natural that they did not see the sales opportunities for the machines in the accounting field.

It was perhaps because of my background of accounting experience that, when I ordered the machines for American Steel and Wire in 1909, they were installed for accounting work primarily. In that installation, the statistics were a by-product of the accounting work. Therefore, in every order I took as a salesman in the Cleveland district, I would always work in some accounting features. My theory was that there was less chance of discontinuance if the machines were part of the company's accounting processes, rather than merely being used for gathering statistics. I always insisted that the installation be under the control of the company's accountant—this assured greater accuracy and it also established friendly relations with the accounting department.

In the natural development of things, my discontinuances were very few. In 1915, I took 12 new contracts and installed them personally. There was no discontinuance in my territory for the whole year.

Jones took a four-year hiatus from the company between 1918 and 1922 to work for the Canton Foundry, a division of Morgan Engineering, in Alliance, Ohio. In 1918, Morgan's production was totally devoted to armaments, and Jones was hired to manage the foundry. The foundry was bought by Morgan to ensure a consistent flow of raw materials. World War I was over before the end of 1918 and there was severe retrenchment at Morgan. Jones returned to CTR as Cleveland district manager in 1922. In 1924, the year the name CTR changed to IBM, he became the assistant comptroller of IBM. In 1927, he became treasurer, comptroller, and a director of IBM.

In the mid-1920s, Jim Bryce (development engineer for TMC) was developing a high-speed calculating machine, which was later added to the electrical accounting machine line as the multiplier. Because of its speed and capacity, there were doubts as to whether such a machine could be used commercially by existing customers. The Sales Department was consulted as to its potential. I was drawn into the discussion and asked for an opinion. In conversation with Bryce, Joseph Wilson (TMC vice president), and L.H. Lamotte (TMC sales manager), I pointed out that although there was little or no work in the present installations that could support such a multiplier, there were fields that we had not touched where the multiplier would be invaluable.

I cited the case of the municipal tax bill. The

bill must show the property valuation, which is calculated by three different rates, that is, school rate, municipal rate, and the county rate. I estimated there were between 500 and 3,000 cities in the US that could use a multiplier to advantage. This angle interested Bryce, as well as the Sales Department, with the result that Lamotte asked me to write out my ideas about municipal tax accounting. My ideas were turned over to the Research Department. The subject of municipal accounting was one with which I was quite familiar, having worked four years for the Town of Westmount, Quebec, writing out by hand, and calculating, the tax bills for the entire town. [Ed. note: Jones was the town clerk in Westmount, Quebec, between 1897 and 1900.]

In 1922, Jones was manager of the Cleveland district office. The following excerpt from the 11 July 1922 issue of "Business Machines," the employee newsletter, provides a glimpse of the work ethic at the time.

Mr. W.D. Jones, in charge of the TM (Tabulating Machine Company) office in Cleveland, has devised a plan which is of great assistance to the salesmen in that territory. The members of the Cleveland Office meet each Friday night at 7:00 o'clock for the purpose of increasing their knowledge of accounts by study and interchange of ideas and experiences. The plan of the meetings includes a comprehensive study of the main classes of accounts to which Tabulating Machines are particularly adaptable. Selling problems are discussed, and in complicated cases the roles of President, Auditor, Treasurer etc. are assumed by the salesmen while another salesman presents his proposition for constructive criticism. Mr. Jones believes that these meetings help them to better understand the customers' and the prospects' problems and so enable them to make a more intelligent application of the machines to the requirements of the users. The meetings are followed by bowling matches, in which we understand that Moesta and Jones are the stars. The plan which has been accepted in the Cleveland office may contain some helpful suggestions to offices in any of the divisions of our company.

In 1928, while having lunch at the Bankers Club in New York with Mack Gordon, one of my old Cleveland customers, I was discussing with him the marvel of being able to send Mr. Watson's photograph through telegraph wires to Chicago.

The thought occurred to me that if a photograph could be sent through space, it should also be possible to transfer a figure from a document through a punching machine to a hole in a card and thus eliminate the human error in punching.

In other words, the transferring of facts and figures from the document of original entry would be done electrically, thus completing the cycle of electric accounting. Upon my return from the Bankers Club, I dropped into Mr. Watson's office and found him in conversation with Andrew Jennings, an IBM executive who subsequently became European general manager, and explained my idea. Mr. Watson's comment was, "If it can be done, it will be worth a million dollars to The Company." I was told to discuss it with Bryce. I did so, and afterward an appropriation was issued for the experimental work to develop an electric-eye principle, which Bryce thought would be the best medium to experiment with.

Jones had a strong accounting background. Before joining TMC he had been chief accounting clerk for US Steel Corporation in Cleveland. He became responsible for invoicing and accounts receivable when he was appointed assistant treasurer of TMC in September 1917. He was treasurer of IBM between 1927 and 1929.

Bill collecting in New York

Collecting delinquent ITR [International Time Recording] and EAM [Electrical Accounting Machine] accounts was a bit different from collecting delinquent accounts in other businesses because of the close and continuing relationship that existed between The Company and its customers. Instead of pressure letters and calls from lawyers representing the interests of the head office, it was customary to have the EAM manager or salesman assume the role of bill collector when an account was past due (see Figure 4, next page).

This often placed our representatives in a difficult position, and a representative's frequent dunning calls to collect the money did not tend to improve his standing with his customers.

Coming out of the 1920s, a great many EAM customers were delinquent. In addition, the accounts with the government in Washington had become hopelessly in arrears for a number of reasons, one of which was the failure of the billing department to put in sufficient information to allow proper accounting

Figure 4. A photo of Jones in 1925. (Photo courtesy IBM Corporate Archives.)

account. Hence, it becomes a matter of how and when to make a compromise agreement or settlement with a customer.

To an ingenious negotiator, it is almost always possible to effect some form of agreement to protect The Company's interests and to ensure that the customer does not disregard his obligations to pay. In certain cases, treasury stock or bonds have been accepted.

> Jones moved to Paris in 1929 and became the European general manager.

The French taxman arrives

TMC was never legally established as an operating company in France. It operated in the offices of Société Internationale des Machines Commerciales (SIMC), at 29 Boulevard Malesherbes in Paris.

The work of rendering the bills to the customers throughout all Europe, outside Germany, and the collecting of the amounts due, was done by SIMC employees. TMC paid a fee to SIMC for this work. TMC maintained no bank account in France. The payments for rentals by customers in Europe, outside of Germany, were made out in US dollars and sent to Paris. They were then sent by registered mail to New York. The Company paid no taxes of any kind in France. I was assured by Jennings that this arrangement was entirely legal.

One of the SIMC employees, for reasons of personal spite, denounced TMC to the French Treasury Department in 1933. The result was that two officers of the French Treasury appeared in my office one day and demanded full information in regards to the operation of TMC, from the date of its inception. Because this looked to be serious business, I stalled the agents and made an appointment with them for the following day. I went down to see Mr. Marion, our solicitor, and reviewed the case with him. Marion stated that in his opinion the French tax authorities had grounds to impose a tax, and its size depended upon the nature of our defense. He offered his assistance, but I had found from contact with him that he lacked force as a negotiator, and besides, his attitude showed that he had already prejudiced the case. I then got in touch with the IBM head office in New York and asked that Mr. Kennerly, a tax specialist, be sent to Paris to assist in the defense of the Company's interests.

to be made for the public monies expended. Something had to be done and it was decided to make a change.

W.C. Sieberg, who was the general bookkeeper of the EAM Division, was given the job. His first task was to straighten out the Washington situation and then he was to move on and clean up the rest of the accounts throughout the country. Sieberg spent about four months in Washington and got the government accounts up to date. At the same time that Sieberg was chasing down delinquent customers, we brought in Mr. Brown to do Sieberg's old job. Brown had been an accountant at a factory, and we brought him in so that he would gain a thorough knowledge of head office accounting, which he could then take back to the factory.

By way of commentary, it is my opinion that a good EAM accountant, of broad commercial training, should always work as the liaison man for the collection of delinquent accounts rather than the salesman. The Company has never, to my knowledge, prosecuted a customer for the nonpayment of an

A 1 May 1933 letter from Jones informs Watson of the French situation. In part, the letter (courtesy IBM Corporate Archives) says:

Dear Mr. Watson,

The Tabulating Machine Company's operations in Europe are controlled from Paris. The Company is not registered in France and has never paid any taxes here. The SIMC acts as an Agent or Correspondent and charges TMC a nominal fee for the office space and the work of making out the invoices and the collection of the customer accounts. The fact remains, however, that the effective control of the European business of the TMC is located in Paris and on account of the fact that we are not registered here, the trend of the present legislation will undoubtedly make our position vulnerable for the future with the possibility of fines and taxation for a period of past years. This latter condition to be considered in the way the German tax authorities have interpreted tax laws and made them retroactive. ...

I am bringing this matter to your attention as I think it of the greatest importance to establish the operations of the TMC on a more secure basis. I doubt very much whether we could do this in France, on account of the possibility of fines and back taxes and I think England or Holland offer the best possibilities. I am investigating these countries under cover. I have already investigated Switzerland, Luxembourg and Liechtenstein, the two latter on account of low taxes, but neither one of the three would be suitable. Mr. Battin informed me in his letter of June 24, 1931 that he had discussed my letter of June 12, 1931 with you on this subject, and I am bringing it to your attention so as to receive your advice and instructions in case it is necessary to act in a hurry.

With kindest regards, I remain,
Yours very truly
W.D. Jones

In the meantime the agents, armed with the authority of the French law, conducted a cursory investigation. During this preliminary investigation, I got as much information out of them as possible in order to get a line on the scope of how, and pertinent facts by which, they hoped to prove their case. When they presented their initial findings, they had arrived at a tax of between 50 million and 60 million francs. They were very decent, however, and when I explained that a representative from New York was coming over to go into the matter in greater detail with them, they agreed to hold off making an arbitrary tax demand until the representative arrived. As a result of Kennerly's proficient presentation of our case, together with whatever assistance I was able to provide, the tax was reduced to about 2,300,000 francs. This sum included all penalties.

Euro-graft

The following illustrates the mentality of a certain type of French government official, and their attitude toward what is commonly known as graft.

One day in 1932 I received a phone call from Mr. Lawrence, a SIMC salesman. He wanted me to authorize a payment of 30,000 francs to a French government official. Lawrence told me that this payment would secure an order for six complete installations in six different departments of the French government. This one order would provide us with an annual income of 30 million francs. Lawrence further stated that once the order was signed, we would also be required to make a one-time payment of 3 million francs—to be divided among the higher-ups. My reply to Lawrence was "Not one centime!" Not surprisingly, the order went to a competitor.

In due course, a million and a half dollars' worth of competitor's equipment arrived at Le Havre. It was unloaded and placed in a warehouse. The French government refused to accept delivery. The equipment remained in storage for a couple of years, at which time our competitor tried to sell it throughout Europe for half price.

Graft was flagrant and open in the Balkan countries—no doubt a hangover from the days of Turkish domination. Graft was even carried to the point where a government official would give an order to a company for goods which the government had no intention of buying. The contract would carry stiff penalties for contract cancellation. When the official cancelled the order, the penalty would be paid by the government and divvied up among the interested parties.

When I arrived in Paris, Jennings explained to me that all tabulating machine price lists for the Balkan countries were 10 percent higher than the rest of Europe. This 10 percent represented the amount of money that we would return to the "interested parties." He even had a rubber stamp made up for Balkan price lists that said simply "10 percent of prices added."

When I became European manager, I countermanded these instructions. I gave orders that EAM prices were to be the same in the Balkans as in the rest of Europe and no orders to be accepted on which The Company was required to pay anything other than the salesman's regular commission.

Figure 5. Watson toured Europe in 1933. Jones arranged this banquet at the Adlon Hotel in Berlin in Watson's honor. Dehomag manager Willy Heidinger is front right, Jones is third from right, and Watson is fifth from right. (Photo courtesy IBM Corporate Archives.)

The Block Brun Company—Warsaw

The TMC agent in Poland was the firm of Block Brun Company, appointed by Jennings in 1927 or 1928. The principals were highly respected and wealthy, third-generation Moscow Jews. The headquarters of the firm was still in Moscow. The Warsaw branch was managed by Stefan Brun, one of the partners who looked after the EAM business.

Jennings was quite frank in stating one particularity about Block Brun. As well as being our agent for EAM equipment, it was also the agent for typewriters and adding machines of a competing company. This was rather disturbing news to me, and I made an early trip to Warsaw to see how the company operated. My investigation convinced me that the two agencies were run by separate organizations of Block Brun. I was also convinced that they were honorable in every respect concerning their obligations to the two companies.

The following is an example of just how honest they were. I was acting as chairman of a German banquet honoring Mr. Watson at the Hotel Adlon in Berlin in 1933 when a messenger brought in a note from Stefan Brun saying that he had to see me at once on urgent business (see Figure 5).

I excused myself to Hermann Rottke, general manager of Dehomag, which was the IBM German subsidiary. Brun told me that while he was waiting in an anteroom of the competitor's office, he overheard their managers and patent attorneys discussing plans to bring a patent suit against Dehomag. The facts were passed on to Rottke, and to Willy Heidinger—who had licensed Hollerith's machines and who had created Dehomag in 1910—and Dehomag made a quick investigation. After a meeting between Dehomag attorneys and the competitor's attorneys, the proposed suit was shelved. Brun had nothing to gain from this personally, but his actions portrayed his loyalty.

The story of Tauschek in Europe

The advent of Gustav Tauschek into the electrical accounting field makes interesting reading. Tauschek lived in Vienna and worked as a bank clerk. In 1926 or 1927, the Powers Accounting Company was a client of the bank. One of Tauschek's duties was to scrutinize checks, including those from Powers Accounting, whose checks required two signatures.

On one occasion, Tauschek failed to note that only one signature was on a check destined for New York. The check came back and Tauschek took it to the Powers' office to have it signed. Tauschek had never seen Powers' accounting machines, and he asked the company manager to explain the machines to him (see Figure 6).

Tauschek made one or two visits to get additional information, and in the course of conversation, he found that the mechanical tabulating machines were being sold in Europe for between $15,000 and $20,000. Tauschek decided that the price was too high and that a cheaper machine could be built that would do the same work.

He then got in touch with patent offices in Germany, Great Britain, and the US. Tauschek had copies of all patents, which had been issued concerning tabulating machines, sent to him. He then took a course in English so that he could read and comprehend all the material.

As a result of investigations, research, and model building, he secured patents from Germany, Great Britain, and the US in and around existing patents. He then manufactured a model of a key punching machine, a sorter, and a tabulating machine, the principles of which were slightly different from the existing types.

With this beginning, Tauschek entered into a contract with the Rhein Metalls Company (Rheinischen Metall-und Maschinenfabrik) to develop his patents and build the machines for commercial use. This contract was entered into around 1929.

Dehomag, our German subsidiary, was somewhat disturbed by Tauschek's being a potential competitor and was in favor of negotiating with him.

During a trip to Europe in 1930, Mr. Watson had Rottke and Tauschek come to London, to meet with himself, Jennings, and myself (as the newly appointed European general manager). The negotiations were held in Grosvenor House in London. After a week of negotiating, the IBM Company bought out Tauschek's patents, and the models he had developed, with the exception of one set of machines that Tauschek presented to the Vienna museum. As well, Tauschek secured five years of employment with IBM, seven months of each year to be spent at the IBM labs in the US. As additional consideration, Tauschek also agreed to unreservedly convey all his ideas and patents with regards to electric accounting machines.

At about the time of the end of his contract with IBM, it was discovered that he had secretly proceeded with certain patents concerning the development of an electric-eye principle. He had not turned this work over to IBM, as per the terms of his agreement with us. Tauschek was brought sharply to task by The Company but it began to look as if the only way The Company could get redress would have been through the courts. In the midst of negotiations, he fled, returning illegally to Germany. The rumor was that he had been called back to Germany to complete work on a new type of machine gun that he had developed for the German government. [Ed. note: Tauschek died in Switzerland in 1945.]

German capital structure, Nazis on staff

There are a number of reasons that led up to the increase of the capital structure and the consolidation of the three companies in Germany: Dehomag, Ingomag (the scale company), and the Sindelfingen Scale Factory. The capital of these companies was nominal. I think that Dehomag's amounted to something like 300,000 marks. We had kept the capital of the companies low on purpose, because the German government taxed on capital stock. In fact, the two scale companies had never shown a profit. Dehomag was different, though, and in 1932 and 1933 its profits soared to four and five times its capitalization. The German Treasury began careful scrutiny of firms such as ours, and of course this scrutiny was aided by supplementary information provided by Nazi "observers." The observers were assigned by party leaders to all industrial plants throughout Germany. There was always one observer keeping track of things

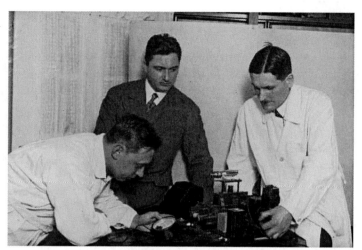

Figure 6. Gustav Tauschek and assistants looking over a new machine. (Photo courtesy of Bildarchiv der sterreichischen Nationalbibliothek [National Library of Austria], Vienna.)

and in some cases two or three, depending on the size of the plant.

At Dehomag we had a young Nazi by the name of Fredericks who was on staff as an observer. I later learned that Fredericks was one of the party of six Nazis who broke into General von Schleicher's residence during the infamous June 1934 "Night of the Long Knives" purge of Ernst Röhm and 70 or 80 others.

The fact that Dehomag was paying out annual dividends many times the amount of its capital had resulted in certain questions being asked by the German Treasury. At the same time, Dehomag had been made the target of abuse and criticism from the Nazi-controlled press throughout Germany on the grounds that the use of Dehomag electric accounting machines threw clerks out of work. In government offices in Hanover in 1932, civil service employees went on a bit of a rampage and partially destroyed their newly installed Dehomag machines. This incident received widespread publicity.

About this time our agent in Munich, a Mr. Pappenburg, had caused Rottke and Heidinger some concern due to reports coming in to the Munich office concerning Pappenburg's unexplained absences from work. They asked me if it would be all right if they put a "tail" on Pappenburg. Because they seemed quite worried, I agreed. The reports we got back showed that Pappenburg was an active Nazi and that his absences were due to his attendance at various conferences and meetings of the Nazi party. This gave Heidinger the idea of using Pappenburg to meet Hitler at Hitler's Nazi headquarters. He wanted to establish friendly

Figure 7. IBM had a large display at the Canadian National Exhibition in 1941. When Watson visited, Jones ushered him around. In this photograph Jones (with technical help) explains the latest IBM technology to Watson. (Photo courtesy IBM Corporate Archives.)

Jones returned from Europe to become vice president of IBM in Canada in 1934. His family was Canadian, his wife's family was Canadian, and he was very happy to receive the appointment.

In Canada

Between 1935 and 1939, the income and profits of the Canadian company increased 70 percent. From 1935 to 1943, the income and profits increased 800 percent. Although it is true that this remarkable growth has taken place during the war years, it should not be overlooked that the extreme confidence, both on the part of business and the government in Ottawa, led them to place their orders with our company.

This confidence was based upon the performance of the machines, as well as the character and ability of the personnel in the Canadian organization. These people, through lean years and good years, have worked conscientiously in the building of the good name of IBM in the minds of customers and prospects. It may also be said that the government, in searching for the mechanical means to fill its needs during the war for accounting and statistical requirements has, with one exception, considered only our company as a source of supply.

The prestige of The Company was greatly increased by Mr. Watson's visits to Canada prior to and following 1937. In 1937, as in each year thereafter, he met the most prominent men in Canada. He also made many public addresses. On 2 September 1941, he took IBM's entire executive staff to the Canadian National Exhibition in Toronto (see Figure 7). The Company was being honored at the Exhibition's International Day.

That evening, entertainers Lily Pons and Lawrence Tibbett gave a concert at the band shell in front of some 60,000 people. This large audience was addressed by Mr. Watson, Mrs. August Belmont [Eleanor Belmont was the widow of American banker August Belmont], and myself. At that concert, a generous donation of $10,000 went from The Company to the Canadian Red Cross to help in the war effort. Although this large sum was given without publicity, the kind comments of the officer and directors of the Red Cross would have been heartwarming to any IBM executives, could they have heard them.

During Mr. Watson's visits to Toronto (see Figure 8), many changes were made to the form and conduct of the business. In the latter part

relations with Hitler and the Nazi party so that the party would discontinue its attacks on Dehomag.

The result of this meeting relieved The Company from further investigation by the German government, and hostile criticism of The Company by the Nazi-controlled press stopped. In addition, the capitalization of the German companies was increased to 7,000,000 marks. All the losses at the Sindelfingen plant and at Ingomag were also capitalized. Over time, Dehomag and the Sindelfingen plant became the only active units in Germany. The small scale factory (Ingomag) gradually folded. In 1934, the output of the Sindelfingen plant was 85 percent weaving machines, most of which were sold to the Russian and German armies for the making of military uniforms.

Rottke did not become a Nazi until 1933. In the fall of that year I called a meeting in Paris of all European managers, which Rottke attended. During the meeting, he took me to one side and said that a demand had been served on him by the Nazi party to become a member. He wanted my advice and showed me the letter and stamped, self-addressed envelope that the Nazis had given him. Rottke told me that he had been given 24 hours in which to answer their demands. From his manner, I surmised that he was hoping that I would advise him not to join. But this was clearly a matter for Rottke and his family to decide, on their own. I understand that he mailed his application to join the Nazi party the next morning.

Figure 9. Rhoda Jones (wife of W.D. Jones), Watson, and Jones at a luncheon held at the King Edward Hotel to celebrate the opening of the Toronto offices on 28 Nov. 1938. (Photo courtesy IBM Corporate Archives.)

Figure 8. Watson (left) and Jones (right), late 1930s in Toronto. (Photo courtesy IBM Corporate Archives.)

of 1937, he purchased the property on King Street, and the executive offices were separated from the factory. IBM executives could thus be located in the heart of the city's financial district. The offices were officially opened in 1938 (see Figure 9).

Another factor that had a lot to do with the welding of The Company personnel into a united team was Mr. Watson's authorization for the purchase of a country club. This property, purchased in 1942, consists of 100 acres just outside Toronto city limits. Fully equipped, it has a playhouse and playgrounds so that the entire family can enjoy themselves. Mr. Watson authorized the purchase of an additional 100 acres adjacent to the country club. This property crosses the main feeder line for the Canadian National Railroad (CNR) and will make a suitable site for a manufacturing plant as needed in the future.

The story of the British war orphans

Following the German invasion of France in May and June of 1940, when England was in great danger, Mr. Watson, with characteristic thoughtfulness for others, cabled Stafford Howard, managing director of the ITR in London, inviting the wives and children of employees to take refuge in Canada at The Company's expense.

In response, nine mothers and 19 children arrived in Toronto on 5 July 1940. This first group was followed by a second group of three mothers and four children on 9 October of the same year. They were temporarily housed at the Sisters of St. John the Devine hostel at 49 Brunswick Street in Toronto.

Mr. Watson then authorized the purchase of lake frontage at Bronte, about 28 miles west of Toronto. This property consisted of eight acres, including fruit and market gardens and two fine houses. When Mr. Watson and a Mr. Nichol visited Toronto on 15 July 1940 to inspect the property and make the necessary arrangements, certain reservations on the part of some of the evacuees caused him to abandon his plan—and the property was sold without loss.

The evacuees were then lodged in boarding houses in the west end of Toronto. Now that return permits are being granted by the British government, some of our families have returned home, and there will no doubt be others in the near future.

Costs and profitability during the war

On 2 March 1943, the Canadian company was asked by the Department of Munitions and Supply to submit a statement of income, costs, and profit on any installations that might be considered war business with the department. This request was later broadened to include all government business, which could be classified as war business. The object of the inquiry was to renegotiate our contracts with all government departments to establish fair and reasonable profits on installations arising out of the war and to arrive at the portion of the profit to be refunded.

At that time, the Canadian company purchased EAM equipment from the parent company on the basis of flat factory cost. We therefore brought to the attention of department officials that we were unable to submit an accurate statement of costs. This flat factory cost

Figure 10. Watson addresses the troops at the Toronto office in 1943. Rhoda Jones, an IBM employee during World War II (daughter of W.D. Jones and mother of Don Black, this article's editor), is seated at the desk, Jones is standing at the far right of the picture. (Photo courtesy IBM Corporate Archives.)

did not include administrative overhead, or the costs of engineering, patents, development, or research (see Figure 10). The department indicated that it would be perfectly reasonable to include any such items in our estimate of our costs and that the department would have the right to scrutinize such items to determine whether they were fair and reasonable.

On 4 June 1943 our controller, A.L. Williams, furnished a statement that showed the amount of such expenses, applicable to the Canadian company, expressed in terms of percent, would approximate 5 percent of the total revenue of the Canadian company for the year 1942.

The increase in cost of the overall picture of the Canadian company, had the expense been included, would have amounted to Can $167,687 (gross Canadian income: $3,563,917) of which about $50,000 would be the amount to be added to the cost of our war installations with the government. Government installations were approximately Can $1,000,000 per year, about 25 percent of total installations.

In view of the known losses we would sustain when the war ended by discontinuances and cancellations, plus the unamortized value of the machines that would be returned to us, I did not consider that the figures being presented were fair for The Company. It was not enough for us just to build up our cost figures.

I therefore decided to fight for the inclusion in our costs of the 25 percent royalty paid by other subsidiary companies. We were finally able to convince department officials to agree to the inclusion of this 25 percent fee and an agreement was reached by May of this year [1944]. On $1,000,000 of revenue, the royalty cost will amount to $250,000 as against $50,000 had we decided to include IBM Corporation overhead as an item of cost.

Bounders need not apply

The policy inaugurated by Mr. Watson to encourage employees to mix in community affairs and join business and trade associations has had much to do with establishing the prestige and reputation of our company, as well as the development of the individual. The Company's employees represent a standard of intelligence and character that fits them all for such a role. The very nature of the business permits and demands constant development along business lines. This is characteristic of the suc-

In Conclusion (Things Discovered In the Archives)

I believe that my grandfather was, first and foremost, a very successful salesman. The significant accounting experience he had prior to joining TMC helped him apply the company's technology in innovative, profitable ways. Because of this success he advanced quickly in the organization and had a rewarding career. His climb up the ladder was put on hold between 1918 and 1922 when he left CTR to work for the Canton Foundry Division of Morgan Engineering in Alliance, Ohio. When he returned to IBM (after the foundry floundered), he became manager of the Cleveland district. By 1927, he was in New York and on the IBM board. He became European manager in late 1929, staying there until late 1934. He then became vice president of IBM in Canada, then became chairman of the board of directors of the Canadian corporation. My grandfather was a rabid IBM'er for more than four decades until he retired (see Figure A), and he had certainly helped IBM become one of the first true multinationals. He had extensive contact with Watson Sr. throughout his career.

Figure A. W.D. Jones died in 1963, age 85. This picture, taken in 1959, shows Jones, his daughter Frances Henderson, granddaughter Rosemary Henderson, and his wife Rhoda. He's looking at his pocket watch, probably wondering if it wasn't about time that he should go back to the office.

I wondered at the overly obsequious tone of his communications with Watson. Certainly a personality cult surrounded Watson, but my grandfather seemed to take it a bit too far. For example, here is a typical excerpt from one of the sales wrap-ups that he sent to all the European offices every month while he was European manager:

Paris, January 3, 1931
I am very pleased to note the excellent results produced by many of the offices. Your efforts have resulted in a volume of business which has made December one of the best months of the year. All business houses have just completed their inventories in order to find out how they stand. Let us therefore take an inventory of our Company, ourselves and our organisation. First, consider the supreme effort on the part of Mr. WATSON and his Executive staff to give to the world the best machines that brains can design and money can build ...

Family history had it that "WD" (like many other American businessmen) had lost all his money in the October 1929 stock market crash. A series of letters in the IBM Corporate Archives details a close relationship between "WD" and IBM and perhaps provides some context behind my grandfather's devotion to the company:

New York, June 21, 1933
The Chase National Bank of the City of New York

Gentlemen:
You have a loan to Mr. W.D. Jones as evidenced by his note for $88,874.35 [*Ed. note:* goods and services that cost $88,874 in 1933 would cost just over $1.25 million in 2002] dated May 11, 1933, the present balance of the principal of which is $61,946.40, secured by 691 shares of capital stock of the International Business Machines Corporation and referred to in our letter of May 11, 1933. We understand you have received instructions from Mr. Jones to deliver from the collateral 400 shares IBM stock, upon payment to you of the proceeds, 400 shares at 132 1/4, the net proceeds to be applied in reduction of the loan. This is to advise you that we agree to the delivery of the stock and application of the proceeds, as set for the above and reaffirm that if the note is not paid at maturity we will, on demand, purchase from you the remaining collateral, securing the note at the amount due upon the note – principal and interest.
O.E. Braitmayer,
Vice President, International Business Machines Corporation
270 Broadway, New York

By October 1933, at the height of the depression, the debt had been cleared up and IBM Secretary George Phillips wrote to Jones:

Mr. W.D. Jones
International Business Machines Co. Ltd.,
112 Strand, London WC2
October 13, 1933
Dear Walter:
I have your letter of the 2nd. Enclosed herewith are the stock powers which were at the Empire Trust Company. I am sorry that you disposed of some of your stock so quickly but on the other hand I congratulate you on being out of debt. I did the same thing and it is a grand and glorious feeling.
With kindest personal regards.
JGP

Correction

In the April–June 2003 issue of *Annals*, Figure 1 (p. 3) from David Caminer's article "Behind the Curtain at LEO: A Personal Reminiscence" contained an error regarding the date of the Lyons payroll job. It should have been 1954, as follows. *Annals* regrets this error.

1949—Decision made to design and build an electronic computer to serve the Lyons business.

1951—The world's first business computer job starts running regularly on the basic LEO.

1954—The world's first full-scale business computer job, the Lyons payroll, ran on the completed LEO I computer. LEO Computers set up as a subsidiary of J. Lyons and Co.

1962—The multiprogrammed, solid-state LEO III was delivered three years ahead of its IBM equivalent.

1963—Merger of LEO Computers and English Electric computer division.

1969—The final deliveries of LEO 326 computers (the fastest of the LEO III range) were made, completing 61 LEO III deliveries in all.

Figure 1. Key milestones in LEO development.

Web Extras

Additional, online-only material about Walter Jones and IBM—correspondence between Thomas J. Watson and Jones, a timeline of Jones's life, and IBM songs—can be found at http://csdl.computer.org/comp/mags/an/2003/03/a3toc.htm

cessful IBM man and stamps him with qualities of leadership, both in public speaking and leadership. He attracts attention wherever businessmen gather. In the US and Canada you will find IBM men in the forefront of sales executives' clubs, chambers of commerce, manufacturers' associations, and boards of trade. Honors and preferments seem to come to them naturally. This is the natural product of the educational system fostered and promoted by Mr. Watson. The Company is no place for the bounder or the philanderer. We have had some in the business, but they don't stick.

Don Black is a policy advisor for the Saskatchewan government, concentrating on public-sector electronic service delivery and electronic governance issues. He has undergraduate degrees in journalism from Carleton University in Ottawa, English literature from the University of Calgary, and an MSc in management from Purdue University.

Readers may contact Don Black at dblack@1stcounsel.com.

Walter Dickson Jones (1878–1963) began work for IBM in 1912. His first contact with the Tabulating Machine Company, a precursor of IBM, was as a customer in 1909. He became a salesman for the Tabulating Machine Company in 1912 and ended his career as chairman of the board of IBM Canada some 40 years later. During those 40 years, he worked at the head office in New York, as a district sales manager in Cleveland, as European general manager, and as Watson's representative on the board of Dehomag, the German subsidiary. This article was written by Jones in 1944.

A Large-Scale, General-Purpose Electronic Digital Calculator: The SSEC

A Large-Scale, General-Purpose Electronic Digital Calculator— The SSEC

JOHN C. MCPHERSON, FRANK E. HAMILTON, AND ROBERT R. SEEBER, JR.

This paper, written and intended for publication in 1948, describes IBM's Selective Sequence Electronic Calculator (SSEC), which was placed in regular operation that year. The machine combined electronic computation with a memory system that included electronic, relay, and paper-tape sections. It executed programs stored exactly as data in any of the sections of memory, and could select, compute, or modify the program in a variety of ways. The speed and flexibility of the SSEC permitted it to solve many of the largest scientific problems of the day, including the generation of astronomical tables still used in space flight.

*Categories and Subject Descriptors: K.2 [**History of Computing**]— hardware, SSEC, software*
General Terms: Design, Experimentation
Additional Key Words and Phrases: relay memory, paper-tape memory, electronic memory, stored program, IBM Corporation

---

The Selective Sequence Electronic Calculator (SSEC) built by IBM and dedicated recently to the use of science is a new tool for the convenient handling of complex and burdensome computational problems that occur in many fields of science, engineering, and research. Recent articles[1] have described other large-scale devices built, or proposed, and outline the general characteristics of this class of machine and their field of usefulness.

---

[1] For example, see the following articles in *Electrical Engineering:* Aiken, H. H., and G. M. Hopper, The Automatic Sequence Controlled Calculator. *Electrical Engineering*, Part I, *65* (1946), 384–391; Part II, *65*, 449–454; Part III, *65*, 522–528. Large-scale computer developments discussed. *Electrical Engineering 66* (1947), 289–290. Tumbleson, R. C., Calculating machines. *Electrical Engineering 67*, (1948), 6–12. Brainerd, J. G., and T. K. Sharpless, *Electrical Engineering 67* (1948), 163–172.

Author's Address: John C. McPherson, P.O. Box 333, Short Hills, NJ 07078.
© 1982 AFIPS 0164-1239/82/040313–326$01.00/00

1. Design Objectives

The SSEC is noteworthy for realization of electronic speed in a general-purpose calculator, for the extent of its number storage or memory, and for its ease of use. The critical problem in the design was to integrate satisfactorily a high-speed electronic computing unit with a sufficiently large number memory to keep the computing unit supplied with numbers and store the results as rapidly as they were produced. This calls for not only an effective computing and memory unit, but also a carefully worked out system for routing numbers to and from the computing unit, and a system of control and automatic instructions adequate to keep the machine in continuous operation for the rapid solution of a problem.

It has been estimated that an adequate memory unit must remember from 1000 to 5000 ten-digit numbers, or say 50,000 digits. By combining (1) electronic storage for rapid recovery of numbers, (2) relay storage for numbers that must be recovered not quite so rapidly, and (3) storage in punched holes for recovery in relatively longer intervals of time, this machine achieves a memory capacity far in excess of this requirement.

To make the machine easy to use, a system for controlling the machine based on standard IBM punched cards is used. The series of instructions by which the computation is to be made are transcribed from a code sheet to punched cards. These instructions are in the form of decimal numbers. As the plan for the computational procedure progresses, the cards can be rearranged, extra steps added, and any changes made that are necessary. When this card file of instructions is completed, it is used to punch sequence (instruction) tapes automatically on a card-to-tape punch. These sequence tapes set up all number paths, controls, and electronic operational commands needed to permit the machine to perform each step of the computation.

John C. McPherson graduated from Princeton University in 1929 with an electrical engineering degree. He joined IBM in 1930 and began his lifelong interest in novel applications of punched-card machines and computers. He was a pioneer in the use of electromechanical machines for scientific computing. During World War II he was instrumental in the establishment of a punched-card computing facility at the Ballistic Research Laboratory at Aberdeen Proving Ground. As director of engineering at IBM from 1943 to 1946, he participated in the early planning of the SSEC. He was elected an IBM vice president in 1948. McPherson was chairman of the 1951 Joint Computer Conference, the first in a series of which the 1981 National Computer Conference was the 50th. He was first director of IBM's graduate-level Systems Research Institute, from 1960 to 1965. He retired in 1971.

Frank E. Hamilton joined IBM in 1923 and spent most of his career in the Endicott, New York, engineering laboratory. He participated in the development of a number of punched-card accounting machines and had a major part in directing the design and construction of the IBM Automatic Sequence Controlled Calculator, which became known as the Harvard Mark I. He managed the development of the SSEC and shortly thereafter the IBM 650 drum computer, announced in 1953. Hamilton became manager of the Endicott Product Development Laboratory in 1954. He was named an IBM Fellow in 1963, and retired in that same year. He died in 1972.

Robert R. Seeber, Jr., a mathematician with experience in large-scale calculation, took an active part in the planning of the SSEC immediately upon

2. Units Composing the Calculator

The SSEC consists of an electronic computing section that includes a multiplying and dividing unit, an accumulator, a shift unit, electronic memory units, and the necessary electronic controls.

The relay memory section provides the means for storing data in electromagnetic relays, including the necessary relay switching for transferring numbers into and out of the unit, sequence-controlled signals, and a series of removable plugboard control panels to provide flexibility in transmission of numbers.

The card readers serve as a means for introducing problem data and instructions into the machine directly from IBM standard punched cards.

Three tape memory units provide extensive and rapid storage for intermediate results that will be required in the problem at a later time.

The table-lookup unit, using punched paper tapes prepared automatically from punched-card mathematical tables, makes available any desired value of any one of six different mathematical functions.

Two multiple bar printers, each capable of printing a line of 80 digits at one time, record as much of the computation as is desired to permit the user of the machine to follow the course of the computation.

Card punches serve to make a perfect machine record of the final results of the computation or other results as are deemed necessary for use in future computations.

The various main sections of the calculator are arranged around three sides of a room approximately 30 × 60 feet, with the card-reading tubes, control tubes, and table-lookup unit along the left wall. The three tape memory units are across the rear of the room, with the main relay memory and table-lookup controls on large racks immediately in back of them, the electronic calculating and electronic memory units along the right wall, and the printers, card readers, card punches, and manual control console grouped on

---

joining IBM in 1945. As a senior staff member of the Watson Scientific Computing Laboratory at Columbia University, he contributed a number of important ideas to the organization of the SSEC. Among them was the concept that instructions should be in the same form as data and that the machine should be able to operate on them. Having been interested in associative memory for a number of years, he spent his last several years in IBM on that subject. He retired in December 1968 and died only a few months thereafter.

Figure 1. General view of the calculator.

the machine floor where they are easily accessible to the operators (see Figure 1).

The principal connections between the units of the calculator are multiwire buses, each consisting of four circuits for each of the 19 digits of the number plus two circuits for the algebraic sign and two circuits carrying interlock signals.

3. Number Representation and Number Paths

The four circuits representing a digit have the values 1, 2, 4, and 8, with the number 6, for example, represented by energization of the 2 and the 4 circuits. Since the representation is binary within each decimal digit, we refer to it as the binary-decimal notation. Each of the multiwire buses thus contains 82 parallel channels. Between the electronic unit and the other parts of the calculator there are 8 of these multiwire buses bringing numbers out of relay and tape units to the electronic unit designated as the main *"out"* buses, and a corresponding group of 8 main *"in"* buses to transfer computed results from the electronic unit into

relay storage or the table lookup unit. Connections between any storage unit or other source of information and the electronic unit can be made by using any of the 8 *in* or *out* buses. Two of each of these buses are usually assigned to reading instructions and the other six to supplying number data to the electronic unit as directed by instructions from the sequence control.

The electronic computer is basically designed to handle 14-digit numbers, with suitable arrangements to carry out computations to more places when desired. The multiplying unit accepts 14-digit factors and produces 28-digit products. The dividing unit accepts dividends and divisors of 14 digits and produces a 14-digit quotient. The accumulator permits adding or subtracting of 19-digit numbers and produces a 28-digit sum. (A sum of this size can be produced only by a series of accumulations because the bus capacity is but 19 digits.) The individual relay memory units are capable of storing numbers of 19 digits and algebraic sign, and the tape memory units also record 19 digits and a sign in a line of punching across the tape. The

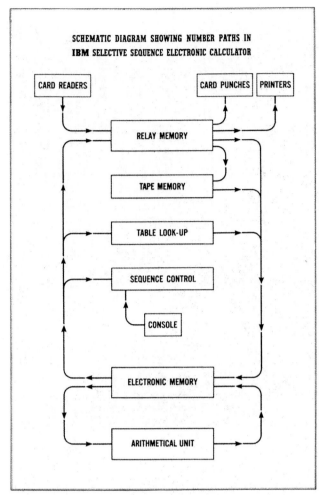

Figure 2. Calculator component connections.

table-lookup unit uses paper tapes similar to those used in the tape memory unit with a maximum of 5 digit positions normally assigned to the argument for selection and 14 digits to the functional values.

As shown in Figure 2, the tape memory, card readers, card punches, and printers are directly connected to the relay memory. This simplifies the timing relations between the mechanical units and the electronic unit, because the time of transmission of numbers into and out of the mechanical units is relatively slow, and traffic over the main buses should not be held up waiting the completion of their operation. This direct connection also takes care of the conversion between the decimal representation of the input and output devices and the binary-decimal representation used in the calculator. Similar circuits are used to check all punching on either cards or tapes by reading information from relay memory and comparing it with the number that had been punched in the preceding operation.

All of the arithmetical operations performed by the calculator are carried out in the electronic computing section, schematically shown in Figure 3. This section consists of multiplying-dividing unit, accumulator, independent column-shift unit, and eight electronic memory units. Numbers from the other parts of the machine are simultaneously imposed on the main *out* buses, then simultaneously stored in the electronic memory units directly associated with these buses in successive electronic cycles. A single internal *in* and *out* bus of 28-digit capacity transfers numbers electronically between the various computing units and from and to electronic memory units by repeated high-speed use of the single channel.

4. Electronic Computing Section

All arithmetical operations are performed through the use of electronic counter units employing the Eccles-Jordan circuit of the general type used in commercial IBM electronic calculators (see Figures 4 and 5).

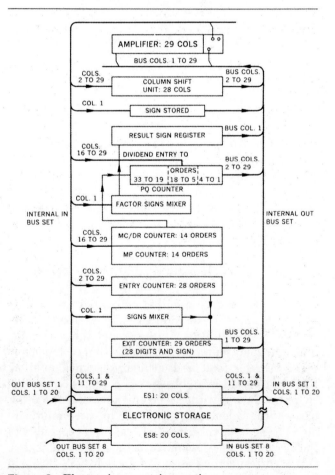

Figure 3. Electronic computing section.

Figure 4. A pair of counter units. (The nine tubes represent two decimal positions.)

4.1 Electronic Accumulator

Two groups of 28 each of these counter units comprise an accumulator. One group is designated the "entry" counter; the other is the "exit" counter. A number that is to be added is stored in the accumulator entry counter by opening electronic gates from the particular electronic storage unit in which the number resides, followed by the opening of a similar set of gates to the accumulator. All decimal positions of the number are stored simultaneously in binary decimal notation.

Whether the operation is to be adding or subtracting is determined by a combination of the algebraic sign of the number that accompanies its transmission and the operational sign indicated by the sequence coding. If the operation is to be adding, each decimal position of the number is simultaneously counted into the exit counter. If the operation is to be subtracting, this counting is done so as to express the number in the exit counter as the complement to 9 in every decimal order except the units, which is expressed as the complement to 10.

The adding cycle consists of 14 pulses, the first 9 of which are used to designate the value of the digit. A later pulse in this cycle is used to cause the carry. Those positions that have passed to, or beyond, 0 in the process of adding cause a 1 to be added into the next higher order at carry time. If one or more orders to the left of a position that has gone to 0 stand at 9, that order *and* the order immediately to its left are advanced one. This operation is simultaneously performed in all decimal orders.

A 29th position in the accumulator detects whether the number is positive by the presence of a 0 or negative by the presence of a 9. This same position is used to indicate a sum that is over the capacity of the accumulator by the presence of digits from 1 through 8. The detection of this condition or incorrect algebraic sign interrupts computations so that the reason may

be investigated. Computation can be resumed by a proceed signal manually initiated from the control console.

When a sequence order is given for the computer to read out a sum, the 29th order of the accumulator is examined; if a 9 is detected, a series of operations ensue that cause the negative complement number standing in the exit counter to be transferred in a single operation over channels directly to the entry counter. It is then counted back into the exit counter as the complement to 9 for every order but the units, which is counted as the complement to 10. The result is a "true" negative number (absolute value) with an associated negative algebraic sign.

4.2 Column Shift

The transmission of all sums out of the accumulator is coded to pass the number through the shift unit. Figure 3 shows this path to be from the accumulator through electronic gates to the *out* internal bus, through a power amplifier, and thence through the shift unit where a number may be shifted to the right or left. The number may be recirculated within the shift unit where each passage of the number causes it to be shifted one column. The sequence code may indicate a shift with or without rounding. If rounding is desired, with a shift of N columns, the sum is routed

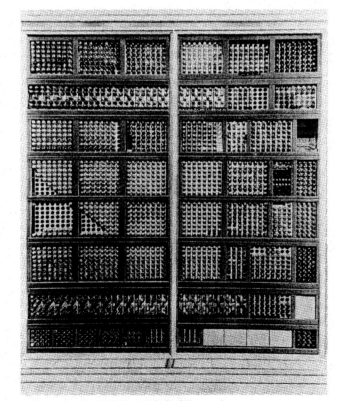

Figure 5. Multiplying and dividing unit.

through the shift unit $(N - 1)$ times, during which time a 5 is added in the units order of the accumulator. After the $(N - 1)$th shift, the sum is transmitted to the accumulator and added to the 5. The number is then routed through the shift unit once more and then along the *in* internal bus to whichever electronic memory unit is indicated by coding.

4.3 Electronic Multiplying and Dividing System

The electronic multiplying and dividing unit is an individual unit having its own internal operational control and timers, so that it can carry out its designated operations on receipt of an external programming signal. Counters receive the number to be multiplied or divided. Sixty-one counter units are grouped to form three counters. There is a 14-digit counter for the multiplicand and divisor, another 14-digit counter for the multiplier, and a 33-digit counter for the product, dividend, and quotient. In multiplication, the multiplier and the multiplicand are successively entered in their respective storage units from electronic memory over the internal *out* buses and through the power amplifier by operation of the proper *in* and *out* gates.

Interlocks are provided to prevent the starting of the operation until the storage units are reset and the factors stored. New numbers cannot be stored in the factor counters while the computation is being made, as the operation has to be completed to indicate that a new line of instruction is to be read. The product is formed by over-and-over addition of the multiplicand under the control of a respective multiplier digit. The addition of a number here, as in the accumulator, is performed by actually counting all decimal positions simultaneously into the product counter. As soon as the proper number of additions has been made for a particular column of the multiplier, a shift selector is changed to add the multiplicand into the product counter position to the right, where adding continues under control of a new multiplier digit. The length of time required to complete a multiplication is therefore dependent on both the number of digits in the multiplier and their value. Multiplication by a 14-digit multiplier will average 20 milliseconds. Multiplication by a smaller multiplier or one with lower digit values can be effected more rapidly.

When the product has been formed, a "complete" signal indicates to the sequence control that the result may be read out under its direction. If required, the rounding of a product is effected by a sequence coding that indicates and controls in which position of the product counter a 5 is to be added.

An algebraic sign control accepts the sign of each factor and combines them to give the sign of the product. If no sign is received with either factor or if an erroneous combination is made, the readout of the product will be interrupted so that the reason may be established.

To divide, the divisor is entered in its entry counter by operation of the proper internal *in* and *out* selectors. The dividend is entered into the product counter similarly and division initiated. The quotient is developed by over-and-over subtraction of the divisor from the dividend. The multiplying shift circuit is used to alter the relative position of the divisor and remainder as each column is exhausted. As the remainder is reduced, the quotient digits are produced in the counter in the positions to the left of the remainder. Circuits similar to those for rounding a product are used to round quotients. These circuits also stop division. A sign control unit operates as in multiplication to form the sign of a quotient and interrupt computation if signs are missing or erroneous.

After a product or quotient has been produced, it is transmitted from the quotient or product counter over the internal *out* buses to the power amplifier and shift unit. The same sequence coding that indicated where the rounding was to occur establishes how many passages it will make through the independent shift unit. When the operation is completed, the shifted results are transmitted over the internal bus to the electronic memory unit, as indicated by the sequence coding.

4.4 Electronic Memory and Switching

The eight electronic memory units provide 160 digits of memory. Each electronic memory unit consists of 19 digits and an algebraic sign and is permanently connected to one of each of the main *in* and *out* buses through electronic gates. These main *in* and *out* buses connect to the various number storage and tape units. All the electronic memory units are connected to a single internal *in* and *out* bus through electronic gates. These memory units serve generally as temporary storage between arithmetical units and relay memory units, both for numbers coming into the arithmetical unit and the calculated results going out. They also serve as high-speed storage for all computations carried out within the arithmetical unit. The transfer of numbers in the electronic unit is performed by two pulses each of ¼ millisecond duration. In normal operation the electronic memory units are loaded with numbers to be processed in accordance with the instruction of each line of sequence. The numbers are taken out one by one at high speed over the internal bus to the calculating units, which then proceed to perform the operations they are instructed to do. When complete signals are returned, results are read out over the internal *in* bus and reentered in electronic memory units. For example, two numbers *A* and *B* are in electronic memory; they are to be multiplied and the result transferred through the column-shift unit to return the decimal point to the same location it had in number *A*. This product is then temporarily stored in an electronic memory unit. Following this a similar multiplication of *C* and *D* is performed. This result may also be shifted and returned to a different electronic memory unit. These products, under sequence control, are then transmitted to the accumulator; their sum is returned to an electronic memory unit from which it will be transmitted wherever needed, under control of sequence coding.

5. Memory and External Data

The numbers required in a problem fall into three classes: external data, including constants, coefficients, and specific numbers defining the problem itself; intermediate results required later in the computation; and mathematical table values. The first two classes of numbers we will consider in this section; the last class will be described separately under table lookup (Section 6).

5.1 Card Readers

External data are entered in the machine in either of two ways: by punched cards or by punched tapes. Direct entry from punched cards is effected through two card readers mounted on a common base. Any column of the card may be read in any arrangement desired by suitable plugging between the reading brushes and the storage hubs. Reading is at the rate of 200 eighty-column cards a minute in each reader.

A bank of card-reading tubes is provided for converting from the decimal notations of the card to the binary-decimal notation of the calculator.

The determination for the value of a hole in a card is by differential time relationships of the card to a timing emitter. That is, when a 9 hole is under the reading brushes, the emitter is at "9 time."

Each of the four tubes in a set representing a decimal order has one of its two grids connected in common to a column of the card by pluggable connections. The other grids of all the tubes for a unit of relay memory are so connected to the emitter that all the 8 tubes are pulsed at 9 and 8 time; the 4 tubes at 7, 6, 5, and 4 time; the 2 tubes at 7, 6, 3, and 2 time; and the 1 tubes at 9, 7, 5, 3, and 1 time.

Thus the coincidence of the emitter pulse with the pulse supplied by the brush contact through a 7 hole in the card, at 7 time, causes the 1, 2, and 4 tubes for that particular column to conduct and energizes the corresponding relays in the memory unit.

The card feed is caused to operate and read a new card by the sequence control. Two types of coding are provided for readout of data from the relay memory units associated with the readers: one that causes a readout followed by a card-feed operation and one that causes only a readout. When the former is indicated, a timed signal from the card feed causes all the related relay units to be reset before 9 time. During the time the card is being read, an interlock signal prevents transmission of numbers from the relay memory units. At a definite time in the cycle, this signal is restored and transmission may occur. If, during the time this signal is open, coding demands another transmission from the card feed, calculation will be interrupted until the first operation is completed. Of course, if possible, the coding should be so arranged that two successive card-reading operations are not required.

5.2 Tape Readers

When certain numbers are required repeatedly in the course of a problem or at very close intervals or in great numbers, a tape is automatically prepared in advance from cards in an auxiliary reproducing punch (see Figure 10), which is arranged to read 300 cards and punch 300 lines of tape a minute. The punching that is done by this unit is checked in the same operation to give complete assurance that the tape is a true copy of the punched-card data. Using tapes for introducing numbers required in a sequence of operations simplifies putting a problem on the calculator, since all the preparatory work can be done in advance. The tapes are formed in loops if the numbers they contain are to be used repetitively, and the tapes may be placed on any of the 66 tape-reading stations (see Figure 9). The numbers on the tapes are read into the calculator directly over the main buses without the aid of special relay memory units.

Two readout relays are associated with each reading station. The output sides of all the *A* relays in each of the three units are common to a set of *A* plug hubs, as are the *B* relays to *B* hubs. Sequence codes are provided for either readout; it is possible to read out simultaneously from two tapes to the main *out* buses.

5.3 Electronic Memory for Intermediate Results

The storage of intermediate results produced by the electronic calculating unit is effected in four areas: electronic memory, relay memory, tape memory, and card memory. The first three are entirely automatic, and when cards are used the only operator attention required is transferring cards from punch to the card

Figure 6. IBM 12-point relay showing pluggable connections. Standard tube is shown for comparison.

feed from time to time. The electronic memory units and their uses were described earlier in connection with the operation of the electronic calculating unit.

More extensive use of electronic storage in the calculator was not attempted because of the bulk and power requirements of electronic storage and switching in comparison to other available methods.

5.4 Relay Memory

Extensive use of relay memory was practicable because of the availability of the wire-contact relay illustrated in Figure 6. This relay is fast, compact, and reliable. It operates, under normal conditions, in 4 milliseconds or less and has an expected life of over 250 million operations. The relay shown transfers twelve independent circuits and takes up about the same room as an electronic tube. Other smaller relays of the same design have six and four transfer points. Each circuit is completed by double independent wire contacts of silver on silver. These relays are provided with either a pickup coil or pickup and hold coils.

The relay memory section of the machine contains 150 relay memory units of 20-digit capacity and the necessary switching to connect any relay memory unit to any main *in* or *out* bus. A single 20-digit relay memory unit requires 80 storage relays, 7 unit-*in* relays, 7 unit-*out* relays, plus some additional controls. It is arranged so that the 20-digit unit can be used as two independent 10-digit subunits with independent reset of each subunit. A group of 15 of these memory units are connected in common through their unit-*in*

and unit-*out* relays. There are ten of these groups, each capable of being connected to any of the main *in* and *out* buses through eight group-*in* and eight group-*out* relays.

When it is desired to enter a number in relay memory, the sequence-control coding closes the group-*in* relay for the bus on which the number is to be transmitted and the unit-*in* relay for the relay memory unit in which it is to be stored. For instance, to store a number on bus 5 in relay memory unit 029, we close group-9 *in* relay for bus 5 and unit-029 *in* relay. When these circuits are set up, a "back" signal is sent out from the relay memory unit to the sequence control indicating that the group-*in* and unit-*in* relays are closed. A reset signal is transmitted from the sequence control to the relay memory unit restoring it to zero, and then transmission can occur. Electronic time-delay circuits provide a transmission pulse of sufficient duration to pick up the memory relays. The "back" signal is sent to the electronic unit initiating transmission of the number from the electronic memory to the relay memory. The relay is held energized by a circuit through a point on each relay that is independent of the pickup circuit.

To read out a number from relay storage, the proper unit-*out* and group-*out* relays are picked up by sequence control; when these circuits are set up, a forward interlock signal to the sequence control initiates reading out of the number from the relay memory to electronic memory.

5.5 Tape Memory

Additional intermediate results to be stored beyond the capacity of the relay memory units are punched in paper tapes on one of the three tape memory units. Numbers to be stored in this fashion are sent to designated relay memory units associated with each of the tape memory units—namely units 134 and 144, 135 and 145, and 115 and 125 for tape memory units 1, 2, and 3, respectively. The instruction to store in tape memory unit 1 causes the tape punch on the tape unit to operate after the number has been stored in one of two alternate relay memory units. While one number is being punched, the punching of the previous number is being checked against the number standing in the alternate memory unit (see Figure 7).

The punched tape from the tape punch may pass in a continuous strip over as many of the tape readers as are required. Numbers stored on the tape must be read from any one station in the same order that they were punched, but since each tape reader can be independently actuated, and a multiple number used, considerable flexibility in the order of reading stored numbers is afforded.

5.6 Card Punches

Numbers stored in punched cards are usually final results. Eighty-column cards may be punched at the rate of 100 per minute on each of the two punches. Punched cards may be used as additional memory for intermediate results, especially when the numbers require rearranging in some systematic way before being reused in the same or a later calculation.

Numbers to be stored on punched cards are placed in specified relay memory units equipped with decimal readout circuits in addition to their normal connections. As in the case of tape punching, these memory units are used in pairs, automatically selected by the calculator when it is desired to store and check.

Four pairs of relay memory units are associated with each punch, which permits punching of all 80 columns of the card. When more than one pair of memory units is used, the entry of the last number before punching is done by a sequence code that directs the unit to store and also initiates the operation of the punch.

5.7 Special Uses of Relay Memory

Of the 150 relay memory units, 110 are solely memory units. The remaining units all have the basic ability to operate as relay memory units; in addition, they have auxiliary uses in connection with the input and output devices of the calculator. The relay memory section acts as the central storehouse for numbers in the machine—receiving them, holding them until used, and disbursing them as they are required.

The memory units are arranged in 10 groups each consisting of 15 units. The code numbers referring to these units extend from 010 to 159.

The units orders of these codes indicate the group, and the tens and hundreds orders the position of the unit in any of the groups. For example, code 129 indicates the 12th unit in the 9th group.

As already described, the card readers deliver the numbers from the cards they read to memory units 150–154 for card reader 1 and 155–159 for card reader 2. If only one number is to be read from a card, the other eight memory units are available for normal

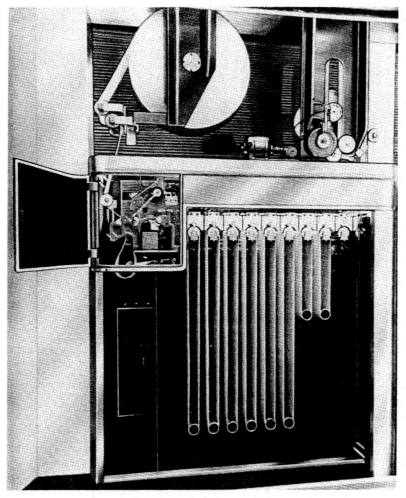

Figure 7. Tape memory unit, showing arrangement of tapes for reading. Punching unit is at left, below paper roll.

relay memory use. Numbers to be punched in tape memory units are delivered to relay memory units 134 and 144, 135 and 145, and 115 and 125 for units 1, 2, and 3, respectively.

When intermediate or final results are to be printed, they are placed in memory units 120–123 for printing on printer 1 and in 126–129 for printing on printer 2.

Results to be punched on tabulating cards for permanent records or for use at a subsequent time in the calculation or for standard IBM equipment are placed in memory units 130–133, 136–139, 140–143, and 146–149.

The relay memory units, and the other forms of storing in the machine, are equally capable of storing numbers, or instructions, and the general design of the calculator is such that, whenever possible, complete freedom to interchange units or functions is maintained. For instance, any tape readers in the tape memory unit that are not required for rereading stored data may be used for reading main-sequence or subsequence tapes, or for sources of the numerical data of the problem.

5.8 Printers

Each of the two printers, which record the printed results of the calculations, prints 80 digits concurrently in a single line, at the rate of 150 lines a minute. The connections between the relay memory units and the printing positions can be arranged in any way desired by changing pluggable connections in the removable control panels, or by changing control panels. This allows the printing in neatly arranged tabular form of all the information needed. With two printers, either a very large amount of information can be printed, or one printer may record the final results and the other give a running record of the calculation itself—various intermediate results, records of tolerance checks, values of subsidiary expressions, calculated interpolated values of mathematical functions incorporated in the problem, and other information useful later to the user in testing the work done to obtain complete assurance that the final results are accurate and reliable.

Zero printing controls print zeros to the right or to the left of significant figures as desired. The lines can be printed with single, double, or triple spacing. The printer will double-space after printing a fixed number of lines (up to 12) to make the form easier to follow, or the extra space can be controlled from the sequence tape to mark sections of the computations. The paper-feeding mechanism separates the continuous printed record into pages by automatically advancing the paper, after one sheet is full, to the desired first line on the following sheet. Sheets up to 12 inches in length can be so handled.

Interlocks are provided to interrupt computation if the paper runs out, or if a printing operation is initiated but not completed.

6. Table Lookup

The table-lookup unit makes available for use in the calculator mathematical tables of six different functions. A group of 36 tape readers (see Figure 8) and their associated selection apparatus will automatically furnish any desired value of these functions. The tables themselves are in the form of punched paper tapes prepared on the special reproducing punch used also for sequence tapes and numerical problem data.

6.1 Possible Arrangements

There may be a maximum of 5400 values in any combination of the six tables. The maximum time to search and find any of these values is 3 seconds. The searching principle is based on that of the IBM standard collator in which the argument for which a value is being sought is continuously compared against the arguments in the tapes until one is found that is immediately lower or equal. This principle permits tables to be arranged in varying intervals, thus providing a table of optimum size.

A single table value may consist of a maximum of 38 digits, of which not more than 5 digits are used to represent the argument for selection of a value. The 38 digits are recorded in a pair of tapes. In constructing a table of a function the greatest possible number of tapes is used, which correspondingly reduces the number of values on each tape since the searching time is a function of how many positions any tape may have to move and not of the number of tapes.

6.2 Method of Operation

The searching procedure consists of three steps: (1) selecting a particular table, (2) selecting the tape in which the required value is recorded, and (3) selecting the value in the tape.

The first selection is initiated by sequence coding, which will call for the table required in the computation and prepare circuits so that subsequent phases of the search will include only those tapes in the required table.

The second selection is made by simultaneously comparing the computed argument against a group of values stored in relays, representing the highest value of the argument in each tape. These stored values have previously been prepared by positioning each tape, when the table is first put on the unit, so that this highest value is beneath the reading brushes; a button connected to each station is depressed and the

Figure 8. Table-lookup unit with 24 tapes mounted.

value of the argument is read into the relays, which are arranged in the binary-decimal notation. These relays are of the latching type; once they have been energized they are mechanically held by a latch, and thus no current is consumed to maintain this closed position. The relay may be returned to its normally open position by energizing an unlatching magnet. By the use of this type of relay, the values are continuously held in the relays as long as a particular table is being used, even though there may be power interruptions, or though the use of the table may be required after a period in which the calculator may be used for other problems.

When this comparison has been made, the station in which the stored value is greater than the computed argument is selected, and the selection operation starts the tape moving past the reading brushes in continuous movement at the rate of 17 milliseconds per value.

The third selection is performed by a continual comparison of the computed argument with the tape arguments as they pass selecting brushes. The mechanism used in this selection consists of an advance set of brushes of 5 digits capacity, capable of reading the argument. Two tape positions beyond these selective brushes is a set of reading brushes for the full 19 digits, capable of reading both the argument and the function value. As the tape passes the sensing brushes, 5 digits of comparison relays are successively set up on one side of the comparison circuit. The relays on the other

side of the comparison circuit hold the computed argument. The first comparison that indicates a tape argument greater than the computed argument following a "lower than" causes the tape to stop spinning. This positions the greater-argument value between the two sets of brushes. Thus the argument value that is standing under the reading brushes must equal or be lower than the computed argument.

The preceding procedure is used except when successive lookups require arguments located in the same tape. In this circumstance it is desirable to know whether the argument under the reading brushes or the one between the reading brushes and the selective brushes is the one required. In these two cases the circuits are arranged so that the function is read out immediately, or the tape is moved one space, followed by a reading of the function. This avoids spinning the tape completely around to relocate the same function.

To accomplish this purpose, two additional sets of comparing circuits are provided: one set to represent the argument at the reading brushes and one to represent the argument standing between the two sets of brushes, called intermediate storage. Under these circumstances the procedure will be as follows.

When a selection procedure has been initiated by sequence control and a table selected, immediate comparisons are made between the computed argument and both the values under the read brushes and the value in the intermediate storage. If the read brushes

Figure 9. Tape reader, showing clutch mechanism.

indicate a "lower than" and the storage a "higher than," it is immediately apparent that the proper value lies under the read brushes and no further selection is required. If this comparison indicates that both values are low, then a similar comparison is made of the value under the selection brushes; if it is "higher than," the value between the two brushes is the one required, the tape is moved one space, and reading of the numbers proceeds under direction of the sequencing coding.

6.3 Readout of Numbers

The circuits for reading of information are similar to those for the tape memory units; two circuits are provided, the A readout and the B readout, so that information from two tapes may be read out to the main *out* bus simultaneously.

Reading stations not in use for lookup purposes may be used for the readings of values or instructions from the tapes by intermittent movement of the tapes under control of sequence coding.

7. Selective Sequence Control

The sequence or program controls of the calculator, in addition to the fundamental purpose of instructing the machine as to the operations it is to perform, must provide interlocking to prevent conflicts and timing to allow each unit to complete its assigned task. Since the complete calculator is an integrated system of three basic types of elements (electronic, relay, and mechanical), interlocks and controls are of these same three types. Tube circuits are used for combining

control pulses as well as for timing. Relays are a space-economical means for multiple control. Cam-operated electric contacts relate the timing of the mechanical units to the rest of the machine.

To secure maximum speed of overall operation, some of the units operate on a semi-independent basis. For example, if it is desired to print a result on the printer, the number is delivered to the associated relay memory unit and the printing operation is initiated. Then the rest of the calculator may resume other computations while the printer proceeds at its (slower) mechanical pace.

There would be no interruption of the calculating process unless a second printing operation were called for before the completion of the first. In that case the interlocks would indicate that the printer was in operation and no new number could be transferred to the associated relay memory units until the first printing operation was completed.

7.1 Use of Tapes and Relays

The basic unit of instruction is a "sequence line" consisting of 40 digits of information and usually presented to the calculator in the form of a line of punched information on each of two parallel sequence tapes. These two tapes can be read from any available tape-reading station via a pair of *out* buses to electronic memory and from there via a pair of *in* buses to sequence-storage relays.

The sequence-storage relays store the sequence numbers in the usual 8, 4, 2, 1 arrangement as explained for relay memory, except that more relays may be used to represent particular elements to provide more relay points for setting up the control circuits. It is through the points of the relays, generally arranged in pyramidal array, that the controls for selector circuits, both electronic and relay, are initiated. The sequence-storage relays appear in duplicate so that overlapping of operations is possible, with one line of sequence controlling the operation of the machine while a second line is being brought from tape to relays.

7.2 Composition of Orders

Each line of sequence can ordinarily be subdivided into two half lines, each of which contains sufficient instructional information for performing one elementary arithmetic operation. If it is desired to perform a multiplication, the instruction essentially must show the source and routing of the two factors, the type of operation, and the delivery point of the result.

The line of sequence shown in Table 1 illustrates the type of selection under control of the sequence

Table 1. Coding for Performing Two Algebraic Operations: $A \times B = C$ and $C - D = E$

| P | | | Q | | | R | | | shift (1) | oper (1) | seq (1) | T | | | U | | | V | | | shift (2) | oper (2) | seq (2) |
s	b	r	s	b	r	s	b	r				s	b	r	s	b	r	s	b	r			
2	1	010	2	2	011	4	3	012	5	15	13	2	3	000	1	4	013	4	5	014	0	02	14

coding for the expressions $A \times B = C$ and $C - D = E$. In detail, the line of sequence is divided into six similar principal fields: P, Q, R, T, U, and V. Four of these fields are used to supply instruction for sources of numbers and two fields to supply instructions for delivery of results. Each of these fields is subdivided into the subfields s, b, and r, where the coding indicates whether the field is a "source" field or a "delivery" field and also indicates, in the case of the source field, operational sign of the factor or term involved. Subfield b indicates the routing by supplying the bus number and electronic memory number for the transmission involved. Subfield r names the individual unit involved.

Thus in the sample coding the P field indicates that the quantity A of the formula is brought from relay memory 010 (Pr = 010) via *out*-bus 1 to electronic memory 1 (Pb = 1) and is to have the plus operational sign +(Ps = 2). The quantity B is read from relay memory 011 (Qr = 011) via *out*-bus 2 to electronic memory 2 (Qb = 2) with plus operational sign +(Qs = 2).

The R field is a delivery field (Rs = 4), and the result is to go from electronic memory 3 via *in*-bus 3 (Rb = 3) to relay memory 012 (Rr = 012). The *shift(1)* coded 5 indicates that the output is to be shifted 5 columns to the right, and the code 15 in the *oper(1)* field shows that the operation involved is multiplication with rounding in the fifth from right column as also indicated by *shift(1)* coded 5.

Since Tr = 000 no new number will be brought into electronic memory 3 (Tb = 3) under control of the T field. This means that for the second half line of operation $A \times B$, which was delivered to electronic memory 3 under control of the R field, will be available. Us = 1 indicates that the number D coming from relay memory 013 (Ur = 013) is to be considered with negative operational sign and brought to electronic memory 4 via *out*-bus 4 (Ub = 4). Vs = 4 indicates the delivery of the result of the second half line of operation from electronic memory 5 via *in*-bus 5 (Vb = 5) to relay memory 014 (Vr = 014). The operation is accumulation without rounding [*oper(2)* = 02] without shift [*shift(2)* = 0]. Thus $C = A \times B - D$ is delivered

to relay memory where it will be available for further computation at some later stage of the problem.

It should be noted that the relay paths for the transmission of numbers for the entire line of sequence can be set up simultaneously because different bus systems are used for each such transmission. On the other hand, the tube paths for transmission of numbers between the electronic memory units and the arithmetic units must be set up on a successive basis since there is only one internal pair of buses.

7.3 Sequence of Operation

The actual order of operation then is as follows. After the relays of the sequence storage have been set up, circuits through their points operate the group and unit *out* and *in* relays in relay memory as called for by the P, Q, R, U, and V fields. Numbers are entered in electronic memory units 1, 2, and 4 under control of P, Q, and U. The multiplicand goes from electronic memory 1 to multiplicand storage unit in the arithmetical

Figure 10. Reproducing punch for making tapes from cards.

unit. Multiplier goes from electronic memory 2 to multiplier storage unit. Multiplication is initiated. When the product is complete, the result goes to the column shift unit where it is shifted five times to the right and then delivered to electronic memory 3. Transmission from electronic memory 3 to relay storage is initiated at the same time that this intermediate result is also delivered to the accumulator under control of the T field. The second term in the accumulation goes from electronic memory 4 to the accumulator. The result of the accumulation is delivered to electronic memory 5, and transmission from electronic memory 5 to relay memory is initiated.

7.4 Subsequencing

The fields *seq(1)* and *seq(2)* indicate the source of the next line of sequence. Thus in the table the sequencing is being taken from the pair of sequence tapes 13 and 14. These numbers are repetitively coded as long as the instructions come from the same source. Most complicated problems can be broken down into sections where some of the sections occur repetitively either a fixed or a variable number of times. When this occurs the repeated patterns are coded as subsequence tapes, thus eliminating the repetition within the main sequence tape. When, in the course of the computation, a pattern computation is required, the appropriate subsequence on tapes 15 and 16 might be used to compute the sine of an argument delivered to the table lookup unit. The last line of the main sequence preceding this computation would then be coded *seq(1)*

= 15 and *seq(2)* = 16. The last line of the subsequence would be coded *seq(1)* = 13 and *seq(2)* = 14, thus returning control of the calculator to the main sequence.

7.5 Modification of Orders

It should be noted that the lines of sequence are numbers of the same form as the ordinary numerical quantities handled by the transmission and computing sections. The point is important in that sequence lines can be operated on by arithmetical operations and hence can be modified or computed from the arithmetical results of the problem. This in effect provides an additional dimension in the selectivity of the sequence unit, allowing the calculator to exercise a large degree of judgment in the choice of a routine as determined by the results of computation.

As an example, it may be desired to compute several cube roots at different points within a main sequence of computation to save repetition of coding. The cube-root computation will be coded as a subsequence called in by the main sequence as required. But more than that, the cube root can be found by a simple iteration process, itself a repetition of a pattern. Here we will not know how many times the iteration is to be repeated to achieve a prescribed accuracy. The computed line of sequence is therefore used to determine the point at which repetition of the iteration is to be discontinued and control returned to the main sequence, all based on the numerical criterion of having achieved sufficient accuracy in the computation.

Early IBM Computers: Edited Testimony

Early IBM Computers: Edited Testimony

CUTHBERT C. HURD

This paper describes the principal computers designed by IBM beginning with its first computer, the 701 delivered in 1952, through its first transistorized computer, STRETCH, and its first commercial process-control computer, the 1710 delivered in 1961. The ideas behind some of IBM's methods and decisions are described.

Keywords: *IBM computers, Defense Calculator, 701, 650, 702, 704, 705, RAMAC, STRETCH, SAGE, 1710*

CR Category: *1.2*

Editors' Note: We have not previously published in the *Annals* an unrefereed article that consists solely of one witness's edited trial testimony. We found Cuthbert Hurd's view of early computer developments at IBM so interesting and important, however, that we chose to break with past practice.

Introduction

This paper was edited by Rosamond W. Dana from testimony given in U.S. Federal Court, Southern New York District, in 1979 in the antitrust trial of the U.S. Department of Justice versus IBM. The original written testimony was prepared in a pseudo-courtroom environment with limited access to personal papers, professional journals, or library facilities. Every word was carefully scrutinized by attorneys for both the Department of Justice and IBM. The complete testimony, including the record of cross examination, direct examination, recross, redirect, etc., is in the public record.[1]

Excursions that would have acknowledged many persons and many other ancillary products at IBM and elsewhere were not encouraged. Neither was it permitted to acknowledge the hundreds of other companies, laboratories, and universities that were heavily engaged in computing by 1962, the end of the time period covered in my testimony.

In the process of condensation for publication, the names of the following individuals who made contributions to the early days of computing were deleted and should be mentioned: John Grist Brainerd, George Brown, Tom Burks, John W. Carr III, Herman H. Goldstine, Harry Goode, John Haanstra, Carroll Hochwalt, Harry D. Huskey, Walter Johnson, Don Mason, John W. Mauchly, Nicholas Metropolis, George Petrie III, Emanuel Piore, Louis Ridenour, Claude Shannon, Donald Spaulding, Abraham Taub, Charles West, Theodore Williams, and William Woodbury.

1. Precomputing Environment

When I began working at IBM on March 1, 1949, the company had revenues of approximately $180 million. It was primarily engaged in the manufacture, marketing, and servicing of punched-card equipment, time equipment, and electric typewriters.

A number of universities and government-related laboratories were designing one-of-a-kind general-purpose computers that were funded by government agencies. By "one-of-a-kind" I mean that each project concerned the design of a single computer, rather than multiple copies of that computer, and that the computer being designed was to be installed at the university or laboratory that was designing it.

Author's Address: 332 Westridge Drive, Portola Valley, CA 94025.
Note: A portion of this paper was first presented at the International Research Conference of the History of Computing held at the University of California Los Alamos Scientific Laboratory in June 1976.
[1] The testimony is on pages 86272 to 88274, dated January 3 to February 1, 1979, United States v. IBM Tr.
© 1981 AFIPS 0164-1239/81/020163-182$01.00/0

The one-of-a-kind projects with which I was familiar (including the name of the computer being designed) were the following:

University of California at Berkeley (CALDIC)
University of California at Los Angeles (SWAC)
Cambridge University (EDSAC)
University of Frankfurt
Harvard University (Mark III)
University of Illinois (ORDVAC; ILLIAC)
Institute for Advanced Study at Princeton (IAS Computer)
University of Manchester (Mark I)
University of Michigan (MIDAC)
Massachusetts Institute of Technology (Whirlwind)
University of Pennsylvania (EDVAC)
University of Rome
University of Vienna
A university in Sweden
Los Alamos Scientific Laboratory (MANIAC)
Patrick Air Force Base (FLAC)
The RAND Corporation (JOHNNIAC)
National Bureau of Standards (SEAC)
Naval Research Laboratory

As of March 1, 1949, none of the machines being developed as part of these projects were yet operational, and only one—the EDSAC, built by Maurice Wilkes at Cambridge—had become routinely operational by the end of 1950.

In addition, the Eckert-Mauchly Computer Corporation, Engineering Research Associates, and Raytheon had announced their intentions to build general-purpose computers for delivery to customers, although by the end of 1949 none had been delivered.

I had become familiar with these developments while I was at the Atomic Energy Commission facility at Oak Ridge, Tennessee, working on the solution of complex scientific and production problems and problems requiring the manipulation of large volumes of

Cuthbert C. Hurd took a Ph.D. in mathematics at the University of Illinois followed by postdoctoral study at Columbia University and MIT. After teaching and serving as a technical research head at the atomic energy facility in Oak Ridge, Tennessee, he joined IBM in 1949 and formed the Applied Science Department, which was responsible for introducing the 701, the 650, the 704, and FORTRAN. In 1962 he became chairman of Computer Usage Company. Since 1974 he has been applying simulation and control techniques to the design and construction of innovative, energy-efficient housing.

data in connection with the development of nuclear technology. As a result of these experiences, I believed that general-purpose computers held the promise of playing a significant role in our society.

I was one of the first Ph.D.'s IBM had hired, and when I began work I had no title. Among the first things I did when I went to work at IBM was to convene a symposium, held in November 1949 under IBM's sponsorship. I invited people who were involved in computer research and development. One paper presented at the symposium was by John von Neumann, whom I had known from my Oak Ridge days and who was one of the most brilliant and respected mathematicians and scientists in the world. At the Aberdeen Proving Ground during World War II, he had performed research as a consultant leading to the description of the organization and method of control of the "von Neumann type of computer."

The computers described by von Neumann in 1946 and being designed in 1949 and 1950 by the various organizations listed were a new class of object the world had never seen before. Compared to IBM's punched-card equipment, for example, computers differed in terms of components, method of control, amount of human intervention required, and the problems that could be solved.

2. Punched-Card Equipment

The components of punched-card equipment included brushes that detected the presence of a hole in the punched card and produced an electrical signal, commutators that divided an electrical signal into a number of timing intervals, relays that were activated by magnets, electromechanical counters, mechanical devices for punching holes in cards, and mechanical printers. Relays could be opened and closed a few dozen times a second and were subject to unreliable operation because they were mechanical and because of dust particles, for example. IBM had built a variety of machines using these components, including a keypunch, verifier, interpreter, reproducer, gang-punch, collator, tabulator, sorter, and calculator.

These devices were controlled by control panels or "plugboards," which looked much like old-fashioned telephone switchboards. Such a control panel might measure three feet by two feet and contain perhaps a thousand holes. Each machine type had a different control panel. It was desirable to memorize the functions of each of these holes. For example, a given hole on the control panel might correspond to column 1 on a punched card. Using a wire with two metal ends, a connection could be made between the reading of column 1 of the card and a particular counter within the machine. The wiring and testing of such a control panel might require several months from the time the proposed connections began to be drawn on a picture of the control panel, called a planning sheet, to the time the panel was operational.

In operation, it was necessary to place the proper control panel in a particular machine, physically pick up a deck of cards (hoping that you didn't drop them and destroy their order), insert the deck in the card reader, allow the cards to pass through that machine, wait a few minutes, go around to the other end of the machine, pick up the deck of cards, possibly thumb through it quickly, possibly decide to divide that deck of cards into one or more packs, pick them up, carry them to another machine for which another control panel had been wired and inserted, put them in the card reader of the second machine, etc. In order to solve a particular problem, it might be necessary to go from one machine to another a dozen or more times. Operators became specialists in a particular machine and therefore might hand the output deck of cards from one machine to the operator of another. At Los Alamos, I remember watching in amazement as Ph.D.'s moved from machine to machine for hours performing these manual operations on the punched-card equipment that was installed there to perform nuclear calculations. Their presence was necessary because of the decisions that had to be made when work was completed on individual machines. The scientists also looked for errors before proceeding to the next operation or machine.

Because of manual intervention and because of the mechanical nature of the devices, results were slow and unreliable. Consequently, there was a sharp limit on the size and kind of applications or tasks that could be performed. Thus, although simple arithmetic operations and sorting and merging were possible, the machine operations were only an elementary assistance to individuals, who were responsible for coordinating the sequence of operations in the course of completing the applications. If one of the specialized operators in a particular application was absent, it might not be possible to process the application at all.

3. General-Purpose Computers

By comparison, general-purpose computers relied on electronic technology, which utilized vacuum tubes and diodes that were being introduced in radio and radar applications. Vacuum tubes were thousands of times faster than the electromechanical components then being used in punched-card equipment, and the electronic technology permitted high-speed random-access storage on cathode ray tubes (CRTs), high-

speed magnetic recording on media such as tapes and drums, and high-speed communication between various portions of the machine.

Not only were the components different, but the method of control was also completely different. The concept of a modifiable stored program meant that a completely automatic machine could be built. For example, a general-purpose computer, when turned on and fed a few instructions, can call for more instructions and data, can consider a number of subprograms that have been written independently and assign addresses for each and assemble them into a single program, and can then generate new instructions and new data as the processing proceeds, while at the same time discarding instructions and data that are no longer needed. These differences held the promise for solving problems that could never be solved on any other kind of machine then in existence.

4. IBM in 1949 and 1950

At the time I joined IBM, those of us within the upper management levels of the company talked to each other a great deal. These people included: Thomas J. Watson, Sr., chairman; Thomas J. Watson, Jr., executive vice president; John Phillips, president; John McPherson, vice president of engineering; Wallace McDowell, director of engineering (in 1950); James Birkenstock, special assistant to Tom Watson, Jr.; A. L. Williams, vice president and treasurer; Charles Love, general sales manager; T. V. Learson, sales manager of the Electric Accounting Machine Division; and Gordon Roberts, manager of product planning.

Within this group, there were differences of opinion as to whether and to what extent IBM should enter the computer business. These differences persisted in one form or another until 1955 or 1956, at which time the company became dedicated to this business.

Tom Watson, Jr., was young and aggressive. In 1946, he had visited the Moore School of Electrical Engineering of the University of Pennsylvania from which the ENIAC and EDVAC came and had attended portions of the 1949 symposium I have described. He had also been a pilot during World War II. I met with him every month or so during 1949 and 1950 to discuss my activities and thoughts for the future. In these meetings and conversations, he told me that he had gained experience with radar and vacuum tubes during World War II, and that he felt that magnetic tapes would soon make punched cards obsolete and that electronics represented the way of the future.

In December 1949, Thomas J. Watson, Sr., gave me my first raise and formally appointed me as IBM's first director of the Applied Science Department (in contrast to the Pure Science Department then under the direction of Wallace J. Eckert). At that time Watson told me that the one IBM Selective Sequence Electronic Calculator (SSEC) then in existence (the largest machine IBM had built and for whose operation I later had responsibility) could solve all the important scientific problems in the world involving calculations. In occasional subsequent meetings with him and as a result of conversations I had with Birkenstock and others, I understood that Thomas J. Watson, Sr., was concerned about a too-hasty leap into the new, expensive, and unproved field of computers—even though he was one of the most intelligent and forward-looking men I have ever met. By the mid-1950s, of course, he had become an enthusiastic supporter of the IBM decision to enter the computer business.

In discussions in 1949 and 1950 with persons in the Engineering Department, including McDowell, Ralph Palmer, and Nathaniel Rochester, I learned that there were differences of opinion within that department. Endicott, New York, was the location of the principal factory and engineering laboratories of IBM. These laboratories had produced IBM's punched-card equipment for many years, the Mark I at Harvard between 1939 and 1944, and the SSEC in 1946 and 1947. In 1949 and 1950, persons in these laboratories, including J. Dayger and O. B. Shaeffer, were interested in obtaining funds to continue making advances in punched-card equipment. A much smaller laboratory in Poughkeepsie had begun to experiment with electronics in approximately 1948 and had incorporated some electronic components in punched-card equipment called the 604 in 1948. By 1949, individuals in the Poughkeepsie Laboratory, including Palmer and Rochester, had also begun to think seriously about the stored-program concept and were interested in obtaining funds to permit them to experiment in general-purpose computers. In 1949 Palmer and Rochester told me that their efforts to move in that direction were opposed by individuals in the Endicott organization who feared that the loss of funds to Poughkeepsie would jeopardize Endicott's ability to continue making advances in the punched-card area.

Throughout 1950 I had many conversations with persons within the Electric Accounting Machine Division, the sales and service organization for punched-card equipment, concerning whether IBM should undertake development of a general-purpose computer. These people, including Gordon Roberts and Roger Bury, told me that computers would not be used in great numbers by IBM's customers and would not contribute significantly to IBM's profitability. They also told me that computers had nothing whatsoever to do with IBM or IBM's main line of equipment and profitability, IBM's customers, or the problems those customers wished to solve. They said they could not imagine that enough problems or applications could ever be prepared by IBM's potential customers to keep a computer busy because such machines were to have the capability of performing several thousand operations a second, and customers in industry would never spend the money to acquire such a machine. Roberts, Bury, and others told me that magnetic tape could not be used as a reliable input/output or storage device because, unlike punched cards, it could not be checked manually to verify the accuracy of the data it contained. This was the "unit record" argument.

My colleagues in the Applied Science Department, who were recent university graduates, many with advanced degrees in electronic engineering, were sometimes referred to as "longhairs" and "double domes." I was not particularly disturbed by the "double dome" apellation. I did fret, however, when friends including John Curtiss, head of the National Bureau of Standards computer activities, and Alston Householder, a former close colleague at Oak Ridge, asked me in those days, "Why did you ever join IBM? That punched-card company will never produce a computer."

Roberts and Bury, because they could not imagine classes of problems different from those treated by punched-card equipment, told me throughout 1950 that no computer could ever be marketed at a price of more than $1000 per month. They reached this conclusion based on experience with the 604 punched-card machine, which rented for $600 per month. Their experience had been in the sale of punched-card equipment, including the 604, to electric utilities. In this application the 604 read a punched card in which was recorded the name and address of a customer and, for example, the number of kilowatt hours consumed during the month. The 604 analyzed the step function representing the relation between number of hours used and cost per hour and computed the bill, which was punched in the same card. The sixty program steps available on the control panel and the thirty-seven digits of storage available were sufficient for this calculation in a single pass. I detail this calculation because many members of the sales and planning departments kept the utility calculation in this form in mind in the early days when considering the feasibility of computers.

5. Developing the Defense Calculator

After the outbreak of the Korean War, Thomas J. Watson, Sr., sent a telegram to President Harry S Truman offering IBM's services for whatever was needed for the war effort. Watson informed IBM employees over the public address system at the World Headquarters Building (590 Madison Avenue in New York City) that he had done so and had an "IBM-O-GRAM" sent to all IBM locations describing the telegram. Shortly after the telegram was sent, Tom Watson, Jr., held a meeting with me, Birkenstock, C. E. McElwain (director of military products), and others in which he emphasized that the telegram offer was not limited to IBM's existing products or services and was to be a priority undertaking. I can remember the excitement the telegram and the subsequent meeting caused within the management group because we realized we would be responsible for recommending what new products IBM should develop to carry out the offer made in the telegram.

During the late summer and fall of 1950, a number of us thought and worked very hard to identify activities that might most appropriately implement Watson's offer to Truman. McElwain, Birkenstock, and I, sometimes together and sometimes separately, visited government contractors and spent many days in the Pentagon, knocking on doors to ask in what fashion IBM's abilities and resources might best be utilized. The company's participation in the design and manufacture of the bombsight for the B-52 bomber was an outgrowth of these visits.

These visits verified my view that government agencies had problems whose solutions required large amounts of processing and calculations. Some of these problems were being solved on large-scale analog machines, but I concluded that most could be performed better on a general-purpose computer. I explained my reasons and my conclusions to Birkenstock as we traveled around together, and he was convinced that IBM should build a computer for the defense industry. During this same period Palmer and I visited several defense laboratories and contractors, and he too was convinced of the need for a high-performance general-purpose computer, which was to be binary.

Technical discussion during the summer and fall revolved principally around the question of whether a decimal or binary system should be built. John McPherson, an IBM vice president and an active participant in the construction of the SSEC, believed strongly in the need for decimal representation. Moreover, based on work performed by Byron Havens and others at the Watson Scientific Computing Laboratory at Columbia, he had initiated conversations with the Naval Ballistics Laboratory at Dahlgren, Virginia, looking toward the construction of a high-performance computer, later called the NORC.

Concurrently, a group headed by Nathaniel Rochester and including Werner Buchholz, M. M. Astrahan, and S. W. Dunwell (a product planning representative) was hoping to produce a serial-by-alphanumeric character machine that was later the 702.

A key influence on me was John von Neumann and his colleagues and friends. The reliability of a large assemblage of electronic components was clearly in question, to the extent that von Neumann one time proposed using only sixteen instructions in the IAS machine. It was evident that the number of components in the binary equivalent of a ten-decimal digit machine was smaller than in a machine using decimal representation and that therefore it could be manufactured more quickly. Thus, I favored a binary machine, even though I realized that programming would be required to communicate with the decimal and alphanumeric world.

Tom Watson, Jr., called a meeting in his office a few days after Christmas 1950 to hear our recommendations. Birkenstock stated his belief, and his concurrence with Palmer and me, that our greatest contribution to the defense effort would be to design and manufacture a machine whose general specifications Rochester, Palmer, and I had developed. I then described the proposed machine in terms of its operating characteristics and capacities and stated that I felt it to be a superior machine that would certainly serve the purposes of the prospective customers whom I knew. It was to be a general-purpose computer, perform a thousand complete multiplications in a second, contain 2048 36-bit words of random-access storage, and utilize subsystems IBM had never delivered to a customer before—CRT storage, magnetic drum, and tape storage. Palmer said he believed that the machine could and should be built. He also emphasized the proposed packaging of the machine that would permit easy shipment and rapid installation.

Many questions were asked by those at the meeting concerning the risks involved. How could we possibly recruit enough electronic engineers to work on such a program? How could we find enough applied science personnel to carry out the functions of programming, testing, manual preparation, and preparation of the customers for installation? How could we be sure that, having devoted tremendous resources to the program, the machine would run at all or would be reliable enough or would be delivered in time to be of help to the defense effort?

John McPherson opposed the Defense Calculator for reasons described earlier. The representatives from the Product Planning Department, including Gordon Roberts, David Rubidge, and S. W. Dunwell, opposed our proposal. Their objections were that the machine could never be sold commercially to any organization that was neither a government laboratory nor involved with the defense effort, and the resulting dead-end project would waste IBM's resources. In the meantime, punched-card developments would suffer. They argued that if IBM were to enter the field, further study and engineering should be undertaken.

A. L. Williams expressed his concern about the financial aspects of the program and its ability to pay its own way. The new machine would require the development of high-speed circuitry, a new form of high-speed storage, and major subsystems such as magnetic drums and magnetic tapes, which IBM had not delivered in any machine, and the cost estimates of each of these projects were at best fragmentary. In the end, however, Williams said that he was in favor of proceeding with the program.

T. V. Learson was on the fence at this meeting. He had assisted tremendously in hiring personnel for the Applied Science Department and was impressed by the intelligence and understanding of these people. On the other hand, his product planning and sales advisors were emphasizing the difficulties of the project and their view that the computing field would be neither large nor profitable to IBM.

From my point of view, and particularly in light of my earlier experience in atomic energy and the visits Birkenstock, Palmer, and I had made, I was convinced that the greatest single contribution to the war effort IBM could make—and should make despite the great risk involved—was to design and produce a set of completely identical computers and to produce software to assist customers in their use. In addition, my colleagues in the Applied Science Department, who were located across the country, were indicating the need defense customers had for such a machine.

Finally, after an assessment of the risk of making commitments to the defense effort that we might fail to meet from a technical and systems point of view, Tom Watson, Jr., concluded the meeting by asking Birkenstock and me to visit agencies within the defense establishment, describe our proposed design, and ask if they would be interested in such a machine. Watson also instructed those in the meeting who were opposed to the project to refrain from participating in it. Essentially, Palmer and I were to be in charge.

In the following month, Jerrier Haddad was appointed manager of component development and Nat Rochester was named manager of engineering planning. I assigned William McClelland to be in charge of planning from the standpoint of customer requirements and software. The members of this group made preliminary component counts and estimated the cost of the proposed machine based on the limited experience at our disposal. Williams set the rental price of $8000 per month.

Birkenstock then visited Washington, D.C., and Byron Luther, an assistant sales manager assigned to me, and I visited a number of government agencies and defense contractors, the latter primarily in the aircraft field. We were able to secure thirty letters of intent for a computer that would perform according to the specifications Palmer and I had discussed at the December 1950 meeting. (I might add that when Luther came back from the trip he told me that he agreed that IBM should build the computer proposed.)

Tom Watson, Jr., then authorized us to proceed with development of the computer. Significantly, Palmer and I were told to hire the people we needed and to complete the task as quickly as possible and to let nothing stand in our way. Because of the resources we devoted to the project, in one year an engineering model had been completed and in less than two years IBM was shipping machines at the rate of one a month. To the best of my knowledge, no other computer manufacturer had achieved this shipment rate at the time IBM achieved it. The machine, ultimately called the 701, was originally called the Defense Calculator. This name helped to ease some of the internal IBM opposition to it since it could be viewed as a special project (like the bombsights, rifles, etc., IBM had built during World War II) that was not intended to threaten IBM's main product line.

In March 1951, when our group had actually completed the detailed design work for the computer and had constructed the engineering model, it was found that a much greater performance than had been anticipated could be achieved—and also that the cost would be much higher than the original estimate. When the customers who had signed letters of intent learned that IBM was increasing its price to $15,000 per month, all but six canceled their letters of intent. Despite this, I obtained approval to order parts to build eighteen machines and to assemble the resources necessary to produce and install them. This was a risky thing to do because of the possibility that the company would lose its investment unless it found more customers. The risk was compounded because the technology was so completely different from what IBM had done in the past and the parts could not be used elsewhere at IBM. I lost a lot of sleep in those days, wondering whether the warnings of Roberts and the other opponents of the Defense Calculator would come true.

6. The 701 Computer

The official announcement letter for the Defense Calculator was dated May 21, 1952. It described the machine as an "electronic data processing machine." The term (coined by Birkenstock) was chosen after

Machine No.	Destination	Date
	Original 701 Customers (from manufacturing records, Poughkeepsie)	
1	IBM World Headquarters, New York, N.Y.	12/20/52
2	University of California, Los Alamos, N.M.	03/23/53
3	Lockheed Aircraft Company, Glendale, Cal.	04/24/53
4	National Security Agency, Washington, D.C.	04/28/53
5	Douglas Aircraft Company, Santa Monica, Cal.	05/20/53
6	General Electric Company, Lockland, Ohio	05/27/53
7	Convair, Fort Worth, Tex.	07/22/53
8	U.S. Navy, Inyokern, Cal.	08/27/53
9	United Aircraft, East Hartford, Conn.	09/18/53
10	North American Aviation, Santa Monica, Cal.	10/09/53
11	RAND Corporation, Santa Monica, Cal.	10/30/53
12	Boeing Corporation, Seattle, Wash.	11/20/53
13	University of California, Los Alamos, N.M.	12/19/53
14	Douglas Aircraft Company, El Segundo, Cal.	01/08/54
15	Naval Aviation Supply, Philadelphia, Pa.	02/19/54
16	University of California, Livermore, Cal.	04/09/54
17	General Motors Corporation, Detroit, Mich.	04/23/54
18	Lockheed Aircraft Company, Glendale, Cal.	06/30/54
19	U.S. Weather Bureau, Washington, D.C.	02/28/55

much thought, and the number 701 was given to the machine, first, to imply that this computer was to be followed by others, and, second, to distinguish it from the punched-card machines (calculators) that had numbers in the 600s. The technology (electronics) and methodology (stored program and automatic control) for the 701 were sharp breaks from IBM's previous technology (punched cards and relays) and previous methodology (control panels and manual operation). Punched-card equipment could do about two complete multiplications a second, whereas the 701 as delivered performed one thousand times faster. Punched-card equipment could carry out multiplications for only a limited period of time and until the card feed was empty. The stored-program computer, on the other hand, could carry out the multiplications indefinitely

for all practical purposes. Moreover, under stored-program control, a computer could automatically and instantaneously change from one set of instructions to a completely different set of instructions. As opposed to the central role played by humans in punched-card operations, the stored-program concept allowed, for the first time, the automatic processing of hundreds of thousands—and millions and billions—of operations with no human intervention whatsoever.

6.1 Programs. People in the IBM Technical Computing Bureau wrote several programs for the 701, including the following:

1. A program to process "supply" information at the Naval Aviation Supply Depot in Philadelphia. "Supply" applications involve the assembly of data describing the number and location of a given weapons system, a similar description of the spare parts, maintenance manuals, and maintenance personnel, and the scheduling and ordering of such facilities to meet the needs of a particular defense agency. This program was written in 1953 and was run on the Supply Depot's own 701 for two years thereafter. It experienced some problems because of a lack of expertise among the programmers who were employed by the Supply Depot and the relatively slow speed of the Supply Depot's printer.

2. A program to assemble financial data from various departments and divisions within the Monsanto Chemical Corporation and to process the data and produce and print the quarterly financial statements. This program was written in 1953 and was run successfully by IBM on a service bureau basis.

3. A program to assemble seismic and well-logging data and to process the data using statistical techniques in such a fashion that likely locations for petroleum drilling were identified. This program was developed in 1953 in conjunction with E. K. G. Kogbetliantz of Columbia University, an IBM consultant who visited a number of oil companies, including Humble and Shell.

4. A program to analyze election returns and make early forecasts during a presidential election. George Gallup and Joseph Harsch appeared on television with me during the 1956 election and successfully used the computer to predict the outcome.

5. A payroll program at North American Aviation, under Frank Wagner's general direction, where input was the number of hours worked by employee, task, and contract number. The 701 computed the amount of pay and appropriate deductions, wrote the checks and check registers, and distributed costs by department and contract.

6.2 Hardware Innovations. The following hardware innovations were included in the 701 at the time of first delivery (unless otherwise specified):

1. An improved cathode ray storage tube (of the Williams tube type) with the following advantages:

(a) Twice the storage capacity of existing CRTs—1024 bits compared to the existing RCA product containing 512 bits—and therefore the ability to provide at machine delivery time the unprecedented amount of 4096 words of high-speed random-access storage.

(b) Blemish-free tubes, which meant that any storage location could be used without restriction.

(c) Greater reliability and longer life than existing tubes because a storage pattern was developed that together with associated read-write circuitry sharply reduced the "spill" problem—the tendency of electrons to spill into neighboring areas and destroy the signal.

2. A tape drive that utilized plastic-coated magnetic tape (the UNIVAC I, for example, used metal tape in 1951 and thereafter; metal tape was more difficult to handle than plastic-coated tape).

3. A vacuum-column control magnetic-tape-handling device (developed by James Weidenhammer of IBM's Poughkeepsie laboratory) that allowed the drive to start and stop more quickly than had been possible previously; it also permitted changing reels easily.

4. The NRZI ("non return to zero IBM") recording method, which improved the reliability of recording on magnetic tape and improved the reliability of checking information that had been recorded.

5. Half-word logic, which allowed the machine to operate on either 18 or 36 bits of information. This was a start toward variable word size.

6. A magnetic drum provided intermediate or backup storage for the CRT storage.

7. A punched-card reader, punch, and line printer.

8. Packaging in such a way that every box would go in a standard-size elevator, would go on a standard-size dolly, would go through a standard-size door, and could be removed or replaced box by box.

9. Multiple-tube pluggable units that enabled a service person to remove all the circuitry associated with an elementary operation, such as a 1-bit addition, simply by pulling it out manually and replacing it with another one almost instantaneously.

10. Some amount of choice in systems configuration in the sense that a customer, depending on requirements, could have 2048 or 4096 words of CRT memory, or 4096 or 8192 words of drum memory, or a choice of two tape units or four tape units.

11. A "cycle-stealing" capability that allowed processing to proceed as the CRTs were refreshed, thus increasing the processing speed.

12. Direct addressing of I/O devices under programmer or operator control, instead of by fixed circuitry.

13. An extended instruction repertoire that eased the programming of the machine. This included:

(a) A "copy-and-skip" instruction that allowed the handling of records of any length.

(b) A "sense-and-skip" instruction that provided the ability to select alternative programs according to the setting of frontpanel "sense" switches.

(c) A convenient method for handling the sign of zero.

(d) A convenient method for handling overflow from the accumulator.

(e) A method that allowed a programmer to regard the binary point in any arbitrary position.

6.3 Software Innovations. What I now call "software" was called "programming aids" in the 1950s. Some software innovations in the 701 were:

1. A capability to continue to execute instructions while data were being transmitted between I/O devices and main storage, thereby increasing the effectiveness of the system.

2. SPEEDCODE, developed in 1953 by a group led by John Backus. It was a three-address interpretive code that automatically implemented what are now known as "macros" and that speeded programming.

3. An assembly program in which the machine assembled its own code and could assemble code of several programs into a single new program.

4. A trace program that followed a computer program step by step and printed results.

5. Programs that translated from binary to decimal, binary to alphabetical, alphabetical to binary, and decimal to binary.

6. A binary loader.

7. A "bootstrap" or self-loader that facilitated loading the starting program.

6.4 Applications Programming Innovations. Beginning in 1953 and for several years thereafter, both within IBM and in cooperation with universities or nonprofit organizations that wanted to cooperate, the Technical Computing Bureau programmed computers with new applications and tested and demonstrated the breadth of problems that a general-purpose computer system could solve. The following innovations in applications programming are noteworthy (all done during the period 1954–1955):

1. Preparation of three-layer weather forecasts for North America, to the specifications of von Neumann and Jules Charney.

2. Proof of the feasibility of computing the trajectory of a missile in "real time" on a computer (in this case the 701), to specifications by Helmut Sassenfeld.

"Struggle for Existence," by William P. Leigh
(1866–1955)

3. Translation of Russian into English, in cooperation with Georgetown University.

4. A demonstration of Euclidean plane geometry theorem proving (demonstrated on the engineering model in Poughkeepsie) by Herbert L. Gelernter and Nat Rochester.

5. Simulation of the IBM Punched Card Collator production line in Endicott, which included the detailed scheduling of parts through a job shop.

6. Playing checkers by Arthur Samuel.

7. Nerve net simulation by Rochester and John H. Holland.

6.5 Manufacturing Innovations. Prior to delivery of the 701 in 1953, no general-purpose computer had been manufactured on a multiple assembly-line basis. Production of the 701 involved the release to production of 4000 sets of drawings, the creation of uniform machine and service manuals and stores of spare parts, and an engineering change-order system through which engineering innovations could be quickly implemented in manufacturing and transferred from manufacturing to the field service organization. Because of IBM's ability to manufacture multiple identical 701s and to maintain current engineering and software status, it was possible for a customer who had not yet received a 701 to test programs on a nearby 701 and to know that the tested program would run on the new 701 when it arrived. Even the magnetic tapes would run on other 701s. This was particularly valuable to the defense industry because customers could run programs on machines at other installations.

6.6 Education Innovations. At the time IBM delivered the 701 in 1952 to the Applied Science Technical Computing Bureau in New York City, very few people in the United States had any experience with computers. The Applied Science Department therefore began a program of educating customers on how to use the 701 hardware and software and how to recruit and train personnel in-house. This training consisted of the following:

1. In 1951 persons from my staff were assigned to particular installations. D. W. Pendery, applied science manager of the IBM western region, assumed the largest management responsibility because twelve of the eighteen customer 701s were installed in the West.

2. Starting in the summer of 1952, the Applied Science Department periodically brought groups of customers to be trained on an engineering model in Poughkeepsie, and later on the 701 in New York City.

3. Starting in 1951, the Applied Science Department arranged for groups of customers to meet together to discuss their problems and their actual applications and to interchange libraries of programs if they wished. The department established a newsletter to help customers help each other. The organization SHARE, which was formed by customers voluntarily and without any participation by IBM, was an outgrowth of these efforts.

The 701 project was highly successful, but it and projects following placed great financial demands on the company. In the early 1950s Thomas J. Watson, Sr., in a meeting with his son, Williams, Birkenstock, McDowell, Learson, and me, displayed a chart indicating that the company had suffered a dip in profits. As he held up the chart he said, "You fellows get your heads together because you are spending too much money; we can't afford it and we've got to get the profits up." We went back to our offices, and he sent each of us a picture of horses being attacked by wolves. The horses were getting their heads together and kicking the wolves. A note attached to the picture said, "Now I want you fellows to get your heads together."

7. The 650 Computer

By late fall of 1952, IBM was well on its way to delivery of the first 701. There had been a formal announcement describing the 701 in May 1952. The number of firm orders had increased from six, and I began to wonder if eighteen machines would be enough.

The machine that was to become the 650 had been started in 1948 shortly after the announcement of the SSEC by a group under the direction of Frank Hamilton, who had also been in charge of the Mark I for IBM. The 650 program progressed by fits and starts and was at its low ebb in 1952 when work had practically stopped. I spent a week in Endicott writing sample programs and uncovered a key system design flaw: of the thousands of words of storage then contemplated, only a fraction were for general-purpose storage. This decision had been made for reasons of economy and perhaps also because of Hamilton's earlier association with Howard Aiken and because of the tendency to design machines to solve problems in the manner that was effective for punched-card machines. Following my assignment of Elmer Kubie and George Trimble to the project, the storage assignment was quickly improved. Ernie Hughes was assigned as chief engineer, and the development of the machine proceeded. Two other improvements were the invention of a high-speed drum that obviated the need for revolvers, a feedback device on the track of a drum, and the development of optimum programming techniques by Kubie and Trimble.

By late fall 1952, those of us in the Applied Science Department began to feel that there was a need for a medium-priced general-purpose computer (in the rental range of $3000–4000 per month). We believed that such a computer could be marketed in larger quantities and that it could be so easy to use that individuals from many different departments of a customer's organization would apply it to the solution of their problems.

The opposition within IBM to this idea was even stronger than the opposition prior to the decision to build the 701. Roberts, Bury, and Rubidge continued to make statements such as, "You can never sell a machine that rents for more than $1000 a month, except to scientists." People from the engineering and product planning departments were arguing for the development of more powerful punched-card machines. At a week-long engineering meeting at the Harriman estate, the debate continued without resolution 20 hours a day.

In the spring of 1953, I spoke with McDowell at great length about my views, and he eventually agreed with me. McDowell and I then met with Tom Watson, Jr., who approved our plan for announcing the machine, later called the 650.

The question of pricing arose. The market forecast procedure consisted of obtaining forecasts from the sales, product planning, and applied science departments. Forecasting for the 650 was done in the late spring of 1953. Roberts, Bury, and Rubidge said that the forecasts from sales and product planning were zero because the machine we had in mind could not be produced for $1000 a month, and therefore no customers would buy it other than the kinds who had bought the 701. The forecast from applied science was based on experience, and also on customer requests to applied science representatives who were by this time present in principal cities of the United States and Europe. We forecast 200 machines at $3500 a month with the bulk of the machines to be used by scientists and engineers. In the IBM Washington Federal office, M. B. Smith, the manager, had been impressed by the performance of the 701 on the Philadelphia Supply Depot application. Customers in the Defense Department continued to ask Washington Federal for a machine that would help in the important "supply" area (described earlier). With the help of applied science representatives in Washington Federal, M. B. Smith and L. H. LaMotte, an IBM vice president who had recently been promoted from Washington to New York, supplied a forecast of 50 machines to be used by Supply. Based on the combined forecast of 250 machines, we negotiated an announcement rental price of $3250 a month for the 650 Model 1 with 1000 words of storage and $3750 a month for the 650 Model 2 with 2000 words of storage. Although Roberts, Bury, and Rubidge, who were members of Learson's staff, were opposed to the 650, Learson in fact signed the announcement letter with me on July 2, 1953. The 650 was first delivered to customers in 1954. Subsequently, changes and modifications to the 650 were announced and additional programming aids were developed. The 650, the first computer to be produced in quantities greater than a few dozen, became the Model T of the computer industry.

7.1 Hardware Innovations. The 650 had many hardware innovations, including the following:

1. Condenser storage to provide a modest amount of random-access memory and thus alleviate the inherent deficiencies of all circulating devices, such as drums and acoustic delay lines, in which the desired instruction or data is, on the average, one-half circulation away.

2. A 12,500-rpm drum, which was faster than drums then included in machines delivered to customers by

other companies, including Electrodata, Computer Research Corporation (CRC), and Engineering Research Associates (ERA).

3. A two-address instruction that simplified programming by indicating both the present operation to be performed and the location of the operand and the location of the next instruction.

4. A method of internally checking operations and transfers of information based on the biquinary (or abacus) system of representation.

5. A table lookup operation to facilitate the automatic searching of rate tables used by companies in the fields of utilities and transportation.

7.2 Software Innovations. SOAP (Symbolic Optimizing Assembly Program) was developed to simplify the programming further and increase the speed of the machine. SOAP allowed the following methods of optimizing the performance of the machine:

1. Performing calculations during the wait time for the drum storage; this method supplemented the use of condenser storage.

2. Examining the instruction stream and attempting to order the instructions in the most expeditious fashion given the latency characteristics of the drum.

7.3 Manufacturing Innovations. The demand for the 650 was such that the manufacturing operation in Endicott became the first large-scale manufacturer of general-purpose computers in the world. The engineering change-order system, which had been developed for the 701 but was done manually for that product, had to be enlarged in 1954 to handle the increased volume of 650s and in 1955 was computerized and implemented on a 650. This work was done at IBM's Technical Computing Bureau.

7.4 Service Innovations. Because of the ultimate popularity of the 650 and its installation by several thousand customers scattered throughout the United States and abroad, IBM had to develop maintenance and customer support services that were uniform and interchangeable. Manuals, education of the customer engineers, test instrumentation, and spare parts inventories were so uniform that the IBM policy of promoting customer engineers within and between offices could be continued. Of equal importance was the development of documentation procedures for software and systems for incorporating changes that were analogous to the engineering change-order system developed for the 701.

7.5 Education Innovations. Representatives from the Applied Science Department trained customers in systems analysis and programming, use of software, installation planning, and machine operation for the branch offices installing 701s. The practice was extended and eventually became worldwide with the Department of Education within IBM assuming full responsibility.

8. The 702 Computer

The 702 was IBM's next computer. It was announced in September 1953 and first delivered to customers in 1955. Fourteen were installed during the mid-1950s. IBM offered the 702 to customers who had participated in joint study programs with IBM in late 1952 and early 1953 and had concluded that the machine would serve their needs. Those joint studies (instituted at the insistence of Roberts and Rubidge of the Product Planning Department, who continued to tell me that general-purpose computers could not be successfully marketed by IBM) included one with Lockheed Aircraft, one with Prudential Insurance, one with Chrysler, and one for departments of the Hanford Engineering Works. Early installations of the 702 were carried out under the direction of applied science personnel.

The 702 utilized the same types of circuit components, memory, pluggable unit design, and I/O as the 701. Substantially all of the innovations of the 701 were carried over into the 702 and were improved. The major difference between the 701 and the 702 was that the 702 was a serial, character, variable-word, variable-record-length machine, while the 701 was a parallel, binary, semifixed-word, variable-record-length machine.

The innovations of the 702 included the following:

1. Variable word size, which made the 702 more flexible and easier to use and maximized the utilization of memory.

2. Common I/O cable, which permitted the attachment of its I/O devices in any sequence.

3. Off-line tape-to-line printer, with tape-to-card or card-to-tape capability.

4. The 727 tape drive, which was announced with the 702. This tape drive had the fastest speed of its day. It had twice the recording density and data rate of the IBM 726 tape drive, which had been introduced with the 701.

9. The SAGE System

In late 1952, IBM was selected by MIT and the U.S. Air Force to work on the design of a computer to be used in the SAGE (Semi-Automatic Ground Environment) system. (SAGE was a cooperative program between the United States and Canadian governments for the air defense of North America.) I participated in the early meetings in late 1952 at MIT's Lincoln Laboratory (the laboratory acted as systems manager for the SAGE project on behalf of the Air Force and was responsible for the overall systems design) in which the design specifications for SAGE were discussed. Among those participating in some or all of the meetings from MIT were James Killian, Jerome Wiesner, Jay Forrester, Albert Hill, George Valley, and Carl Overhage; from IBM were Tom Watson, Jr., Arthur K. Watson, Williams, Birkenstock, McDowell, Palmer, and occasionally Thomas J. Watson, Sr. I supplied personnel from the Applied Science Department to the project and visited the SAGE lab, the IBM High Street Laboratory, and the IBM factory periodically, although I did not have any direct management responsibility for the project.

IBM, under Lincoln Laboratory's general direction, had responsibility for the design, manufacture, installation, and servicing of the central twin computers, consoles, and I/O devices and certain programming aids in the SAGE system. Other prime contractors included:

1. Western Electric, which had responsibility for the construction of the site.

2. Burroughs, which had responsibility for converting radar input into digital signals and assembling bit patterns to feed the modems and for associated operators' consoles and displays (I do not remember if Burroughs used a computer for these tasks).

3. System Development Corporation (SDC), which was an offshoot from the RAND Corporation and had responsibility for the application programming to be used in the system.

The SAGE system was to take radar input and flight-plan information and track airplanes automatically as they traveled across North America. It would dispatch fighter planes in case of suspected unauthorized entry. The system involved the development and interrelationship of a large number of highly complex technical devices—such as sensors, communications links, displays, consoles, and computers—that were all interconnected despite the fact that they were in many different geographic locations. A project of such size and complexity had not been attempted before, and SAGE was certainly the largest undertaking by IBM until that time. The general systems design by Lincoln Laboratory, based on systems research performed by Jay Forrester and his colleagues on Whirlwind, took a great deal of imagination and boldness, as did the design and implementation of the major subsystems for which IBM had responsibility.

IBM's proposal to build the SAGE computer involved substantial risks. Many of the concepts had been tried only in a laboratory. There was no guarantee that IBM could hire the numbers of people who would be needed to carry out its responsibilities. Failure to deliver the computers successfully, because the project was so massive, could have led to adverse financial repercussions and damage to IBM's reputation. A. L. Williams, for example, asked if a mistake in computation might result in the accidental destruction of one of our own country's airplanes, with the resultant financial exposure and publicity such an accident might entail. All of us were concerned in 1953 about the diversion of key engineering and systems persons and applied science persons who were barely completing the design of the 650, 701, and 702. Moreover, IBM would need to construct a completely new factory to build the SAGE computers, and all of us in the highest management group wondered what would happen if the contract were canceled in midstream. The internal debate within IBM was great, and I remember, for example, a day-long meeting chaired by Thomas J. Watson, Sr., that resulted in no progress whatsoever toward a decision.

We finally began work on SAGE, however, and carried out design and manufacturing engineering from 1953 through 1956, when SAGE computers were first delivered. IBM's work on the SAGE system resulted in a number of innovations in the computer industry that led to reduced manufacturing costs, improved reliability and serviceability, and reduced size and power requirements. Some of these innovations were:

1. IBM developed a method of manufacturing uniform, high-speed, reliable, and inexpensive core memory. While core memory had been implemented on the Whirlwind computer at MIT prior to SAGE, IBM developed methods for removing impurities and for developing manufacturing techniques to make millions of cores available with uniform electronic characteristics, making memory more quickly, more easily, and more cheaply. IBM developed new devices that partially automated the stringing of core planes (using such devices as hypodermic needles); designed improved packaging techniques to ensure proper signal propagation; and developed semiautomatic core testers. Prior to these developments, it had taken weeks to produce small quantities of raw cores, and the probability of those cores having identical specifications had been extremely low. The need to build and test cores and to string and test core planes manually had resulted in a cost of approximately $1 per core, which made it too expensive to use core memory in computers built in production quantities

(more than one or two). As a result of IBM's improvements and developments, the cost of core memory was decreased almost 100-fold, and main memory consisting of magnetic cores became available for the first time in production computers.

2. SAGE was a real-time computer system in that data acquisition and communication and computing could keep up with the aircraft under observation. It incorporated the first use of computer-to-computer communications by telephone lines over a distance of miles and had the capacity for simultaneous use by over a hundred persons in real time.

3. SAGE used a keyboard terminal and had the capability for direct human-to-machine and machine-to-human communication.

4. SAGE incorporated the capability of duplexing in that two processors were available to work on a problem. In SAGE, the second processor kept track of the operations of the first processor and was able to begin processing if the first machine malfunctioned. This capability improved serviceability and reliability.

5. SAGE incorporated the ability to remove certain functions from the main processor and put them on a processor located remotely, in order to ease the burden on the main processor and to accomplish certain results locally rather than centrally. A magnetic drum with associated processing circuitry was located near a remote operator and contained information concerning the airspace for which the operator had responsibility. Information could be selected and displayed at the command of the operator using either a keyboard or a light pen, and the display proceeded independently of and concurrently with the operation of the twin processors at the central site.

6. Printed circuit boards were used throughout for control and computation. Every logic element of the SAGE system was on a pluggable unit, and every component except the vacuum tubes was mounted on a printed circuit board. The printed circuits were double-sided cards having plated holes through them.

7. SAGE had an interrupt system.

8. As part of SAGE, IBM developed diagnostic programming and preventive maintenance techniques in the form of computer-assisted marginal checking. Maintenance programs could be inserted into the system to look throughout the system and give early warning with respect to possible failures of vacuum tubes, diodes, magnetic core memories, magnetic drums, magnetic tapes, consoles, card readers or punches, or any other elements of the system. This early warning could minimize failures.

9. Work in associative memory was done by Larry Sarahan, from the Applied Science Department, in connection with SAGE.

All of this work was done with the close cooperation of MIT, which, for example, assigned Kenneth Olson as its project leader on-site in Poughkeepsie.

The experience IBM gained from its work on the SAGE system was significant to the future success of the company. IBM improved its techniques and abilities for designing and building computer systems. The several thousand engineering, programming, and maintenance personnel who were hired to work on SAGE added greatly to the company's store of technical knowledge and expertise. These people worked on developing and maintaining many of IBM's subsequent computer systems.

Many of the hardware and software features developed during SAGE were introduced into subsequent IBM computer systems starting with the 704 and 705 and continuing through STRETCH and SABRE. IBM replaced the CRT memories in its 701 and 702 with the cores that were produced using the techniques developed for SAGE. Those same techniques were used to produce cores for the 704 and 705.

10. The 704 and 705 Computers

The 704 was announced by IBM in May 1954 and was first delivered to customers in 1955. The 705 was announced in October 1954 and was first delivered to customers in 1956. More than one hundred 705s and some fewer 704s were delivered. The 704 was a successor to the 701 and the 705 was a successor to the 702. The innovations of the 704 and 705 were:

1. The 704 and 705 had larger instruction sets than the 701 and 702. While the 701 had approximately 33 instructions, the 704 had approximately 75. These new instructions permitted, among other things, the following points:

(a) The 704 incorporated into hardware floating-point arithmetic and three addressable index registers (which simplified programming).

(b) The 705 was able to read and interpret all five characters of the operation part of an instruction in a single cycle, increasing the speed of decoding of instructions.

2. IBM, under John Backus, developed FORTRAN for use on the 704—an innovation that led to a huge expansion in the uses and users of computers.

The development and installation of the 704, 705, and 650 finally ended the IBM debate as to whether the company should enter the computer business. These machines, because of their speed and reliability and wide customer acceptance, were enthusiastically embraced by IBM's sales force; opposition to computers ended for all practical purposes.

In 1954 T. V. Learson was named by Tom Watson, Jr., as IBM's first director of electronic data processing machines to serve as the "czar" coordinating all the company's computer activities for the purpose of developing the 705. In 1955 he was appointed vice president of sales, reporting to L. H. LaMotte, executive vice president. I had had responsibility during 1953 and 1954 for the 704 and served as Learson's technical advisor in connection with the 705. In 1955 I took on the title of director of electronic data processing machines, also reporting to LaMotte, with responsibility for coordinating the engineering, manufacturing, sales, and service of all of IBM's computer systems offered to the public.

11. The RAMAC

The 305 RAMAC (Random-Access Memory Automatic Computer) was announced by IBM in September 1956 and was first delivered to customers in 1957. The RAMAC was the product of IBM's San Jose Laboratory, which had been established as a result of a decision made in 1951 to take advantage of the engineering and scientific talent that was graduating with advanced degrees from West Coast universities. The San Jose laboratory acted both as an engineering facility and as a place where scientists and engineers could work on computing concepts and designs without the need to focus them on any particular product or product development effort.

The 305 RAMAC was announced with a random-access disk drive, the first magnetic disk drive to be delivered to a customer by any computer manufacturer. The introduction of the disk drive by IBM had profound and continuing significance to electronic digital computing. It involved a whole new way of storing and accessing data and offered yet another subsystem that could be compared with the cost, performance, and maintainability of competitive subsystems existing at that time, such as magnetic cores, magnetic drums of various sizes, magnetic tapes, and punched tapes. By the time I left IBM in 1962, disk drives were being used as part of almost every IBM computer system and most other computer systems.

Beginning with the delivery of the RAMAC, IBM became the leader in the design and manufacture of disk drives, magnetic materials research, recording media, reading and writing heads, search methodology, error detection and correction, and software to assist the customer to utilize all of the above effectively. IBM's competitors did not provide disk drives comparable in performance or reliability to the RAMAC until several years after the RAMAC was first delivered to customers. By that time IBM had made additional innovations in technology and design, including the first removable disk pack, announced in 1962.

In contrast to IBM's development and early use of the disk drive, other computer manufacturers experimented with other forms of random-access storage. For example:

1. NCR utilized a magnetic card device called the CRAM for random-access storage. The CRAM device never worked reliably and was abandoned.

2. RCA utilized a device called the RACE file for random-access storage. The RACE file contained strips of magnetic tape enclosed in magazines carried to a rotating drum on which they passed by a reading head. The RACE file also never worked reliably and was abandoned.

One of the most important system innovations of the RAMAC derived from the fact that it was the first general-purpose computer in which in-line processing of transactions became practical. In in-line processing, each transaction is processed sequentially. For example, every order arriving at a factory could be processed as it arrived, and every file affected—inventory, sales statistics, accounts receivable, commissions on sales, etc.—could be adjusted to take account of the transaction before the next transaction was processed. Another in-line application in engineering departments involves the processing of engineering change-orders and resultant new part numbers.

12. Other IBM Computers

The 709 computer was announced by IBM in January 1957 and was first delivered to customers in 1958. The following innovations were connected with the 709:

1. The channel, which permitted processing and I/O functions to proceed simultaneously, thereby increasing the speed at which an application could be performed by the system.

2. The 729 magnetic tape drive, which was announced in 1957 and contained two read/write heads, very close together, that permitted magnetic writing and almost instantly thereafter the reading of what had been written for checking purposes. Prior to the first delivery of the 729 in 1958, it had been necessary in tape drives to stop the tape and backspace to check or rerun the whole tape. The dual read/write capability of the 729 greatly increased the effective speed and reliability of tape operations.

3. The delivery by IBM in 1961 of COMTRAN (commercial translator), a language in which the words were familiar to accountants, and an associated compiler—software that translated the statements made in COMTRAN into machine language.

Left to right: Tom Clemmons, director of electronic data processing sales at IBM, Cuthbert C. Hurd, director of electronic data processing at IBM, and John von Neumann at the NORC dedication, Watson Scientific Computing Laboratory, December 2, 1954.

The 1401 was announced by IBM in October 1959 and delivered to customers beginning in 1960. More 1401s were installed than any computer to that time—between 15,000 and 20,000.

Delivered in early 1961 for use with the 1401 was RPG (report program generator), an innovative software procedure for performing the programming needed to produce reports. A FORTRAN compiler was also made available on the 1401 in 1961. The 1401 was used by customers as a stand-alone computer system. It was also used, as early as 1960, as part of an off-line tape-to-print facility in computer installations containing 7090s, 7080s, 7010s, 7040s, and 7044s, which were larger than the 1401. By 1961, the 1401 was being used to communicate between these machines and I/O devices.

The 1401 had high-quality output, high speed, and ease of use, all of which contributed to the number of installations of 1401s. No competitive machine as of 1960 processed tape as fast as the 1401, and no other high-speed line printer as of 1960 came close to matching the quality of the 1403 chain printer, which was announced with the 1401.

The 1403 printer utilized a new chain-printing technique that was superior to competitive drum-type techniques. The advantages of the chain-type printer were the following:

1. It operated at a speed of 600 lines per minute with multiple copies and with printed lines that were straight to the naked eye. Prior to the 1403, high-speed printers had printed wavy lines, which made the printers of limited utility to companies concerned about the print quality, especially of bills and invoices to be sent to customers.

2. Cartridge packaging of the chain, a feature added in 1961 that permitted quick change from one character set to another.

The 1403 had not been equaled by competitors by the time I left IBM in 1962.

Among the research and development projects of IBM was the NORC (Naval Ordnance Research Computer), designed and built between 1950 and 1954 at the Watson Scientific Computing Laboratory at Columbia. The NORC, to which I referred earlier, was a powerful, one-of-a-kind system undertaken by IBM in response to a request from the Naval Proving Ground at Dahlgren, Virginia. The NORC was dedicated in December 1954 at a ceremony at which John von Neumann spoke. Part of what he said is as follows:

The last thing I want to mention can be said in a few words, but it is nonetheless very important. It is this: In planning new computing machines, in fact, in planning anything new, in trying to enlarge the number of parameters with which one can work, it is customary and very proper to consider what the demand is, what the price is, whether it will be more profitable to do it in a bold way or in a cautious way, and so on. This type of consideration is certainly necessary. Things would very quickly go to pieces if these rules were not observed in ninety-nine cases out of a hundred.

It is very important, however, that there should be one case in a hundred where it is done differently. . . . That is, to do sometimes what the United States Navy did in this case, and what IBM did in this case: to write specifications simply calling for the most advanced machine which is possible in the present state of the art. I hope that this will be done again and that it will never be forgotten.

The NORC was the fastest computer in the world at the time it was delivered in 1954 and had the fastest tape drives. Its Williams tube memory had an 8-microsecond access time, the fastest of the day. The 1-microsecond delay line, which was also used in the 701, grew out of research by Byron Havens, director of the NORC project and an IBM employee.

The NORC was used to calculate the orbit of the earth and other heavenly bodies with greater accuracy than had yet been achieved. It was also used in the study and design of new weapons systems, missiles, rockets, nuclear reactors, and fleet exercises. The NORC was used by the Naval Proving Ground for over a decade.

13. The STRETCH Computer

In 1955 McDowell and I had a conversation in which he emphasized the need to challenge IBM engineering in a sizable way, the need to incorporate as directly as possible the ideas of customers, and the need for a contrast to focus the challenge. Thus, in 1955 IBM decided to proceed with a development project that led to what became known as the STRETCH computer. As part of my work as director of electronic data processing machines, I was responsible for the STRETCH project during 1955 and 1956, and I was directly involved in securing a research and development contract with the Atomic Energy Commission (AEC) for STRETCH. After the contract was signed in 1956, I actively participated in the development of STRETCH on a systems level—I worked with engineers, physicists, and applied science personnel in deciding on the features and specifications for STRETCH—until IBM reorganized later and I was named director of automation research. The name STRETCH was intended to signify a "stretch"ing of the state of the art and was coined by Haddad in 1955. IBM worked on the development of STRETCH (later called the 7030) for about five years. Of the hundreds of persons involved, special mention should go to Ralph Palmer, Jerrier Haddad, S. W. Dunwell, Werner Buchholz, B. O. Evans, Gene Amdahl, Lloyd Hunter, John Backus, and John Sheldon for their initial conceptualization.

The first customers for STRETCH were the AEC and the National Security Agency (NSA). Working with Norris Bradbury, Carson Mark, Bengt Carlson, and Roger Lazarus, and with Louis Tordella, Solomon Kullback, and their associates at Los Alamos and NSA, respectively, I told them that IBM wanted an objective and a focus for the high-speed technology it would develop and a partner to help define the characteristics for a high-speed computer based on the problems the partner wished to solve.

Negotiations for a second STRETCH-type machine began with NSA in 1955. NSA needed a machine to manipulate vast quantities of alphabetic characters and other symbols in connection with activities such as cryptography. The equipment installed at NSA in 1962 included a STRETCH computer and a special unit called HARVEST.

In addition to AEC at Los Alamos and NSA, other STRETCH users included the Livermore AEC facility, the atomic energy facilities in England and France, the Naval Proving Ground at Dahlgren, the Weather Bureau, Mitre Corporation (which performed research for the Defense Department), and IBM.

In 1955 and early 1956, the objectives set for STRETCH had been the following:

1. It was to have 100 times the performance of the IBM 704, which was the most powerful computer available in 1955.
2. It was to be equally useful and powerful for problems requiring vast amounts of computation, vast amounts of data handling, or both.
3. It was to be constructed of transistors instead of vacuum tubes.
4. It was to have very high-speed main memory.
5. It was to have a large high-speed supplemental memory device.
6. It was to have improved I/O devices.
7. It was to have innovations in machine organization that would enhance the high speed of the proposed components and subsystems such as disks.
8. It was to be developed by means of computer-aided design to the greatest extent possible.

When the STRETCH project began, these objectives had never been achieved in a general-purpose computer, and IBM achieved them in STRETCH. It was the fastest machine in the world at the time it was delivered in 1961, although there was some dispute about whether STRETCH was actually 100 times faster than the 704.

STRETCH included the following innovations, developed from 1955 to 1958 and first delivered between late 1959 and 1961:

1. A fast, diffused-base, alloyed-emitter transistor, known as the drift transistor. Developed by Lloyd Hunter, whom I had known at Oak Ridge and who came to IBM in the 1950s, the drift transistor offered improvements in quality, consistency, and speed over prior transistors.
2. A logic circuit design called transistor current switching or emitter-coupled logic that permitted faster operation than prior logic circuit design.
3. A memory having an access time of about 2 microseconds (compared to the fastest memories available in 1960—about 6 microseconds).
4. A method of memory interleaving of up to four 2-microsecond memories, which permitted an average memory access time of about ½ microsecond.
5. A "lookahead" feature that increased the speed at which an application could be performed by the

system. The lookahead feature read instructions that were three levels ahead of the one being performed and determined the appropriate memory references and memory allocations for these instructions.

6. An interrupt system that was more sophisticated than any interrupt system to that date.

7. The incorporation of multiprogramming, by which a computer could process two or more applications simultaneously. To implement this feature, IBM developed a system of memory protection to ensure that each task being performed would stay within its memory space.

8. A disk drive, which had a set of parallel read/write arms contained in a single mechanism to provide high-speed writing on and reading from the disk. One or more disks could be attached to STRETCH. Each disk had the capacity of 2 million words, and the data rate was several million bits per second for a single channel—approximately 100 times faster than the bit rate of a 727 tape unit. This performance specification exceeded those of any competitive storage products—tape drives, disk drives, magnetic drum devices, punched-card devices, and paper-tape devices.

9. A mass storage device, developed for use with the HARVEST computer and delivered with STRETCH to NSA in 1962. This device, called TRACTOR, used large tape cartridges and a mechanical means for storing and retrieving them. The use of proportional sensing within a vacuum-tube tape drive enabled the tapes to accelerate, reach high speeds, decelerate quickly, and stop without breaking the tape.

10. Error-correcting codes were used to a great extent in STRETCH. A single error in data read from the disk was corrected automatically before the data were transferred to memory. This error detection and correction was also employed in operations involving high-speed memory.

11. IBM developed methods of computer-aided design for STRETCH. For example, the 704 was used to produce backpanel wiring diagrams and instructions to accomplish the wiring. The 704 was also used to simulate the operation of the lookahead feature within STRETCH and thus compare the productivity of various levels of lookahead. STRETCH probably could not have been built without computer-aided design.

12. During the late 1950s, when STRETCH was being constructed, methods were developed for the automated assembly and testing of printed circuit boards. These innovations contributed to the consistency and standardization of STRETCH's componentry.

13. STRETCH eliminated the distinction between character and decimal and binary machines, fixed-word-length and variable-word-length machines, and fixed-record and variable-record machines.

In 1958, after the development of STRETCH had begun, the U.S. Air Force issued a request for proposals for computers to be used in the DEWLINE air defense system. In response, IBM proposed a computer designated the 7090 in December 1958. After a competition involving several other companies, IBM was selected for the system, and in late 1958 the Air Force ordered four 7090s, to be delivered starting in November 1959. Components being built for STRETCH—including transistors, memories, tape controllers, circuit cards, backpanels, frames, cables, power generators, etc.—and engineers working on STRETCH were diverted to the 7090, and the 7090s were delivered on schedule.

The 7090 was lower in price than STRETCH and offered an operating system, the IBSYS system. At the same time, it did not have certain STRETCH features—such as lookahead and mass storage—and was therefore less powerful than STRETCH. The 7090 could solve less complex problems more cheaply than STRETCH and thus reduced the demand for STRETCH.

STRETCH was used at Dahlgren in connection with the International Geophysical Year to assemble data from the satellites of all participating countries, including Russia, and to compute a new map of the surface of the earth with accuracy improved by two orders of magnitude.

14. The 1710 Computer

In 1956, shortly after the STRETCH project was launched, I was appointed director of automation research with the responsibility of using whatever resources were needed within IBM to develop new fields of application and define new computing systems if so required. A group of engineers, planners, and programmers working under me conducted, as an example, an investigation into the possibility of using computers for air traffic control. Air traffic control had clear similarities to the problems addressed by SAGE, although it was enormously more complicated because of the thousands of private planes in use at the time in the United States as well as the hundreds of daily flights by commercial airlines.

In 1957 my group became intrigued with the possibility of installing computers in factories of various kinds to improve the efficiency of production processes and to assist in preventing malfunctions or even disasters. My group thought that this was a substantial business opportunity because a larger amount of money was being spent on manufacturing than on research and development or accounting.

I organized several study teams that participated with companies in a number of industries, such as

Standard Oil of California, Standard Oil of Indiana, Inland Steel Company, and Du Pont Chemicals, in projects to determine the degree to which the functions then being performed by those responsible for controlling plant processes could be performed by a computer more responsively, more cheaply, and more efficiently. The studies proceeded from fundamental physics and chemistry and continued through detailed observation of the actions operators performed and the subsequent results. The operators of the plants had only modest formal educations but had long experience, and they "knew" what to do to improve plant performance by observing certain characteristics in the product being produced or in the instruments measuring such variables as pressure, temperature, flow, or chemical composition. For example, a person at a steel mill would view the color of the steel in formation and then make one or more adjustments in the process until the color was correct. By using mathematical models that employed partial differential equations, the study teams were able to describe some of the processes and develop mathematical optimization methods, such as linear programming, that would permit computers to improve the efficiency of the processes without human intervention. In approximately 1959, the companies with which the study teams had been working stated their wish to install computers on-site to allow a complete feedback control system for optimization purposes.

During 1959 I suggested to the companies that they use one of IBM's then-existing computers to which analog devices and appropriate interrupts (or, in the alternative, software in the form of a program-directed scanning system) would be added. In 1961 IBM announced the 1710 to perform process-control applications. The 1710 consisted of a 1620 computer, an interrupt feature in the hardware (added in August 1961), and a device connected to analog measuring devices that entered digitized analog signals into the 1620, took digitized signals from the 1620, converted them to analog, and returned them to the process.

During 1960 there was a discussion about the number of these machines that could be installed. This discussion was among Tom Watson, Jr., Williams, Learson, Haddad, and several people responsible for forecasting. Executives at IBM, including Williams, looked at the number of factories and thought the potential was several thousand. The machine was finally priced in early 1961 based on a quantity of 250. The first machines went to the customers who had participated in our studies. They were pleased with the machines, operated them for a number of years, and believed they had fulfilled their expectations.

My experience in the computer business is that once a machine is installed in any location, nearby employees immediately use it for purposes other than the one for which it was originally installed. Robert Jacobs of Standard Oil of Indiana and Enias Kane of Standard Oil of California told me that when the 1710 was installed in their plants, the operators began to consider how their other responsibilities could be expedited, given the capabilities of the computer. Accounting functions such as preparation of data to enter the payroll system were performed on the computer, and engineering and manufacturing personnel who were located nearby also used the computer.

15. IBM Innovations

Many innovations were introduced by IBM in the years 1949 to 1962 that went beyond those mentioned previously. Innovations in packaging, leasing, bundling, and educational support are discussed below.

15.1 Physical Packaging. As mentioned earlier, the 701 computer was packaged in boxes in such a fashion that any box would fit in a standard-size elevator, go through a standard-size door, and fit on a standard-size dolly. Until the 701, machines had to be built in place. Now the 701 could be installed quickly, and a customer who wanted to replace one of the units—or even the whole system—could do so quickly and without great expense.

Another packaging approach first embodied in the 701 was to place in a given box as many related functions as possible with the upper limit defined only by size and by quick and easy servicing of that unit. This method was used flexibly for different machines. For example, the main memory of the 701 was in a separate stand-alone unit because the main memory and the arithmetic and logic unit were both so bulky that they could not be packaged together in a single standard-size box. In the 650, the space required for the arithmetic and logic unit and for the main memory was small enough that they could both be put in one box. In the 1401, a portion of the main memory was integrated within the box containing the arithmetic unit and logic unit, while additional memory that could not fit in that box was put in a separate box.

15.2 Leasing. During the time I was at IBM, I always believed that, from the point of view of a customer, leasing was the most appropriate method of acquiring all or part of a computer system. My reasons were the following:

1. Leasing helped customers avoid the risks of technological obsolescence. During my years at IBM, the company announced some twenty computers. Users had to be able quickly and easily to substitute more advanced equipment as it became available.

2. Leasing gave customers the flexibility to dispose

of or reconfigure their systems by replacing subsystems as applications or workloads changed or improved products were announced. Users could simply call a sales representative and ask that a rental machine be removed—easier than remarketing a used machine.

3. Leasing involved a smaller financial investment than purchasing. This was especially important during the years I was at IBM when computing was new and relatively untried and users did not have sufficient confidence in the reliability of computer systems to warrant committing large capital to purchases.

4. By 1962 so many companies were offering computer systems and subsystems that a person responsible for data processing within a company or government organization was forced to consider many alternatives in arriving at the systems design best for that organization. I believed that it was not a good use of the technical capabilities of data processing personnel to enter also into the financial studies necessary to make lease-versus-purchase decisions. I saw no reason for asking that systems personnel, who were in short supply, spend time on such financial calculations.

5. Leasing fostered a relationship in which the vendor was required to respond rapidly to user needs because users who were not satisfied with the equipment or services provided by the vendor could simply demand that the equipment be removed at once.

15.3 Bundling. Most customers requested that IBM and other manufacturers provide users with hardware, software, maintenance services, education, and customer support on a bundled basis. Without the practice of bundling, many users would not have installed and manufacturers would not have been able to market computer systems in any quantity. At least through the late 1950s, computers were still a curiosity to most potential customers. Many of those who were acquiring computers simply did not have sufficient expertise with or understanding of the new concepts and techniques involved to enable them to use computer hardware efficiently and effectively in the absence of support from the manufacturers. Nor did they wish to write programming aids or software because they were busy enough performing systems analysis, writing application programs, instituting project control, and dealing with their own customers—members of various departments. Also, systems programmers were rare, and few customers had such people on their staffs even by the late 1950s. Moreover, acquisition of computer systems constituted a substantial financial and business risk. Customers were being asked to rely heavily on machines that were very expensive, novel in design, and of unproved reliability. Bundling enabled customers to predict more accurately the costs of their installations, to increase the probability of successful installations, and to share the risks of difficult or unsuccessful installations with the vendor.

I regarded software as an integral part of IBM's computer systems, essential to the operation of those systems. IBM's software was so intimately related to the hardware that the two were designed simultaneously. Decisions as to whether functions should be performed by hardware or software depended on numerous trade-offs made at the time the system was developed, since almost everything that was capable of being implemented in hardware was also capable of being implemented in software. For example, some machines built in the early days had no divide instruction in the hardware, while others did. For machines without a divide capability, programs could be written to divide using other instructions that were in the hardware such as multiply, subtract, detect a negative number, etc., much like the familiar algorithm of a person performing division.

Until the time of final testing of a machine and its software, such trade-offs were continually made between hardware and software by the systems designers and by the engineering and software designers. When the machine entered final test, it rarely performed exactly as planned, and changes had to be made to assist the performance. At that time a trade-off was again made: "Shall we modify the software or shall we modify the hardware?" No matter how exhaustive, expensive, or time-consuming the product test period, logic and operational malfunctions were detected during the early period of installation and in fact continued in decreasing numbers throughout the life of the machine. Again, then, during early installation phases when faults were detected and reported to the engineering laboratory, trade-offs were made between software and hardware adjustments.

Because of the integral nature of software and the hardware-software trade-offs, it was impossible to draw a line that separated hardware functions and software functions, and as a result it was not sensible to try to price software separately from hardware.

As rental agreements ended and computer equipment was returned to IBM (this began to happen in the early 1950s), IBM necessarily had to worry about remarketing that equipment to other customers. Accordingly, to ensure that its equipment would be returned in good condition, IBM maintained rental equipment itself, and it was therefore not sensible to price maintenance of leased equipment separately.

Independent software and applications programming vendors began to emerge in the second half of the 1950s, and their number increased steadily over time. (In fact, I joined such a company when I left IBM.) These companies offered their products to both users and manufacturers. The companies came into existence because of a shortage of programmers, particularly systems software programmers, on the part of both users and manufacturers, and because some users found it substantially less expensive or otherwise more desirable to purchase programs from independent companies than to develop them in-house.

15.4 Educational Support. I first became aware of IBM's support of higher education in 1938 in connection with my position at Michigan State College, where I worked with the registrar to install IBM punched-card machines. IBM offered an educational allowance—a lower price—to colleges and universities using IBM products for teaching or research.

IBM's earliest contribution to an educational institution was in connection with research in genetics that Henry Wallace, later vice president of the United States, was conducting at Iowa State College leading to his Ph.D. and to the development of hybrid corn. He was allowed to use punched-card machines in Des Moines to further his research. In 1929, at the urging of Benjamin Wood of Columbia, Thomas J. Watson, Sr., donated punched-card equipment to Columbia to help assemble and evaluate a nationwide educational research project. The success of this project proved extremely useful to educational institutions generally.

In the 1930s Wallace J. Eckert of Columbia's astronomy department requested that IBM modify its traditional tabulating equipment to make it more effective in performing the operations to calculate the moon's orbit. Eckert and persons from IBM devised a means of rolling the counters in the tabulating equipment that significantly speeded performance and enabled the equipment to be used more effectively to calculate orbits. The equipment was donated to Columbia and installed at the Thomas J. Watson Astronomical Computing Bureau, established in 1937 as a joint enterprise of the American Astronomical Society, the Department of Astronomy at Columbia, and IBM.

In the late 1930s Howard Aiken of Harvard visited the Computing Bureau at Columbia in search of assistance on one of his projects. At Eckert's suggestion, Aiken called on Thomas J. Watson, Sr., who offered to build the Automatic Sequence Controlled Calculator (ASCC) to Aiken's design. The ASCC was built at IBM's Endicott plant between 1939 and 1944 and was the fastest calculator of its time. After its completion it was donated to Harvard, along with a gift of money to assist in its operation. It was called the Mark I and was used for 15 years, mainly by government agencies.

During the mid-1940s, IBM aided John Gibbon, Jr., of the Jefferson Medical College in Philadelphia, in the development of the heart-lung machine. Thomas J. Watson, Sr., supplied funding for the project and made IBM's laboratory facilities available to Gibbon, and several IBM engineers designed parts for the device. After the machine was built, IBM published a description of it and made its design specifications available to anyone interested in building a similar machine. IBM did not receive any payment for its work on the heart-lung project.

At the request of Robert Millikan, president of the California Institute of Technology near the end of World War II, Thomas J. Watson, Sr., agreed to build devices that would automatically read results from the Cal Tech wind tunnel and punch the data into cards. The device, which was built by IBM either at cost or for a one-percent profit, was the first automatic punched-card data-acquisition system. After the war IBM built similar systems for Cornell and Consolidated Vultee—again, either at cost or at one-percent profit—and these systems were of great significance to the United States missile and space efforts.

After World War II, IBM founded the Watson Scientific Computing Laboratory at Columbia. This was IBM's first full-time research facility. Wallace J. Eckert became the first head of the laboratory and was hired as IBM's first director of pure science.

In January 1948, the SSEC was installed at IBM headquarters in New York City, and the company allowed educational and research institutions to use the machine without charge.

In the mid-1950s IBM established data processing educational centers with a 704 on the campus of MIT and a 705 on the campus of UCLA, with the understanding that any person from any college or university in the Northeast or West, respectively, could apply for time at the centers. No charge was made for the use of these centers, and IBM provided funds to help with installation and operation.

IBM supported data processing activities in higher education for the following reasons:

1. To contribute to the expansion of human knowledge generally.

2. To help educational institutions to improve the quality of instruction and instructional materials.

3. To contribute to the training of students in the methods and concepts of computing.

4. To expand the uses and users of computing.

5. To facilitate the interchange between IBM and universities of scientific knowledge resulting from their respective research and development efforts.

6. To develop a class of trained engineers, scientists, systems analysts, and programmers who would be potential employees of IBM as well as customers.

Pioneering:
On the Frontier of Electronic Data Processing, a Personal Memoir

Pioneering: On the Frontier of Electronic Data Processing, a Personal Memoir

James W. Birkenstock

This personal memoir is essentially an insider's view of IBM—how it worked, the road to its success, and the major decision-making processes IBM used.

Introduction

I have always thought that my career at IBM, my sole employer, was the most challenging and wonderful work any person could ever have. However, I never thought my life's work would be interesting to others beyond my family and friends.

In the spring of 1979, Irwin Tomash, a computing pioneer from Engineering Research Associates and the founder of the Charles Babbage Institute (CBI), visited me to acquaint me with the role and purpose of the CBI and to invite me to serve on the Board of Trustees. During an interview the following year with Tomash and Roger Stuewer, CBI's executive director, for the purpose of recording my oral history, they suggested that I write a more comprehensive account of my role in the evolution and use of digital computing.

Probably the most persistent urging that I prepare a personal memoir came from the then editor-in-chief of the *IEEE Annals of the History of Computing*, J.A.N. Lee. He suggested that I record my memoirs and permit the *Annals* to consider publishing them. My trepidation persisted, however. I did not want to commit myself to writing a lengthy piece on my extensive business career until my consulting activity began to wane in 1996 and I had time to review memorabilia and to think about events I could record in a memoir.

Responding to the urging of my family members—and especially from my daughter-in-law Susan-Marie Birkenstock, who turned out to have a flair for literary criticism—I finally committed to documenting my career in the form of a personal memoir and later submitted it to the *Annals*. The next editor-in-chief, Michael R. Williams, and his advisory board deemed the result appropriate and accepted it for publication.

My Boyhood and School Years

When I was born on 7 May 1912 in Burlington, Iowa, to Anna and George Birkenstock, I suspect I was a bit of a surprise, since my sister Elsie was 20 years old and my brother Roy was 17. My father was a furniture buyer and salesman for Wyman and Rand Department Store, and my mother was a homemaker. Both sets of my grandparents immigrated to the United States in the mid-19th century. My maternal grandparents, the Flynns, arrived from County Tipperary, Ireland; my paternal grandparents were from Magdeburg, Germany.

While I attended elementary school in Burlington, my family's financial circumstances led me to enter the workplace at the age of nine. I began as a caddie at the Burlington Golf and Country Club. With age and experience, I was promoted to caddie master. During the summer of 1928, touring pros Johnny Farrell and Gene Sarazen, on their way to Chicago to play in the U.S. Open, stopped in Burlington to play an exhibition match. As caddie master, I chose to carry Farrell's bag. When we reached the ninth hole, Farrell asked me to make a club selection for the uphill approach to the green. Embarrassingly honest, I said, "I don't know." Undaunted by my response, Farrell chose a four iron and put his ball hole high on the green. The next week at the Olympia Fields course, Farrell tied Bobby Jones in the U.S. Open at the end of regulation play. Farrell then beat Jones in the play-off. Little did I know that 28 years later, I would become a member of the Country Club of Florida, where Farrell served as head pro.

I continued working as caddie master through my high school years, which included the Great Depression of 1929. These were hard times for most Iowa families, including mine. However, the greatest depression I experienced was when my mother passed away on 21 December 1929, leaving me in the care of my sister. My father was devoted to my older brother, who was a professional baseball player. As a result, he showed little interest in me and seemed pleased that my sister, who was childless, took responsibility for my upbringing. While not estranged, we did not have a close father–son relationship. Dad died in 1937.

When I graduated from high school with honors in 1931, I was pleased with myself in my first store-bought suit. I could not help but think of my self-sacrificing mother, who had made all of my clothes. Just after graduation, still wearing my new suit, I went on a date with another new graduate. We stopped in Corso's Drug Store for a milk shake. As I looked across the room, I noticed Jean Hale, a sophomore at Burlington High. I did not know then who she was, but I did know she was the prettiest girl in Burlington. The next week, I arranged an introduction through a mutual friend. Four years later, we were married. My accomplishments over the past 64 years of our married life are, in great part, the result of Jean's support, companionship, and understanding.

Even though I graduated from high school and went on to Burlington Junior College (now Southeastern Iowa University), I never left the building. The junior college shared the same facilities with Burlington High. When school was in session, I held two jobs in addition to my caddying position, while maintaining a full course load. I worked as a busboy in the school cafeteria and also worked for Mrs. McFarland, a wonderful elderly widow and cultured lady, whose guidance and philosophy helped to shape my adolescent years. One of my duties was to take Mrs. McFarland on daily afternoon drives, weather permitting, through the beautiful countryside and farmlands. During one of those drives, Mrs. McFarland asked, "James, do you know how you can tell who is boss of the household?" I answered, "No, Mrs. McFarland. How would I know?" She responded, "Look at the property, James. If the barn is larger than the house, the man is the boss." I gathered how I could tell if the woman was the boss. Whenever she was ready to go home, Mrs. McFarland always delighted in saying, "Home, James," to which I always replied, "Yes, Ma'am."

During the summers, I served as assistant to Scottish golf professional Bonnie Weaver at the Burlington Golf and Country Club. Because of my caddie and caddie master experience, I became a good golfer. Weaver, who called me "Jimmy boy," thought I had the potential to be a professional golfer. On his recommendation,

I was given the pro job at a start-up, nine-hole municipal golf course. Unfortunately, 1932 was the year of the Iowa bank closings and a Dow Jones that dropped to 50 points. As a result, people stopped playing golf, buying clubs, and taking lessons. With no money coming in, I was forced to seek other work. A member of the country club saw my situation and offered me a job painting billboards that yielded an average income of $2 a day. I supplemented this employment by pumping gas at a DX filling station, working evenings and weekends.

I graduated with honors from junior college in 1933. Then, Sterling Lord and Max Conrad, country club members who knew me as a caddie master, sponsored me for a scholarship at the University of Iowa in Iowa City, their alma mater. As a result of their sponsorship and my academic record, I was granted the scholarship. With this and my summer earnings, I entered the university with encouragement from my sister Elsie and her husband Art Friedel, with whom I had a home and as much financial assistance as they could manage. My first and biggest challenge on arrival at the university was to find a part-time job. I had heard that the Iowa Memorial Union was interviewing for cafeteria employment and that the person to see was the dean, Rufus Fitzgerald. During my interview, Fitzgerald said that all cafeteria positions were filled except one: a job on the meat counter, the most difficult one on the cafeteria line. He asked if I could handle such an assignment. With bravado, I cited my previous work experience at the Burlington Junior College Cafeteria. I assured him that I could handle the position, stressing how much I needed employment.

Fitzgerald hired me, and I immediately went to work under Ted Rehder. Mrs. Ebert, a warm and lovable Irish woman who was a cook in the cafeteria, recognized my inexperience at the meat counter and bailed me out. "Don't worry, James," she said. "I'll teach you the ropes." Mrs. Ebert took me under her tutelage and set up a temporary carving station behind the refrigerator that adjoined the cafeteria line. From there, she taught me to carve and supply the counter with meat. In a short while, I was able to master the carving of large roasts, turkeys, and hams with dexterity, at which point Mrs. Ebert returned to the cafeteria kitchen.

In the summer of 1934 before I began my senior year, I returned to Burlington to court Jean, my bride-to-be, and to work as a bookkeeper for the Burlington Beverage Company. The following fall, I returned to Iowa City for my senior year at the university and was pleased to learn from Rehder that I had been promoted to operate the cash register at the end of the cafeteria line. Additionally, I was to replace George Byce as maitre d' on his days off, operating the cash register and greeting the diners. One day, shortly after spring break, Clark Kusterer, an IBM vice president, was dining in the cafeteria. Apparently impressed by the way I was greeting the customers and handling the job, he asked my name and informed me that IBM representatives would be at the university in the near future to conduct employment interviews with graduating students. While I was pleased to have been informed of this opportunity, Chester Philips, dean of the College of Business Administration, had already advised me that he had selected me for employment at Northwestern Bell, an AT&T subsidiary. This company had a policy of hiring one senior, who was selected annually from the College of Business Administration on the dean's recommendation. Philips had become my idol during my junior and senior years at the university and was my good friend, mentor, and confidant both before and after graduation. Naturally, I was honored that he had chosen me for the position. Philips, aware that I was to graduate magna cum laude, also knew that I had a strong work ethic. That I was a near-scratch golfer also helped, since he and his wife were avid golfers. Philips sometimes invited me to play with him and his wife at the university golf links, a rare treat.

A Pivotal Career-Launching Decision

Based on Philips's recommendation, Northwestern Bell offered me a position starting at $125 a month. Therefore, believing I need not pursue a job opportunity with IBM, I dropped Kusterer's business card in the wastebasket. Little did I know how important IBM would eventually become in my life. About a month later, scarcely remembering Kusterer, I received a call from Philips telling me that Gordon Thomas from IBM was conducting interviews at the university with prospective graduates and was asking for me. This created somewhat of a dilemma, since my first reaction to this request was that perhaps Philips would be offended, thinking I had instigated the interview and was unappreciative of what he had done for me regarding Northwestern Bell employment. I explained to Philips what had happened. To my great relief, he urged me to proceed with the interview, saying it would be a good experience to do so and assured me that I was free to accept employment from IBM, if its offer was more appealing. During my interview, Thomas described the position of IBM Electric Account-

ing Machine salesman as one in which I would be studying customer business problems and devising solutions utilizing IBM's electric punch card accounting machines. Thomas described the dress code for IBM salesmen as white shirt, solid color tie, and pin-striped suit. Since I owned only one business suit, the one I was wearing, I found this disconcerting. When I explained my situation to Thomas, he said that I should not be concerned and that if I joined IBM, I could buy a new suit and put it on my first expense account. Incidentally, the IBM Accounting Department disallowed the suit when I submitted my first expense account. A decade or more later, I reminded Thomas of this promise not kept. He just laughed and shrugged his shoulders.

In contrast to Northwestern Bell's accounting job, IBM's offer appeared far more attractive, challenging, and intriguing, despite the fact that the starting salary was only $100 per month, $25 less than Northwestern Bell's offer. Nevertheless, I accepted the IBM offer, with Philips's concurrence. This proved to be one of the most important decisions of my life, launching me on a career with IBM that lasted 38 years. I eventually earned the position of IBM corporate vice president in 1958 and an appointment to the IBM World Trade Corporation's Board of Directors in 1963. I held both positions until 1973, when I retired from the company.

In this memoir, I will attempt to highlight my most poignant experiences. While some were frustrating, many were rewarding and, at times, afforded me peer recognition both inside and outside IBM. When I joined IBM in 1935, the company was small, generating annual revenues of $25 million with fewer than 4,000 employees. I had only two weeks at home after graduating from the university before I left Burlington by train for the 24-hour ride to the IBM sales school in Endicott, New York. I had never taken a sleeper train before, and this was quite a thrilling experience for me and likewise for Carl Gamrath, another University of Iowa hiree. Because lower sleeper berths were designed to accommodate two people, we shared a berth, concerned that to do otherwise would appear extravagant to our new employer. In Iowa there is a saying: "You can take the boy off the farm, but you can't take the farm off the boy." This was certainly the case for the two of us.

When Gamrath and I reached Endicott to begin the six-week sales school, we were joined by George Teyro, another University of Iowa graduate. We reported to the IBM Educational Center, about the size of a small elementary

Figure 1. IBM Sales School Number 125 trainees and instructors.

To Thos. J. Watson, President, IBM
(Tune: "Happy Days Are Here Again")
Happy days are here again!
And every heart in I.B.M.,
All loyal T.J. Watson men,
Love our noble President.
His leadership stands out alone;
He's honored everywhere he's known;
We proudly claim him all our own;
In our worldwide I.B.M.,
By him we are all inspired,
To do whate'er he desires.
Happy men of I.B.M.,
Throughout the world good citizens,
With faces bright as Diadems,
Happy days are here again!

Ever Onward
(IBM rally song, written especially for the International
Business Machines Corporation)
There's a thrill in store for all,
For we're about to toast
The corporation that we represent.
We're here to cheer each pioneer
And also proudly boast

Of that "man of men," our sterling president.
The name of T.J. Watson means a courage none can stem:
And we feel honored to be here to toast the "I.B.M."
Chorus
Ever onward—ever onward!
That's the spirit that has brought us fame!
We're big, but bigger we will be,
We can't fail for all can see
That to serve humanity has been our aim!
Our products now are known in every zone,
Our reputation sparkles like a gem!
We've fought our way through—and new
Fields we're sure to conquer too
For the ever onward I.B.M.
Second Chorus
Ever onward—ever onward!
We're bound for the top to never fail!
Right here and now we thankfully
Pledge sincerest loyalty
To the corporation that's the best of all!
Our leaders we revere, and while we're here
Let's show the world just what we think of them!
So let us sing, men! Sing, men!
Once or twice then sing again
For the ever onward I.B.M.

---

school, where IBM conducted training for customer engineers, factory workers, engineers, and office personnel. Two classrooms were designated for sales trainees. The smaller room was assigned to a class of 25 recently hired female college graduates. The larger classroom was allocated to Sales Class Number 125 and was comprised of 67 men (see Figure 1). The 25 women were housed at the IBM Homestead on the outskirts of Endicott, a facility normally used to house customer VIPs and dignitaries. The men stayed at the Hotel Frederick in Endicott. The venerable Glen Armstrong, the instructor, was a veteran of the IBM sales executive team. "Army," as he was affectionately

known, was 100-percent salesman and 50-percent educator and was loved by all who met him. Bill Wiselogel and George Hedendorf, two experienced IBM instructors, assisted Army as guest instructors. The class was immediately indoctrinated in IBM's dress code, its rules regarding drinking and smoking, and, most important, the need for a studious attitude, coupled with enthusiasm and "pep." To instill pep, each class session opened in song. Usually, we sang a patriotic song first, such as "America," followed by one of the five songs dedicated to Thomas Watson, Sr., that was in the IBM songbook (see the sidebar). If a trainee's attention wavered, there was always the threat that he or she would have to sing a solo of "Ever Onward" (see the sidebar). Singing aside, the curriculum of the sales school focused, for the most part, on learning to use IBM punch card machines and applying them to solve customer problems. Everything was user-oriented. Sales training usually followed within a year.

When Watson, Sr., IBM's founder and CEO, visited the IBM Educational Center, he noticed there were 67 men and 25 women in separate classes. With his insistence, classes were merged and from then on were coeducational. Watson, Sr., visited the classroom about every other week. Having a class of young women was a novelty that he seemed to enjoy. Accordingly, he had the staff at the IBM Homestead arrange social activities, such as picnics and dinner dances, where he could enjoy observing the female sales trainees having fun. The women caught on quickly and played up to the "Old Man," as the employees affectionately nicknamed him. The women performed skits and composed songs especially for these occasions. In one skit, the setting was a slumber party in which the women wore "Dr. Denton's" (sleepwear).

Just before the course was completed in September 1935, Armstrong, vice president of education, asked the trainees to indicate their first, second, and third choices for branch office assignments. I listed Peoria, Illinois; Des Moines, Iowa; and St. Louis, Missouri. Armstrong, admired for his humor and wit, commented on my choices, saying that this was the first time anyone asked to be sent to Peoria, the IBM version of Siberia. As it turned out, I was assigned to St. Louis as a sales trainee.

Following a brief stopover in Burlington, where I was able to visit my sister Elsie and my fiancée Jean, I reported to Paul Maxwell, IBM's St. Louis branch manager. While in Burlington, Jean and I agreed that courtship by telephone and mail was not conducive to a satisfactory relationship and that we needed to marry as soon as I could afford it. On the basis of a $25-per-month salary increase after six months of employment, which was promised at the time of hire, Jean and I set a goal of marrying six months hence. I loved my job in the St. Louis office, and Maxwell was very supportive of me. If it had not been for him, my IBM career would have been snuffed out before it began. He reassigned me as manager of the IBM service bureau, where I worked late into the night. During the day, he allowed me to make sales calls with him and prospect his territory, giving me sales training I would not have experienced otherwise. At the time, I did not realize that he was protecting my employment with IBM. I learned much later that Watson, Sr., annoyed at IBM field sales management's resistance to accepting the 25 women on the marketing staff, had ordered termination of all 67 men in my Sales Training Class Number 125.

Jean and I Marry

Anxious that Jean and I fulfill our promise of marriage, I pressed Maxwell for the promised raise as my six months' employment approached. Maxwell assured me that he would send his recommendation for the raise to IBM headquarters in New York. Based on this reassurance, Jean and I proceeded with our marriage plans. Because IBM's policy in 1935 did not include time off for marriage, we scheduled the event for Thanksgiving weekend. In a car Gene Gilbert (a St. Louis IBM colleague) loaned to me, I arrived in Burlington on Thanksgiving Day and had dinner with my family. The following day, Jean and I took out a marriage license. On Saturday morning, 30 November 1935, we married in a ceremony in St. Paul's Church that one could characterize as a "hometown elopement." On 30 November 1997, Jean and I celebrated our 62nd wedding anniversary.

Several months after my marriage, I was shocked to learn from Maxwell that my promised six-month salary increase had been denied. After meeting with Maxwell's manager, Mr. Worthington, the Midwest IBM regional sales manager, I was told that he had approved the increase and that it had been denied by Mr. Farwell, IBM sales manager at headquarters. Not long after that, I learned Farwell planned to visit St. Louis. I went back to Worthington and received permission to seek an appointment with Farwell. When Farwell arrived, I met with him and inquired why my salary increase had been denied. He replied that I should consider myself fortunate to still be employed, explaining that of the 67 men in my training class, only 14 were still with IBM. I responded that if I could not sell IBM management on honoring its commitment to me, I doubted I could be successful selling IBM systems.

Following the Farwell meeting, I explored alternative employment opportunities. In the meantime, Maxwell was transferred out and replaced by Harry Eilers, which was the purpose of Farwell's visit to St. Louis. Eilers allowed me to continue the dual work assignment Maxwell had arranged. A month or so after Eilers became manager, I surprised him by bringing in a signed contract for a $128-a-month punch card accounting machine installation with Tom

Boy Stores, a St. Louis wholesale grocery chain. I had secured this account prospecting on my own in the manager's sales territory. Eilers considered this no small accomplishment. He said that such an unassisted sale by one who was not yet a junior salesman was "unprecedented." I further surprised Eilers with the news that I had accepted an employment offer from Shell Oil Company as assistant manager of its Tabulating Machine Department for $125 a month. Since I had never resigned from a job before, I asked Eilers for his advice regarding the appropriate procedure for tendering my resignation. He suggested that before resigning, I take three days off, implying that my decision to leave IBM was more the result of my fatigue from handling dual job assignments than from my irritation with IBM for failing to honor its commitment to me. I followed his suggestion. After taking the time off, I met with Eilers for further discussion.

At this point, Eilers said that the IBM home office was impressed by the sale I had made and that if I would remain with IBM, I would receive an invitation to IBM's two-month advanced sales school, scheduled to commence in a few weeks. Additionally, I would receive my $25 increase and be assigned back to IBM St. Louis after my training concluded. I told Eilers that while this offer was appealing, I had made a commitment to Mr. Baker, the controller of Shell Oil Company, and that I felt duty-bound to honor it. Eilers suggested I discuss the matter with Baker. When I spoke with Baker, he said, "Birkenstock, I think you love your work at IBM and, in due course, will be a successful salesman. You have no obligation to me or to the Shell Oil Company. I think you should stay with IBM." Years later, Eilers informed me that during my three-day sabbatical, he had contacted IBM headquarters and obtained approval for his plan to retain me. He also had contacted Baker relative to the Shell job offer. This was my first introduction to business intrigue as well as the beginning of my association with one of the highest-principled salesmen and managers I have ever known. Eilers and I bonded as friends and business associates throughout Eilers's lifetime. As a salesman and manager, Eilers was a role model I did well in following.

All IBM marketing representatives operated on a sales quota that was established at the beginning of each year. Good sales achievement was marked by making 100 percent or more of the sales quota and becoming a member of that year's Hundred Percent Club. At year's end, all club members were invited to New York for a series of motivational sales meetings (see Figure 2). Members enjoyed various cultural activities and a banquet featuring famous Broadway or opera performers. Each member was invited to address the assembly, presided over by Watson, Sr., who was assisted by the president of the Hundred Percent Club, the highest achiever of that year.

Early Success Interrupted by Tragedy

During my seven years in St. Louis, I advanced from senior salesman to special transportation representative. In this capacity, I handled the railroad, trucking, and airline accounts in the St. Louis area and qualified for five IBM Hundred Percent Clubs. The only year I failed to make the club was in 1939, the year our one-year-old son Michael was tragically killed in an automobile accident that my wife and I experienced outside Peoria while on our way to visit Jean's parents. Jean sustained a concussion, while I suffered a broken sternum and jaw. While in the hospital, Mr. O'Malley, branch manager of the Peoria office, showed me a telegram from Watson, Sr. It authorized O'Malley to set up a $5,000 account to pay our hospital expenses, if needed. This was my first introduction to Watson, Sr.'s compassion toward his employees, whom he considered family members. Though we had been badly injured, Jean and I recuperated from the accident; however, we never fully recovered from the trauma of the death of our precious infant son. The grief over the loss of Michael was softened with the birth of our second son Robert Hale on 5 May 1940 and with the arrival of our daughter Joyce Ann on 6 October 1943.

The year before the accident, Charles Kirk had succeeded Eilers as branch manager. Kirk, a free spirit with a knack for business politics, showed me the importance of the "lighter" side of selling. Kirk served as St. Louis branch manager until 1940, when he was promoted to manager of IBM's Endicott plant. My tenure in St. Louis, especially the first five years, was a period of challenge, growth, and development. During this period, several junior salesmen were assigned to me for training. This responsibility,

Figure 2. The author addressing 1937's Hundred Percent Club Convention in the Grand Ballroom of the Waldorf-Astoria Hotel, 26 January 1938.

Figure 3. St. Louis branch manager Larry Flick (left) presenting me with my Five-Year Medal.

small as it was, was my first experience in personnel management. However, I feel fortunate to have had a part in the career development of two IBM employees in particular. O.M. Scott, a 1938 graduate of the University of Missouri, and Warren C. Hume, a 1939 graduate from Rollins College, were both assigned to me as junior salesmen for training. Both men later had long and distinguished careers as IBM executives and corporate officers. Before their retirement, Scott was president of IBM's Field Engineering Division, and Hume was an IBM group vice president.

In 1940, Larry Flick (see Figure 3) succeeded Kirk. Flick's management style was entirely different from the managers who had preceded him. He was alternately pessimistic and wildly optimistic and did not control these emotional swings. Moreover, Flick became jealous of Harry Strait and me for being the most successful salesmen in the St. Louis office and for the tribute World Headquarters (WHQ) paid us for our accomplishments. Needless to say, our relationship with Strait was somewhat strained. In the spring of 1941, Bob Brownell, IBM special representative to the U.S. Army, asked me to undertake a special assignment, the rescue of a failing IBM installation at Fort Leonard Wood in the Ozark Mountains. The assignment began after IBM's Washington office, dealing directly with the Army, sold the IBM accounting machine installation to the Fort Leonard Wood contractors to perform payroll accounting and camp construction logistics. Thousands of people had been hired to construct this new Army base. However, the IBM tabulating machine installation could not keep pace with the personnel growth and, therefore, could not produce a timely weekly payroll. Consequently, disgruntled employees were picketing and were on the verge of rioting.

To cope with this problem and to save the installation, IBM branch manager Flick assembled a six-person task force of St. Louis branch office systems service and sales personnel. Because this attempt was unsuccessful, the Army lost faith in IBM, sent a discontinuance notice to the IBM Washington office, and ordered new payroll equipment from the

Burroughs Corporation. As a result, Brownell went to the site and quickly concluded that Flick's task force leadership was ineffectual and that a different strategy was required to save the installation. At that time, I was functioning as an IBM special representative with a sales territory in St. Louis that was not geographical but transportation industry-specific. St. Louis was a transportation hub and the home of four major railroad companies, several trucking companies, and an airline. The railroads I served all had large IBM accounting and payroll installations. My experience in planning and installing payroll systems in the area prompted Brownell to call Washington and request that I be assigned to the project. He advised Flick of his action.

On Brownell's instruction, Flick ordered me, via telephone, to go to Fort Leonard Wood. On my arrival there, I discovered Flick was still on the site and that he had made his growing animosity toward me and his predecessor Kirk evident to the members of his task force. Believing it would be impossible to work with Flick, I stated to Brownell that I would accept the assignment only on the condition that Flick and his task force return to St. Louis. I further requested that Hume, a junior salesman assigned to assist me, remain. Brownell agreed. As a task force of two, Hume and I worked in the succeeding weeks from Wednesday through Saturday with little sleep, making system and procedure changes that produced an on-time payroll and saved the installation. The Burroughs equipment remained in its crates and was subsequently shipped back to Burroughs. Needless to say, IBM headquarters considered this quite a feat. As a result, both Hume and I received an IBM headquarters commendation. After the assignment, I returned to working my normal territory and had already made the 100 Percent Club for that year. Hume was promoted to senior salesman and went on to an outstanding IBM career.

In the fall of 1941, presumably due to the Fort Leonard Wood achievement, Watson, Sr., called me to New York and assigned me as an IBM civilian advisor to the Army on maneuvers near Fort Bragg, North Carolina. The assignment placed me in charge of one of the two 12-hour shifts for the operation of an experimental IBM Mobile Accounting Machine Unit utilizing IBM punch card equipment. This occurred during what was then the Army's largest simulated warfare maneuvers, which Major General Hugh Drum commanded. T. Vincent Learson, an IBM employee from the Boston office, managed the other shift. IBM's experimental Mobile Accounting Machine Unit was programmed to manage ammunition logistics and inventory control on the battlefield during simulated warfare. As a result of this experiment, the military recognized the great potential of IBM's mobile accounting units. The Army subsequently employed IBM for not only ammunition control but also field personnel records, logistics, and frontline military applications during World War II.

The early days of this assignment did not exclude physical discomforts. As civilians, Learson and I and our staffs, comprised of recent sales trainee civilians, were unaccustomed to both the simulated battlefield environment and our exposure to the extremely cold temperatures. We were required to sleep on cots in tents, wearing civilian clothes far from weatherproof. More often than not, I found myself cold and damp. Fortunately, my discomfort was cut short. The Blue Army captured the commanding officer of a Red Army division. Embarrassed and infuriated, Drum blamed this surprise capture on the presence at the "front" of the civilian contingent that, he contended, disclosed the Red Army headquarters' position. In retaliation, the general ordered all civilians to "move to the rear."

The "rear" for all IBM staff members meant bivouacking at the Southern Pines Hotel. How wonderful my warm hotel bed felt, especially after a 12-hour work shift. (Some 40 years later, I revisited Southern Pines on a golfing holiday. For nostalgic reasons, I had hoped to stay at the Southern Pines Hotel. To my disappointment, I found the hotel closed and the building in a shambles.) The mobile unit experiment was completed on 1 December 1941. I arrived back home in St. Louis on 6 December 1941, awakening the next day to the news of the Japanese bombing of Pearl Harbor.

World War II opened a new era for IBM and its people. The company's punch card equipment was in great demand by both the armed forces and military contractors. New IBM equipment rental for nonmilitary use was restricted to government contractors and military applications. In addition, many IBM personnel not serving in essential industries were drafted into the military and commissioned as officers. Almost immediately, IBM's branch office activities shifted from sales to the service of defense contractors and customers classified as "War Emergency Enterprises."

My First Promotion

Flick, in his idiosyncratic manner, began running his branch office in a paramilitary fashion, and his relations with me became even more strained. With what appeared to be excessive patriotism, he assembled the sales personnel at 9 a.m. daily for a brief sales meeting. Prior to the meeting, we were required to stand and salute the flag and sing "America" and the "Star-Spangled Banner." On occasion, Flick, who loved ceremony, would wear his Army Reserve uniform to the office. A major in the Army Reserve, Flick was called to active duty in the summer of 1942. Having the best sales record in the St. Louis office, I thought I might be named as his replacement. However, Flick advised New York against this and, instead, recommended Mike Petkus, the C.E. Manager, be appointed. As it turned out, in September, Thomas was named St. Louis branch manager, and I was appointed branch manager of Kansas City. Shortly after my move to Kansas City, the U.S. Navy, aggressively recruiting IBM employees to take command of Navy IBM tabulating machine installations, offered me an ensign's commission. Not wanting to be drafted, I was eager to enlist. Unfortunately, I was unable to serve, having flunked my physical due to a hyperacidic stomach. Later, the U.S. Army drafted me; however, I once again failed my physical, was declared 4-F for the duration of the war, and remained the Kansas City branch office manager. An extraordinarily large number of defense contractors resided in this territory, including the Army base at Fort Leavenworth, Kansas.

Wartime restrictions notwithstanding, my days in Kansas City were among the happiest and least stressful of my IBM career. I had the full cooperation of two other managers in the office. Ed Vincent, International Time Recording Division branch manager, and I shared 7 May as our birthday; Vincent turned 60 the day I became 30. Vincent never once resented working under a man so much younger than he was and gave me his full cooperation, as did Ken Van Antwerp, the typewriter branch manager. As Kansas City branch manager, one of the most challenging problems I faced was the renovation of Kansas City's Baltimore Bank building into an IBM office. During a brief stopover in Kansas City in the spring of 1942, and prior to my becoming manager, Watson, Sr., hearing that the bank building was for sale, bought it because of its splendid location. Unfortunately, the building had structural problems, which I discovered when I engaged an architect to plan the remodeling. Since the building would be housing heavy IBM accounting machines, the floors had to be strengthened. This became a major problem due to wartime restrictions. Steel construction that was nonessential to the war required a certificate of necessity from the military that was difficult to obtain.

While having lunch with IBM customer Fred Detweiler, comptroller for the new Pratt and Whitney aircraft plant being built in the Kansas City office territory, he and I commiserated over our mutual construction problems and his start-up problems. The Pratt and Whitney plant was nine months behind schedule, with IBM accounting machines due to arrive in a few weeks, and he had no facility in which to train key punch and accounting machine operators. Detweiler and I collaborated on a solution to both of our problems. Since Pratt and Whitney could easily obtain a certificate of necessity as a defense contractor, I agreed to give that company a one-dollar-a-month, short-term lease to the bank building. Pratt and Whitney, at IBM's expense and to its design, would remodel and reinforce the premises. Furthermore, I agreed as a quid pro quo that Pratt and Whitney personnel would be given a free training course at the leased bank building on the new IBM accounting machines scheduled for use at the Pratt and Whitney plant when its construction was completed. What a stroke of luck for both of us. When the work was completed, Pratt and Whitney personnel moved out of the building, and IBM personnel moved in.

At IBM headquarters in New York, Pete Pennell, in charge of branch office facilities nationwide, thought I was a magician, a super negotiator, or just darn lucky. I suspect a little bit of all three were involved. On completion of the Pratt and Whitney plant, and after Detweiler's accounting machines and staff moved, only minor alterations were required to make the former bank building serve as IBM's Kansas City branch office. The Kansas City IBM branch operation won high acclaim from both IBM management and the U.S. government for its wartime service to both industry and the military in the Missouri/Kansas area.

Career Crisis

All of my experiences during my Kansas City days were not always this positive, however. During wartime, and particularly toward the close of the war, IBM adopted a practice of occasionally inviting branch managers to Endicott as guest instructors at an IBM training facility. In the fall of 1944, headquarters invited me to teach a two-week sales and management course. While I was there, Watson, Sr., and his wife were visiting and staying at the IBM Endicott Homestead, where I was residing as well. At dinner one evening, Watson, Sr., sensing that the war might be ending soon, posed questions relative to the future of our defense contractor customers. I responded that they already were looking for commercial applications for their wartime technology and manufacturing capability. I further commented that IBM was assisting our customers in this regard to avoid IBM having to requisition "packing cases." This terminology was field jargon for preparing discontinued IBM machines for field transfer to other users. Under IBM policy, machines discontinued by a customer ceased to be under branch office control and became part of field transfer inventory administration, which George Richter headed at IBM headquarters. IBM filled equipment orders from both factory production and field transfer inventory, and the delivery sequence was established according to the date of the customer's order under a delivery schedule Richter controlled. When I used the term "packing cases," I did not realize that, for Watson, Sr., it carried a negative connotation or that he was unaware that discontinued equipment ceased to be under the control of branch office management. In other words, he did not understand the field transfer system the company utilized.

Several days later, I visited New York to obtain some sales material before returning to Kansas City. While in New York, Kirk called to inform me that in two days, a meeting was being held in Chicago for all IBM branch office managers and that I should stop there for the meeting on my way home to Kansas City. Two days later, Kirk opened the meeting by telling the assembled group that Watson, Sr., had posed a question to one of his branch office managers regarding the future of IBM wartime defense contractor installations. He said that Watson, Sr., perceived a negative attitude by a branch manager in the response to his question. When the meeting broke for lunch, I said in private to Kirk that I was, undoubtedly, the branch manager whom Watson, Sr., thought had exhibited a negative attitude. I then asked Kirk how he thought I should handle the situation. He responded that I needed to write Watson, Sr., a letter of apology. I said that I felt I had done nothing wrong and that Watson, Sr., had misunderstood my comment. Upset, I left before the meeting had concluded and boarded a sleeper train for Kansas City.

I tossed and turned all night in my berth, mulling over the problem. I finally decided prior to my arrival in Kansas City that I could not and would not offer Watson, Sr., an apology. In my heart, I did not feel that I had anything for which to apologize. I decided that I would write him what turned out to be a two-paragraph letter, explaining that unfortunately he had misinterpreted my comment to him regarding the packing boxes. I further stated that I had no negative feelings regarding IBM's pursuit of postwar equipment sales. I concluded my letter stating that my positive attitude could be easily ascertained by examining my sales record and history with the company. Within a week, I received Watson, Sr.'s response. He thanked me for my letter and agreed that my sales record resolved the issue. As far as he was concerned, the incident was "behind us and forgotten."

Called to IBM Headquarters, New York City

That incident certainly was behind us, for in August 1945 (when the end of the war was in sight), I received a telegram from Watson, Sr., requesting that Jean and I meet him in Endicott the Tuesday following Labor Day. While en route and during a stopover at the IBM Midwest district office in Chicago, VJ Day occurred. Although the euphoria that followed presented some travel difficulties, Jean and I managed to arrive in Endicott on schedule. When I met with Watson, Sr., he informed me that I had been promoted to the IBM headquarters staff as assistant to Kirk, who was recently appointed as IBM executive vice president. Naturally, I was thrilled, even though Jean and I regretted leaving Kansas City. We knew we were fortunate, by IBM standards, to have moved only twice in 10 years.

In the ensuing fall of 1945, I spent considerable time getting acclimated to the role of assistant to the executive vice president. Kirk's job was challenging, since he was the principal operating executive responsible for "retooling" IBM from a wartime to a peacetime operation. One of my assignments was to develop a peacetime sales plan along with retraining programs for the IBM sales and management personnel returning from military service. Others in Kirk's office were assigned to engineering and manufacturing changes. Jean and our children stayed in Kansas City during the several months it took me to locate an apartment for my family in Bronxville, New York. During these same months, Kirk, who also was house hunting, invited me to share with him a Ritz Tower suite in Manhattan. Through my many after-hours conversations with Kirk, I gained a broad insight into both the present problems and future opportunities IBM faced as we spent considerable time planning the wartime-to-peacetime transition.

In December 1945, Watson, Sr., announced the convening of an IBM branch managers' school at Endicott on 6 January 1946 to update and train IBM's postwar branch managers, many of whom only a few months earlier had been on military duty. The group included Tom Watson, Jr., whom, although not a branch manager, his father invited to attend. On the opening day, Kirk, who was to have been the principal instructor and discussion leader, was occupied with the "Old Man," Watson, Sr., relative to a glitch in factory production that suddenly had come to his attention. As the only WHQ executive present, the role of classroom instructor fell to me.

A Stunning Promotion

During the third day of the weeklong school, Watson, Sr., and Kirk joined the assembly and seated themselves in the back of the room. At that point, I was making a presentation about the need to double the existing number of IBM branch offices to maximize sales potential and the related, though unpopular downsizing of sales territories in order to enhance customer service. After listening to my presentation for about half an hour, Watson, Sr., moved to the podium and stated that he had just discovered his postwar general sales manager. With that, he announced my appointment as IBM general sales manager, filling a six-month vacancy. At 33, I became IBM's youngest general sales manager. In my new position, I felt a great responsibility to IBM and its customers and a tremendous sense of challenge in meeting the demands of the postwar period. Besides the "retooling" and restaffing necessary for IBM's Marketing department to adjust promptly to a postwar operation, the marketplace was experiencing a pent-up customer demand for punch card tabulating systems. Additionally, with the help of the government's financial support, competition was growing.

During my first week in my new position, Executive Vice President Kirk assigned me to a highly sensitive regional sales management personnel problem. A year or more had passed since IBM had promoted Eilers from Minneapolis branch office manager to manager of the Midwest regional office in Chicago. Eilers was still residing in Minneapolis, however, and commuting to Chicago each week. Kirk said that Watson, Sr., strongly disapproved of a regional sales manager living in a city other than the one in which he was headquartered. He made his feelings known to Kirk and told him he wanted the matter resolved immediately. Consequently, Kirk instructed me to go to Minneapolis and give Eilers an ultimatum either to move his residence from Minneapolis to Chicago or to resign as regional manager. This was the same Eilers who was my St. Louis branch office manager and, later, the district manager to whom I had reported when I was the Kansas City branch office manager. Knowing Eilers's respect for authority, I could not imagine him disobeying Watson, Sr.'s order.

When I arrived in Minneapolis, I discovered the reason Eilers had not moved to Chicago. He was receiving treatment at the nearby Mayo Clinic for a partial blockage of his carotid artery. Under these circumstances, rather than issuing Eilers the ultimatum, I encouraged him to undergo further Mayo Clinic diagnostic procedures and arranged for assistance in the Midwest region. I expressed my concern to Eilers that his health might be impaired by travel time between his Minneapolis home and his Chicago office. I asked him to consider moving to Chicago at the earliest feasible date.

On arriving at my next destination, Seattle, Washington, I called Kirk and explained Eilers's situation and my rationale for not taking Eilers out of the Midwest region job. Kirk was displeased by my failure to follow orders, especially, as he said, "when they came from the top." He characterized my handling of the situation as a "bad beginning" and said he would take care of the matter himself. As a result, Eilers, who refused reassignment, retired from the company prematurely and remained in retirement until 1953, when Watson, Jr., found a way to partially rectify Eilers's harsh treatment. Watson, Jr., put Eilers in charge of IBM/3M relations, reporting to me. To facilitate the IBM/3M relationship, IBM opened a small magnetic computer tape finishing plant near 3M's St. Paul, Minnesota, plant that supplied IBM with "raw" computer tape. In 1970, IBM closed its St. Paul tape finishing plant when IBM's Boulder tape manufacturing plant supplied all the company's magnetic tape requirements. At this time, Eilers retired for good, however, but not without Watson, Jr.'s personal hand in restitution for Eilers's lost pay and retirement benefits.

Years later, after I left the general sales manager position and after Kirk's death, Watson, Jr., told me that he held me blameless for the "terrible injustice done to Eilers" and assigned Eilers to a management position reporting to me. This confirmed my suspicion that the reason behind Watson, Sr.'s order to remove Eilers from his position was that he wanted his nephew Charlie Love appointed as Midwest sales manager. Watson, Sr., eventually assigned Love to succeed me as general sales manager in 1947, a position Love held until 1952. By then, Watson, Jr., had convinced his father that a position should be arranged for Love in an affiliated company.

On my January 1946 visit to Seattle, another noteworthy incident occurred. Art Brambach, Seattle manager, asked me to interview a young applicant, recently returned from the military, whom he considered to be outstanding. The applicant was Dean McKay. However, Watson, Sr., had initiated a hiring freeze that would remain in place until all former staff returning from military duty were absorbed into IBM's sales organizations. As a result, Brambach's request necessitated a policy exception. Believing that the hiring freeze would soon be lifted, I interviewed McKay, was greatly impressed with him, and authorized his hiring. When I reported this to Kirk, he replied that within my first month as executive sales manager, this was the second time I had disregarded the orders of "the boss" (Watson, Sr.). I am pleased to say, however, that I never regretted making the policy exception to hire McKay, whose brilliant career with IBM culminated in the position of IBM vice president of communications. As IBM's chief information officer, McKay was adept at public relations and, later in his career, was elected to the IBM Board of Directors.

Since postwar IBM was experiencing a surge in customer demand for systems and service, coupled with a "tired" product line, my life as general sales manager was quite hectic, particularly with Watson, Sr., acting as my chief critic. Consequently, each day I was confronted with new and diverse challenges. Meeting market demand for IBM systems from government, industry, and academia drove the company to a phenomenal expansion of branch offices—from 85 to 135 in a single year. This growth in marketing capability was achieved due to the support of Gordon Lovell, Ed Zollinger, Don Gamel, and, to a lesser extent, Love, all regional sales managers. These men were supported by a staff of special department executives such as Jack Kenny, Gordon Roberts, Al Lishawa, Paul Shakelford, and Barney Freeman. Freeman's loyalty and expertise were outstanding. Generally, a manager had the prerogative to select his own assistants. However, while away on my first trip to the West Coast, Watson, Sr., appointed C.E. McKittrich as my assistant without my knowledge or concurrence. This appointment was Watson, Sr.'s way of rewarding McKittrick for tracking down the dog that had bitten his wife during the Watsons' visit to the Winston–Salem, North Carolina, branch office that McKittrick managed. He made another appointment without my concurrence. Fortunately for me, this was a good choice, as Norma Trabold was a loyal and capable assistant.

Previously, on my 33rd birthday, Watson, Sr., convened a meeting of executives in his office to read to them a letter he had received from a disgruntled salesman. The salesman complained that his commission statement was tardy, inaccurate, and prepared on Burroughs machines. Watson, Sr., asked A.L. Williams, in charge of accounting and finance, if indeed our commission statements were produced on Burroughs equipment rather than our own machines. Williams acknowledged they were. Watson, Sr., responded that he wanted all commission statements prepared on IBM machines by 1 June—less than a month away. Williams said he did not believe this was a feasible request.

Watson, Sr., then turned to me and, acknowledging my many years of experience with this equipment, handed the assignment to me. I told him that I did not believe I could meet that deadline any more than Williams could. Besides, I told him I had many problems retooling our sales organization from wartime to peacetime operation and felt it inadvisable for me to neglect them. With that, Watson, Sr., turned to my newly appointed assistant, McKittrick, and asked him to undertake the assignment. McKittrick responded, "Yes, sir." Watson, Sr., then added, "I won't be asking you to undertake this project alone, because I will help you, Mr. McKittrick." As it turned out, neither Watson nor McKittrick solved the problem. A Mr. Bray, manager of payroll records, fulfilled the assignment; however, it took him months, not weeks to accomplish it.

Penalty Box for Crossing Watson, Sr.
That same afternoon, Watson, Sr.'s secretary, Byron Waters, notified me that Watson, Sr., felt I needed a vacation. Accommodations, I was told, had been arranged for Jean, the children, and me at the Buck Hill Falls Resort Hotel in the Pocono Mountains. Waters also told me he had called Jean; asked her to pack bags for herself, the children, and me; and told her that a car would be picking them up at 3:00 that afternoon to drive them to the resort where I was to meet them. I knew this was Watson, Sr.'s way of demonstrating to me that I was not indispensable. I also knew that I had little alternative but to accept this "vacation." My fami-

ly and I spent a week in a resort that would have been far more enjoyable had it not been in May. It was cold and damp in the mountains, and the resort was almost empty. I, along with my family, suffered out the week, all the time cursing myself for not having the fortitude to refuse Watson, Sr.'s enforced vacation.

One of the most pleasurable experiences I encountered as general sales manager was the placement of many men and women returning from military assignment who had become qualified in IBM punch card systems. Those with a marketing background needed to be integrated into IBM's sales and service operation. Each week, all top-level managers were furnished a list of IBM personnel returning from the armed services that indicated the IBM position they had held prior to their military service. Drawing from the returning military service personnel, we staffed the new offices we needed to open in every state of the union. Many were moved immediately into management positions, and some became important WHQ executives.

Due to the branch office growth during 1946, new sales territories were established, while others were realigned. New sales and compensation plans were announced to replace those terminated during World War II. Another complication I had to resolve was when older salesmen were reluctant to share sales territories with the new hires or returning employees. Also, several new rental products were announced, requiring training and sales promotion. I faced these challenges as general sales manager for just under a year.

Watson, Sr., in most ways, was a great person. Many considered him America's greatest business leader. He was an exponent of world peace through trade and was a confidant of U.S. presidents. In spite of this, or perhaps because of this, he was not easy to please and wanted the final say in all facets of the business. Unless he gave his full concurrence in advance, he was prone to disapprove decisions subordinates made, especially decisions his general sales manager made. He did not like to delegate authority and, at the same time, had a reputation for making impulsive appointments (as was the case with my appointment as general sales manager). He was also known to terminate management or sales personnel just as impulsively, as was the case with Eilers and the entire male contingent of Sales School Number 125 in 1935.

Greatest Career Crisis
Toward the end of 1946, Kirk called me to his office and, in the abrupt, "hatchet-man" man-

ner for which he was noted, told me I was being relieved of my position of general sales manager. When I asked why, he said it was because I had too often opposed Watson, Sr. When I inquired about a place for me in the company, Kirk suggested I could have any marketing management position anywhere in the field I wished. This meant, of course, that someone else would have to be removed from that position before I could occupy it. At the time of my appointment, I had accepted the possibility that my term of office might be short. What I could not accept, however, was the type of job reassignment Kirk proposed. I was filled with anger, disgust, and disappointment because of the ruthless manner in which Kirk handled my removal. I was not willing to play his game and told Kirk as much. After a brief and heated exchange, I advised Kirk that I was resigning from the company, packed up, and went home.

In apparent disagreement with Kirk's handling of the matter and wanting to retain me in IBM, Watson, Jr., called my home. He spoke with Jean, who told him that I was too upset to converse with him. Watson, Jr., asked Jean to relay to me his nonacceptance of my resignation and his desire to meet with me later in the week. When we met, Watson, Jr., said IBM should not lose a man with my record and executive capability. He offered me the position of manager of the IBM Future Demands department, reporting to him. In this new position, Watson, Jr., said, I would be able to utilize my knowledge of customer requirements and what he believed to be a flair for systems design and innovation. This gave me the opportunity and privilege of working with him directly. I admired him and his greater concern for IBM's future rather than for its present.

Career Rebound Begins

In 1947, when I was only six months into my Future Demands position, Kirk suffered a heart attack and died while on IBM business in France. Watson, Jr., promptly was named executive vice president, succeeding Kirk. Following his appointment, he began to talk to his father about decentralization, encouraging him toward lessening his control over all IBM functions and divisions. In 1949, as one of the first steps in that direction, Watson, Jr., believing his father had too many people reporting to him, persuaded his father to allow Bob Noll, IBM's patent manager, to report to him. In that same year, as Watson, Jr.'s workload as executive vice president increased, he added staff and promoted me from manager of Future Demands to

his staff as executive assistant with responsibility for certain functional areas, such as Intellectual Property (then called the Patent department). With the Intellectual Property responsibility came John Hayward as an advisor. Hayward was a wonderful, elderly, legal statesman who, together with Noll, schooled me in the world of intellectual property. On occasion, Noll was somewhat pedantic. Nevertheless, this highly capable attorney was particularly adept at selecting younger attorneys who reported to him, such as John Shipman, John Hanifin, Charlie McTiernan, Dewey Cunningham, and Jerry Etienne. Roger Smith, Paul Enlow, and Paul Carmichael joined the department over the next several years. Later, Shipman became second in command, responsible for international patents and the development of foreign patent policy and staff. All of these attorneys were highly professional and, I believe, the best in their field. In the years to come, each attorney achieved manager status. McTiernan left to head Sperry Rand's patent department, and Enlow was hired away by AT&T to direct its intellectual property activity with distinction.

The era following my assignment to Watson, Jr.'s staff coincided with a tremendous surge in the growth of engineering throughout IBM, which came about at Watson, Jr.'s insistence. This, coupled with the emphasis Watson, Sr., had placed on patenting, resulted in a patent workload glut. IBM was filing patent applications on 47 percent of inventive disclosures received from engineering. I foresaw that if IBM were to continue filing at that rate, based on its growth potential, there would come a day when such a filing rate would require the company to hire all the available patent attorneys in the United States and more. In search of a solution, Noll advised me that "publication" was a secondary and infrequently used form of protecting IBM's engineering accomplishments. But this, some reasoned, would mean prematurely telling the world, and especially the competition, what we were doing or about to do. A legal study of the problem suggested the innovative procedure of adopting a form of early publication that would serve as a "statutory bar" against others claiming they were the first to invent something. Such a procedure would require only limited publication in, for example, an area newspaper or a technical journal.

To further ensure that we met legal requirements, we devised a limited-publication document called an *IBM Engineering Disclosure Bulletin* that would be filed in the Library of Congress and several university libraries throughout the country, such as the Massachusetts Institute of Technology, Princeton University, California Institute of Technology, and Carnegie Tech. Consequently, the IBM Patent department changed its filing practices, and our filing rate dropped to 11 percent. The patents IBM filed represented the very best of the inventions coming out of the laboratories. The remaining approximately 36 percent of IBM's previously filed internal invention disclosures were published in our new *IBM Engineering Disclosure Bulletin*. This procedure reserved exclusive patent monopoly rights for IBM's best invention applications while preserving IBM's freedom of action to practice all its inventions and to assert them as prior art when they were challenged. Not only did this practice become a first in U.S. industry, but also it enabled IBM to concentrate its patent firepower on its best inventions and to protect them worldwide. This process would have been too expensive had we been filing applications on all patentable inventions. The strength of our worldwide patent portfolio became, in 1960, the tool we used to retain 100-percent ownership of IBM Japan and, subsequently, through cross-licensing, to gain freedom of action worldwide under the inventions that IBM competition held.

The scarcity of patent attorneys throughout the free world caused me, in collaboration with Noll and Shipman, to create another first for the profession. Instead of hiring attorneys away from other companies, analogous to today's professional athlete's free agency, we established IBM's own patent attorney school in Washington, D.C., staffed by IBM attorneys Jan Jancin and Maury Klitzman. Within IBM, Jancin recruited engineers with an ambition to become patent attorneys. They were then relocated to the Washington, D.C., area for training, spending part of their workday studying patent law at either Georgetown University or George Washington University. During the remainder of their day, Jancin and Klitzman taught them in IBM classrooms. They trained on real IBM patent searches, analyzing engineering disclosures and drafting patent applications on some of IBM's lesser inventions. After obtaining their law degrees and completing the IBM school, these new attorneys were assigned to various IBM laboratories.

IBM's Patent Operations department also played a role in stimulating the company's research and development. As a result, Emmanuel Piore, IBM vice president of research and engineering, asked me to devise an invention award system. Calling on the talented Hanifin and Cunningham, we came up with an award system that gave points for patents filed and articles published in the *IBM Engineering Disclosure Bulletin*. Annually, a patent award committee evaluated new patent issues, chose the most outstanding inventions, and gave the inventors cash awards, ranging from $20,000 to $100,000 and even higher. IBM Engineering Management sponsored an annual dinner to honor the most outstanding and prolific inventors. This patent award system was another first within the computer industry and, perhaps, for industry at large.

Historic Fumble

After the death of Clem Ehret—the elderly IBM veteran and manager of market research—I, as Watson, Jr.'s assistant, was also responsible for receiving and handling submissions from people outside the company who hoped to sell their inventions or technology to IBM, a legally sensitive, but only rarely fruitful procedure. Each of these submissions was given careful review, even though most proved worthless. But, one of them I received, had it been accepted, could have steered IBM in yet another profitable direction. Sometime in either late 1946 or early 1947, Chester Carlson, a freelance patent attorney, presented IBM with a rudimentary electrophotographic printing device that he proposed IBM manufacture and market, paying him royalties for the use of his patents. I was impressed with his development model, crude as it was, and saw the invention's potential, not as an adjunct to the punch card machine, but as a new office product: a plain paper copier. Carlson wanted a large sum up front and royalties for exclusive rights to his invention. In order to make a commitment to him in a deal of the magnitude he was proposing, I had to obtain a higher level of management approval. Since Watson, Jr., was away, I went to Watson, Sr. After I described the Carlson invention to him and what I believed to be its capability, he queried, "What has this got to do with the punch card?" "Nothing," I replied, "but it will give us a new product for the office machines market." He responded, "Now let me tell you something, young man. When my wife Jeanette tells me I'm the smartest man in the world, I respond, 'No, Jeanette, I'm only smart in spots; and I'm wise enough to stay on those spots.' Birkenstock, you should know that the punch card is one of those spots, and this Carlson invention isn't; so tell Mr. Carlson we're not interested in his invention." This time, to my later regret, I suppressed my inclination to debate the issue and turned down Carlson's offer. My becoming a yes-man to Watson, Sr., in this instance was a huge mistake.

Carlson's next visit was to Battelle Institute, which undertook product development of a plain paper printer/copier and obtained a license under the Carlson patents. Sometime later, Joe Wilson, president and CEO of Haloid Company, saw the rudimentary electrophotographic printer under development at Battelle and instantly recognized its potential. For an undisclosed sum and future royalties to both Battelle and Carlson, the Haloid Company purchased exclusive rights to the invention. Thus, xerography was born. Several years later, Haloid changed its company name to Haloid Xerox and subsequently dropped the name Haloid.

Prior to Xerox's enormous success, Wilson appeared as a guest on a TV program and discussed what he called "a document processing technology breakthrough." Watson, Jr., saw the TV program, so the next morning, I was "on the carpet" in his office. I explained how my proposal to accept Carlson's deal was turned down. Watson, Jr., responded with, "What a pity. Well, let's see if we can still get some part of the action. Haloid is a small company and may want our help." I contacted Wilson, who was extremely candid with me. This invention, he said, was the "find of the century, a technology that will give us a plain paper copier and a Haloid exclusive." Wilson continued that he would welcome a partnership with IBM regarding any other xerographic applications other than copiers. Consequently, IBM agreed to a joint development program for several IBM system products. Regrettably, this partnership did not produce a viable product. The heat fixing of the electrostatic image onto a punch card created dimensional instability relative to the tabulating card, and as a result, the IBM/Xerox technical collaboration died on the vine. It did lead, however, to Wilson's proposing that our two companies join in the manufacturing and marketing of the Xerox 914 in the United States. I thought this would be a means for IBM to enter the copier field. IBM management turned to Arthur D. Little to evaluate the proposal, and the Little firm forecast a modest market for plain paper copiers. Therefore, IBM turned down Wilson's offer, much to my regret and eventually to IBM management's regret. Following the success of the 914, Xerox came to me with a second proposal for a collaboration, this time in Europe. The IBM World Trade Corporation, which Arthur K. Watson (Watson, Jr.'s younger brother) headed, declined the offer, so Xerox formed a company with Rank, Ltd. to capitalize on the European market. In hindsight, I believe if I had waited for Watson, Jr., to intercede with his father before turning down Carlson, IBM would have achieved another goal. Instead, a historic fumble transpired, not only initially, but also twice thereafter.

Emerging Competition and Pivotal Assignment

One of IBM's most sensational growth periods began in the late 1940s and continued into the 1950s. The postwar demand for data processing outpaced IBM productive capacity, and the annual revenue growth was hundreds of millions of dollars. Also growing at a rapid pace in the late 1940s was the competitive threat of vacuum tube electronics and various means of binary computation and storage under development at university and private laboratories. Future competition from these developments concerned Watson, Jr., and caused him to assign me the additional responsibility of monitoring the potentially competitive threat arising from U.S. government-supported electronic development not only in government laboratories but also in government-funded university labs. In particular, I was to monitor the competitive cloud that was forming on the IBM horizon resulting primarily from the vacuum tube computer developments of the Eckert and Mauchly Electronic Company and secondarily from the binary storage capability Engineering Research Associates (ERA) was developing. I reported the results of my monitoring activities to Watson, Jr., every two to three weeks over lunch, viewing with alarm these competitive threats. Watson, Jr., and I both anguished over the publicity coups Univac achieved when CBS forecast election results in 1952 using Univac and when General Electric installed a Univac. The scope of the various new competitive threats required me to visit many of the university and government laboratories engaged in electronic development or research throughout the United States and in Great Britain, France, and Germany.

In parallel, the European branch of the IBM Patent department had a "patent watch" in place for adversely held patent applications that might impact IBM's future. From what I saw and learned from both sources, coupled with my knowledge of unfulfilled IBM customer requirements, I soon realized that the work going on in university, government, and private laboratories constituted a substantial threat to IBM's future. Watson, Jr., accepted this outlook and voiced his opinion to others. However, Watson, Sr., while not averse to IBM's experimenting with higher speed electromechanical processors, felt that there would never be a successor to the IBM punch card systems, which were so much in demand that our plants were working three shifts. He would publicly say, "IBM is an institution that would live on forever, based on the punch card."

In regard to shifting engineering emphasis toward electronics, Watson, Jr., soon found himself running interference between his father on one side and himself and me on the other. Because of his concern for IBM's future, Watson, Jr., with the passive approval of his father, issued instructions to IBM engineering departments that new IBM hires be electrical engineering graduates, preferably with a doctorate in mathematics, physics, or electronics. Because of this, IBM's electronic technology development capabilities were rapidly enhanced, and IBM began moving away from electromechanical accounting machine development toward electronic processors, with considerable emphasis as well on electronic memory and tape drives. This set the stage for the company's bold move into a crash program of electronic computer development in 1951. At that time, the emphasis on electronic development could not have been accomplished by anyone in the company other than the son of the founder. Watson, Jr., could, and often did, oppose his father's views. On occasion, he countermanded his father's orders and got away with it. Eventually, he persuaded his father to change some of his views regarding IBM's future.[1]

In 1948, IBM Poughkeepsie's electronic engineering laboratory staff demonstrated an innovative development called a Magnetic Tape Processing Machine Test Assembly. Only a few of those who appraised the Poughkeepsie test assembly believed Poughkeepsie's laboratory technology could give IBM an early entry into the electronic computing industry. We "believers" with marketing experience—none of whom was at a top management level—argued that the Tape Processing Machine could be the platform for a machine that would outperform both the ENIAC installed at the Aberdeen Proving Grounds and its successor the Univac being installed at the General Electric Company. Both products were the developments of the Eckert and Mauchly Electronic Company. I championed magnetic tape for processor input and storage because of its greatly enlarged digital storage and high-speed input/output capability, as did other supporters. Admittedly, as supportive as I was, I visualized it only as an alternative to the punch card as an operating medium. The primary need, as I envisioned it, was for a high-speed processor with

> ## In regard to shifting engineering emphasis toward electronics, Watson, Jr., soon found himself running interference between his father on one side and himself and me on the other.

large-capacity storage capability to use with IBM printer systems and punch card peripherals. I was confident that IBM's customers would pay a rental price many times higher than for punch card system rentals because such equipment would be far more cost-effective. This was especially true for the larger customers whose enormous data input required complex processing applications, recording more than 80 digits in a single entry, and whose output required "acres" of storage capacity.

Several major problems, however, needed to be addressed: the cost of development, the initiation of the program, and the introduction of such a new development into the market in competition with proven electromechanical punch card accounting systems. Most of all, we had to face the obsolescence factor, namely, the specter of outdating the company's lucrative equipment-rental machine inventory, the main source of IBM revenue and profit. We also needed to be concerned that we not lose our proprietary intellectual property rights if we accepted U.S. government funding to pursue a new development course.

Another threat to IBM's dominance that surfaced in mid-1947 was an advanced magnetic storage drum development, accomplished by a group of elite engineers originally assembled by the Navy in Dayton, Ohio, during World War II as part of the Navy's highly confidential wartime cryptology effort. These engineers developed stored-program potential and provided large-capacity, intermediate storage capability, something the ENIAC and the IBM Defense Calculator (mentioned later) lacked. Such potential was particularly worrisome to Watson, Jr., and me, because we considered this group of computer scientists and engineers to be some of the most talented engineers, outside of those at IBM. When General Bud Talbot, a Dayton resident and friend of Watson, Jr.'s, suggested IBM acquire the group as a separate entity along with its related contractual obligations to the Navy, Watson, Jr., declined for antitrust reasons. Watson, Jr., asked me to assist Navy Captain Ralph Meader, who was in charge of the cryptology project, in finding a solution to the antitrust dilemma. Meader found John Parker, a retired Navy officer with a defunct glider factory in St. Paul, Minnesota, and convinced him to incorporate the group and to locate it in Parker's factory, offering him lucrative Navy development contracts as an inducement. Parker became president of the new company (ERA). William C. Norris became the chief operating officer. (Some years later, Norris founded Control Data, Inc.)

In early 1950, ERA had cash flow problems and was unable to raise sufficient venture capital. Parker came to IBM and, ultimately, to my office. Parker's approach to IBM was quite timely. A few months earlier, I was at a meeting when Watson, Jr., expressed his dissatisfaction with the IBM Endicott Magnetic Drum Project, which was vital to the company's introduction of a new calculator for its punch card line. (This planned IBM Intermediate Calculator was later introduced as the highly successful IBM 650.) When I informed Watson, Jr., of Parker's offer to sell us ERA, he said, "Jim, as much as I would like to, we can't acquire ERA because of antitrust reasons; but see if we can buy rights to their technology." I suggested we hire ERA to do drum development for us. Watson, Jr., liked the idea of IBM's funding a magnetic drum calculator design at ERA, because, he said, the Endicott drum project was "going nowhere and needed a kick in the rear." He added, "I think a competitive design by ERA would stimulate Endicott drum development and be good for the business. Go ahead and see what you can work out with Parker."

Over the next several months, with the aid of Stephen Dunwell, a highly innovative engineer handling electrical specifications, I began negotiations with Parker and his staff regarding the terms and conditions for IBM's funding an ERA development of a computer to IBM's design objectives. Further, we discussed IBM's acquiring rights under ERA patents. On 8 March 1950, Watson, Jr., signed an ERA–IBM agreement, a development contract that was the first ever for IBM with a potential competitor. This became a milestone agreement, particularly for IBM, since it provided the company with an alternative drum computer design to the Endicott project. Equally, and perhaps more importantly, it contained a clause that gave IBM the right to purchase for $150,000 a nonexclusive, paid-up patent license to all ERA inventions conceived prior to

and during the development done for IBM. Needless to say, Parker was delighted with the agreement because of the recognition it gave ERA. Moreover, the agreement provided ERA with an advance of working capital and a 20-percent profit to ERA above total cost. For IBM, the ERA development served several purposes. It motivated IBM's engineers at Endicott to furnish the company with an innovative drum design, a stored-program concept, and checking capability compatible with IBM's punch card input and output peripheral equipment. Of landmark significance was the freedom of action that the patent license clause afforded IBM. (In 1951, the Remington Rand Corporation acquired ERA. Within days of the acquisition, I notified Remington Rand that IBM was exercising its purchase option to a nonexclusive license under all ERA patents.) IBM could now move forward technologically, unhindered by ERA's patents.

The decade of the 1950s was arguably the most significant in IBM's history and, certainly, in the so-called Watson years. The Korean War, the cold war, and other geopolitical events provided IBM and other technically oriented companies with new opportunities. These opportunities were so abundant that IBM's chief problem was selecting the right project. When IBM seized the opportunity to serve its country, it grew and prospered as a result. Fortunately, I was in the right place at the right time, a blessing for which I am grateful. Below, I will attempt to describe how the U.S. government and IBM's customers turned to us for solutions to both military and commercial problems. As a result, the marketing of solutions was becoming as important as the marketing of products.

As this important decade began, I found myself in a position to know what calamity any missed opportunities could bring and to understand the rich rewards that innovation and creative solutions could bring. I needed people with skills and backgrounds similar to mine, people who believed in themselves enough to take risks and dare to fail. As was my good fortune, Watson, Jr., chose me from his immediate staff to recruit, organize, and conduct a unique Corporate Staff operation that moved IBM into the frontier of electronic data processing. In planning for the future, Watson, Jr., gave me more authority than his division managers.

IBM's Korean War Effort

In 1950, when the Korean War started, IBM Poughkeepsie had not yet obtained IBM management support for a proposed program to develop an electronic computer, based on the Magnetic Tape Processing Assembly. The Poughkeepsie staff were chafing at the company's decision to fund the Endicott magnetic drum calculator (a punch card system project) in preference to Poughkeepsie's proposed development of a much larger tape processor. As fate would have it, only hours after the onset of the Korean War, Watson, Sr., notified President Truman that an unlimited amount of IBM personnel and facilities would be available to serve our country's war effort. Promptly thereafter, Watson, Sr., decided to reactivate IBM's Military Products Division, which had been deactivated at the close of World War II. He did so by calling Watson, Jr., and me to his office to say that he was reestablishing this division, whose sole function would be the design and manufacture of products, systems, and material for the U.S. government's war effort. Furthermore, he said that IBM would make its engineering and manufacturing capability available for any program directed and approved by the War Production Planning Board in Washington, D.C.

Next, Watson, Sr., informed the two of us (although I am sure he had prior discussions with his son) that he was appointing me to organize and direct this new activity under the title of IBM manager of military contracts. My assignment was to contract with the U.S. government for research and development projects and to start a new IBM division to provide IBM services and products of a military nature. All existing IBM divisions, Watson, Sr., said, would be instructed to assist in the staffing of the new division. Because of this, I had access to divisional promotion lists, enabling me to recruit and staff the infrastructure of a brilliant team effort from within the company. I was able to bring in people with outstanding management and sales records, like Cy McElwain from Factory Management; Zollinger, a former regional sales manager; and branch office managers Glen Solomon, Phil Whittaker, and Phil Coulter.

Watson, Jr.'s first comment to me after we left his father's office was that this could be IBM's "window of opportunity" to utilize the Poughkeepsie tape processing assembly technology in a government contract. He suggested that a large-scale computer development I had been advocating (similar to those being funded at several universities) be a part of the military products effort his father had just authorized. Watson, Jr., cautioned, "Our first priority, of course, must be to follow my father's orders and to meet whatever requirements the U.S. government's War Production Planning Board

> ## I had access to divisional promotion lists, enabling me to recruit and staff the infrastructure of a brilliant team effort from within the company.

places upon IBM." Then he said that after this was determined, I should see what I could do about contracting for a suitable government-supported computer project. This was the green light I needed, and I gave this equal, and perhaps greater, priority to determining what the government had in mind for IBM's war effort. My first move relative to selling the government on the concept of funding an IBM electronic development was to explore the possibility of the government funding an electronic computer, based on IBM Poughkeepsie's electronic test assembly expertise.

I promptly communicated to Ralph Palmer—manager of IBM Poughkeepsie's Electronic Development Laboratory and leader of the group that had developed the Magnetic Tape Test Assembly—the good news that IBM would undertake new computer development under the auspices of a government contract related to IBM's activation of a Military Products Division. Palmer and his people were delighted at this prospect, as was Cuthbert Hurd, a skilled mathematician heading IBM's Applied Science department and a former employee of the U.S. Atomic Energy Commission. Palmer, Hurd, and I quickly decided that the first development contract we should seek would be for a "scientific computer" because of the known pressing need for such equipment for military applications. Following such development, our second effort, we reasoned, would be to produce a commercial computer to counter our arch technology rival: Univac.

In 1951, in parallel with my efforts regarding what became the Defense Calculator Project, I spent considerable time and effort in Washington, D.C., ascertaining what the U.S. Department of Defense and the related War Production Planning Board perceived to be IBM's role in the Korean War effort. I pursued this at the same time I was alerting the Defense Department of IBM's interest in fulfilling part of its war effort by undertaking the custom design, under government contract, of several scientific electronic calculators. I inquired about contract terms and conditions and probed to see how much government money might be available for computer development. My second step toward obtaining a computer development contract was to conduct a nationwide survey of the military's need for high-speed computation rather than to rely solely on estimates given to me in Washington. To accomplish this, I asked for and received what proved to be invaluable assistance from Hurd. Together, Hurd and I conducted a nationwide survey of U.S. military and government computational requirements, looking at the same time for prospective government funding to support the development of several electronic high-speed magnetic tape computers at IBM. In so doing, we visited numerous computational sites from coast to coast. Palmer had provided us with block engineering diagrams of the Magnetic Tape Processing machine, along with an estimate of his group's capability to develop a maximum of four custom-built computers under contractual terms and funding by government agencies or defense contractors.

As I recall, Hurd and I visited 22 government contractors, laboratories, and computational facilities, including the Long-Range Proving Ground at Coco Beach, Florida, later known as Cape Canaveral. At the close of this study, we concluded that a single electronic scientific computer architecture, well within IBM Poughkeepsie's engineering design capability, could meet 80 percent of all the government and contractor market requirements. With this new concept of what was best for both IBM's future and the Military Products effort, I ceased my quest for several separately funded computer development contracts and concentrated on convincing IBM management to do the unprecedented: skip the trial by development stage and proceed immediately into production. Therefore, on 15 December 1950, I wrote to Watson, Jr., recommending that IBM pursue a strategy of corporate funding of IBM computer development. I reasoned that this move would protect IBM's patent rights and, at the same time, enable the company to focus its efforts on a single computer architecture that would jump-start us into the electronic computer business. I asked Watson, Jr., to authorize an estimated $3-million investment in a proprietary IBM Electronic Magnetic Tape Computer, based on the Poughkeepsie laboratory's technology, to be rented, not sold. I further proposed that due to program urgency, IBM skip the design model phase and build a production lot of 20 machines to be leased at $8,000 a month. Of the production lot, 18 machines were to be leased to customers, and two were to remain in IBM. Admittedly, this was a huge gamble and a bold step never before attempted by IBM—or any other company, as a matter of fact. I played down the risk factor and emphasized our need to maintain our leadership in the data processing field.

My memorandum also endorsed the appointment of a committee comprised of Engineering department, Applied Science department, and Watson Laboratory personnel to establish system architecture and specifications for the machine capable of meeting all or almost all the current military scientific computational needs. Additionally, I suggested the project be named the "IBM Defense Calculator" to comply with Watson, Sr.'s desire to give government needs first priority over IBM commercial market requirements and to avoid the appearance of challenging Watson, Sr.'s belief that punch card system technology was IBM's future. In the 15 December 1950 letter proposing the IBM Defense Calculator development, I assured Watson, Jr., that my recommendations had the full support of Palmer and Hurd. In spite of this, the IBM Sales department members, ordinarily short-term oriented, were not enthusiastic about a proposal they viewed as taking away engineering from punch card systems that were still in great demand. Nevertheless, Watson, Jr., acted on my proposal for the Defense Calculator Project a few weeks later with the provision that Hurd and I demonstrate to him that a market existed for an electronic scientific computer at the projected $8,000 monthly rental.

With Watson, Jr.'s provisional authorization and admonition to be discreet, in February 1951, Hurd and I revisited the government installations and the military contractors, carrying with us block engineering diagrams of the proposed architecture for the Defense Calculator. Our purpose was to secure letters of intent from 18 future customers for a machine that would meet the proposed capability of performing high-speed arithmetic calculations at an $8,000-a-month rental. When we returned with 18 letters of intent, Watson, Jr., promptly gave his consent to the program. Some months later, Watson, Sr., approved a $3-million budget for the development and production of the Defense Calculator, thus launching IBM full force into what was to become our first production of an electronic computer. We would also become the first company to offer a machine of such power and magnitude on a rental basis. Apparently, this project required a gamble some were unwilling to make.

Opposition mounted within IBM, enhanced by Learson's quite vocal disapproval. Midway through the Defense Calculator Project, Williams, vice president of finance, called a meeting and suggested to Watson, Jr., that the project be halted because, at the $8,000 monthly rental, he projected the machine would generate staggering losses for the company. He further projected that for IBM to break even, the Defense Calculator had to be priced at a monthly rental ranging from $11,900 to $17,600. Sensing the demise of the project, the IBM Electric Accounting Machine Division assumed an I-told-you-so attitude.

Dismayed but undaunted, Hurd and I returned to the customers from whom we had received letters of intent and advised them of the revised rental price. In most cases, the customers accepted the rental increase. Fortunately, the several letters of intent that were canceled were soon replaced by orders from new prospective customers, the production lot was reestablished at 18, and the Defense Calculator Project was not only continued but also publicly blessed at the IBM annual meeting in April 1952. Watson, Sr., by this time having become a convert, announced to the stockholders that the company was building an electronic machine (the Defense Calculator) 25 times faster than any previous IBM development.

With Watson, Sr.'s acceptance of the project, I reasoned that the name Defense Calculator had served its purpose. With Hurd's concurrence and my eyes to the future, I selected "electronic data processing" as more descriptive of our new capabilities. Besides, it was different than the terminology our competitor used. In December 1952, the Defense Calculator was renamed the "IBM 701 Electronic Data Processing Machine" and was marketed under rental contract by that name as were its successors, each with a different number prefix. At the same time, Watson, Jr., astutely put Learson in charge of both the production and marketing of the 701 and the follow-on data processors. With Learson in charge, the IBM Sales department and its Electronic Data Processing Machine Division quickly became supporters. This marked the inception of a new era of IBM electronic data processing that initially supplemented and eventually replaced the punch card systems in IBM's product line, the total replacement of which, I must confess, I did not envision at the outset. In the same year, the U.S. Department of Justice filed an antitrust suit against IBM, charging the company with market dominance in punch card systems. One of

> **IBM's strength in both the quality and quantity of its patents gave the company a trump card to use later in its "freedom of action" negotiations with both companies and countries, particularly market access in Japan.**

IBM's defenses was the availability of magnetic tape data processing systems and the emerging competition offered by the new companies joining the data processing industry.

Following the 701, IBM quickly embarked on two other magnetic tape data processor projects, designated the IBM 702 and 704, targeting the commercial market rather than the scientific computer market. These second-generation products were designed to process business functions as well as scientific computing applications. At the outset, Watson, Jr., took personal charge of the marketing of IBM's new data processors. Every Monday, he held a meeting of all the principals involved in the development, manufacturing, education, servicing, and marketing related to the data processors. IBM was on its way to becoming the dominant computer manufacturer due to the intensity of management interest. Sperry Rand's Univac Division, notwithstanding its earlier technical leadership, failed to make a matching marketing commitment and became an also-ran.

All of IBM's technology utilized in its computer system architecture remained the company's intellectual property because of IBM's business strategy of supporting research, development, and production without the benefit of U.S. government funding. This policy decision gave IBM an unparalleled patent license trading capability industry-wide, furthered IBM's growth, and positioned it for world dominance in what was to become known as the Era of Electronic Information Processing. IBM's strength in both the quality and quantity of its patents gave the company a trump card to use later in its "freedom of action" negotiations with both companies and countries, particularly market access in Japan. Another important factor that contributed to the company's achieving such dominance was the excellence of IBM's peripheral units (e.g., tape drives and

Figure 4. The author (left) and Ed Zollinger (right) in a SAGE discussion with Lt. Col. Townes at ARDC headquarters in Baltimore, Maryland.

high-speed printers) compared with those of its competitors. Consequently, IBM became a supplier to its own customers as well as to its competitors. This often caused problems, such as when our competitors requested discounted prices and expedited deliveries. In all cases, we denied these requests, on the grounds that such action would discriminate against IBM's own customers. Consequently, this exacerbated our already sensitive relations with our competitors.

At the same time IBM was developing these new data processors, the War Production Planning Board recognized both our electromechanical capability and our systems management skills. The board asked us, as prime contractor, to manufacture high-speed bombing systems. Additionally, the Army wanted us to produce tank gun stabilization systems, and the Navy asked us to undertake the design of a sonar detection system. Early in this time frame, we learned by chance that MIT's Lincoln Laboratory was engaged in coupling its prototype Whirlwind computer with a prototype AT&T radar-tracking system. The Air Force was funding this project, and MIT was considering Sperry Rand as a partner in the production phase of the computer and display portion of the air defense system. My immediate challenge was to dissuade MIT from utilizing Sperry Rand/Univac and to accept IBM as a partner, sharing development responsibility with MIT and as the sole manufacturer and installer of the production versions of the system. This project was a perfect fit for IBM because it was a rare opportunity for us to display our innovative capability and manufacturing know-how relative to sophisticated computer and data display technology. Production versions of these prototypes were to be integrated into an air

defense system that would protect the North American continent from hostile planes—a huge and complex undertaking.

Not wanting to be outsold in obtaining a project of such prestige, Sperry Rand called on five-star General Douglas MacArthur, its "biggest gun" and a member of its Board of Directors, to join its sales effort, particularly at the Pentagon level. Believing that the Pentagon would not make the ultimate decision, I focused our sales effort on the system's architect, MIT's Lincoln Laboratory. To convince a self-assured laboratory like MIT that IBM had a unique capability, my first step was to establish a high-level contact at MIT's Lincoln Laboratory. As a result, I met with laboratory manager Al Hill and expressed IBM's interest in becoming MIT's industrial partner in the project, with MIT retaining its systems design leadership. Several of IBM Poughkeepsie Laboratory engineers and I met with Jay Forrester and Ken Olsen, MIT Lincoln Laboratory engineers responsible for the Whirlwind computer. Since it was apparent that an intensive selling and corporate management effort would be required, I first alerted Watson, Jr., of the opportunity. Assisted by IBMers Zollinger and Solomon, I quickly organized a series of demonstrations of IBM research, development, and production capabilities, showcasing our personnel in particular and utilizing our Poughkeepsie factory 701 computer production site as the focal point. Watson, Jr., eager for an MIT–IBM collaboration, personally participated and did a superb selling job on MIT management, an achievement to which he proudly alludes.[1]

Zollinger and Solomon, two of our most capable marketing executives whom I recruited to assist me, coordinated IBM's continuing sales effort. Their assistance in directing the company's contract negotiations with MIT's Lincoln Lab and the Air Force officers made IBM the successful bidder. The MIT–IBM partnership became known as the Semi-Automatic Ground Environment (SAGE) defense system project, with the U.S. Air Force as our customer (see Figure 4). Arguably, SAGE was the most significant U.S. government-sponsored electronic computer development in history (accomplished by the blending of talented university and industry scientists) and the largest and most costly special-purpose computer project ever attempted. It provided IBM with invaluable product know-how and experience, an electronic development laboratory at Poughkeepsie, and a new plant site at Kingston, New York. Project SAGE became a pioneering technical effort, utilizing breakthrough technology in many areas, such as ferrite magnetic core memory. The SAGE system was a massive duplexed computer operation, making large-scale use of telephone lines for digital data acquisition, cathode ray display terminals for data and graphics, and much more. As IBM's *Federal Systems Division Magazine,* printed in honor of the division's 25 anniversary, describes it:

> With SAGE, the Pentagon planned a network of digital computers fed by ground-based radar, ships, early warning aircraft and ground observers. IBM was responsible for the digital computers to process the data and, if an attack were imminent, pictorially display the battle situation for the human controllers.

At the same time that the Military Products Division was making MIT's SAGE systems, it was also engaged in developing and manufacturing Bombing Systems/Navigational computers for the Air Force. IBM was awarded a design contract for more-advanced bombing and navigational systems for the B52. This activity evolved into IBM's Federal Systems Division with manufacturing headquarters in Gaithersburg, Maryland, but only after the initial bombing and navigation systems project had provided IBM's Poughkeepsie manufacturing site with a quantum expansion in production facilities and personnel.

My Most-Cherished Moment

My efforts during my term as Watson, Jr.'s assistant and beyond were recognized when, in early 1953, Watson, Jr., arranged a luncheon in the IBM boardroom to commemorate the birth of the electronic computer industry and to recognize its pioneers. He invited J. Presper Eckert, Jr., and John W. Mauchly (inventors of the Univac) to meet with IBM's Board of Directors on this occasion. He also invited George Brown from the California Institute of Technology; John von Neumann; James Madden, vice president of Metropolitan Life; and several other government and industry computer innovators. Watson, Jr., paid equal tribute to all the computing engineers and scientists present. In my view, however, the greatest of all was Palmer, whom I considered to be without peer. Besides Palmer, Nat Rochester (noted for his capability as a systems architect), several other IBM staffers, and I were also invited. Watson, Jr., spoke of the financial and technical problems of the fledgling industry and its great future promise with benefits to government, industry, commerce, and humankind in gener-

al. He also spoke of the contributions of each of the attendees. To commemorate the founding of the electronic computer industry and the invitees' contributions to its beginning, he presented to each an inscribed Tiffany gold electric watch. Its unique design made the watch capable of serving both as a desk clock and as a money clip. The inscription on my watch reads:

> *J.W. Birkenstock*
> *1946–1952*
> *IN APPRECIATION OF YOUR CONTRIBUTION TO*
> *THE COMPUTER INDUSTRY IN THE EARLY YEARS*
> *IBM*

I consider the watch a treasured memento. Many years later, at a CBI meeting, Mauchly's widow Kay said that her late husband had felt the same way. She praised Watson, Jr., for the recognition he had given her husband and others both in and outside IBM who pioneered during an uncertain era. In any event, competitors, academicians, customers, and businessmen attended this unique and historic meeting. They were all recognized collectively as founders of an industry that historians later credited as having done more for humankind than any other industry. This was a memorable occasion in which Watson, Jr., shared the credit with other pioneers for the inauguration of an industry. Many years later, Kay Mauchly and Eckert commented it was a pity that no photographs or video recordings had been made. I agreed.

Another Pivotal Assignment

In 1953, Watson, Jr., in a reassessment of what he called "an almost near miss" in IBM's early electronic computing, asked me to look into how IBM assessed electronic computing technology and to recommend a strategy to prevent another policy error. After careful study, I suggested the establishment of two new corporate staff departments, to be known as IBM Product Planning and Market Analysis, to replace IBM's Future Demands department. These departments were to be staffed with specially skilled, career-oriented personnel selected from both within and without IBM. Watson, Jr., accepted the recommendation, but with one criticism. He said, "I like your recommendation, but I don't like the fact that you didn't finish your assignment." I asked him why I had not. He said, "Because you didn't name an individual to head the operation." I replied that I was not aware this was part of my responsibility. He said, "All right; I'll complete the assignment by naming you." While I was pleased to accept this appointment, I told Watson, Jr., that I was reluctant to give up my responsibility for IBM Intellectual Property Management and Patent Licensing. Watson, Jr., suggested I retain responsibility for these functions in my new position as executive director of product planning and market analysis. I did, however, willingly relinquish my responsibilities in Military Contracts, renamed the Military Products Division, to which McElwain was appointed director. Zollinger, Solomon, and Coulter, who had previously assisted me in the SAGE program, were appointed assistants to McElwain. Whittaker left SAGE and joined the newly created staff department. For administrative assistance, I turned for help to Herb Keith and named him assistant director of recruiting, organizing, and establishing this new IBM corporate departmental function.

From 1953 to 1956, the Product Planning and Market Analysis departments shifted IBM product and systems development emphasis toward Electronic Data Processing Systems and away from Electromechanical Punch Card Accounting Machine Systems. Additionally, subdepartments were added, focusing on electric typewriters and time recording equipment as well as product testing and special products. This marked a new era of business guidance to IBM Engineering, Manufacturing, and Marketing that emphasized new and more cost-effective solutions to customer problems in both small and very large enterprises. Heretofore, IBM Engineering developed technology and then sought problems for this technology to solve. Now, we focused on locating the customers' problems and then planning, in concert with IBM Engineering, to apply invention, innovation, and technical solution to these problems. What had been a feeble voice in the past now became a loud and persistent cry with full management support. This significant shift in IBM practice required a different composition of personnel than that utilized in the disbanded Future Demands department. As a result, I became immersed in building a staff of future-market-oriented professionals, recruited from both within IBM and without, that was fully compatible with my intellectual property management.

During my entire career at IBM headquarters, I was blessed with exceptional secretarial support, but particularly in the Defense Calculator and Product Planning days. Two people in particular come to mind. I was continually amazed by Don Skelly's fantastic memory. His efficiency was exceeded only by his tremendous loyalty. When I moved to director of product planning and market analysis, Skelly was the logical choice for my office manager. His first assignment was to find me a secretary as capable as he was. I was recuperating from abdominal surgery at the time when he came to my hospital room to tell me he had found "just the right person." When he told me it was Ulla Rundberg, I said I had serious reservations about hiring an 18-year-old. Additionally, knowing the many long hours this position often required, I suggested Skelly find a male secretary who could handle the physical rigors of this assignment. However, he persisted, convincing me to give Rundberg an opportunity to demonstrate her abilities. She did just that. While Skelly was the best male secretary I have ever had, Rundberg was my best female secretary. She was a devoted employee who expertly balanced her work schedule with her personal life. She married Paul Mangodt and had a son before leaving IBM to become a full-time mother. Both Skelly's and Rundberg's support greatly aided my transition from Watson, Jr.'s staff to manager of defense contracts and then to vice president–executive director of product planning and market analysis.

The Birth of the Saber System

From 1953 to 1956, the Product Planning and Market Analysis departments planned, guided, and supported many landmark developments, such as the IBM 702, 704, and 705 computers; the IBM 305 RAMAC; the IBM 1401, 1410, and 1620; the early planning phase for the 7090; the 1710 control system; teleprocessing; and the Saber (Semi-Automatic Business Environment Research) system. The Saber system was a joint development between American Airlines and IBM directed toward an automated interactive reservation and ticketing system. Its architecture was conceived under the leadership of Product Planning's Perry Crawford. Blair Smith, manager of Market Analysis, was the IBM liaison between the two companies, and Charlie Amin was his counterpart from American Airlines. This was the first of such business relationships between IBM and one of its customers in the Electronic Data Processing Machine era. The business agreement for the IBM–American Airlines collaboration, a brief memorandum of understanding, was negotiated and agreed to between C.R. Smith, president and CEO of American Airlines, and me. Blair Smith assisted in the negotiation. The Saber system development was significant because it marked the first convergence and use within a commercial system of interactive display, teleprocessing, random access disk and drum storage, cache storage, keyboard terminal input, data transceivers, and a variety of data processors. Although smaller than the SAGE system, it rivaled it in system complexity. Today, all airlines use Saber or Saber-like systems. As a result of this shift in emphasis and our new class of products, beginning in the mid-1950s, IBM's rental revenue gave the company a quantum growth in earnings.

Coping with Adversely Held Patents

In the early era of electronic computer development, there was a preponderance of inventions originating in university and government laboratories and in private facilities. Coping with adversely held patents that might be read or could be alleged by the patentee to be infringed by IBM-installed computer equipment worth billions of dollars was an immense problem. Inventors' patent infringement claims grew by leaps and bounds and seemed to be coming out of the woodwork. A patent infringement suit filed against the computer lessor invariably carried the threat of an injunction against our customers' future use of the patent embodied in IBM equipment, should the plaintiff prevail against IBM. This created an awesome responsibility for IBM as the lessor. How did we cope? We did so through our intensive patent watch, discussed above, particularly abroad where patent applications, by law, must be laid open for opposition within 18 months of filing. In the United States, where no opposition procedure exists, the problem of ascertaining which patents had issued or were about to issue became a real challenge—a guessing game not unlike the commodities market.

As soon as an adversely held or potentially held patent or patent application came to our attention, our contracts and licensing personnel, after thorough evaluation, attempted to buy a paid-up, nonexclusive license to make, use, and sell the device as insurance. In some cases, as a last resort, we entered into an option agreement to a royalty-bearing license, based on a percentage of the manufacturing cost. Sometimes we bought patent licenses not used in our products, but on balance, what we spent on paid-up licenses was millions of dollars less than what it would have cost us had we waited for the inventor to assert his claims against us. During my 25 years of Intellectual Property department management, only a single serious patent infringement suit was filed against IBM, the aforementioned Research Corporation–MIT

suit. While I was vice president of commercial development, IBM's Intellectual Property attorneys and our contracts and licensing personnel accomplished a great deal. Each day produced a new challenge and put an old one to rest.

It is worthy of mention that toward the end of the 1960s, IBM unbundled software from its equipment lease agreements, due to pressure from the U.S. Department of Justice's Antitrust Division and the mounting customer demand for software innovation beyond the operating system. About the same time, IBM began shifting its marketing strategy from leasing to sales. IBM's pricing policy made outright purchase more attractive than rental. These two shifts took a great deal of antitrust heat off the company and, more than anything else, paved the way for the Department of Justice to eventually drop its antitrust suit in 1983, originally filed by Ramsey Clark late in the Johnson administration.

Early Problems in 700 Series Computers

The early 700 Series, however, had its problems. After the 701/702 data processors reached the field, Watson, Jr., began hearing negative reports about their reliability. After intensive engineering review and consultation, Watson, Jr., made an epic command decision that was crucial to the success of electronic data processors within IBM. He ordered all data processors operating with electrostatic storage (whose patent rights I had purchased from NRDC of Great Britain for $290,000) to be retrofitted with magnetic core memory, pioneered in the SAGE computer. For a commercial (nonmilitary) core memory first used in the SAGE project, IBM's design and manufacturing capability was not sheltered under a government "save harmless" clause. While the U.S. government provided "save harmless" patent rights for SAGE memories, this was not applicable to commercial use. From a patent standpoint, IBM lacked freedom to produce ferrite cores for use in commercial products, blocking our use of the SAGE composition ferrites as a substitute for electrostatic memory in the 701 and 702. I attempted to obtain patent license rights from the patentee, General Ceramics Corporation, but failed because it insisted on retaining exclusive make rights and on supplying 100 percent of IBM's core requirements, making us a captive customer. My offer to purchase 50 percent of our core requirements from General Ceramics Corporation with IBM retaining the right to produce the other 50 percent at a reasonable patent royalty was rejected by Hans Arnold, the CEO. This seemed to me a short-sighted decision. I understand Henry Arnold, Hans Arnold's nephew and president of General Ceramics, did not agree with his uncle's decision.

At this point, IBM's "patent watch" discovered a substitute noninfringing Dutch ferrite core composition, developed by the Philips Company of Eindhoven, Holland, and alerted the Engineering department. Philips Company had the capability to manufacture cores to IBM specifications and was receptive to giving IBM a make, use, and sell license under its core composition patents. In 1956, Mr. Loupard, managing director of the Philips Company, and his deputy, Mr. Thromp, and I negotiated a comprehensive cross-license and technology transfer agreement stipulating that North American Philips would supply 50 percent of IBM's commercial magnetic core requirements for a period of time. Near the conclusion of our negotiations, Loupard, an interesting personality, suggested that the contract signing take place after lunch at the Eindhoven Golf Club. "This way," Loupard said, "we can have lunch and watch a historic event on television—the wedding of Prince Rainier and Grace Kelly." I was surprised that Philips, an early leader in the European TV industry, did not have a TV in its executive offices.

The contract with Philips, however, did not solve all our commercial-use ferrite memory patent problems. Several other patent licensing negotiations of import in which I was deeply involved occurred during the core storage era. IBM patent operations uncovered the existence of two patent applications about to be issued to An Wang, a graduate student at Harvard, and Frederick W. Viehe, a public works inspector in Los Angeles working out of a home basement laboratory. Wang's rights were clouded by certain claims in the Viehe patent, filed prior to the Wang application. IBM patent operations predicted that, in due course, the U.S. Patent Office would declare an interference between Viehe and Wang and that a legal battle would ensue to determine who was entitled to what. A further cloud over the Wang patent was Dr. Woo's contention of being a coinventor. (Woo was Wang's research partner at Harvard.)

After long and tedious negotiations with all the parties, Viehe sold us his patent rights in 1956, making IBM a party to the interference, if and when the U.S. Patent Office declared it. Next, we bought Woo's claim of coinventor's rights. Finally, we took a paid-up, nonexclusive license under Wang for $500,000 with a stipulation that $100,000 of the payment could be withheld if the interference was declared and Wang lost one or more of the claims in his patent, as predicted. The Patent Office declared interference, and Viehe won the claim. In the course of the interference, Wang learned that IBM had bought the Viehe patent and was, therefore, the opposing party in the interference. As a result, Wang became critical of me because of the ruling and expressed himself accordingly in his autobiography.[2] This was notwithstanding the fact that subsequent to the 1956 IBM–Wang agreement, IBM paid the cost of having Wang's outside patent counsel defend the Wang patent claims in the interference action in the U.S. Patent Office. Viehe put the money we paid him for his patent right in 72 savings and loan banks, so his neighbors would not learn of his wealth. Unfortunately, he never got to see his patent issued or enjoy the money we paid him. During a rock collecting expedition in a California desert, his car broke down. Viehe became lost while seeking help and perished from exposure. Wang used the money from the sale of his patent rights to found Wang Laboratories, which ultimately made him a fortune.

Midway into IBM's ferrite core memory production, IBM's patent watch activity discovered another adversely held patent. This was a magnetic core systems patent awarded to Gerhard Dirks in Germany and filed in the United States and elsewhere. Dirks was a rare character with inventive genius. During World War II, he became a Russian prisoner of war and was incarcerated for several years in a building in Russian-occupied Germany. The building contained a technical library, and Dirks, with nothing else to do, spent his time reading and studying in the library. In the course of his studying there, he conceived his version of a magnetic drum and magnetic core storage system. When the war ended, he returned to his former employer, the Krupp Company, but failed to interest it in taking a license to his German patent application. A small German company, Siemag Fein Mechanische Werke GmbH, that manufactured bookkeeping machines did show interest and, in return for an exclusive German license, paid Dirks a modest sum, enough to enable him to file his patent application worldwide.

Following this, Dirks came to the United States and contacted Sperry Rand, which paid him $1,000 for a one-year option to an exclusive U.S. license that the firm allowed to lapse. Next, Dirks contacted the British Tabulating Machine Company, which, for a substantial sum, took an exclusive license to Dirks's patent rights for the British Commonwealth. At this point, IBM patent operations informed me that several IBM memory developments would infringe on Dirks's patent rights. I contacted Dirks and conducted a long series of negotiations that involved several trips to Germany and Great Britain. IBM also financed Dirks, along with his wife, to come to the United States for negotiations. During this time, Dirks became enamored with California and the IBM San Jose research laboratory. In due course, I was able to obtain a license from the British firm for the rights Dirks had granted it. This was accomplished as part of a comprehensive cross-licensing agreement between IBM and the British firm. IBM paid Dirks $1 million and assigned him a research position in our San Jose laboratory. In return, IBM obtained a paid-up, nonexclusive license under all the rights that remained under Dirks's patents. In his early advocacy of "distributive processing," Dirks was ahead of all others.

IBM was particularly interested in a cross-license under RCA patents because of the inventions Jan Rajchman of RCA had made in the field of magnetic core storage. RCA, pursuing its Busmark computer development, was in need of freedom of action under various IBM patents. Accordingly, a cross-license agreement between RCA and IBM was one of the first that I negotiated with a major company aspiring to be an IBM competitor. After RCA Vice President Anderson and I concluded negotiations, and I was poised to sign the agreement, Anderson explained that RCA's CEO (General Sarnoff) wanted the agreement signing to be between himself and Watson, Jr., in Sarnoff's office. Watson, Jr., and I went to Sarnoff's office, at which time Sarnoff advised Watson, Jr., that a complete exchange of know-how between RCA and IBM would solve IBM's antitrust problems. Needless to say, Watson, Jr., declined Sarnoff's self-serving advice. The following year, RCA abandoned Busmark.

The most politically sensitive and legally complex patent licensing negotiations I conducted regarded obtaining a license under the Forrester patent. In 1955, Research Corporation, functioning as patent licensing agent for MIT, charged IBM with infringing a Forrester magnetic core array storage patent. Research Corporation proposed IBM pay two cents per bit of core memory—an exorbitant royalty. IBM refused to take a license under the MIT–Forrester core memory patent for two reasons. First, we questioned the validity of the patent because Rajchman of RCA claimed to have conceived the same invention at an earlier date and had an application on his conception pending at the Patent Office. IBM was licensed under the Rajchman patent due to the IBM/RCA cross-license. Second, we considered the running royalty to be exorbitant. Research Corporation contended that the proposed royalty was reasonable and refused to acknowledge the fact that the Rajchman patent cast an invalidity cloud over the Forrester patent. I suggested that negotiations resume after the interference had been adjudicated in the U.S. Patent Office. Then, without sanction from MIT or prior notice to IBM, Research Corporation filed suit, charging IBM with willful infringement of the Forrester patent. Besides the question of validity and the exorbitant royalty fee demands, this became a sticky issue between the heads of IBM and MIT. Watson, Jr., was on MIT's board, and MIT's president, John Killian, was on IBM's board. The lawsuit caused both men to resign from each other's boards. Because I had stood firm against both the validity and royalty issues, I became the black sheep and the man in the middle of a legal drama involving two nonconsenting corporations drawn into a lawsuit by a greedy licensing agency.

An early action on the part of MIT was to notify Research Corporation that MIT would settle the Forrester patent issue directly with IBM. This accomplished, Watson, Jr., and Killian moved quickly to terminate the lawsuit. IBM agreed to pay $13 million to MIT for a paid-up, nonexclusive license under the Forrester patent. Huge as the sum was in the minds of some people, it turned out well for IBM. Over the life of core storage, IBM's estimated usage was several trillion bits of memory. However, it was not a sweet deal for Research Corporation. MIT made a private settlement with Research Corporation and then fired that firm. This incident reinforced my belief in a patent licensing policy I had adopted. I was convinced that the most practical licensing procedure for IBM was to purchase a paid-up license in lieu of a running royalty rate based on future sales or product usage for the life of the patents.

In addition to his resolve to replace electrostatic tube memory with ferrite core memory, Watson, Jr., made a second technical command decision, perhaps the most epic in mid-century IBM history. During the production phase of the 701 and the planning stage of the 702, Watson, Jr., became concerned with field reports regarding the failure of vacuum tubes in the 701. He ordered all vacuum tube assemblies in 700 series machines to be retrofitted with transistorized circuits. This bold decision was made notwithstanding that IBM lacked transistor production facilities, making it necessary to find a manufacturing source that could meet

IBM's requirements. While IBM's Engineering department believed that Texas Instruments (TI) would be the best source, it feared we would become captive to an outside supplier. Therefore, following a strategy meeting in Watson, Jr.'s office, it was decided to seek the collaboration of TI. Watson, Jr., assigned me to pursue this course with TI's CEO Pat Haggerty, being careful to reduce the risk of IBM becoming wholly dependent on TI. I was authorized to arrange a technical partnership and to handle contractual relations pertaining to a collaborative transistor design and manufacturing program. This led to TI's becoming IBM's computer circuit design collaborator and sole source of transistor circuitry during the IBM era of 700 series electronic computers. TI also remained a partial supplier during 1958 and into the mid-1960s. With TI's assistance, IBM developed the manufacturing capability, enabling IBM to meet most of its own transistor requirements, should it choose to do so. Consequently, IBM became a world leader in the development and manufacture of microelectronics. The mutually beneficial relationship between TI and IBM made TI a powerhouse in semiconductor manufacturing, both in the United States and abroad. Additionally, the TI–IBM collaboration made IBM's computers more reliable and orders of magnitude faster. Bringing solutions to both the U.S. government and industry was now more affordable and cost-effective.

The Sperry Rand Antitrust Suit Settlement

In the early 1950s, the U.S. government became concerned about IBM's dominance in the punch card equipment market. Consequently, the government filed an antitrust suit against IBM, alleging it was a monopoly. Our powerful competitor Sperry Rand also filed a private antitrust suit against us. This constituted a major harassment to IBM management and affected business practices until, on 22 January 1956, IBM signed a consent decree with the U.S. government that terminated its antitrust litigation. Among other things, to make the market more competitive, the consent decree stipulated that IBM establish a patent licensing policy, opening up its existing patents to competition. In regard to its manufacturing know-how of the tabulating card itself, the decree mandated providing a royalty-free transfer to all applicants for those rights as well as selling card manufacturing equipment to all comers. The tab card manufacturing know-how was the only know-how mandated under the decree. That in itself was a victory for IBM.

Following the IBM consent decree, patent interference negotiations continued with Sperry Rand, where I sensed the climate was less tense. Frank McNamara, Sr., Sperry Rand general counsel, confirmed this to me during a negotiating session in March 1956. He began to hint that a settlement—much broader than settling the pending patent interference issues we were currently negotiating—might be considered. I assumed this meant an out-of-court settlement of Sperry Rand's antitrust suit against IBM might be possible. When I brought this to Watson, Jr.'s attention, he called a meeting in his office, attended by Hank Trimble (IBM legal counsel) and attorneys from the law firm of Cravath, Swain & Moore. Trimble was opposed to a nonlawyer's involvement in settlement negotiations with Sperry Rand, no matter how skilled a negotiator that person might be. Former District Court Judge Bruce Bromley, Cravath's lead attorney, took the opposite view and offered his support to me. "Why not let Jim have a go at it," he said to Watson, Jr. "We lawyers can always take over if he fails." With that, Watson, Jr., authorized me to proceed with the negotiations.

Soon after, negotiations began between McNamara, Sr., and me and proceeded without rancor. While he was a hard-nosed negotiator, he was also one of the highest-principled men with whom I have ever dealt. During the six months of negotiations, I received great encouragement from Bromley and George Turner, Cravath's lead attorney to IBM. In September 1956, McNamara, Sr., and I initialed a consent decree settlement. However, a problem developed before IBM and Sperry Rand management could sign it. The Eckert–Mauchly people at Sperry Rand were displeased with the agreement, believing it was not compensatory enough for ENIAC patent rights. McNamara, Sr., stood by his commitment that the agreement we had reached represented a quid pro quo: $10 million for a patent cross-license and the settlement of the antitrust suit. With only minor alterations in terms to appease the Eckert–Mauchly dissenters, Mr. Vickers for Sperry Rand and Watson, Jr., for IBM signed the agreement. Although the Sperry Rand settlement cost IBM a substantial sum of money because it included a royalty-free cross-license between the two companies, it was worth many times its cost. The settlement permitted IBM patent freedom, particularly under the Eckert–Mauchly patents assigned to Sperry Rand. Many years later, during a Sperry Rand–Honeywell patent litigation, Honeywell attorneys characterized this settlement as a "sweetheart deal for IBM," since it included a paid-up license under valuable ENIAC patents.

The year 1956 was a pivotal one for IBM in several other respects. In May, at a top management luncheon in the St. Regis Hotel dining room, Watson, Jr., gave a stirring talk about his father's "golden years of leadership" as IBM's founder and leader for the past 41 years. To commemorate the occasion, the invitees were given a $20 gold piece, minted in 1914. Watson, Sr., also spoke, announcing his decision to step aside as CEO and declaring IBM's good fortune to have his son Watson, Jr., as his successor with the title of president and chief executive officer. Watson, Sr., also said he would retain the title of chairman of the board. This was the last time I saw Watson, Sr., since he passed away some weeks later.

The Birth of Line and Staff at IBM

Shortly after taking over as CEO, Watson, Jr., made known his concern that IBM's centralized management system could not adequately cope with the challenges of the company's growth and the resultant customer requirements. Accordingly, he brought in Booz, Allen & Hamilton to study IBM's present organization and to propose a decentralized management plan. In October 1956, Watson, Jr., at a meeting of all IBM executives, revealed the Booz, Allen plan to create a line/staff management concept with himself as CEO and Williams as president and chief of staff. Product divisions functioning under a decentralized management concept were to report to Watson, Jr., as the CEO, and those divisions were given greater autonomy. Corporate staff under Williams would provide functional review of divisional operations and establish a system of management by contention. Under this concept, IBM's Product Planning and Market Analysis departments ceased to exist as a corporate function. Thereafter, all operating divisions would be responsible for their own product planning and market analysis.

The Booz, Allen study, however, recommended that Intellectual Property Management and Contracts and Licensing activities become entities within the IBM corporate staff. Under powers reserved to the corporation, Commercial Development was to function outside the proposed line/staff system of management contention on a worldwide basis, serving all IBM divisions and subsidiaries. The Booz, Allen study further recommended that Commercial Development, under powers reserved to the corporation, be responsible for IBM's worldwide intellectual property management, all technology transfer in and out of IBM, contracts and licensing, and other related responsibilities. As a part of the plan, I became IBM director of commercial development. While I regretted I would no longer be associated with planning IBM's future products and would no longer report directly to Watson, Jr., I supported the recommendation and accepted my new position with alacrity, reporting to Williams and, through him, to Watson, Jr. Two years later, because of both the growth and importance of IBM's patent licensing activity and the magnitude of the company's intellectual property resources, I was elected IBM corporate vice president for commercial development.

One key set of a vice president's responsibilities was to administer IBM's policies and practices regarding divestitures; two major ones occurred on my watch. In 1958, Watson, Jr., in consultation with Learson, decided that IBM should divest itself of the International Time Recording Division, which Simplex Corporation had shown an interest in acquiring. I arranged an appointment whereby Learson initiated discussions that led to IBM's transfer of all the physical assets of the International Time Recording Division to Simplex. Commercial Development handled the administrative details of the divestiture of the division's physical and intellectual property assets to Simplex.

In the late 1960s, Watson, Jr., Learson, and Nick Katzenbach (IBM general counsel) decided it would be in IBM's best interest if a settlement were reached in Control Data Corporation's antitrust action against IBM. Accordingly, I arranged for secret meetings between IBM President Learson and Norris, president and CEO of Control Data. They reached a settlement that included IBM's divestiture of the Service Bureau Corporation through Control Data. For the most part, Paul Knaplund—acting on behalf of IBM's general counsel (with Commercial Development attorneys assisting with intellectual property, transfer, and cross-licensing matters)—administered the divestiture. Industry Relations, a subdepartment of Commercial Development under Tom Spain, monitored competitive marketing.

Slow Death of a Visionary Acquisition

A second key responsibility of Commercial Development was acquisitions. IBM was offered an average of one acquisition possibility a week. Such propositions required in-depth study and analysis, a function assigned to Vilar Kelly and Dick Geeson from my staff. Kelly also had the responsibility of seeking out acquisition possibilities. In this capacity, he suggested the acquisition of Science Research Associates (SRA) in Chicago. SRA developed, published, and distributed elementary education teaching materials. Its math, science, language, and history courses were highly regarded in the education community. Kelly visualized computerization of the SRA material, with IBM achieving a leading role in both elementary and secondary institutions of education.

Watson, Jr., bought the idea and approved my embarking on negotiations with Lyle Spencer, president and principal owner of SRA. The negotiations that I conducted with Kelly's assistance resulted in the acquisition of SRA for $20 million in IBM stock. Shortly after the acquisition closing, the value of the IBM stock doubled because of a two-for-one split. Unfortunately, Spencer, the founder and inspirational leader on whom we were counting, died several years later. To replace him, Watson, Jr., appointed Geeson as SRA's president and managing director. For various reasons, however, the SRA acquisition never flourished as Watson, Jr., and I had intended. The chief reason was the company's attempt to "IBMize" SRA, a process that stifled its growth. As a result, IBM sold SRA in the mid-1980s for $150 million. Although IBM's lofty goals for SRA were never realized, its acquisition and divestiture were, nonetheless, profitable to IBM.

A World Trade Directorship and the Perks

In 1963, I was elected to the IBM World Trade Corporation's Board of Directors. This, coupled with my promotion to IBM corporate vice president, facilitated my dual roles of director of Commercial Development staff operations and IBM chief negotiator with governments, such as Japan's Ministry of International Trade and Industry (MITI), as well as companies and individuals seeking rights from IBM or offering to license IBM under their property rights. As a world trade director, I had the privilege of attending the annual joint board meetings with the IBM parent Board of Directors. These meetings were held throughout the world at the major IBM subsidiary sites in Canada, South America, Great Britain, France, Germany, Italy, Switzerland, Scandinavia, and Japan. This afforded IBM directors the opportunity not only to meet the management personnel abroad but also to become acquainted with our important customers and government officials. The directors and their wives were always royally entertained in each country. For example, in France,

we were entertained at the Palace of Versailles; in Great Britain, at the U.S. ambassador's residence; in Peru, at the president's palace; and in Japan, at the former Imperial Palace in Kyoto. A great deal of public relations value was achieved through the association of the directors with the foreign dignitaries and especially with the customers due to the prominence of IBM's outside directors, who had careers in education, government, law, finance, and industry. Among these directors were Bromley; Grayson Kirk, president of Columbia University; Merske Mueller, Danish shipping magnate; Amo Houghton, CEO of Corning Glass; Tom Hoving, director of the Metropolitan Museum of Art; William Scranton, governor of Pennsylvania; Cyrus Vance, U.S. ambassador; and William Moore, CEO of Bankers Trust. For my wife and me, this was an opportunity to develop personal relationships with several of the outside directors and their wives.

A Professional Staff—Key to My Success

As director of Commercial Development, I am too often given disproportionate credit. The achievements of this corporate function must be shared with the professionals on my staff who assisted me. One credit I can solely claim, however, is the development of a recruitment technique that enabled me to promote from field sales positions a number of highly qualified men for jobs in Contract Relations and Intellectual Property management. To accomplish this, I gained access to the IBM sales department's "high-potential personnel" list, guarded closely at the divisional and district sales manager levels. Prior to the meeting of each IBM 100 Percent Club, I would arrange a luncheon meeting for approximately a dozen high-potential employees from this list. During the luncheon, I would discuss with the invitees IBM's challenges and opportunities from a field marketing perspective. I also would intersperse into the discussion several hypothetical problem situations, bordering on the ridiculous, to solicit spontaneous responses. Almost invariably, one or two people stood out at the luncheon meeting. Since I taped each session, I would return to WHQ and have my staff listen to the taped responses and select whom they thought were most likely to succeed in Contract Relations. Without prior knowledge of my selection, the staff, by consensus, always chose the same people as I did. Through this means, I was able to recruit such outstanding men as Bill Miles, Gordon Williamson, Tom Birchfield, Kelly, and Dave Luening.

The early computers that resulted from the

work accomplished through IBM's frontier efforts, like all IBM equipment from the Hollerith days forward, were offered on a lease-only basis. Even IBM computer peripherals, ordered by competitors such as Burroughs, Control Data, NCR, and Honeywell for use in their early systems, were leased, not sold. Our customers preferred leasing over outright purchase because it reduced their initial capital investment and protected them from obsolescence resulting from the rapid pace of electronic development compared with an earlier era of electromechanical computing, when change had been slower. Under the lease plan, the customer received free maintenance, installation, and programming assistance. Software furnished with the installation was "bundled" into the rental price.

While IBM's competitors, especially those offering electronic computers, disliked leasing their equipment, market forces compelled them to offer their machines on a lease basis as well. IBM continued its lease-only marketing practice until the 1956 consent decree that terminated the U.S. government's antitrust suit and that compelled IBM to sell as well as lease equipment to help stimulate competition. The leasing concept of marketing computer systems, in which monthly rentals ranged from $20,000 to $1 million or more per system, put a great strain on IBM Intellectual Management and related patent licensing activity for which I was responsible. Leasing created a huge lessor field inventory that became a vulnerable target for patentee claims of lessor infringement. In the punch card era, infringement claims were rarely asserted against IBM, chiefly because invention was made mostly by company employees within the industry and patent rights were assigned to the company. Consequently, patent licensing was between companies; and cross-licensing solved most of the licensing problems, especially for IBM, due to its large patent portfolio. Toward the end of my career, IBM's punch card line was beginning to become subject to infringement claims from independent inventors.

Since both small and large European companies were engaged in computer development, a considerable number of inventions under which IBM needed a patent license originated in Europe. I closely monitored this activity with assistance from Shipman, director of International Patent Operations, and two extremely capable and talented patent attorneys, Harold Aspden, the U.K. patent manager at Hursley, and Walter Hoffmann, IBM patent manager based in Boblingen, Germany, who also later coordinated the IBM patent system in Munich.

Research Involvement

In the late 1950s, Watson, Jr., asked me to tour Europe with Arthur Samuel from the Yorktown Research Laboratory to look for a site for a European research laboratory. We selected Zurich and hired Ambrose Speiser, a noted Swiss professor of engineering, to head the facility. Watson, Jr., approved both selections. Subsequently, I hired Thomas Speckert as attorney for the laboratory and as a contract relations representative to assist the talented and capable Claude Wiley, whom I named European manager of Contract Relations, based in Zurich. Speckert became known throughout IBM and the World Trade Corporation for his charisma and for his ability to arrange joint board of directors meetings in every part of the world. IBM European research began in rented facilities until, in 1963, our permanent laboratory in Zurich was completed. I traveled to the new facility to share the honor of dedicating it with Williams and Arthur Watson.

The Japanese Challenge

The business, legal, and political challenges facing IBM seemed to be growing at a pace equal to, if not exceeding the company's growth in revenue and scope of operations. In late 1957, Arthur Watson, president of the IBM World Trade Corporation, had a visit from Mr. Komai, president of Hitachi, Ltd. Arthur Watson perceived early that Komai was wearing two hats: one for Hitachi and one for the Japanese government. Komai wanted to ascertain the availability of an IBM 705 computer for installation at Hitachi, allegedly to do nonmilitary scientific computing such as weather forecasting. More importantly, however, Komai wanted to inform IBM management, on behalf of MITI, that the Japanese government considered IBM Japan an unlawful foreign subsidiary. Komai further advised us that IBM Japan, Inc. was violating Japan's foreign investment and foreign exchange laws that forbade 100-percent ownership of a Japanese subsidiary by a foreign national. The background follows.

On 7 December 1941 (Pearl Harbor Day), the Japanese had confiscated IBM Japan as an enemy alien company; during World War II, Toshiba operated it. After VJ Day and during the Allied occupation, IBM Japan was operated under the direction of the Supreme Commander for the Allied Powers (SCAP). When the occupation concluded, SCAP ordered the Japanese government to return to

IBM Japan its assets and facilities, along with revenues held in escrow. In the postwar occupation period, SCAP had assumed direction of IBM Japan, with the cooperation of IBM U.S., from which SCAP procured equipment and personnel. These resources were utilized in order to administer SCAP's occupation and to perform SCAP studies pertaining to the economic reform of Japan.[3]

In October 1950, by orders from SCAP to the Japanese government, IBM took over the operation of IBM Japan as a wholly owned, foreign-resident subsidiary. Three years later, Japan enacted its foreign investment and foreign exchange laws requiring foreign-resident enterprises to be validated by the Japanese government to transfer technology and products into Japan, to manufacture and market products in Japan, and to remit royalty payments and dividends to the foreign parent. In order to be validated, foreign companies were required to be only a minority owner of the enterprise, with the majority owned by a Japanese organization. Because it had existed prior to these laws and was established by SCAP order, IBM Japan believed it had grandfather rights, making it exempt under the 1954 law. Komai informed us that the Japanese government held a different view and proposed that IBM form a jointly owned subsidiary with Hitachi as a 51-percent partner so the enterprise could achieve validation. He further proposed that the partnership be licensed to make, use, and sell under IBM's patents worldwide and that an IBM know-how transfer from IBM U.S. to the jointly owned Japanese subsidiary be a part of the license grant. This later stipulation brought me into the picture as the IBM executive responsible for contract negotiations and patent licensing. Arthur Watson told Komai that all patent licensing and technology transfer matters were my responsibility, as the director of IBM Commercial Development, and that I would handle directly with the Japanese government the matter he had brought to our attention.

During several visits to Japan during 1957 and 1958, I made contact with MITI, observed what other companies had done in similar situations, and concluded three actions were fundamental to the successful conclusion of negotiations. First, IBM initially had to avoid any form of renegotiation with Japanese companies seeking partnership with IBM and had to negotiate only with the Japanese government. Other U.S. companies, I observed, had initially negotiated with a potential Japanese business partner only to have MITI renegotiate many of the terms and provisions when those

U.S. companies sought government approval. Second, IBM had to prolong the negotiations, allowing the company sufficient time to build up a sizable patent portfolio in Japan. Third, IBM had to make known to MITI that the term of any license granted would not exceed the term of validation granted to IBM Japan.

It did not take me long to realize that MITI wanted to build a Japanese computer industry and that MITI's demands on IBM comprised the first step in that direction. I knew that the aspiring Japanese computer manufacturers could not be successful without violating IBM's intellectual property rights. I also was aware of MITI's policy to seek a license under intellectual property rights rather than have Japanese companies violate them and risk being charged with infringement both in Japan and abroad. Therefore, it was evident that, most of all, MITI wanted freedom under IBM patents not only for Hitachi alone but also for other companies that would comprise Japan's computer industry in the future.

Against this background, I concluded that it would not be in IBM's interest to seek a speedy resolution. Both Watson, Jr., and Arthur Watson concurred and allowed me as many months or years as I deemed necessary. Accordingly, I established the following Japanese negotiation policy guidelines:

- We would allow the Intellectual Property staff approximately four years to build a strong intellectual property rights position in Japan, sufficient to block manufacture, use, and sale of electronic computers and punch card peripherals.
- IBM would not negotiate directly with any proposed Japanese partner, regardless of the terms of any proposed offer.
- IBM would not transfer know-how, except that shown in a patent, to a Japanese company other than the wholly owned IBM Japan, with the right for IBM Japan to exclusive-license subcontractors for limited production for IBM Japan only.
- IBM would reject MITI's demands that 50 percent of IBM product content be of Japanese manufacture, and IBM would substitute a balanced import/export product shipment between IBM subsidiaries.
- IBM would not reduce the 10-percent royalty rate that it uniformly collected from its subsidiaries that were manufacturing and selling in foreign countries.
- IBM would not acquiesce to MITI's request that IBM delay shipment of its latest model computers until three years after U.S. introduction.

- IBM would offer the Japanese government as quid pro quo for validation the company's pledge to grant a patent license for all MITI-approved prospective Japanese computer makers at a reasonable 2-percent cross-license royalty rate, applicable to both parties under a MITI-approved cross-license agreement. But, we would not agree to transfer know-how to the Japanese companies.
- IBM would agree to a 99-percent equity interest, with the remaining 1 percent to be held by the directors of IBM Japan as nominee stockholders—all of whom were Japanese nationals. (This provision was made so MITI could save "face," in respect of MITI's contention that it had never validated a 100-percent-owned company.)

The free hand that both Watsons had given me—along with the authority the IBM Board of Directors gave me—was invaluable, especially during the difficult and protracted negotiating sessions that ensued over a span of almost four years. During this time, MITI threatened to impose restrictions on IBM Japan regarding importing technology and products, raising capital, hiring employees, and purchasing land for plant expansion. MITI contended that a validation of IBM Japan as a wholly owned subsidiary would set a precedent with which Japan could not live, as many other U.S. multinational companies would seek similar treatment.

The stalemate that developed in the negotiations between MITI and IBM made life difficult for Ko Mizushina, president of IBM Japan, and the other Japanese nationals managing our subsidiary. However, this was reasonably tolerable to the parent IBM World Trade Corporation that was willing to accept short-term "extreme administrative guidance" with an eye on the long-term benefits of complete control of its Japanese subsidiary. While negotiations were dragging on, prospective Japanese computer makers were becoming anxious and impatient with the passing of time, and MITI was chafing at the bit, eager to inaugurate the Japanese computer industry. Manufacturers like Hitachi turned to partnership with RCA, NEC partnered with Fairchild Semiconductors and Honeywell, Toshiba with General Electric, Fujitsu with Siemens, and Oki Denki with Sperry Rand. The Japanese partners eventually dissolved all these partnerships, leaving the foreign partner with but a short-term monetary gain. All the while, however, the Japanese companies were aware of IBM's Intellectual Property strength and its tremendous investment in research and devel-

Figure 5. Jim and Jean Birkenstock at an NEC-hosted dinner.

opment. Consequently, they continued to woo IBM (see Figure 5), hoping that IBM's position would weaken under pressure from MITI and that IBM would accept a Japanese partner in response to MITI's threats of sanctions and restrictions on IBM Japan.

My negotiations with MITI consumed a great deal of my time and stamina, notwithstanding the able assistance I received from Wally Doud as assistant director, Williamson and John Gosselin from Contract Relations, and Shipman, successor to Noll as Patent Department manager. These last three men spent a disproportionate amount of time in Japan. With all negotiations taking place in Tokyo, plus negotiations here and abroad with European companies, I had to maintain a heavy travel schedule. Despite my many visits to Japan, I never learned to speak the language. My Japanese vocabulary was limited to several hundred phrases, sufficient to help me communicate on the golf course or at the geisha dinners my wife and I found interesting and sometimes amusing. (Due to my excessive time away from home, the company allowed my wife to accompany me occasionally.) During negotiations with MITI, I overcame the language barrier through a professional interpreter. I saw to it that my interpreter was always an American, because I chose not to put IBM Japan personnel in a position that might test their loyalty between company and country. Additionally, I felt that utilizing a Japanese national interpreter might compromise my negotiating capability. Translating technical language is a problem for the best of interpreters. I want to emphasize, however, that at no time during my negotiations did I have reason to doubt the loyalty of any of my Japanese fellow IBM employees. Mizushina, Ono-san (IBM Japan's highly capable patent manager), and Kudo-san not only gave me their complete loyalty but also offered me their unstinting effort. Interestingly, when the negotiations became tense, members of the opposition who spoke fluent English began to utilize an interpreter. In this way, the Japanese negotiator was able to remove himself from any discomfiting direct confrontation with me while, at the same time, continuing the negotiation process.

Cultural Differences

The difference between Japanese and U.S. culture was more of a hindrance than the language. Therefore, I became a student of the Japanese culture, believing this would help me better understand and predict how the Japanese would respond during our negotiations. Most helpful in this regard were the cofounders of Sony, Akio Morita and Maski Ibuka, whom I met soon after one of my early visits to Japan. Since Sony was not a contender as a computer maker for IBM affiliation or license rights, and because of Morita's fluent English, I felt comfortable talking with and learning from him and his brother-in-law Iwama-san and became well-acquainted with them both. Trust and confidence developed among us, certainly to my benefit and, I believe, also to theirs and Sony's. The knowledge I gained regarding the various aspects of Japanese culture gave me further insight into the intricate Japanese business strategies. During almost every visit to Japan, I visited Sony headquarters and laboratories, where I was privileged to see its most advanced developments.

My personal relationship with these men eventually led to technical collaboration between Sony and IBM. When Leo Esaki, Sony's Nobel Prize-winning electronic engineer, desired to work in the United States for a U.S. firm, Morita approved IBM hiring him because, he said, "his employment was handled in a Japanese-like manner." In the late 1960s, Morita was elected a member of the IBM World Trade Board of Directors and served in this capacity for a number of years. In 1965 and beyond, IBM and Sony collaborated on a number of projects of mutual interest, the most significant being the manufacture at IBM's Boulder, Colorado, plant of magnetic computer tape utilizing Sony tape manufacturing know-how. This collaboration, like the one with Philips in Holland, ceased when Sony's products became competitive with IBM's.

As IBM maintained its negotiation strategy, the fledgling Japanese computer makers, anxious for a license under IBM's patents, were putting pressure on MITI to conclude negotiations with us. MITI reacted by requesting IBM refrain from discussing with these Japanese companies any details pertaining to the negotiations. The MITI–IBM negotiations were also receiving attention from the Japanese press. To suppress coverage of IBM's position, MITI ordered IBM not to communicate in any manner with the Japanese media. We strictly adhered to this policy, giving MITI freedom to provide its own version of how negotiations were proceeding. At a certain point, MITI became so sensitive to media pressure that it arranged for secret meetings at various locations of its choosing.

Impasse and Its Resolution

Finally, in mid-December 1960, IBM and MITI reached a total impasse. Akasawa-san, chief negotiator for MITI, attempting to bully me into acquiescence, stated that unless IBM accepted MITI's terms, MITI was prepared to impose severe sanctions on IBM Japan, crippling its current operations and clouding its future. Akasawa-san requested I make IBM's Board of Directors in the United States aware of this situation. I flatly refused. I responded to this threat by telling Akasawa-san that if MITI wished to play hardball, IBM was prepared for the game. I further told Akasawa-san that I had written authorization from the IBM Board of Directors to resolve the validation issues on terms and conditions that would be in the best interests of IBM and the Japanese government.

Until this was accomplished, all negotiations would remain at my level. I then advised Akasawa-san that I considered the negotiations to have reached an impasse that only a period of time would heal. Meanwhile, I said, I considered negotiations suspended. I also advised Akasawa-san that I no longer felt obligated to maintain confidentiality regarding IBM's position in the negotiations. I informed him that I would be leaving Japan at 11:00 p.m., the following Monday night. In accordance with Japanese protocol, I requested a 30-minute "sayonara" appointment on Monday afternoon. I hoped, I said, that both sides would benefit from a cooling-off period. Akasawa-san scheduled the appointment for Monday at 3:00 p.m.

After departing from the MITI office, I met with IBM's outside legal counsel, Dick Rabinowitz, and Mizushina to suggest they devise a short-term strategy for IBM Japan to continue operations, should MITI's threatened sanctions be imposed. After the meeting, I returned to my hotel to receive a telephone call from Mr. Kurata, CEO of Hitachi, inviting me to play golf with him and several of his staff at the Three Hundred Club in Tokyo on Sunday afternoon. From this, I sensed that word of the negotiation impasse had already reached Hitachi via MITI.

During my round of golf, Kurata pressed me for my views of the MITI negotiations. With confidentiality lifted, I was able to apprise him of the impasse, as if he did not already know, and of IBM's position relative to it. After I hit one particularly long drive of over 200 yards, Kurata asked me how I hit the ball so far. My "un-Japanese" reply was that I imagined the insignia on the ball to be "MITI" rather than "Titleist" and "hit the hell out of it." This evoked a hearty laugh from my host. During the cocktail hour that followed our golf session, Kurata said that it was a pity for me to leave Japan without the other prospective Japanese computer makers having had an opportunity to hear IBM's position regarding the negotiations and the impending impasse. I responded that, regretfully, I could not, due to commitments at home and my departure the following evening. Kurata then asked if I would agree to Hitachi's arranging a dinner meeting comprised of top executives from the other prospective Japanese computer makers, at which time I could present IBM's views and, in general, its position relative to the MITI–IBM negotiations. I agreed, provided IBM host the dinner. Prior to leaving the clubhouse, Kurata insisted I not dine alone but have dinner with his aide, Mr. Haraguchi, to which I agreed. At dinner, Haraguchi suggested I might enjoy the company of a "dancing partner." I refused. After dinner, I went directly to my hotel.

I was awakened at 8:00 a.m. the next morning by a knock on my door. When I opened it, Mr. Ando from Akasawa-san's office greeted me. The first thought that flashed through my mind was Haraguchi's offer of the night before. Although Ando-san said he had come to inquire if I could meet with Akasawa-san at 11 a.m., I reasoned that he could have more easily contacted me from his office. Nevertheless, I asked Ando-san to join me for breakfast in my room and then inquired whether or not it was Akasawa-san's intention to reschedule my 3:00 p.m. "sayonara" meeting. Ando-san explained that this meeting had not been rescheduled but that Akasawa-san wished to have some further discussion with me prior to it. While this puzzled me, having learned to accept the unexpected during these negotiations, I agreed to the dual appointments.

At the 11 a.m. meeting, after a few minutes of sipping green tea with Akasawa-san and his aides Hiramatsu-san and Ando-san, Akasawa-

san took a paper from his jacket and, reading from it, fully capitulated to IBM's position, without precondition. Concealing my surprise with great difficulty, I thanked Akasawa-san for removing the impasse prior to my departure and discussed with him a near-future meeting to be arranged at a date that would give both sides sufficient time to prepare the definitive legal agreement. At 3:00 p.m., I revisited MITI for the "sayonara" meeting. Not surprisingly, we discussed nothing substantive other than my assurance that IBM would develop a definitive agreement applicable to the general terms to which we had agreed. We sipped more green tea and exchanged pleasantries for about half an hour. I said "sayonara" and departed.

While I was delighted with the turn of events, I now faced a new dilemma: how to deal with this unexpected reversal at the 7:00 p.m. dinner meeting that Kurata had arranged with the five prospective computer manufacturers. On the way to my hotel, I had a brainstorm. By good fortune, I had brought with me a golf practice putting clock, golf balls, and several putters that I had intended to give as gifts to my Japanese golf hosts. I visualized a hastily arranged putting contest among the dinner invitees as a means of consuming much of the time set aside for discussion at the dinner meeting. Prior to the dinner, on the reception area rug, I announced a putting contest involving only the dinner guests, with IBM employees as scorekeepers. Mr. Degawa of Nippon Electric Corporation (NEC) won the contest and the prize: a new Ping putter. Degawa-san was ecstatic. With the contest concluded, we sat down to dinner with only a little time left for me to address the group prior to my departure. In my brief remarks, I informed my guests that I was pleased to say that IBM and MITI had reached an accommodation that had broken our negotiation impasse, the details of which I was sure they would learn shortly from MITI (as if they did not know already). I then departed for the Tokyo airport with a smile instead of a frown for the first time in three years of negotiations.

My joy on this occasion was enhanced by a touching event that had occurred just prior to dinner being served. I was called to the hotel lobby by a surprise visit from Hiramatsu, who said, as best he could in English, that he came to compliment me on my "honorable manner of conduct" during the long negotiations. With that, he presented me with a gift of bamboo rosary prayer beads, hand-carved by his father-in-law, the mayor of Beppu City and a Roman Catholic. I still use this treasured gift.

Some weeks later, following MITI's abrupt

capitulation, I returned to Japan with legal papers pertaining to IBM Japan's validation and the terms and conditions of a patent cross-licensing agreement in both Japanese and English. With minimum alterations, Japanese government officials agreed to the terms and conditions. Consequently, IBM Japan was validated without restriction for a period of five years. In due course, IBM executed patent cross-license agreements with five prospective Japanese computer makers, giving both IBM and the Japanese licensees a worldwide patent cross-license for a corresponding period of five years under each party's respective patent at a reasonable royalty rate. No know-how was to be exchanged, only the gold fountain pens each party used to sign the agreement. By this time, MITI's confidence in my integrity had reached a high point. Because of this, MITI asked me to be the principle spokesperson at the press conference regarding the agreement between MITI and IBM.

Follow-on Negotiations

Approximately three years following our initial cross-licensing activity, the Japanese computer makers began to manufacture products and systems similar to IBM's and, in many cases, not unlike their competitors. As they began remitting royalties to IBM, we discovered a major problem. The Japanese licensees were ascertaining in a disparate manner the patented portion of their product or system covered by IBM patents and subject to royalty. For example, Licensee X manufacturing a product almost identical to Licensee Y considered the portion of its machine subject to IBM patents to cover a much smaller area than did the competitor Licensee Y. As a result, Licensee X was paying smaller royalty fees to IBM per unit than Licensee Y under the same patent. It became an administrative nightmare for IBM to contest and prove validity and equity of its royalty base. Additionally, this became a serious legal and accounting issue between the licensor and licensee. The language barrier exacerbated the problem.

Due to the frequency of dispute over the patented portion and the technology swing away from discrete componentry in subassemblies to solid-state integrated circuitry, conventional royalty-bearing cross-licensing procedures—even at nominal royalty rates—became inadequate. To solve the problem, I proposed a new form of cross-licensing between IBM and the licensees wherein the licensee could pay a single rate per machine and be licensed under all patents that pertained, thus avoiding the administrative costs of determining patent coverage on various portions of a machine and computing each portion's costs or selling price. This simplified the royalty computation for both IBM and its licensees and became known as the "*Table d'Hote* Option." I was deeply concerned that the language in our Japanese license agreements might be troublesome, should the pending U.S. government antitrust suit force IBM to break up into several separate companies. Therefore, in 1971, I embarked on a rather comprehensive revision of our Japanese license agreements with the aid of IBM's legal counsel. As an incentive to the Japanese, particularly MITI, I conceived the idea of a royalty payment procedure that became known as the "Five-Year Balancing of Royalty Payment Cross-License." The negotiating procedure required both parties to exchange measurements that reflected their research and development and manufacturing capabilities for the present and for a projected five-year period, along with the size of their respective currently issued patent portfolios.

The first step was to sell MITI on approving the new license plan, which MITI agreed to with a few questions regarding the language changes vital to IBM concerning the licensing of separate business entities. Because of the U.S. government antitrust suit brought against IBM on the last day of President Johnson's administration, it was essential that we incorporate language in our Japanese license agreements to take care in the event the U.S. Department of Justice was successful in breaking up IBM through the antitrust action. The language I was able to incorporate stipulated that all parts of IBM could retain the benefit of a Japanese license as that part (of IBM) had prior to any segregation. (Fortunately, the U.S. Department of Justice dropped its suit against IBM in 1983, and segregation was never forced on IBM.) The focus was almost entirely on simplification of royalty payments and assurance of complete "freedom of action" for both parties to cross-license for a five-year period. The five-year period was chosen because of the corresponding five-year validation IBM Japan received from MITI and the Japanese Ministry of Finance. IBM was now in the comfortable position that if the U.S. Department of Justice broke up IBM into separate companies, each would be licensed under the patents of our Japanese cross-licensees

From measurements, and through negotiation, the two parties agreed on a dollar amount to be paid annually by the party with the lesser number of issued patents and smaller research and development capability. This was done to compensate for the current and projected difference in the patent strength between the parties. Because the relative patent and research and development strength was expressed in U.S. dollars and paid annually, this practice became known as an annual balancing of payment for a specified term of cross-license. Due to IBM's sizable patent portfolio and the magnitude of its research and development effort, compared with the cross-licensee, in each case IBM became the recipient of an agreed-on annual royalty of six or more figures. With MITI endorsement of the new "Balancing of Royalty Payment" plan, the only issue that remained was negotiating separately the balance of payment applicable to each licensee. These negotiations occupied most of my time following my relinquishment of management responsibility for the day-to-day operation of Commercial Development and becoming fully retired by mid-1973.

Because of the equity of this form of cross-licensing and its relative freedom from both an administrative burden and contentious royalty calculation issues, our Japanese licensees accepted this practice and frequently employed it in their licensing relations with third parties. IBM's innovative "balancing of payment cross-licensing" procedure eventually was adopted by some U.S. corporations, especially those possessing patent portfolios that covered technologically complex products and systems. As a result of recommendations from consultants, myself included, U.S. companies became aware of this procedure. My postretirement activities as a consultant specializing in the management of intellectual property assets and licensing enabled me to suggest this innovative cross-licensing practice to a wide number of companies facing similar cross-licensing problems.

As negotiators, the Japanese are about as tough as they come, especially MITI officials. However, on one occasion, when MITI officials could have taken advantage of IBM, they showed great understanding and compassion. In April 1970, after having just arrived in Tokyo, I was preparing to engage in yet another round of sensitive negotiations with MITI officials concerning revisions to our patent cross-licensing agreements, particularly changes MITI proposed concerning "administrative guidance." Just as the negotiations were commencing, I received an urgent telephone call from my wife in Florida. She advised me that our New Canaan, Connecticut, home had caught fire and had burned almost to the ground. All but a few of our home furnishings were destroyed.

Fortunately, the house had been unoccupied; Jean was at our Florida residence and was unharmed. The circumstances obviously required my returning home as quickly as possible. Without any request to do so, MITI officials responded to my plight by expediting discussions around the clock. Without haggling, they made all the contract concessions I wanted.

When word of my loss of home and furnishings became known in Tokyo among high-level government and computer industry executives, expressions of regret and sympathy poured in. In several cases, these expressions were accompanied by the replacement of our Noritake dinnerware, Japanese artifacts, and other household items the fire destroyed. Jean and I will always be grateful for the unsolicited show of compassion and sympathy by both friends and business adversaries in Japan. It gave us an understanding of still another side of Japanese nature.

Japanese Government Recognition

The licensing of the Japanese computer makers was considered an epic event in Japan, since these companies became the core of the Japanese computer industry. Japan has on occasion publicly stated that the Japanese computer industry arguably has been more beneficial to its society than any other industry. In 1980, at a ceremony commemorating the 20th anniversary of the Japanese computer industry, Hiramatsu, by now governor of the Oita Prefecture, arranged for me to attend ceremonial events in Tokyo and to be honored by the Japanese computer industry. (Hiramatsu, for three decades following his MITI career, has served as governor of the Oita Prefecture on the island of Kyushu. Even to this day, we frequently correspond with one another and have exchanged visits at our respective homes.) In 1994, Asahi TV made a documentary on the Japanese computer industry and its origins. A camera crew came to the United States and interviewed me as part of the program.

Travel

My life as a negotiator in foreign lands was not all work. My wife accompanied me abroad on several occasions. My travels were sometimes fascinating and other times rather boring, especially when I found myself alone in a large city that I had previously visited and whose places of interest I had already seen. To relieve weekend boredom and to get some exercise, I played golf. I stored a set of clubs at IBM Europe headquarters in Paris, and that office shipped the

IBM Japan kept a set of clubs on hand for me, and over the years, my golf playing became one of my "tools" of negotiation.

clubs to the IBM facility nearest me during each business trip. Over the years, I was able to play golf in Scotland, England, Holland, Denmark, France, Switzerland, Germany, and Italy. IBM Japan kept a set of clubs on hand for me, and over the years, my golf playing became one of my "tools" of negotiation. Additionally, when I was hosting foreign negotiators in the United States, I would play an occasional round of golf at the Westchester Country Club (in New York) or the Country Club of Florida, where I had my second home. The Japanese particularly loved this experience.

The Japanese were not the only ones interested in becoming licensees under IBM's patent portfolio. The British, French, German, Dutch, and Italians wanted to enter the electronic data processing market as well. Additionally, patents were issuing in Europe, particularly Germany, France, and Great Britain, that were adversely held advancements in the art and under which it would be prudent for IBM to acquire license rights. As a result, I spent considerable time in Europe as IBM's chief negotiator for patent licensing and technology transfer during the Electronic Data Processing Machine's frontier days and beyond. In addition, administrative responsibility for the management of the IBM patent departments located in IBM's foreign subsidiaries doing product manufacturing and development frequently took me to the European cities in which these facilities were located.

Watson, Jr., while a fierce competitor, saw the computer as a God-given tool for the benefit of humankind. With this viewpoint, he was among the first, if not the first, of the computer company CEOs to advocate industry standards—both de facto and anticipatory. This did not set well with the IBM engineering infrastructure that endorsed standards as long as they were IBM-dictated. Watson, Jr., fought this in his own company and instructed me to organize and conduct an anticipatory standards effort within the industry, working with the U.S. Bureau of Standards and IBM competitors, or would-be competitors, large or small, without discrimination. I appointed John Rankin

from my staff to be the catalyst for this activity. Rankin organized an industry-wide effort through the Computer and Business Equipment Manufacturer Association. In the mid-1950s, when I needed a counterpart effort abroad, I traveled to Europe and persuaded International Computing and Tabulating, Inc. and Bull (France's Computing and Tabulating Company) to organize and staff the European Computer Manufacturer's Association. By this means, worldwide computing standards were negotiated and promulgated, giving data processing a common program language and unified standards. Thanks to Rankin and other members of my staff, we were able to assist Watson, Jr., in realizing his pioneering goal for "open computer systems." I believe many people overlook this IBM contribution, without which the World Wide Web could not function.

A CIA Point of Contact

In the period following Soviet Premier Nikita Khrushchev's visit to IBM's San Jose plant in 1959, during the Cuban missile crisis, the CIA was contacting Watson, Jr., with increasing regularity with a variety of requests. These contacts became burdensome to him, so he advised the CIA that I would be its contact point. Thus began perhaps the most sensitive and annoying of assignments Watson, Jr., gave me. Because CIA demands were wide-ranging and, for the most part, unreasonable, I refused practically all of them. One request, for covertly placing a CIA agent in the IBM Watson Research Laboratory in Yorktown, New York, I promptly rejected. Another request, to permit a CIA agent to assume cover as an IBM customer engineer assigned to service a customer in Omaha, Nebraska, I also immediately denied. During the peak of the cold war, IBM World Trade subsidiaries unknowingly employed CIA operatives in the Asian Pacific area and Europe in several instances. There seemed to be no limits to the requests the CIA made. It was most aggressive in seeking to obtain information through IBM scientists who attended engineering and technical symposiums abroad. The CIA wanted IBM scientists to covertly contact foreign scientists or to make extracurricular visits to Russian laboratories. Since this type of activity posed serious threats to IBM personnel, I firmly denied all such requests.

At one point, anti-Vietnam War activists were making frequent threats against computer research facilities. In several cases, there were bombings, the most notable at the University of Michigan computer research laboratory and at several IBM overseas facilities. One Westinghouse executive, while visiting a facility behind the iron curtain, was charged with espionage, jailed, and held hostage by the KGB. As a result, I became apprehensive when I, along with other members of the U.S. Patent Commission, visited several communist countries to conduct a patent study. When the commission study group visited Berlin and East Germany in 1966, I declined to make the trip, not wishing to risk being apprehended and accused of a trumped-up espionage charge. When my IBM career was drawing to a close, I was relieved to be able to transfer my assignment as CIA contact to another IBM corporate officer.

My Most Interesting Extracurricular Activity

During the mid-1960s, I was involved in several extracurricular activities, in particular with the U.S. Patent Commission. On 8 April 1965, President Johnson, having become concerned about the complexities and delays arising out of the U.S. patent system, established a bipartisan commission to conduct a study of the system and to make some recommendations regarding its reform. I suspect I was among the 14 appointed to the president's commission for two reasons. The first reason was because the commission would be addressing the controversial issue of the U.S. patent system's permitting software as patentable subject matter. The second reason was because I had become well-known for executive management of IBM's worldwide intellectual property. I served along with members from the legal, industrial, and governmental sectors. Former Circuit Court Judge Symond Rifkind was our chairman, who brilliantly guided the commission to its conclusions and submitted our report to President Johnson.[4] The commission members were greatly pleased that the Johnson administration accepted all of its recommendations. Regrettably, only a few were enacted into law due to the highly influential Patent Law Bar that opposed most of the commission's recommendations. Decades later, however, the U.S. Patent Office adopted a number of the recommended changes; even today, some are being reconsidered and may yet be adopted.

From 1955 to 1970, IBM's annual corporate revenues increased 12-fold from $696 million to $7.5 billion and employment grew from 60,000 to 270,000. Due to the electronic technology explosion, my Commercial Development responsibilities outpaced even IBM's growth within the worldwide computer industry throughout most of this period. In the 1960s, IBM management broadened my responsibilities and corresponding workload by adding such

functions as Industry (Competitive) Relations, managed by Spain; Industry Standards, under Rankin; Government Regulatory Practices; and Trade and Professional Association Activities. Fortunately, I was able to cope with my expanded responsibilities thanks to the support from my "world-class" Assistant Director Doud, who came to me in 1959 after serving as assistant to Williams, IBM president and chief of staff.

During this same period, Birchfield, a transfer from the Kansas City branch office, came into the department as my administrative assistant. Although IBM did not offer the title as such, Birchfield acted as my chief of staff. He directed traffic in and out of my office, never hesitated to be the staff's advocate when differences arose between the staff and the boss, and, in general, brought harmony to the operation. For Birchfield, there was no task too large or too small, and his aid was invaluable. He not only worked tirelessly behind the scenes but also was a loyal friend who was never afraid to tell me when I was wrong. I later learned, after leaving Commercial Development, that Birchfield's peers described him as "the person charged with the responsibility of cleaning out the tiger's cage while the tiger was still in it." On one occasion, he even took my dog Peppy, suffering from an incurable disease, to the veterinarian to be "put down," a task I could not face or bear the thought of turning over to just anyone. After my retirement and after Doud took over, Birchfield went on to an outstanding career as a director in IBM World Trade America's Far East Corporation and domiciled in Japan.

IBM's Astounding Growth

IBM's growth following Watson, Jr.'s becoming CEO in 1956 was, as I mentioned above, phenomenal. In January 1970, to recognize those who helped IBM realize this important 15-year period in IBM's history, Watson, Jr., and his wife Olive gave a dinner party at their Greenwich, Connecticut, home. They invited approximately 25 of Watson, Jr.'s top executives plus their spouses. At the party, each executive was given a small solid silver mantel piece emblematic of the company's revenue growth from almost $700 million in 1955 to over $7 billion in 1970. The polished silver base was inscribed:

Towers We Built Together
Tom and Olive

Affixed to the base was a cluster of silver rods of ascending height, each representing and inscribed with one of the 15 years of IBM's revenue growth. The shortest "tower" was 1/4 inch in height, and the tallest was four inches high. I was honored to be a part of this occasion and, more importantly, a part of this piece of IBM's history.

A Change to Come, Told in Confidence

In late 1971, Watson, Jr., to whom I still reported on most matters, told me in confidence that he was contemplating introducing a mandatory retirement age of 60 for all IBM corporate officers, effective 1 January 1973. He reasoned that this would increase career opportunities for the many highly capable employees in positions below the corporate officer level. Since I would be one of three corporate officers to be retired under the new policy, he wanted my views. I told him I could not speak for the others, but mandatory retirement at 60 would not be unwelcome in my case. I said this because I was beginning to feel "burned out" due to both the breadth of my responsibilities and the added workload I was experiencing since Doud was promoted from assistant director of commercial development to group vice president. Operating without Doud's assistance was having a telling effect on both my effectiveness and my health. My talk with Watson, Jr., provided me with the opportunity to gripe to him about his and my failure over the prior months to agree on the person most qualified to become assistant director.

Some weeks after this confidential meeting, Watson, Jr., informed me that because of a management reorganization in another area of the business, Doud was available for reassignment and suggested he return as my assistant. I viewed Doud as a "perfect fit" for my job and reasoned that if he were asked to resume his former position as assistant director and to await my retirement before he could become a vice president and director, he would resign and go to another company. Therefore, I reasoned with Watson, Jr., that it would be in IBM's, Doud's, and my best interests for Doud immediately to take my job. This would enable me to phase gracefully into retirement and provide me, in my remaining time with IBM, an opportunity to focus my efforts primarily on high-level corporate negotiations such as IBM/Western Electric Corp. cross-licensing rather than on administrative activity. I also could devote more time and energy to concluding the balancing of payment agreement negotiations in Japan that I estimated would take 18 months. Watson, Jr., accepted the logic behind my recommendation, and Doud returned and took charge as vice president of commercial development, renamed Commercial and Industry Relations to better

reflect the scope of its operations. My title, consistent with the management change I had proposed, was now IBM vice president, corporate relations, under which I functioned in parallel with Doud in the aforementioned areas. This facilitated the management transition and the negotiating responsibilities left with me.

I turned the Commercial Development department over to Doud on 24 May 1971, leaving behind a wonderful staff, and moved my office to the third floor of our Armonk, New York, corporate headquarters facility. On the occasion of my move, my staff, who had always enjoyed an opportunity to have an after-hours gathering, arranged a party in my honor at one of the neighborhood restaurants. We had enjoyed other social functions as well, such as our annual golf outing with the Patent department that I captained and with the Contract Relations department that Doud captained. The rules of the contest were simple: the losing team had to buy the beers. Bob Schuey always made arrangements for office parties and other social events. Frank Chadurjian led the singing and Roy Fougere arranged golf foursomes. It saddened me to think I was leaving all of this behind, and my "going-away" party was most touching as I experienced, one last time, the warmth, good humor, and fellowship of my colleagues. Schuey clearly missed his calling as a writer and was known to the group as the "Phantom Poet." In his capacity as master of ceremonies, he read a poem he had written about my IBM career. I shall always treasure the poem and the memories of the special event that occasioned its writing. Schuey retired several years after I did. Although he moved to California, we managed to keep in touch. Unfortunately, his retirement was saddened by the death of his beloved wife Eleanor. Schuey survived his wife by only a few years. I kept a copy of the poem he wrote and read for my party (see the sidebar).

Another Cherished Moment

When January 1973, my official retirement date, arrived, I was still involved with completing and consummating the MITI–IBM revalidation negotiations in Japan. Therefore, I retained my IBM office for six months beyond retirement in order to conclude the Japanese negotiations. In the middle of 1973, as I was closing my IBM office to become a full retiree from IBM, Frank Cary, who on 1 January 1973 had succeeded Learson as CEO, organized a farewell luncheon in the IBM executive dining room. Following some very complimentary remarks by Watson, Jr., regarding my 38 years

Saga of a Salesman or How to Take License (Poetic, That Is)

Jim B. began his long career back there at SUI,
He studied, worked and played—gave everything a try.
When Jimmy Boy left college, it seemed that he was fated,
For in '35 toward IBM he quickly gravitated.

Now in '35 the times were tough and it was hard to make a living,
A hundred a month, and a little commission, was all that they were giving.
So up to Endicott he went and worked as hard as hell,
He learned the IBM lingo—he didn't need to learn to sell!

Then back to old St. Louis, by the mighty Mississippi,
He made his calls and did he sell—you better bet your bippy.
He did so well it wasn't long before they noticed Jim,
Then good old Harry Eilers said, I'll make Assistant Manager out of him.

Then on to Kansas City, garden spot of all the Midwest,
Jim made his clubs and proved himself to be one of the best.
He was happy and contented with his family, home, and work,
But then one day he caught the eye of big shot Charlie Kirk.

So they took the bull from old Missou and sent him to the city,
But along the way he was to learn, 'twas a city without pity.
Wide-eyed and eager, full of fight, he climbed to greater heights,
He made his mark, and soon became one of IBM's leading lights.

At 33 he reached the top, directing every sale,
What happened then, he'll never know, but that's another tale.
But at this point, he promised himself that in spite of all their snide ways,
If they won't let me grow straight up, I'll do my growing sideways.

Came Future Demands and our boy changed from a doer to a seer,
And overnight he realized, here's a whole damn new career.
Punched cards will ultimately go out, thought their erstwhile greatest rooter,

They'll be replaced, and I predict, by electronic computer.

Today we're faced from every side with status, status, status.
You have to have an E.A. or they'll think that you have had it.
But back in 49'ish, would you believe, I'm sure you'll laugh,
J.W.B. was E.A. to the whole darn corporate staff.

Product Planning was his mission, the future was his game,
EAM or EDP, you name it, his efforts were just the same.
He said, "buy those Haloid patents and we'll do quite well with them."
Tho' "they" said "No," can you imagine, a Xerox-IBM!

Oh, Williamsburg, you changed the ways that we all did our thing,
You decentralized, divisionalized, and overnight did bring
A lot of new and different things—we wondered at their intent,
Everyone quickly started asking, "What the hell is Commercial Development?"

Jim began negotiating, some at home a lot abroad,
And Accounting started yelling, "Those expense accounts, My God!"
They really weren't that bad until he started going to Japan,
I'd like to know the real account of Mr. Birkenstock-san!

Our Jim's had a lot of relations—I mean Contract, Industry and such,
But regardless of the type, he always had the touch.
Now in Corporate Relations, whatever they may be,
He'll do his thing, and you can bet, do it successfully.

For 35 years he made his mark and did all that they required,
But he's still as young—tho' a little gray—as the day that he was hired.
He tried for success and got it—you really just have to want it.
The moral of this story is, if you got it, you just have to flaunt it!

The Phantom Poet
24 May 1971

of IBM service, Cary presented me with a replica of Leonardo da Vinci's 15th-century gyroscope. Watson, Sr., a great admirer of da Vinci, had acquired an extensive collection of replicas of da Vinci's art and innovative ideas. From this collection, Cary chose the gyroscope, one of da Vinci's heralded inventions, as an appropriate memento for me and for the years of service I had given the company. A plaque on the gyroscope's base carries the following inscription:

Jim Birkenstock
Innovator
IBM Corporation
1935–1972

Watson, Jr.'s Personal Note
Another, and perhaps my most satisfying, moment concerning my IBM career came 17 years after my retirement. In June 1990, Watson, Jr., sent me an autographed copy of *Father, Son and Company*. In the text, he named me, along with Executive Vice Presidents L.H. LaMotte and Williams and Vice Presidents Wally McDowell and Whiz Miller and Learson as his management "inner circle" on which he relied to run IBM after his father handed him the reins. What I cherish most are the words Watson, Jr., wrote beneath his autograph:

For the Birkenstocks. From Watson, with great admiration. Lest you don't notice, Jim, I think you are one of a very few of IBM's indispensable men.

These words could not have been more fulfilling, even if they had been written in 1973 or earlier. Regrettably, Watson, Jr., died of a heart attack in December 1993.

Postretirement Consulting and Directorship Activity
When Watson, Jr.'s revised retirement policy became public knowledge, it received a great amount of media attention, especially because, under the new policy, IBM Chairman and CEO Learson was affected. There was considerable speculation regarding his successor as an outcome of this policy. As a fallout of the publicity regarding IBM's retirement policy, a number of companies, both domestic and Japanese, approached me offering employment opportunities. I was not interested because I had envisioned my post-IBM life to be in the consulting field, where I could function at my own pace and apply my experience in contracts, licenses, and intellectual property management. Texas Instruments, Fairchild Camera & Instruments, and Motorola contacted me. Bob Galvin, chair-

man of Motorola, offered me a five-year retainer as a consultant and a promise of a place on the company's board. I chose Motorola over the others and, after a short time, was elected to the board on which I served until I reached Motorola's mandatory retirement age of 70.

Ten Years with Motorola
My work with Motorola was perhaps my most stimulating and rewarding post-IBM consulting effort. Galvin was an outstanding leader and corporate executive. His concept of corporate governance was to have his directors become heavily involved in leadership activities and in planning Motorola's future. Early in my service with Motorola, I was asked to assist in the restructuring of the company's patent and licensing activity as it shifted from outside legal patent counsel, utilized since Motorola's founding, to in-house management of its intellectual property. I had the opportunity to work with fellow directors Ken West, CEO of Harris Trust, and Art Reese, retired vice president of Motorola, in presenting recommendations for the restructuring of Motorola's corporate governance. Galvin accepted our recommendations almost in their entirety. We recommended bringing more outside directors to the board and forming a number of new committees of the board, such as the executive and nominating committees as well as committees for technology, corporate strategy, long-range planning, and human resources in addition to the already existing audit and finance committees.

In the mid-1970s, Galvin decided that Motorola should divest itself of its Quasar Division, which developed and marketed large-screen TVs. Negotiations for the sale of the Quasar Division to Matsushita Electric Company in Japan were proceeding when they reached an impasse. Some months earlier, Motorola had licensed Sony to manufacture a large-screen TV under Motorola's patents and know-how for sale in Japan by a Sony subsidiary. Matsushita contended that it could not live with such an arrangement and, for the acquisition to be consummated, Motorola would have to bring about a dissolution of its Sony arrangement. Galvin sensed that this could be accomplished only at a high level between Motorola and Sony. At that time, Galvin had not met Morita, president and CEO of Sony. Knowing of my long and cordial relationship with Morita, Galvin turned to me for assistance. I knew of Morita's forthcoming visit to the United States for a groundbreaking ceremony for Sony's San Diego plant. I suggested that I arrange a California meeting between Galvin and Morita. Knowing that Morita was continuing to New York, I further suggested that Galvin use his private Gulfstream to fly Mr. and Mrs. Morita to New York. I suggested that while in flight, they would have time to discuss Motorola's problem and work out a solution. The plan worked well, and the two men agreed to a dissolution and asked me to serve as consultant to both companies to mediate the dissolution. I was able to accomplish the dissolution, with Motorola's paying Sony a flat sum of $200,000 for relinquishing the rights Motorola had previously granted Sony. I was pleased that two heads of large corporations were able to place their mutual trust in my ability to devise a fair and objective solution for both.

Consultation at IBM

Like me, other IBM corporate officers became retirees, and Cary thought our skills should be utilized somehow. Accordingly, he invited retirees to meet with the current IBM top management for three days, biannually, at IBM corporate headquarters to discuss IBM's opportunities, challenges, and problems and to solicit input from the retirees regarding these topics. I enjoyed these sessions not only because IBM valued the many years of experience we retirees brought to the meetings but also because these meetings kept us updated in regard to IBM's latest products and business strategies. These meetings continued into John Opal's term as CEO. When John Akers succeeded Opal, he reduced the number of meetings to one a year and eventually terminated them altogether.

Following my retirement from IBM, several Japanese companies wanted to retain me as a consultant. All except Sony were competitive with IBM, so I rejected their offers and accepted Sony's offer of a five-year retainer. In this capacity, I assisted Morita in resolving several technology transfer matters and the particularly sensitive Motorola license termination issue described above. A man of great wealth, Morita asked me to consult with him regarding opportunities for expanding his personal holdings in the United States, particularly in Florida. He also sought my assistance in licensing several patents issued to him in areas outside the interest of the Sony Corporation of America. More than anything else, Morita used me as an advisor on various matters in which he sought an American's point of view.

My ECD Connection and My Consultancy to Others

Stanford Ovshinsky, president of Energy Conversion Devices, Inc. (ECD), offered me a consultancy and a directorship. I had previously met and dealt with Ovshinsky when I was active in IBM and knew him in his capacity as a prolific inventor, as a leader in the synthesis of new materials, and as the developer of advanced production techniques. Intrigued by the Ovshinsky inventions in photovoltage technology, optical memory, and battery technology, I accepted the consultancy. However, I declined the ECD board directorship, citing conflict with my Motorola directorship. After I retired from the Motorola board in 1984, I was free to accept a place on the ECD board. After four years of air travel from West Palm Beach, Florida, to Detroit for monthly board meetings, I reluctantly decided to retire from the ECD board and focus on ECD consulting. My relationship as a consultant with ECD has continued to the present.

My consultancy to the Ricoh Corporation of Japan on intellectual property matters and technology licensing matters was the most extensive, lasting eight years. I assisted M. Tagami, a clever man who had a Japanese law degree and who spoke fluent English. Tagami placed a higher value on my credibility than my logic when dealing with difficult negotiations. He placed too high a value on my broad acquaintanceship within industry in contrast to what I felt was a proven capability on my part as a negotiator. This created tension and usually resulted in my having to prove to him that negotiation in the United States had to be done the American way to be successful, not the Japanese way. Influence seldom had any effect in resolving intellectual property matters. For reasons I never understood, Tagami seldom gave me all the facts when patent infringement was the issue. He sought my opinion and employed me to set up the negotiation; however, with only one exception, he never relinquished his role as lead negotiator. The single exception was a prolonged cross-license negotiation between Ricoh and Motorola in which Motorola alleged that a subcontractor had developed a certain applied specific integrated circuit (ASIC) design using misappropriated Motorola know-how. Ricoh was producing this ASIC for Nintendo in huge quantities and needed the Motorola license to retain its customer. Tagami proceeded with a general cross-license with Motorola that excluded the ASIC. In desperation, he turned over to me the problem of obtaining a license to the excluded technology. It took more than a year to resolve the issue at a cost of $1.4 million, less than Ricoh had anticipated. Notwithstanding this successful negotiation, Tagami never allowed me to assume a concluding role in any of the negotiations in which I assisted. I believe he was fearful of "losing face" with his superiors. My problem and my consultancy were terminated when Ricoh retired Tagami.

Of shorter duration, I served Illinois Tool Works, Franklin GNO, NCR, Vendo Corporation, DASI, Inc., Vari-Lite Corporation, and Katsuragawa Electric Company in Japan, among others. During a 15-year postretirement time span, to facilitate my consulting efforts under a name other than my own, I set up a consulting firm called Intercal, Inc., a contraction of International Contracts and Licensing Consultants, specializing in intellectual property resource management. The challenges of my consulting activity were more intellectually stimulating than they were financially rewarding. I found that for the most part, clients disliked compensating consultants even more than they did attorneys. They were reluctant to pay additional compensation even when the results merited it. I am glad to say that my career as a consultant was accomplished without my having to relinquish too many rounds of golf.

Post-IBM Directorship/Trusteeship

My post-IBM career contained considerable board activity. I accepted election to a local bank board in 1984 when I was named director of the Harris Trust Company of Florida, a directorship I resigned in July 1996. Another directorship I held early in my post-IBM retirement was with Air Sunshine in Florida, prior to its merger with Air Florida. For more than 10 years, while with IBM, I served as a director of the Computer and Business Equipment Manufacturers Association and as chairman of the board for two years. Several years later, the Electronic Industries Association cited me for distinguished service to the electronics industry and awarded me an honorary life membership in the association. Outside the electronics field, I served on the Vendo Corporation board, including a term as interim chairman.

One of my most interesting affiliations began prior to my retirement and continued after I left IBM. As a trustee of the Charles E. Culpeper Foundation, I was privileged to serve under the leadership of Frank McNamara, Jr., whose father is mentioned above. Like his father, McNamara, Jr., is noted for his integrity and great insight that led the foundation to outstanding philanthropic heights. Also on its separate incorporation in the early 1960s, I served Fairfield University as a lay trustee, the first non-Jesuit to be appointed. I am proud to say that I continue as trustee emeritus of this exceptionally fine educational institution. In the mid-1970s, Irwin Tomash asked me to become one of the early trustees of the CBI and president and director of the Charles Babbage Foundation. In this capacity, I chaired the relocation committee that selected the University of Minnesota as the site for the institute.

Other than Motorola, my most active post-IBM directorship was as director of University Patents, Inc. (UPI) in Westport, Connecticut, a firm that managed patent properties for universities. At UPI, I became reassociated with Miles, now chairman and CEO of the company. Both at IBM and at UPI, Miles was one of the most astute and highly qualified executives I have ever known in the field of patent resource management and negotiation. Sid Alpert, president and former IBM patent attorney, served as Miles's alter ego. Together they have formed an outstanding team. This exciting and stimulating enterprise at UPI provided me with office space and secretarial assistance during my five-month annual stay at my Connecticut home, solving the logistics of working as a consultant out of a Florida home office in the winter months and from a Connecticut residence in the summer. I resigned my directorship and relinquished my office when Maxwell Enterprises bought the company. All my consulting and board activities were fruitful in that they provided me with intellectual stimulation, especially when my association was with companies whose activities were at the leading edge of high technology in their respective fields.

Today, at the age of 87, I have only one consultancy and two trusteeships, one emeritus. In 1965, my alma mater, the State University of Iowa, awarded me a Distinguished Alumnus Award. In 1974, I received an honorary doctor of laws degree from Fairfield University. As I wind down from a long and richly rewarded career, I discover that my highest priorities are time with my family and friends and two rounds of golf weekly at the Country Club of Florida, where my home overlooks the 14th hole.

Epilogue

During my business career and throughout my life, I have had the good fortune of associating with some wonderful people, many of whom I had the pleasure of hiring. Others, through God's will, happened to be in my path of life. I cannot recall anything that I achieved entirely by myself; there was always someone close by to encourage, assist, teach, or inspire me. Therefore, when it came time for IBM management to arrange and host my retirement dinner, I graciously declined, but not because I was ungrateful. It was customary for IBM management to arrange and host a dinner in honor of the retiree at which the CEO or a member of upper management would give praise to the retiree for his or her accomplishments and service. IBM management chose the guests as well. Therefore, I chose to host my own retirement dinner so that I could pay tribute not to myself but to the wonderful IBM employees who worked with and assisted me during the various stages of my IBM career.

In January 1973, my wife and I hosted a dinner in the Westchester Country Club ballroom. The only speech was my tribute to and expression of appreciation for my guests. I thanked my colleagues for enabling my career to be what it was and for allowing me to bask on occasion in the light of a success achieved primarily because of their loyalty, diligence, and talented performance. I told these associates and assistants that they were a blessing from heaven. I believe my retirement dinner was a success. Certainly, Jean and I thought so as we dined and danced with my former coworkers and associates.

Although he was not invited, since it was not my intent to include members of IBM top management, I must pay tribute to Watson, Jr., who, in recognizing the harsh treatment I had received from his father and from Kirk in 1946, saved my career in the company. Throughout most of my IBM employment, I reported either directly or indirectly to Watson, Jr. Because he was demanding and sometimes temperamental, working for him was not always easy. Yet, Watson, Jr., had another side that was fair and compassionate. Although I was seldom invited into the Watson social circle, I was an integral part of his inner management team. There I earned his trust and respect. Watson, Jr., will always live on in my fond memory.

Many people made my IBM career a possibility even before I passed through the doors of the company. My parents, particularly my mother, cared for me during my formative years. When I lost my mother, my grown sister, Elsie, continued that care as if I were her son. During my teenage summers, Weaver, head pro at the Burlington Golf Club, kept me well-employed and taught me self-discipline and responsibility. Clara, head cook at the club, made sure I was never hungry.

When I recall my years at the University of Iowa, I think of Rehder, manager of the Iowa Memorial Union's dining services, who was my first boss and whose trust in me increased along with my job responsibilities. As a result, my self-confidence grew, preparing me for even greater responsibilities. I also think of Philips— dean of the university's business college, my teacher, confidant, role model, and source of encouragement. From him, I learned to live a life of purpose and integrity.

My greatest tribute of all must go to my wife Jean, my soul mate and companion for the past 64 years. While I did my best not to bring the office home, there were times when I sought Jean's advice and counsel on matters regarding a troublesome personal relationship or a critical IBM career choice I was facing. Jean was always willing to listen and, invariably, provided me with an objective point of view that assisted me in making the best decision. My worldwide corporate responsibilities required extensive travel and lengthy absences from home. Jean was always tolerant of this as she took on the duties not only of homemaker and mother but also of the head of the household for extended periods of time without my being there to give her a breather. When we were required to host business functions, Jean always stood out as a beautiful and gracious lady.

Acknowledgment

I am particularly grateful to my daughter-in-law Susan-Marie Birkenstock for her patience and assistance during the 18 months I devoted to preparing for and writing this memoir. If she burned out while I fiddled, she never showed it.

References

[1] T.J. Watson, Jr., *Father, Son and Company*. New York: Bantam Books, 1990.

[2] A. Wang, *Lessons*. Menlo Park, Calif.: Addison Wesley, 1986.

[3] M. Mason, *American Multinationals and Japan— the Political Economy of Japanese Capital Controls, 1899–1980*. Cambridge, Mass.: Harvard Univ. Press, 1992.

[4] U.S. Patent Commission, *To Promote the Progress of Useful Arts*. Washington, D.C.: Government Printing Office, 17 Nov. 1966.

James W. Birkenstock's portrait was painted by his daughter Joyce Ann Birkenstock for her father's 85th birthday.

The author can be contacted at
42 Country Road
Village of Golf, FL 33436-5299, U.S.A.

The IBM 650 Magnetic Drum Calculator

The IBM 650 Magnetic Drum Calculator

GEORGE R. TRIMBLE

Editor's Note

As stated earlier, Kubie and Trimble were the first members of the Mathematics Planning Group of Applied Science in Endicott, New York, where the 650 was designed and manufactured. In preparation for this special issue, I wrote to Kubie, who referred me to his paper with Hamilton (preceding) and made the following statement:

The 650 used biquinary for its self-checking capability. Remember, machines at that time were still relatively

unreliable. The little initial software that existed was written by George Trimble and myself. The 650 was probably the last machine where it was feasible to write application software in machine language. Therefore, a great deal of support software was not required.

Trimble has kindly written for us a paper that describes not only the 650 as it was first built, but also the enhancements made to its design.

Introduction

The IBM 650 was a major contribution to the data processing industry in that it was the first computer for which the number of systems delivered was measured in thousands, not in dozens. It was not the first electronic computer, nor was it the largest or the fastest. Its impact went far beyond the 2200 systems eventually installed, however, in that it showed that the market for "reasonably" priced systems was far larger than most people had anticipated. Price was certainly a major factor in the popularity of the 650, but it was only one factor. Ease of use was also of considerable importance.

This paper examines the background of the development of the 650 in the perspective of the technology available at the time, and relative to competing developments within IBM. The rationale for the architecture of the IBM 650, and the reason for IBM selecting it as a product to market over competing architectures, is examined. Figure 1 is a picture of the basic 650.

Early Computers

The IBM 650 was developed during the embryonic stages of the computer industry. The first electronic computer, the ENIAC, was a decimal computer developed during the later part of World War II by the Moore School of Electrical Engineering for the Ballistic Research Laboratory at Aberdeen Proving Ground in Maryland (Burks and Burks 1981). It was placed in operation in 1946, and I used it for rocket trajectory calculations in 1949. Although the original machine was controlled by plugging wires into large fixed-plug panels, it was modified in 1947 to be controlled by 1200 ten-position rotary switches, following a suggestion made by Richard Clippinger (see N. Metropolis in the *Annals*, Vol. 7, No. 2, April 1985, p. 147). These

Author's Address: 4 Peak Lane, Princeton, NJ 08540.
Categories and Subject Descriptors: C.1.1 [**Processor Architectures**], Single Data Stream Architectures; K.2 [**History of Computing**]—*hardware, IBM 650, software. General Terms:* Design. *Additional Key Words and Phrases:* Woodenwheel.

Figure 1. Magnetic Drum Data-Processing Machine, Type 650.

switches had to be set up for every new application. Stored programming had not yet come into use.

The very early computers that employed stored programming utilized a variety of technologies for memory. They were all based on vacuum-tube logic and control circuits, but the memories consisted of mercury delay lines, as in the UNIVAC and EDVAC, or the Williams tube, a CRT with bits stored as charged spots on the surface of the tube. Memory capacities were on the order of 1000 words, but the words were fairly large, typically 36 to 40 bits. Magnetic drums came into play as secondary storage devices for some of these early machines. They were also the basis for the main memory of a couple of dozen early computers (Perlis 1954). The magnetic drum memories used as main memories had a capacity of 2000–5000 words.

Peripheral equipment for these computers was primitive. Input was usually through punched cards, read at speeds of up to 100 cards per minute, or in some cases punched paper tape read at 150 to a few hundred characters per second. Output was to punched cards at 30–100 cards per minute and paper tape at 75–150 characters per second. Line printers were also used, commonly tabulating machines adapted for use as output printers for the computers, ranging in print speed from 100–300 lines per minute. The need for better secondary storage soon resulted

in the development of magnetic tape drives that ran at roughly 12,000 characters per second.

Computers Based on Magnetic Drums

The IBM 650 was based on a magnetic drum. At that stage of the industry development, most magnetic drums rotated at about 3400 revolutions per minute, which meant about 17 milliseconds for a full rotation or 8.5 milliseconds, on the average, to be able to access a piece of information on the drum. Machines based on acoustic delay lines had a delay time of approximately 1 millisecond for a pulse to travel through a mercury tank in the form of a sound wave, thus giving an average access of about 0.5 millisecond. Williams-tube-based machines had access times on the order of 10–12 microseconds. The magnetic-drum-based machines, with an average latency on the order of 8.5–10 milliseconds, obviously had much lower performance levels than the other more technologically advanced systems. The magnetic drum machines, however, were significantly less expensive.

A technique used to improve performance was to put a second read-write head in a track on the drum. Information written by the first head could be read by the second head and then rewritten by the first head. The spacing of the heads was such that the distance

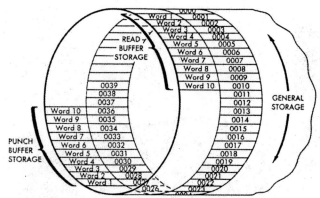

Figure 2. Input-output buffers, shown here to illustrate one application of revolvers.

between the two heads corresponded to 10 or perhaps 20 words of the 50–100 words around the circumference of the drum. Data stored in these tracks with two heads was then available to be reread after the drum rotated perhaps one-quarter to one-eighth of its full rotation. This effectively reduced the access time to those words to one-quarter or one-eighth the access time to words in other tracks on the drum.

Use of this technique was referred to as "revolvers" and effectively provided a form of "high-speed" storage for a few words of data that could be accessed more frequently than any of the other words on the drum. Figure 2 illustrates how revolvers functioned. A similar concept is used today in the form of high-speed cache memories between the main memory and the CPU. Some of the early drum computers provided two or more tracks with multiple heads so that several blocks of words could be available from these revolvers.

Although revolvers did not increase the performance of the magnetic-drum-based computers to the point of competing with even acoustic delay-line machines, they did significantly increase the performance of the basic magnetic drum, as long as the programmer knew how to use them and employed the revolvers effectively. The program had to be analyzed to determine which items of data should be kept in revolvers on the basis of the frequency of reference to an item of data during the computations. As the solution to the problem progressed, data had to be moved from revolvers to main memory to make room for other data that became accessed more frequently.

One technique for moving data was to transfer a full block of data out of or into a revolver. Since the revolvers effectively operated in synchronism with other groups of words on the drum that were recorded in the same relative angular position, the programmer had to be aware of this synchronism in assigning locations and performing block transfers. For exam-

ple, if the drum had 50 words written around its circumference, and a revolver consisted of 10 words, these 10 words corresponded to words 0 through 9, respectively, then 10 through 19, respectively, then 20 through 29, respectively, and so forth. Individual words could obviously be moved from a revolver memory location to any other memory location by going through the main arithmetic register.

Programming to make use of words in revolvers was a tedious, time-consuming, error-prone task. The programmer had to lay out the data, and in some cases instructions, carefully in order to utilize the revolvers effectively. This tended to increase the number of bugs and the amount of time it took to get a program working.

The IBM 650 Approach

Two techniques were employed to improve the performance of the 650: using a higher-speed drum and having two addresses in each instruction (see Hamilton and Kubie in this issue; also Hughes 1954).

High-Speed Drum

One of the early designs of the 650 in the IBM laboratories was based on a 4000-word magnetic drum with a 17-millisecond rotational time and with revolvers. As discussed by Hurd (1980) and Glaser in this issue, there was a question of patent violation if revolvers were used. It was therefore important to develop an architecture based on a magnetic drum that would avoid the use of revolvers (and thus patent problems) while still maintaining a high level of performance.

The solution arrived at was a thoroughly simple and straightforward one. It involved the use of a smaller-diameter drum rotating at a much higher speed than was the standard for the industry. At 12,500 revolutions per minute, the rotation time was 4.8 milliseconds providing an average latency of 2.4 milliseconds, as compared to the 8.5 milliseconds typical for industry at the time. This direct approach to increasing the speed resulted in a decrease in the average rotation latency by a factor of nearly 3.5. Figure 3 illustrates the magnetic drum developed for the 650.

The increase in performance of the drum was not without cost. The higher rotational speed required a smaller-diameter drum. The smaller-diameter drum meant that the number of bits recorded in one track around the circumference was reduced in order to keep the bit density below the maximum achievable with the technology in 1952. A direct result was the reduction in storage capacity from 4000 words to 2000 words. Although this was a rather high price to pay, it was considered justifiable in view of the significant increase in performance.

Two-Address Instructions

Revolvers had a certain latency associated with them. Typical revolvers spaced the heads approximately one-quarter of a revolution apart, resulting in an average access time of one-eighth of a revolution or approximately 2 milliseconds for words in revolver memory, at 17 milliseconds total rotational time, compared to the 2.4 millisecond average access for the 650.

In order to simplify block transfers between revolvers and the main memory, consecutive addresses were normally assigned to consecutive word locations on the drum. With instructions being executed from consecutive memory locations, until a branch or transfer of control took place, each instruction required at least a full drum revolution to execute. Instructions executed from the revolvers required a quarter of a revolution to execute. Data references would occasionally add an additional revolution (or eighth of a revolution if the data were in a revolver) to the instruction execution time.

Although the raw decrease in rotational latency was significant, it was still not sufficient to provide the overall increase in performance required to compete with revolver-based computers. The approach taken with the 650 was to use a two-address format for instructions. One address was used to reference data. The second address was used to access the next instruction. Thus the 650 was continually operating in a state of transfer of control to another instruction. This second address meant that the programmer could place instructions, as well as data, at the optimal location on the drum to reduce the average latency time to effectively zero. A paper by Trimble and Kubie (1954) describes the optimum programming techniques that were developed for the 650.

Reducing the latency to zero was not possible for every instruction. Improvements in efficiency on the order of 10–50 percent were quite achievable, however. In limited but critical applications such as floating-point subroutines, the improvement could result in a factor of between two and three times the speed of a nonoptimally programmed routine. In any case, the combination of the high-speed drum with application of optimum programming techniques resulted in performance that was superior to other magnetic-drum-based computers employing revolvers.

Ease of Programming—A Prime Goal

Elimination of revolvers avoided the necessity of having block transfers and the associated allocation of

Figure 3. Magnetic drum assembly is on the lower left.

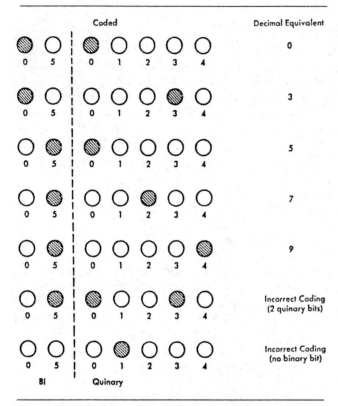

Coded	Decimal Equivalent

Figure 4. Biquinary code representation.

The particular representation used by the 650 was biquinary. This representation used seven bits, two of which represented 0 or 5, respectively, while the remaining five represented 0, 1, 2, 3, or 4. Only one of the two binary bits was on, and only one of the five quinary bits was on to represent a decimal digit. Figure 4 illustrates the biquinary representation.

Debugging in the days of the 650 was done largely at the computer console. The ability to display the contents of the various arithmetic registers, the instruction counter, and the instruction register were standard on most computers. The biquinary representation of numbers in the 650 facilitated the display because it was easy to interpret the lights. The 650 had one additional capability that was very useful for debugging: the address-stop feature. It was the hardware equivalent of the breakpoint capability commonly implemented through software in modern systems. By setting a selected address into switches on the console and setting the controls to address stop, the program would stop execution when that address was encountered. Operators could step through the program rapidly, stopping at selected points, instead of cycling a single instruction at a time. Figure 7 of the Hamilton-Kubie paper in this issue shows the console of the 650 and the control switch.

System Software

In the early 1950s, system software was virtually nonexistent. Programming originally was done in absolute, using decimal instructions on the 650 and other decimal machines, and in binary (or octal) on the binary computers. Early assemblers used mnemonics for the operation codes but relative addresses. Selected addresses would be given a symbolic name and then other locations determined by specifying an increment from that symbolic location. This was quickly superseded by one-for-one symbolic assemblers as the amount of main memory available on computers became large enough to permit reasonably large assembly tables.

Because of the nature of the two-address instruction in the 650, particularly if the program was to be optimized, most of the early applications for the 650 were written in absolute. Within two years of the introduction of the 650, automatic optimization programs became available. One of the first of these was SOAP (Symbolic Optimizing Assembly Program) (see Gordon 1956; Poley and Mitchell 1955). It performed optimization on each instruction, but as the program got larger and the instruction and data locations were fixed, later portions of the program could not be optimized effectively. A total reoptimization program

relative word locations in order to utilize the revolvers effectively. This alone made a significant contribution to the ease with which programs could be developed for the 650.

On the other hand, optimum programming introduced a degree of complexity that reduced the ease of programming. Optimum programming was not a requirement, however. Programs could be written with sequential assignment of addresses, the penalty being simply reduced performance over what could be achieved if optimum programming were used. Consequently, the major impact on ease of use was the requirement for having to specify an additional address in every instruction.

Several other factors contributed to the objective of having ease of use as a primary design criterion. One of these was that the number system used was decimal. The ENIAC was a decimal machine; most of the machines that immediately followed it were binary. Decimal number representation became popular again with the 650 and a few other contemporary magnetic-drum-based computers. Use of decimal arithmetic internally eliminated the need for binary-to-decimal and decimal-to-binary conversions for input/output. It also simplified displays on the console.

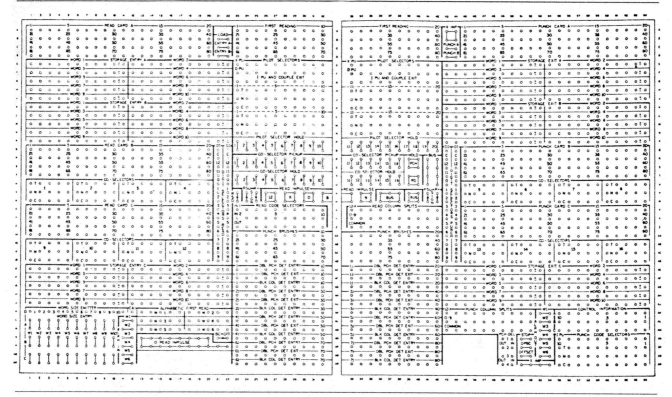

Figure 5. Schematic of control panel (IBM's term for *plugboard*).

that could readjust locations to improve the program performance as a whole was not practical. SOAP was quite effective for small programs, particularly for subroutines called by a main program.

Certain frequently used programs could not be effectively optimized by SOAP, even though they were small. Floating-decimal arithmetic subroutines, complex arithmetic subroutines, square root, trigonometric functions, and other such scientific subroutines needed to be highly optimized. A library of such routines was developed and made available as part of the software support for the 650. They were published in IBM Technical Newsletters (Nos. 7 through 13) and were among the first software support provided by IBM (see the contents of Nos. 8 and 9 in this section and No. 11 at the end of the issue).

A Choice: Ease of Use versus Sophisticated Power

Programming computers has always been an arduous task. It has evolved from wiring plugboards, coding in absolute machine language, and simple symbolic assemblers to sophisticated operating systems, high-level languages, and database management systems. Extensive libraries of applications programs and sub-

routines are tools that have taken many years to develop.

Early Plugboard Control

Electromechanical tabulating machines had been used for many years to perform accounting functions. These machines were controlled primarily by removable plugboards in which electric pulses were directed to a series of plug positions in sequential order and directed by wires placed in the plugboard to control electromechanical devices such as relays, counters, accumulators, and selectors. The "programmer" wired the plugboards to perform the specific sequence of arithmetic functions desired. Some of the earliest electronic computers were based on the same principle.

The IBM 604 had 60 program steps that, through plugboard wiring, could be directed to various electronic registers. The IBM Card Programmed Calculators (CPC) (Sheldon and Tatum 1951) were based on such electronic calculators, as stated earlier. Even the ENIAC as it was originally constructed used plug-wire control before Clippinger suggested using rotary switches on the function panels as a means of control.

One advantage of the plug-wire control in the early development of computers was the possibility of customizing instructions to perform functions efficiently. This technique was, in fact, the basis for the CPC. In a way, it was a precursor of microprogrammed control, which is common today. Data directed to the read-punch unit of the 650 were controlled by a plugboard. Figure 5 illustrates a schematic of the control panel.

650 or Woodenwheel?

Prior to announcement of the 650 by IBM, two products in development in the IBM laboratories were competing for the position of a small computer—that is, small compared to the 701 (see Hurd 1983) and 702, which were fairly large, expensive systems. The internal competitor to the 650 was a development termed the Woodenwheel, an acronym based on the names of the three engineers primarily responsible for its design—Bill Woodbury, Greg Toben, and Truman Wheelock (see Glaser in this section).

Although the Woodenwheel was architecturally comparable to the CPC, it used the much more advanced technology that became available in the five years following introduction of the CPC. Instead of 16 words of electromechanical storage (the CPC's "icebox") or half a dozen words of electronic storage as in the 604 and 605, the Woodenwheel had a couple of dozen words of high-speed electronic storage.

The primary arithmetic processing in the Woodenwheel was performed under control of a plugboard with features much more sophisticated and advanced than were available on the 604 and 605 electronic calculators. The multitude of high-speed registers, large number of program steps, and sophisticated decision-making possibilities made it a potentially very powerful computer once the plugboard had been properly designed and wired. Main memory was still a drum with block transfers between the drum and the high-speed registers.

The Woodenwheel was used in two ways. The first was to have a standard, general-purpose plugboard that would implement the various commonly used functions anticipated in general-purpose applications. For scientific applications this would mean such things as floating-point routines and trigonometric functions. It could then be driven by an interpretive instruction set with a program that could be executed from the high-speed registers using pseudo-instructions to activate the functions wired into the general-purpose board. This approach was certainly feasible, and it would get the problem solved, but it would not take advantage of the power available within the Woodenwheel architecture.

As an alternative, the programmer could design a board with functions specifically oriented toward the type of application being implemented. This obviously would require the design and testing of a plugboard for each of several general classes of applications. In either case, the Woodenwheel was more difficult to program than the 650. The decision of which machine to produce was then reduced to the question of which was more important from the user viewpoint—ease of use or sophisticated power.

To resolve this problem and obtain some kind of quantitative basis for making a decision, several applications were programmed for both computers. They ranged from matrix inversion and solution of differential equations in the scientific area to a simple payroll program in the commercial area. I programmed at least two applications for both computers; one was a matrix conversion, and the other was solution of a set of differential equations.

The programs for the 650 were relatively easy to develop. With the directly addressable memory, I could take a straightforward approach to the solution of both programs, with the result that in less than half a day, each of these programs was written (but not yet debugged).

Programming the problems for the Woodenwheel was quite another matter. First, it was necessary to develop a plugboard that would implement the types of functions required in inverting a matrix or in solving differential equations. Determination of what functions to put on the plugboard depended on the arrangement of data in memory and how it was to be accessed. Then, having determined those functions, I had to design the plugboard itself. Finally, having designed a plugboard (but not actually wired and debugged it), came the problem of writing the actual program. All in all, it took nearly two days to design the board and write the program for each of these applications for the Woodenwheel. Thus, setting up the program for the Woodenwheel took about four times as long as it did for the 650. The same order of magnitude applied to the other applications developed for both machines by other programmers. About half the time was spent designing the plugboard and the other half writing the program using the plugboard. Even writing the program took twice as long on the Woodenwheel, assuming that a plugboard was available that could be used.

The positive side of the Woodenwheel approach was speed of execution once the plugboard was designed and the programs were written. Estimated times of execution on the Woodenwheel were 50–100 percent faster than on the 650.

The choice then became one of a machine in which the programs could be developed from two to four times as fast versus a machine that would execute up to 100 percent faster. Although computer time was quite expensive in the early 1950s, and much emphasis was placed on efficiency of the programs, the time and cost to develop the programs were not insignificant. Programmers were also much more scarce than they are now. The choice was made to produce the 650 instead of the Woodenwheel. The validity of that choice was borne out by the tremendous popularity of the 650.

Major Expansion of the 650

Following the success of the 650, a program was undertaken to add features to it to improve its performance even further. These additional capabilities included a method for handling alphabetic information, indexing accumulators, high-speed memory, magnetic tape, a line printer, random-access disk storage, and floating-point arithmetic.

Alphabetic Information

The basic 650 was a strictly decimal machine. There was no way to handle alphabetic information directly, although with cleverness, it was possible to encode the alphabetic information read from a card and pass it through as decimal information, then regenerate it in the alphabetic form at the punched-card output. Plug-panel wiring on card reader and card punch made it possible, but it was very limited and difficult to do. Hardware options were developed to enable alphabetic information to be represented internally as two decimal digits. A second device permitted special characters to be handled as well. Thus a single 650 word could hold five alphabetic or special characters. Use of this encoding technique in the hardware eliminated the need for complex plugboards and permitted alphabetic information to be passed through the computer. It was still very cumbersome and required skill and experience to manipulate alphabetic information.

Indexing Accumulators

Index registers became quite popular following the development of the "B-box" on the Manchester Mark I in England (Williams and Kilburn 1951). As typically implemented on computers in the early 1950s, they were used exclusively for modifying addresses.

The index registers developed for the 650 had more general utility. In addition to being used to modify the address of the instruction, the registers could be used as limited general-purpose intermediate storage registers for four-digit numbers. Although they could not be used as general-purpose accumulators, they provided high-speed temporary storage registers if they were not being used for address calculations. As such, the indexing accumulators on the 650 were precursors

of the very flexible index registers on the 7030 (Stretch) computers developed by IBM two or three years later (Buchholz 1962). They led to the general-purpose register architecture in common use in IBM equipment today.

High-Speed Memory

Although the use of the high-speed drum and the second address with optimum programming increased the speed of the 650 over other computers of its generation, a more direct approach was used as the technology of magnetic core memory made it possible to have small amounts of core memory. The high-speed core memory developed for the 650 consisted of 60 registers of 10 digits each. Access time to each word of memory was measured in microseconds and was much faster than accessing words in drum memory. Data could be block transferred between the drum memory and the magnetic core memory with no timing or synchronization restrictions on the magnetic core addresses as there are with revolvers. Not only could data be stored in high-speed memory; instructions could be stored there as well. More typically, however, instructions would be kept in drum memory because of the basic limitations on the number of cycles to execute an instruction. The high-speed memory meant that data could be placed in it and achieve close to perfect optimization.

Magnetic Tape

The magnetic tape option used 15,000-character-per-second magnetic tape drives. The high-speed core-memory device was used as a buffer between the drum memory and the magnetic tape. Alphabetic information on the tape was converted to two decimal digits when it was entered into the 650.

Line Printer

Initial input/output for the 650 was strictly punched cards. The addition of the 407 line printer enabled output to be printed as well as punched on cards. The line printer operated at 150 lines per minute. Since the basic 650 could only handle numeric information, the line-printer plug-panel control had to be used to generate any alphabetic column headings that were output.

RAMAC Disk Storage

Random-access disk storage devices (called RAMAC at IBM) for computers in the mid- and late 1950s were bulky and slow compared to those of today. The disk storage device attached to the 650 consisted of 50 disks, each 24 inches in diameter. The two sides of the disk provided 100 disk surfaces, or faces. Each face contained 100 tracks, thus giving 10,000 addressable tracks. Each track in turn contained 60 words, a word being 10 decimal digits and a numeric sign (the normal word in the 650). Note that the number of words in a track was the same as the number of words in the high-speed storage unit. In fact, the high-speed storage unit was used to transfer data to and from the disk unit.

The access arm to read or write data on the disk had two read-write heads, one for each of the two disk surfaces. In order to read or write, the access arm had to be positioned to a particular disk, and then to one particular track on the disk. Having been positioned, either the upper or the lower read-write head could be selected to read or write either the track on the upper surface or the track on the lower surface.

Seek time was a major factor in the operation of the disk. Disk-to-disk seek time ranged from 450 milliseconds to as much as 850 milliseconds. Track-to-track seek time on the same disk varied from 100 to 225 milliseconds. In order to minimize the effect of these long seek times, the RAMAC provided three read-write mechanisms. Obviously, only one could be physically reading from or writing to the high-speed storage unit at one time. Seeks could be performed in an overlap mode of operation, however, permitting processing to occur simultaneously with seeking or having two of the access mechanisms seeking while the third was performing a read or write operation.

Floating-Decimal Arithmetic

Floating-decimal arithmetic was introduced for the IBM 650 to eliminate the need for scaling numbers that varied over a wide range of values. This feature did not involve any change in the means of storing numbers in the 650, but instead in the interpretation of numbers. The same signed 10-decimal digit numbers were used. If a number was to be used to represent a floating-point number, the mantissa or magnitude of the number consisted of 8 decimal digits in which the decimal point was assumed to be just to the left of the leftmost digit. The remaining two digits were used to represent the exponent. Since the sign of the 650 word was already used to represent the sign of the number itself, the exponent could not have a sign directly. The range of these two digits was 00 to 99, and the value of 50 was taken to be an exponent of 0. Positive exponents were represented by values of 51 to 99 (99 representing the value 49), while negative exponents were represented by values less than 50 (49 being −1, etc., to 00 being −50).

One advantage of this representation was that floating-point numbers could be compared for being positive, negative, zero, or non-zero using the standard IBM 650 instructions. Note that a true zero in the floating-point notation would occur when all 10 decimal digits of the number were zero.

Beyond the 650—The 660/7070

Upon completion of the expansion program to increase the capabilities of the 650, a project was undertaken to develop a successor to the 650. This was the 660. The objective was to make use of the rapidly improving technology, particularly magnetic cores, to expand on the basic 650 design. The first obvious improvement was the use of magnetic core for a large main memory of 1000 or possibly 2000 words, still retaining the decimal architecture. With the use of magnetic cores, the need for optimum programming was no longer there, and consequently the use of a second address to indicate the location of the next instruction to be executed was not necessary. Many uses for these four additional digits were considered, including their use as increments and/or limit values in index register operations.

A second consideration was an expansion of the indexing accumulator concept to ten indexing accumulators instead of the three that were implemented on the 650. Expansion of the indexing accumulators to a full 10-digit word was also included. In fact, the 660 design did not include an accumulator register as the 650 had, but the indexing accumulators could be used for any of the arithmetic operations.

One aspect of the 650 was retained in the 660 design: the use of the magnetic drum as a buffer between the magnetic core memory and the slow peripheral devices, namely the card reader, card punch, and line printer.

Technology was advancing so rapidly that it became apparent that the use of the magnetic drum as a buffer was absolutely ludicrous. The 660 project was scrapped, and a new effort was undertaken to utilize fully not only magnetic core memory but also transistor technology, which had been experimental up to that point but had resulted in the 608 magnetic core transistor calculator, a successor to the 604 and 605 electronic calculators. The use of transistors in computers was shown in the TX-0 at MIT (Mitchell and Olsen 1956); the IBM 608 proved the feasibility of using transistors in commercially produced computers. Subsequently, the 7070 project was undertaken to replace the 660 and, more directly, the 650.

The 7070 design eliminated the drum completely with direct transfers of data between the magnetic core memory and the peripheral devices. The concept of general-purpose indexing accumulators that was begun in the 650 and continued in the 660 was an integral part of the 7070 design. The 7070 had 99 indexing accumulators that could be used as general-purpose registers.

The 7070 still retained the decimal arithmetic of the 650. It needed a two-decimal-digit representation of an alphabetic character, and manipulation of alphabetic information remained somewhat cumbersome.

Ease of use was still the key to the architecture of the 7070. In that sense, the 7070 was a continuation of the design philosophy of the 650 and was indebted to many of its concepts. The 7070, however, took better advantage of the advanced technology, not only in its main memory, but also in faster tape drives, random-access memory, a form of magnetic disks, and higher-speed line printers. These concepts were integrated with the character-manipulation capabilities of the 702, 705, 1401 line of commercial computers and the 701, 704, 709 concept of the binary scientific computers to be become the integrated family of System/360, which encompassed both application areas.

Summary

The IBM 650 Magnetic Drum Calculator has sometimes been referred to as the DC-3 of the computer industry. Although it was not as powerful arithmetically as some of its contemporary computers, or even some of its predecessors, it was the first computer where more than two or three dozen copies were sold. It gave a good indication of the untapped potential for computers in business, which many people did not fully believe possible. One of the reasons for its popularity was its ease of use. Programmers could learn how to write code and begin developing applications in a few hours. Debugging, although archaic by today's standards, was relatively easy on the 650 compared to debugging on some of the other equipment available at the time.

One of the major architectures that has become so popular in modern computers is the use of general-purpose arithmetic registers. The 650 was a significant step in this direction through its indexing accumulators, which developed into more sophisticated forms in the 7070 and came to full culmination in the System/360. As such, the 650 not only proved the potential in markets for computers, but also was a precursor of the modern multiregister architecture.

REFERENCES

Buchholz, W. (ed.). 1962. *Planning a Computer System, Project Stretch.* New York, McGraw-Hill.

Gordon, B. January 1956. An optimizing program for the IBM 650. *J. Association for Computing Machinery 3*, No. 1, pp. 3–5.

Hughes, E. S., Jr. February 1954. The IBM Magnetic Drum Calculator Type 650—Engineering and design considerations. *Proc. Western Joint Computer Conference*, pp. 140–154.

Metropolis, N. C. April 1985. Comment in C. C. Hurd, "A Note on Early Monte Carlo Computations and Scientific Meetings," *Annals of the History of Computing*, Vol. 7, No. 2, pp. 141–155.

Mitchell, J. L., and K. H. Olsen. December 1956. TX-0, A transistor computer. *Proc. Eastern Joint Computer Conference*, pp. 93–100.

Perlis, A. J. December 1954. Characteristics of currently available small digital computers. *Proc. Eastern Joint Computer Conference*, pp. 11–15.

Poley, S., and G. Mitchell. November 1955. Symbolic Optimum Assembly Programming (SOAP). *650 Programming Bulletin 1*, IBM Corporation, Form 22-6285-1, 4 pp.

Sheldon, J. W., and Liston Tatum. December 1951. IBM Card-Programmed Calculator. *Review of Electronic Digital Computers, Joint AIEE-IRE Computer Conference*, pp. 30–35.

Trimble, G. R., Jr., and E. C. Kubie. September 1954. Principles of optimum programming the IBM Type 650. IBM Applied Science Division Technical Newsletter No. 8, pp. 5–16.

Williams, F. C., and T. Kilburn. December 1951. The University of Manchester computing machine. *Review of Electronic Digital Computers, Joint AIEE-IRE Computer Conference*, pp. 57–61.

Getting Sabre off the Ground

Getting Sabre off the Ground

Robert V. Head

The Sabre system was developed by IBM in the 1960s to handle reservations and seat inventory for American Airlines. System specification requirements included an unprecedented number of transactions, such as handling 83,000 daily phone calls. This look back at the project's history highlights system problems and achievements.

There is, I have been told, a band of Mohawk Indians adept at high steel construction who travel from project to project throughout the land in pursuit of their high-risk occupation. They are seldom present for the dedication of the structures they erected. I felt some affinity for these migrants as I said goodbye to the remnants of my ERMA programming staff at the San Francisco airport in the fall of 1959 and boarded a flight for New York City to go to work for IBM on the Sabre system.

The original acronym for Sabre was Saber, which was a take-off on the SAGE system then being deployed by the Department of Defense. SAGE, which stood for Semi-Automatic Ground Environment, was a missile early-warning system considered state-of-the-art in its day. Saber was Semi-Automatic Business Environment Research, reflecting IBM's view that, by virtue of its advanced features, it would become the equivalent of SAGE in the business world. At some point in the project's early days, Saber was rechristened Sabre by IBM, which continued the use of uppercase letters, even though the acronym had been divested of meaning.

The history of airline reservation systems, from the earliest manual procedures to the deployment of today's finely tuned and sophisticated systems, has been chronicled in detail in the *Annals*.[1] My objective here is to provide a first-hand account of IBM's struggle to make the Sabre system operational at American Airlines.

Early systems efforts

Before Sabre's installation in the early 1960s, US commercial airlines, particularly American and arch rival United Air Lines, had a long history of computer usage. The principal contenders for this business were IBM and Univac. IBM had successful installations for revenue accounting—the processing of ticket vouchers using 7070 computers—but this was back-office batch processing and had nothing to do with real-time control of reservations and seat inventory, the applications that were the airlines' lifeblood.

At American, passenger reservations were handled by a procedure known as "book-to-board" in which the record of a reservation was maintained at the location that booked the sale if, as was usually the case, that location was also the passenger's boarding point. If the passenger booked a different boarding location, or there was a continuing or return reservation, a copy of the itinerary was forwarded to these other locations by teletype. Seat inventory was controlled by a "sell and report" procedure, whereby flights were listed on a control board at each reservations office. When space was sold, it was reported to a central location where, as the flight approached capacity, a "stop sale" message would be issued.

In an attempt to streamline these cumbersome labor-intensive operations, American had begun to make significant progress in automating seat inventory, so that seat sales for each flight and date could be updated at the time a sale was made. By 1952, a small Connecticut-based firm, Teleregister Corporation, had installed its pretentiously named Magnetronic Reservisor drum computer at American's New York reservations office for this purpose. "Agent sets" were installed to communicate with the computer, which activated display lamps on the set to confirm seat availability.

As passenger bookings continued to increase and computer technology continued to make significant advances, American began to work with IBM to ameliorate its systems workload. In particular, the airline was seeking a means of automating not just seat inventory but also passenger name records (PNRs), which were still being maintained manually, with information communicated to boarding locations by means of punched paper tape on American's extensive teletype network, which routed messages through a massive "torn tape" switching center located at LaGuardia Airport.

Among the more stringent design objectives that American set for Sabre was that information must be retrievable within three seconds 90 percent of the time. This reflected the airlines' fear of lost calls, which occurred when a customer's telephone inquiry could not be answered promptly. The number of end points that Sabre would serve was unprecedented for systems of that era, even among celebrated military systems like SAGE. Sabre would have to be installed at more than 100 locations, without disrupting normal business operations, for use by some 1,100 sales agents. The system would have to support 83,000 daily phone calls and maintain 40,000 passenger reservations. And it would have to generate and receive teletype messages to and from other airlines.

The Smith story

Except for revenue accounting and other batch processing applications, IBM had made little headway in the airline business until the advent of Sabre, which was intended to maintain seat inventory in real time, as well as to automate the larger, more complex task of maintaining passenger records. PNRs could contain an enormous amount of data on each passenger, besides just passenger name and flights booked. Records included contact information such as phone numbers, special meal preferences, whether the passenger had yet been ticketed, wheelchair assistance required, and so on.

According to legend, the problem of automating PNRs was discussed on an American flight in late 1953, when R. Blair Smith, a senior IBM sales executive, found himself seated next to C.R. Smith, American's founder and chairman. As the story (possibly apocryphal) goes, Blair Smith, a soft-spoken but ambitious Mississippian who had made a name for himself in Los Angeles selling computers to aerospace firms, convinced C.R. Smith, a taciturn Texan, that an all-encompassing real-time airline reservation system was indeed feasible. In 1954, American and IBM entered into an agreement covering research of airline reservation systems problems.

From its inception, Sabre was a high-risk undertaking. American, striving to be first to be fully automated and thus free of cumbersome manual procedures, sought reassurance by hiring Arthur D. Little in the person of Martin Ernst to look into Sabre's feasibility. IBM desired an entree into the airline business that would make it competitive with rival Univac. For Blair Smith, success in the airline marketplace could mean ascension into the highest ranks of the IBM executive hierarchy.

IBMer Bill Elmore had programmed a PNR demonstration on an IBM 650, which at 25,000 instructions gave an impressive indication of how powerful Sabre would ultimately be. Unfortunately, there was a bug in the program that caused the 650's drum memory to zero itself out unexpectedly, a possibility viewed with great apprehension by Blair Smith and his marketing staff, which included assistant Bev Brown and account representatives Joe Nemesi (American), Bill Hilton (Pan American World Airways), and Cecil Webb (Delta Airlines).

A flawed strategy

From the beginning, IBM's marketing strategy was flawed. Proposals to American, Pan Am, and Delta focused exclusively on equipment costs with no recognition of the enormous hidden costs in programming each device. Application programming had to be done in assembly language, as higher-level business languages like Cobol were intrinsically unsuited to real-time processing using mass random access storage. Unfortunately, the computers proposed—for American, the IBM 7090; Pan Am, IBM 7080; and Delta, IBM 7070—were strikingly incompatible. For example, the 7090, viewed as a "scientific" processor, was a 36-bit-word machine, while the 7080, IBM's "business" machine, was a variable-length-character device. All were dual processor configurations, with one computer handling the real-time workload and the other serving as backup while processing offline maintenance tasks.

In retrospect, it seems obvious that the best solution would have been to standardize on the more expensive 7090 so that application development costs could have been spread among the three users. In that era, however, we must recall that IBM was in the hardware marketing business only, with application development costs viewed as the customer's responsibility. IBM, of course, provided "system software," such as the then-emerging operating systems, and stood ready to assist its customers in getting their applications operational.

It became increasingly clear that the traditional IBM business model, whereby IBM sold (or leased) the hardware and the customer did the needed application programming with "assistance" from IBM, would not see Sabre through to completion. It became evident that American, for its part, would have to hire a qualified programming manager and augment its programming staff with additional outside hires. And IBM, if it were to assure project success, would have to apply an unprecedented level of effort to support program development.

Thus, even though it had essentially sold hardware to the customer, IBM would have to foot the bill for a large number of onsite programmers. And American—besides expanding its Sabre technical staff—would have to pay for any additional equipment needed as the project proceeded.

Along Fifth Avenue

I joined the Sabre (then Saber) project in October 1959 in New York City, leaving General Electric's Bank of America ERMA project, which was by then beginning to wind down. IBM's Sabre organization was headed by Blair Smith in White Plains, with engineering under Pat Beeby in Poughkeepsie. The group that I joined consisted initially of Bill Elmore, a former divinity student; Dick Casey, who had studied for the priesthood; and Al Scaia, whose novitiate had been with IBM. Our nominal supervisor was John Siegfried, who came out of Cuthbert Hurd's elite "applied science" cadre. We were housed on the 10th floor of a decrepit building at 724 Fifth Avenue, while space more suitable for IBM occupancy was being readied in the new Corning Glass building nearby. Also at 724 Fifth Avenue was American account representative Joe Nemesi (who liked to introduce himself as "Nemesis without the s") and Sandy Olsen, our young secretary. IBM world headquarters was a couple of blocks away, at 57th and Madison, and we often had lunch there in the company cafeteria.

Making the transition from GE to IBM was definitely a culture shock for me. At GE, the managerial hierarchy was carefully structured, and my position as a unit manager carried with it clearly defined perks and responsibilities. GE was a company whose top management was traditionally drawn from either engineering or finance, and this top-down influence and philosophy permeated the organization. At IBM, make no mistake, the salesman was king. (Sales types were wont to tag themselves with the archaic term, "peddler," probably in emulation of the early career of founder Tom Watson Sr.)

On a project like Sabre, which had a high advanced-technology content, the relationship between sales and technical people was uneasy and ambiguous. Sabre was not part of IBM's massive Data Processing (DP) Division, which encompassed most sales and marketing, but was instead a component of the Advanced Systems Development Division (ASDD). I was actually hired by John Siegfried, but first had to be interviewed by Blair Smith. There was little nuance when it came to the customer interface—the account representative had the final

say. In IBM parlance, whoever "held your card" (time card) controlled your future in terms of raises, promotions, and so on. Clearly, marketing held the cards at Sabre. Then there was the starchy business dress code. Even back at GE in California, I usually wore business suits, but at IBM I was viewed as mildly eccentric for occasionally wearing blue shirts and bow ties.

Before we left our temporary digs at 724 Fifth Avenue, there were a couple of memorable occurrences. Our offices there looked directly across Fifth Avenue toward the dressing room windows of Bonwit Teller, the exclusive women's store. Sometimes, in their zeal to try on new finery, Bonwit's customers neglected to lower the dressing room Venetian blinds. When this happened, those of us who had window offices would alert the rest of the staff, and we would all take a break to view and comment on the show under way across the street. Our secretary was convinced that she had been thrown into a den of perverts, and the situation wasn't helped when, at Christmas, we all chipped in to buy her a present—a gift certificate from Bonwit Teller!

Also during the 1959 holiday season, I experienced a fast-fading IBM tradition, a handshake from president Tom Watson Jr., who made the rounds of all headquarters offices to personally extend Christmas greetings. Our elevator operator (yes, we had one) was so impressed by this gesture that he pronounced Watson a "great man. People like him should be running this country." To which Bill Elmore sardonically rejoined, "They are!"

American gets organized

At American, the moving force behind Sabre had long been nice-guy and long-range thinker Roger Burkhardt, but after the contract was signed, managerial responsibility was given to assistant vice president Wilfred (Fred) Plugge—also a nice guy but with a bit of an edge—from the airline's financial side. Burkhardt stayed with the project as director of technical reservation systems and headed up a group writing functional requirements. Later, after strong urging by myself, Elmore, and Siegfried to hire a senior computer professional, American brought in mathematician Mal Perry, who in turn recruited four subordinates: Marvin Rothstein, Dave Kohler, Jonathan Lu, and Dave Sutton. In early 1960, all the IBM people moved over to American Airlines headquarters at 99 Park Avenue (though we occasionally used our IBM offices at Corning Glass).

Plugge's appointment came as a surprise to IBM and certainly must have been a disappointment to Sabre godfather Burkhardt. After Plugge's promotion was announced, another mid-level executive, named Prigge, left American to join National Airlines. The insider's joke at the time was that American was no longer big enough for a Prigge and a Plugge.

As the project got under way in earnest at 99 Park, IBM began adding programmers, including two that I recommended: Bob Sobecki, whom I had known both at Univac and GE, and Ed Liljegren, a Bank of America programmer who had worked under me on the ERMA system. The combined IBM–American staff was organized into four units encompassing the programming workload, each supervised by an American Airlines person. Elmore and I each had cognizance over two of the four groups. The first task was to write programming specifications covering such subapplications as display record, sell space, and end transaction. Elmore and I had the task of reviewing these specifications to make sure that nothing was overlooked and that they tied together properly.

Mal Perry was a talented programmer, but often seemed uncomfortable in his managerial role. Sometimes he would sequester himself in his office to work on some interesting programming problem while the rest of us waited for application specifications to be approved and finalized.

Structuring the software

Elmore undertook defining the basic random access file structure, which was an offshoot of his earlier 650 experience. Passenger records were to be stored and retrieved from disk storage using a gross and a fine index, the gross index containing pointers to all American flight numbers by date, and the fine index referring to individual passengers booked on each flight. Thus, it would take at least three file events to retrieve a passenger's record—possibly more in the case of a complex itinerary. Elmore and others had done extensive hand calculations and, as I recall, at least some primitive computer simulations, to determine the throughput capacity required to retrieve and process these records, based on American's statistics on how far in advance flights were booked. Worst-case situations had to be taken into account, such as heavy seasonal travel.

All file referencing and application program processing was to run under an airline control program (ACP), which was being written by a group in Poughkeepsie under the supervision of Jim Kessler; this group was part of the ASDD engineering department. Coordination with these programmers required me to take frequent train trips from New York to Poughkeepsie, the engineers seemingly reluctant to visit the customer premises.

The application programs themselves were to be "re-entrant," meaning that each routine would have to clean up its processing work even though the passenger booking was not yet complete. Under this multiprogramming approach, several reservation requests could be processed simultaneously, sharing such common tasks as checking availability, entering passenger data, or ordering special meals. Individual PNR data was maintained in an "agent assembly area," and only upon activation of the end transaction program would all the data for a particular PNR be filed away permanently.

As time passed, and we worked to give specificity to the schedule and the programming workload, it became evident to the IBMers responsible for program specification, such as myself, Elmore, and Siegfried, that the programming task was far more complex and sizable than the sales types and engineers realized. Our initial estimate was 100,000 instructions, exclusive of the ACP and offline batch processing.

Sluggish performance

An example of the ambiguity between IBM as system (read: hardware) supplier and American as customer arose when IBM's analysis revealed the need for additional equipment to handle the mainframe and disk file throughput requirements. First, the 7090s had to be augmented with additional core memory, which the engineers in Poughkeepsie grudgingly agreed to provide. More significantly, it became necessary to supplement the system's disk memory with a high-speed, high-capacity drum. This device, which we called the Kingston drum, had been developed by IBM's Federal Systems Division in Kingston, New York, for use on the real-time 7090s used to support NASA's Project Mercury (see Figure 1). Although it was agreed within IBM to attach the Kingston drum to American's 7090s, those of us onsite with American were forbidden for months by the marketers to reveal this extra cost item to the customer. Consequently, programming and file specifications continued to be written without reference to the relocation of frequently used files from disk to drum that would ultimately have to take place. This was an inexcusable deception.

A key to many of the chronic system throughput problems, which required continuing hardware augmentation, lay in the number of file references, or what we called file events, needed to complete a transaction. The

Figure 1. The Kingston drum. (Reprinted by permission from IBM Corporation, *General Information Manual, 9090 Airlines Reservation System,* Poughkeepsie, N.Y., © 1961 IBM.)

Figure 2. Terminal interchange communications processor. (Reprinted by permission from IBM Corporation, *General Information Manual, 9090 Airlines Reservation System,* Poughkeepsie, N.Y., © 1961 IBM.)

Figure 3. Agent's set. The unit above the typewriter is the air information device, with cards used to determine flight availability. (Reprinted by permission from IBM Corporation, *General Information Manual, 9090 Airlines Reservation System,* Poughkeepsie, N.Y., © 1961 IBM.)

end transaction program, which took place once a passenger was booked and his or her itinerary entered, required a massive cleanup of the agent assembly area.

Cecil Webb tried to explain away the sluggish system performance by asserting that agents, once online, had begun to use Sabre in unanticipated ways—for example, retrieving passenger records just to make sure that everything was in order—but this was a smokescreen intended to excuse the system's poor performance.

When engineering changes like those just described were required for an IBM customer, the salesman on the account would have to submit an RPQ (request for price quotation) to determine the additional cost to the customer for his system. One of our staff once estimated that when Sabre was finally configured, it was 90 percent RPQed.

Hardware reengineering was not confined to the mainframe computers. The communications concentrators used in the system were actually reworked IBM 1401s, the company's workhorse data processing product (see Figure 2). This small computer seemed ill-suited to the terminal control and message forwarding task, but was probably the best device readily available that could handle the more than 100 locations and 1,000 agent sets communicating with Briarcliff Manor over 2,400-bps leased lines. The system's primitive nature was also epitomized by the agent sets themselves, which embodied the recently announced IBM Selectric typewriter. No CRT or other visual display was configured for the system (see Figure 3).

None of this constrained IBM from hyping Sabre in advertisements in national publications. For example, in May 1961, a *Newsweek* ad asserted that "By adding the dimension of distance to data processing, IBM Tele-Processing systems are carving out new solutions urgently needed for the data handling problems of business, science and government."[2] But as one observer later put it in a personal conversation with me, IBM had cobbled together an "adequate but not elegant" hardware solution. And IBM, with American's tacit acceptance, had seriously underestimated the size and duration of the programming workload.

This, of course, did not deter outsiders from euphorically describing what Sabre would provide once it became operational. A 1961 "case study" published by the American Management Association lauded the system as

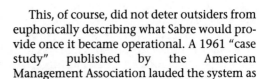

a major step in the evolutionary process at American Airlines which has kept pace with advances in technology and American's information requirements. American's needs, in fact, have caused some marked technical advances.[3]

Also in 1961, IBM announced the 9000 Series Airline Reservation Systems, which redesignated the 7090 computers as part of a 9090 system that "assures that queries and entries from any point in the system, however remote, will receive a response from the data processing center within seconds."[4]

On to Eastern

Because of my misgivings about project direction, as well as some personal considerations, I asked Blair Smith for a transfer off the project, with the result that in February 1961 I was assigned to the IBM branch office in Miami to assist Eastern Air Lines (EAL) account manager Bob Hillstrom in trying to sell a Sabre-like system to EAL. Hillstrom was a veteran of the airline marketing wars in Washington, D.C., where he had gone head to head with Univac star salesman Lee Johnson in selling to Capital Airlines and other accounts. I was enthusiastic about this relocation from ASDD to the Data Processing Division, as it carried with it the newly created title of senior systems engineer, one of only 12 in the company.

Unfortunately, my tenure at Eastern was sporadic, as I was constantly being called back to New York to help shore up the American Airlines programming effort. For several months, I was a weekly commuter between Miami and New York, and had little time to devote to EAL and my staff of three IBM systems engineers. In Miami, I parked my Morgan roadster in the Eastern employee lot, and every once in a while some of my EAL friends would get together and carry this lightweight vehicle to a different section of the parking lot while I was gone.

In August 1961, I was requested by the increasingly nervous IBM managers in New York to undertake a review of the Sabre programming specifications, which were then finally nearing completion. Presumably, the idea was that my divorce from the day-to-day American effort would make me an objective analyst. As Elmore wrote me, in transmitting the massive volumes of program documentation, "As far as things you see amiss are concerned, do whatever seems best about passing the information on to us here. Most any written notation—however informal and unliterary—should suffice."[5] I checked into a motel in Miami and spent several days poring over this mind-numbing documentation, looking in particular for flaws in how the program specifications interfaced. I found no glaring deficiencies, but this was not surprising because most problems of this kind would be more likely to surface during later testing of the programs.

At about this time, I was visited in Miami on an "off-the-record" basis by Fred Plugge, who was seeking insights into just how long the cost overruns and delays American was experiencing were likely to continue. I gave him my candid professional opinion, though I was careful not to reveal any IBM confidential information or say anything critical of IBM's account management. I am certain, though, that he left Miami with a more sobering perspective than the upbeat attitude of the sales types running things in New York.

Westchester County

In May 1961, Plugge announced the letting of a contract for the Sabre central site to be located in Briarcliff Manor, New York, with the building set for completion in October. The site was described as "A wooded sloping area overlooking the Hudson River. This location rests in a fine residential area, with the Sleepy Hollow Country Club directly across the street."[6] What Plugge failed to mention was that American had almost blown its application for site approval by the Briarcliff Manor town fathers when they learned that the facility being insinuated into their bucolic setting included noisy diesel generators for power backup, which blew massive smoke rings when powered up.

As time elapsed, both companies continued to hire—or contract for—additional programmers. An American Airlines organization chart issued on 15 March 1962 showed a programming staff reporting to Mal Perry that reminded me somewhat of recruits drawn into the foreign legion. Divided into four units (Agent Set Programs, Inventory Programs, Passenger Record Programs, and Systems Programs), the groups contained, in addition to American and IBM employees, programmers from the Service Bureau Corporation (an IBM subsidiary), CEIR, and Computer Applications Inc.[7]

In March 1962, I visited American's processing center in Briarcliff Manor and also a rented IBM facility in nearby Ossining, which housed the by-then sizable programming staff. I spent some time with Elmore in his office, which overlooked the exercise yard of Sing Sing Prison. As we looked out the window, he explained to me the difference between the prisoners and the Sabre programmers—the prisoners *knew* when they were going to get out!

After this trip, I sent an IBM-confidential memorandum to Hillstrom containing recommendations for strengthening IBM programming management. In particular, I urged the creation of a strong project manager position to be filled by a qualified systems professional, not a salesman. Incredibly, Blair Smith had placed Cecil Webb, his star salesman on the Delta account, in charge of the programming group in Ossining. This was the same Webb who, when he had the Martin Marietta account, referred to his distribution of Fortran manuals to the programmers there as "slopping the hogs." My memorandum to Hillstrom stated:

> My recent visit to the American Airlines center and my discussions of system checkout with the IBM personnel assigned lead me to conclude that drastic steps must be taken if the system is to become operational in the near future. Since the successful completion of this effort is vital to the whole future of Tele-Processing in IBM, I am asking you through this memorandum to convey [these] recommendations to our management.[8]

Goodbye to Sabre

In the summer of 1962, I was asked by IBM vice president John McPherson, who headed the IBM Systems Research Institute (SRI) in New York City, to help faculty member Al Pietrasanta organize a course in real-time systems for IBM field systems engineers. The course, which had many guest lecturers, was structured around Pietrasanta's experience with the Federal Systems Division on Project Mercury and my experience with Sabre. Among the guest lecturers were Saul Gass from Project Mercury and Project MAC director Fernando Corbató), who annoyed us by condescendingly enumerating what he deemed to be deficiencies in the Sabre design concept.

One of our students was a young systems engineer from IBM UK named Jim Martin who went on to become a prolific writer on real-time systems and a well-known lecturer and consultant after gaining the benefit of our presentation of hands-on experience. Over dinner at Jimmy Johnson's steak house one evening, he proposed a collaboration to author a book on real-time systems. I declined, as I had already begun work on my own book, *Real-Time Business Systems*.[9]

One frustrating aspect of the real-time systems course was the realization that Project Mercury and Sabre, both IBM 7090-based systems, had gone through the harrowing experiences of real-time system development without benefit of any interchange of ideas. No doubt the Mercury Monitor and the Sabre airline control program had many feature dissimilarities, but it would have been useful if those working on this software had known of each other's existence.

Upon conclusion of the real-time systems course, I was invited to join the SRI faculty to teach and conduct research full time. Thus ended my three years of active involvement with Sabre and its problems.

At about the same time as I phased out of Sabre, senior programmer Bob Sobecki left IBM to accept a job at GE in support of MIT's ambitious Project MAC (a double-barreled acronym for *machine-aided cognition* or *multi-access computers*). Shortly after starting his new job, he was invited by Blair Smith to have a drink after hours. Sobecki enthusiastically accepted, certain that this was the prelude to a lucrative offer to return to IBM. Instead, in a darkened lounge deep in the bowels of the Pan Am building, he was warned by Smith not to reveal any Sabre technical secrets under threat of dire legal consequences. In a state of panic, Bob called me at SRI, and I told him to behave professionally and simply forget the meeting.

An overdue—but operational—system

Sabre finally became fully operational in 1964. In an upbeat presentation, Roger Burkhardt cogently outlined the early history of American's efforts to automate its manual and teletype-based systems and correctly noted that these cumbersome systems were natural candidates to be replaced by a centralized, highly automated system like Sabre. He also acknowledged the schedule delays the project had experienced, though attributing many of them to the agent training workload rather than technical implementation problems.[10]

As Burkhardt had rightly envisioned, Sabre, when finally operational, helped to maintain American's industry leadership in information processing. The central processing system, relocated to Tulsa, Oklahoma, from Briarcliff Manor while morphing through numerous upgrades in equipment and software, continues to function to this day, with major applications like electronic ticketing added to the original capabilities.

Within IBM, the overdue and over-budget Sabre system seemed to have taken on some of the aura of the ill-fated Stretch supercomputer project, though not to the point of abandonment and public acknowledgment of problems that was the fate meted out to Stretch. And in truth, Sabre *did* launch IBM into the world of proliferating online real-time systems long before the advent of the personal computer. The airline control program, conceived in the 1960s, has survived conceptually unchanged into the 21st century.

Off we go

I left IBM in the fall of 1963 to become vice president for systems planning at Security First National Bank in Los Angeles and, as often happens, gradually lost touch with many of even my closest colleagues from both American and IBM. Most of those I worked with went on to other pursuits. Here is what happened to a few that I do remember.

Mal Perry died in 1968, just as Sabre was beginning to achieve its full potential. Roger Burkhardt left American, his employer since 1936, and joined R.H. Donnelley, publishers of the *Official Airline Guide*. Walt Pemberton took a job with Univac in Paris. Fred Plugge joined SRI International. Marvin Rothstein was hired by a bank in Hartford, Connecticut, and Dave Sutton helped start a new software company.

On the IBM side, Blair Smith was relegated to a long-range planning position in White Plains. Dick Casey went to work for Teleregister in Connecticut. Bob Sobecki returned to GE in Boston to work on Project MAC. Marge Saxon married and later moved to Bethesda, Maryland. Ed Liljegren took a job with a fledgling software company in New York City. Bob Hillstrom was transferred from Miami to Columbus, Ohio, after Eastern selected a Univac reservations system. Bill Elmore spent a brief period as IBM account manager at Pan Am, an unprecedented assignment for a nonsalesman and perhaps an indicator of how times were changing.

References and notes

1. D.G. Copeland, R.O. Mason, and J.L. McKenney, "Sabre: The Development of Information-Based Competence and Execution of Information-Based Competition," *IEEE Annals of the History of Computing,* vol. 17, no. 3, Fall 1995, pp. 30-57.
2. Inside front cover, *Newsweek,* 8 May 1961.
3. R.D. Norby, "The American Airllines Sabre System," in James D. Gallagher, *Management Information Systems and the Computer,* Am. Management Assoc. Research Study, 1961, pp. 150-176.
4. IBM General Information Manual, *9090 Airlines Reservation System,* 1961. The photos in this arti-

cle are from this IBM publication. Interestingly, the word "Sabre" does not appear in this manual.

5. W.B. Elmore to R.V. Head, letter, 11 Aug. 1961. In possession of the author.

6. W.R. Plugge, director, Technical Reservations Systems, to all Sabre personnel, memorandum on "Central Site," 2 May 1961. In possession of the author.

7. M.N. Perry, director of programming, to all Sabre personnel, memorandum on "Organization," 15 Mar. 1962. In possession of the author.

8. R.V. Head to R.D. Hillstrom, "American Airlines System Checkout," memorandum, 19 Mar. 1962. In possession of the author.

9. R.V. Head, *Real-Time Business Systems*, Holt, Rinehart and Winston, New York, 1964. This book embodies many of the lessons learned about new technology application management while working on the ERMA and Sabre systems.

10. R.F. Burkhardt, "The Sabre System," presentation, 1 Oct. 1964. In possession of the author.

 **Robert V. Head** has worked since 1985 as an editor and journalist for information technology publications. He is the author of seven books and more than 200 papers on information systems management. He was a member of the federal Senior Executive Service from 1971 to 1985. Before entering government service, he was manager of management information technology at Computer Sciences Corporation and vice president for systems planning at Security First National Bank. Previously, he held engineering positions with GE, Univac, and IBM, where he served as a senior systems engineer on the Sabre system. Head is a graduate of George Washington University where he was elected to Phi Beta Kappa. He is also a graduate of GE's Professional Business Management Course, the IBM Systems Research Institute, and the Federal Executive Institute.

Readers may contact Robert Head at 1000 Aquia Dr., Stafford, VA 22554, email rvhead@earthlink.net.

For further information on this or any other computing topic, please visit our Digital Library at http://computer.org/publications/dlib.

The History of Fortran I, II, and III

The History of Fortran I, II, and III

JOHN BACKUS

This article discusses attitudes about "automatic programming," the economics of programming, and existing programming systems, all in the early 1950s. It describes the formation of the Fortran group, its knowledge of existing systems, its plans for Fortran, and the development of the language in 1954. It describes the development of the optimizing compiler for Fortran I, of various language manuals, and of Fortran II and III. It concludes with remarks about later developments and the impact of Fortran and its successors on programming today.

[*Editor's note: This paper originally appeared in the* Annals of the History of Computing, *vol. 1, no. 1, July 1979. The sayings used as "pull quotes" were not in the original paper but were on cards that were distributed during the 1982 AFIPS National Computing Conference, which included a "Pioneer Day" honoring the Fortran pioneers. Readers interested in the topic of Fortran should consult the* Annals, *vol. 6, no. 1, which was a special issue devoted to the history of the language during its first 25 years.*]

Early Background and Environment
Attitudes About Automatic Programming in the 1950s

Before 1954, almost all programming was done in machine language or assembly language. Programmers rightly regarded their work as a complex, creative art that required human inventiveness to produce an efficient program. Much of their effort was devoted to overcoming the difficulties created by the computers of that era:

- the lack of index registers,
- the lack of built-in floating-point operations,
- restricted instruction sets (which might have AND but not OR, for example), and
- primitive input-output arrangements.

Given the nature of computers, the services that "automatic programming" performed for the programmer were concerned with overcoming the machine's shortcomings. Thus, the primary concern of some "automatic programming" systems was to allow the use of symbolic addresses and decimal numbers (e.g., the MIDAC Input Translation program[18]).

But most of the larger "automatic programming" systems (with the exception of J.H. Laning and N. Zierler's algebraic system[27] and the A-2 compiler[29,36]) simply provided a synthetic "computer" with an order code different from that of the real machine. This synthetic computer usually had floating-point instructions and index registers and had improved input-output commands; it was, therefore, much easier to program than its real counterpart.

The A-2 compiler also came to be a synthetic computer sometime after early 1954. But in early 1954, its input had a much cruder form; instead of "pseudoinstructions," its input was then a complex sequence of "compiling instructions" that could take a variety of forms, ranging from machine code itself to lengthy groups of words constituting rather clumsy calling sequences for the desired floating-point subroutine, to "abbreviated form" instructions that were converted by a "Translator" into ordinary "compiling instructions."[29]

After May 1954, the A-2 compiler acquired a "pseudocode" that was similar to the order codes for many floating-point interpretive systems that were already in operation in 1953, for example:

- the Los Alamos systems DUAL and SHACO,[16,40]
- the Massachusetts Institute of Technology (MIT) "Summer Session Computer,"[1]
- a system for the Illiac designed by D.J. Wheeler,[30] and
- the Speedcoding system for the IBM 701.[5]

The Laning and Zierler system was quite a different story: It was the world's first operating algebraic compiler, a rather elegant but simple one. Donald Knuth and Luis Trabb Pardo[26] assign this honor to Alick Glennie's Autocode, but I, for one, am unable to recognize the sample Autocode program they give as "algebraic," especially when it is compared to the corresponding Laning and Zierler program.

All of the early "automatic programming" systems were costly to use, since they slowed down the machine by a factor of five or 10. The most common reason for the slowdown was that these systems were spending most of their time in floating-point subroutines. Simulated indexing and other "housekeeping" operations could be done with simple inefficient techniques, since, slow as they were, they took far less time than the floating-point work.

Experience with slow "automatic programming" systems, plus their own experience with the problems of organizing loops and address modification, had convinced programmers that efficient programming was something that could not be automated. Another reason that "automatic programming" was not taken seriously by the computing community was due to the energetic public relations efforts of some visionaries spreading the word that their "automatic programming" systems had almost human abilities to understand the language and the needs of the user, whereas closer inspection of those systems would often reveal a complex, exception-ridden performer of clerical tasks that was both difficult to use and inefficient. Whatever the reasons, it is difficult to convey to a reader in the late 1970s the strength of the skepticism about "automatic programming" in general and about its ability to produce efficient programs in particular, as it existed in 1954.

In the above discussion of attitudes about "automatic programming" in 1954, I have mentioned only those actual systems of which my colleagues and I were aware at the time. For a comprehensive treatment of early programming systems and languages, I recommend the articles by Knuth and Pardo[26] and by Jean Sammet.[38]

The Economics of Programming

Another factor that influenced the development of Fortran was the economics of programming in 1954. The cost of programmers associated with a computer center was usually at least as great as the cost of the computer itself. (This fact follows from the average salary plus overhead and the number of programmers at each center and from the computer rental figures.) In addition, from one quarter to one half of the computer's time was spent in debugging. Thus, programming and debugging accounted for as much as three quarters of the cost of operating a computer; and obviously, as computers got cheaper, this situation would get worse.

Fortran is a collection of warts, held together by bits of syntax.

Anon.

This economic factor was one of the prime motivations that led me to propose the Fortran project in a letter to my boss, Cuthbert Hurd, in late 1953 (the exact date is not known, but other facts suggest December 1953 as a likely date). I believe that the economic need for a system like Fortran was one reason why IBM and my successive bosses, Hurd, Charles DeCarlo, and John McPherson, provided for our constantly expanding needs over the next five years without ever asking us to project or justify those needs in a formal budget.

Programming Systems in 1954

It is difficult for a programmer of today to comprehend what "automatic programming" meant to programmers in 1954. To many, it then meant simply providing mnemonic operation codes and symbolic addresses; to others, it meant the simple process of obtaining subroutines from a library and inserting the addresses of operands into each subroutine. Most "automatic programming" systems were assembly programs, subroutine-fixing programs, or, most popularly, interpretive systems to provide floating-point and indexing operations. My friends and I were aware of a number of assembly programs and interpretive systems, some of which have been mentioned above; besides these, there were primarily two other systems of significance: the A-2 compiler[29,36] and the Laning and Zierler[27] algebraic compiler at MIT. As noted above, the A-2 compiler was, at that time, largely a subroutine fixer (its other principal task was to provide for "overlays"); but from the standpoint of its input "programs," it provided fewer conveniences than most of the then-current interpretive systems mentioned earlier; it

later adopted a "pseudocode" as input that was similar to the input codes of these interpretive systems.

The Laning and Zierler system accepted as input an elegant, but rather simple algebraic language. It permitted single-letter variables (identifiers) that could have a single constant or variable subscript. The repertoire of functions one could use was denoted by "F" with an integer superscript to indicate the "catalog number" of the desired function. Algebraic expressions were compiled into closed subroutines and placed on a magnetic drum for subsequent use. The system was originally designed for the Whirlwind computer when it had 1,024 storage cells, with the result that it caused a slowdown in execution speed by a factor of about 10.[1]

The effect of the Laning and Zierler system on the development of Fortran is a question that has been muddled by many misstatements on my part. For many years, I believed that we had gotten the idea for using algebraic notation in Fortran from seeing a demonstration of the Laning and Zierler system at MIT. In preparing a paper[8] for the International Research Conference on the History of Computing at Los Alamos, New Mexico, 10–15 June 1976, I reviewed the matter with Irving Ziller and obtained a copy of a 1954 letter[6] (which Dr. Laning kindly sent to me). As a result, the facts of the matter have become clear. The letter in question is one I sent to Dr. Laning asking for a demonstration of his system. It makes clear that we had learned of his work at the Office of Naval Research Symposium on Automatic Programming for Digital Computers, 13–14 May 1954, and that the demonstration took place on 2 June 1954. The letter also makes clear that the Fortran project was well under way when the letter was sent (21 May 1954) and included Harlan Herrick, Robert A. Nelson, and Ziller, as well as myself. Furthermore, an article in the proceedings of that same Office of Naval Research (ONR) symposium by Herrick and myself[11] shows clearly that we were already considering input expressions like "$\Sigma a_{ij} \cdot b_{jk}$" and "$X + Y$." We went on to raise the question: "Can a machine translate a sufficiently rich mathematical language into a sufficiently economical program at a sufficiently low cost to make the whole affair feasible?"

These and other remarks in our paper presented at the symposium in May 1954 make it clear that we were already considering algebraic input considerably more sophisticated than that of Laning and Zierler's system when we first heard of their pioneering work. Thus, although Laning and Zierler had already produced the world's first algebraic compiler, our basic ideas for Fortran had been developed independently; thus, it is difficult to know what, if any, new ideas we got from seeing the demonstration of their system.

(In response to suggestions of the Program Committee, let me try to deal explicitly with the question of what work might have influenced our early ideas for Fortran, although it is mostly a matter of listing work of which we were then unaware. I have already discussed the work of Laning and Zierler and the A-2 compiler. The work of Heinz Rutishauser[37] [1952] is discussed later. Like most of the world (except perhaps Rutishauser and Corrado Böhm, the latter of whom was the first to describe a compiler in its own language[15]), we were entirely unaware of the work of Konrad Zuse.[41,42] Zuse's "Plankalkül," which he completed in 1945, was, in some ways, a more elegant and advanced programming language than those that appeared 10 and 15 years later. We were also unaware of the work of John Mauchly et al. ("Short Code," 1950), Arthur Burks ("Intermediate PL," 1950), Böhm (1951), and Glennie ("Autocode," 1952), all as discussed in Knuth and Pardo.[26] We were aware of but not influenced by the automatic programming efforts that simulated a synthetic computer (e.g., MIT's "Summer Session Computer," SHACO, DUAL, Speedcoding, and the Illiac system), since their languages and systems were so different from those of Fortran. Also, we were not influenced by algebraic systems that were designed after our "Preliminary Report"[34] but that began operation before Fortran (e.g., BACAIC,[22] IT,[33] and Mathe-Matic[4]). Although PACT I[13] was not an algebraic compiler, it deserves mention as a significant development; it was designed after the Fortran language but was in operation before Fortran; it did not influence our work.)

Our ONR symposium article[11] also makes clear that the Fortran group was already aware that it faced a new kind of problem in automatic programming.

The one central attribute of Fortran is its name.

Martin Greenfield

The viability of most compilers and interpreters prior to Fortran had rested on the fact that most source language operations were not machine operations. Thus, even large inefficiencies in performing both looping/testing operations and computing addresses were masked by most of the operating time being spent in floating-point subroutines. But the advent of the IBM 704 with built-in floating point and indexing radically altered the situation. The 704 presented a double challenge to those who wanted to simplify programming; first, it removed the raison d'etre of earlier systems by providing in hardware the operations they existed to provide; second, it increased the problem of generating efficient programs by an order of magnitude by speeding up floating-point operations by a factor of 10 and, thereby, leaving inefficiencies nowhere to hide. In view of the widespread skepticism about the possibility of producing efficient programs with an automatic programming system and the fact that inefficiencies could no longer be hidden, we were convinced that the kind of system we had in mind would be widely used only if we could demonstrate that it would produce programs almost as efficient as hand-coded ones and do so on virtually every job.

It was our belief that if Fortran, during its first months, were to translate any reasonable "scientific" source program into an object program only half as fast as its hand-coded counterpart, then acceptance of our system would be in serious danger. This belief caused us to regard the design of the translator as the real challenge, not the simple task of designing the language. Our belief in the simplicity of language design was partly confirmed by the relative ease with which similar languages had been independently developed by Rutishauser,[37] Laning and Zierler,[27] and ourselves, whereas we were alone in seeking to produce very efficient object programs.

To this day, I believe that our emphasis on object program efficiency rather than on language design was basically correct. I believe that had we failed to produce efficient programs, the widespread use of languages like Fortran would have been seriously delayed. In fact, I believe that we are in a similar, but unrecognized situation today: In spite of all the fuss that has been made over myriad language details, current conventional languages are still very weak programming aids, and far more powerful languages would be in use today if anyone had found a way to make them run with adequate efficiency. In other words, the next revolution in programming will take place only when *both* of the following requirements have been met:

- a new kind of programming language, far more powerful than those of today, has been developed and
- a technique has been found for executing its programs at not much greater cost than that of today's programs.

Because of our 1954 view that success in producing efficient programs was more important than the design of the Fortran language, I consider the history of the compiler construction and the work of its inventors an integral part of the history of the Fortran language; therefore, a later section deals with that subject.

Early Stages of the Fortran Project

After Hurd approved my proposal to develop a practical automatic programming system for the 704 in December 1953 or January 1954, Ziller was assigned to the project. We started work in one of the many small offices the project was to occupy in the vicinity of IBM headquarters at 590 Madison Avenue in New York; the first of these was in the Jay Thorpe Building on Fifth Avenue. By May 1954, we had been joined by Herrick and then by a new employee who had been hired to do technical typing, Nelson (with Ziller, he soon began designing one of the most sophisticated sections of the compiler; he is now an IBM Fellow). By about May, we had moved to the 19th floor of the annex of 590 Madison Avenue, next to the elevator machinery; the ground floor of this building housed the 701 installation on which customers tested their programs before the arrival of their own machines. It was here that most of the Fortran language was designed, mostly by Herrick, Ziller, and myself, except that most of the input-output language and facilities were designed by Roy Nutt, an employee of United Aircraft Corp. who was soon to become a member of the Fortran project. After we had finished designing most of the language, we heard about Rutishauser's proposals for a similar language.[37] It was characteristic of the unscholarly attitude of most programmers then, and of ourselves in particular, that we did not bother to carefully review the sketchy translation of his proposals that we finally obtained, since from their symbolic content, they did not appear to add anything new to our proposed language. Rutishauser's language had a **for** statement and one-dimensional arrays, but no IF, GOTO, or I/O statements. Subscript variables could not be used as ordinary variables, and operator precedence was ignored. His 1952 article described two compilers for this language (for more details, see the article by Knuth and Pardo[26]).

As far as we were aware, we simply made up the language as we went along. We did not regard language design as a difficult problem, merely a simple prelude to the real problem: designing a compiler that could produce efficient programs. Of course, one of our goals was to design a language that would make it possible for engineers and scientists to write programs themselves for the 704. We also wanted to eliminate a lot of the bookkeeping and detailed, repetitive planning that hand-coding involved. Very early in our work, we had in mind the notions of assignment statements, subscripted variables, and the DO statement (which, I believe, was proposed by Herrick). We felt that these provided a good basis for achieving our goals for the language. Whatever else was needed emerged as we tried to build a way of programming on these basic ideas.

We certainly had no idea that languages almost identical to the one we were working on would be used for more than one IBM computer, not to mention those of other manufacturers. (After all, there were very few computers around back then.) But we did expect our system to have a big impact, in the sense that it would make programming for the 704 very much faster, cheaper, and more reliable. We also expected that if we were successful in meeting our goals, other groups and manufacturers would follow our example in reducing the cost of programming by providing similar systems with different, but similar languages.[34]

Fortran—"the infantile disorder"—is hopelessly inadequate for whatever computer application you have in mind today...too clumsy, too risky, and too expensive.

Edsger Dijkstra

By the fall of 1954, we had become the "Programming Research Group," and I had become its "manager." By November of that year, we had produced a paper: "Preliminary Report, Specifications for the IBM Mathematical FORmula TRANslating System, Fortran,"[34] dated 10 November 1954. In its introduction, we noted that "systems which have sought to reduce the job of coding and debugging problems have offered the choice of easy coding and slow execution or laborious coding and fast execution." On the basis more of faith than of knowledge, we suggested that programs "will be executed in about the same time that would be required had the problem been laboriously hand coded." In what turned out to be a true statement, we said that "Fortran may apply complex, lengthy techniques in coding a problem which the human coder would have neither the time nor inclination to derive or apply."

The language described in the "Preliminary Report" had:

- variables of one or two characters in length,
- function names of three or more characters,
- recursively defined "expressions,"
- subscripted variables with up to three subscripts,
- "arithmetic formulas" (which turn out to be assignment statements), and
- "DO formulas."

These DO formulas could specify both the first and last statements to be controlled, thus permitting a DO to control a distant sequence of statements, as well as specifying a third statement to which control would pass following the end of the iteration. If only one statement was specified, the "range" of the DO was the sequence of statements following the DO down to the specified statement.

Expressions in "arithmetic formulas" could be "mixed": involving both "fixed-point" (integer) and "floating-point" quantities. The arithmetic used (all integer or all floating point) to evaluate a mixed expression was determined by the type of the variable on the left of the "=" sign. "IF formulas" employed an equality or inequality sign ("=" or ">" or ">=") between two (restricted) expressions, followed by two statement numbers: one for the "true" case, the other for the "false" case.

A "Relabel formula" was designed to make it easy to rotate, say, the indices of the rows of a matrix so that the same computation would apply, after relabeling, even though a new row had been read in and the next computation was now to take place on a different, rotated set of rows. Thus, for example, if b is a 4×4 matrix, after RELABEL (3, 1), a reference to

- $b(1, j)$ has the same meaning as $b(3, j)$ before relabeling;
- $b(2, j)$ after $= b(4, j)$ before;
- $b(3, j)$ after $= b(1, j)$ before; and
- $b(4, j)$ after $= b(2, j)$ before relabeling.

The input-output statements that were provided included the basic notion of specifying the sequence in which data were to be read in or out, but did not include any "Format" statements.

The report also lists four kinds of "specification sentences":

1) "dimension sentences" for giving the dimensions of arrays,
2) "equivalence sentences" for assigning the same storage locations to variables,
3) "frequency sentences" for indicating estimated relative frequency of branch paths or loops to help the compiler optimize the object program, and
4) "relative constant sentences" to indicate subscript variables, which are expected to change their values very infrequently.

Toward the end of the report (pp. 26–27), there is a section "Future Additions to the Fortran System." Its first item is: "a variety of new input-output formulas which would enable the programmer to specify various formats for cards, printing, input tapes and output tapes." It is believed that this item is a result of our early consultations with Nutt. This section goes on to list other proposed facilities to be added:

- complex and double precision arithmetic,
- matrix arithmetic,
- sorting,
- solving simultaneous equations,
- differential equations, and
- linear programming problems.

It also describes function definition capabilities similar to those that later appeared in Fortran II:

- facilities for numerical integration,
- a summation operator, and
- table lookup facilities.

The final section of the report (pp. 28–29) discusses programming techniques to use to help the system produce efficient programs. It discusses how to use parentheses to help the system identify identical subexpressions within an expression and thereby eliminate their duplicate calculation. These parentheses had to be supplied only when a recurring subexpression occurred as part of a term (e.g., if a * b occurred in several places, it would be better to write the term a * b * c as (a * b) * c to avoid duplicate calculation); otherwise the system would identify duplicates without any assistance. It also observes that the system would not produce optimal code for loops constructed without DO statements.

This final section of the report also notes that "no special provisions have been included in the Fortran system for locating errors in formulas." It suggests checking a program "by independently recreating the specifications for a problem from its Fortran formulation [!]." It says nothing about the system catching syntactic errors, but notes that an error-finding program can be written after some experience with errors has been accumulated.

Unfortunately, we were hopelessly optimistic in 1954 about the ease of debugging Fortran programs (thus, we find on page 2 of the report: "Since Fortran should virtually eliminate coding and debugging ... [!]"), and, hence, syntactic error-checking facilities in the first distribution of Fortran I were weak. Better facilities were added not long after distribution, and fairly good syntactic checking was provided in Fortran II.

God is real (unless otherwise declared in an explicit type statement or in an implicit declaration).

B. Graham

The Fortran language described in the *Programmer's Reference Manual,*[24] dated 15 October 1956, differed in a few respects from that of the Preliminary Report, but considering our ignorance in 1954 of the problems we would later encounter in producing the compiler, there were:

- remarkably few deletions (the Relabel and Relative Constant statements);
- a few retreats, some fortunate, some not (simplification of DO statements, dropping inequalities from IF statements for lack of a ">" symbol, and prohibiting most "mixed" expressions and subscripted subscripts); and
- the rectification of a few omissions (addition of FORMAT, CONTINUE, computed and assigned GOTO statements, increasing the length of variables to up to six characters, and general improvements of input-output statements).

Since our entire attitude about language design had always been a very casual one, the changes we felt to be desirable during the course of writing the compiler were made equally casually.

We never felt that any of them involved a real sacrifice in convenience or power (with the possible exception of the Relabel statement, whose purpose was to coordinate input-output with computations on arrays, but this was one facility that we felt would have been very difficult to implement). I believe the simplification of the original DO statement resulted from the realizations that:

1) it would be hard to describe precisely,
2) it was awkward to compile, and
3) it provided little power beyond that of the final version.

In our naive unawareness of language design problems—of course, we knew nothing of many issues that were later thought to be important, e.g., block structure, conditional expressions, and type declarations—it seemed to us that once one had the notions of the assignment statement, the subscripted variable, and the DO statement in hand (and these were among our earliest ideas), then the remaining problems of language design were trivial. Their solution was thrust on us either by the need to provide some ma-

chine facility such as reading input or by some programming task that could not be done with existing structures. (For example, skip to the end of a DO loop without skipping the indexing instructions there. This gave rise to the CONTINUE statement.)

One much-criticized design choice in Fortran concerns the use of spaces: Blanks were ignored, even blanks in the middle of an identifier. Nutt reminds me that that choice was partly in recognition of a problem widely known in SHARE (the 704 users' association). There was a common problem with keypunchers not recognizing or properly counting blanks in handwritten data, and this caused many errors. We also regarded ignoring blanks as a device to enable programmers to arrange their programs in a more readable form without altering their meaning or introducing complex rules for formatting statements.

Another debatable design choice was to rule out "mixed"-mode expressions involving both integer and floating-point quantities. Although our Preliminary Report had included such expressions and rules for evaluating them, we felt that if code for type conversion were to be generated, the user should be aware of that, and the best way to ensure that he was aware was to ask him to specify them. I believe we were also doubtful of the usefulness of the rules in our report for evaluating mixed expressions. In any case, the most common sort of "mixture" was allowed: Integer exponents and function arguments were allowed in a floating-point expression.

In late 1954 and early 1955, after completing the Preliminary Report, Herrick, Ziller, and I gave perhaps five or six talks about our plans for Fortran to various groups of IBM customers who had ordered a 704 (the 704 had been announced about May 1954). At these talks, we covered the material in the report and discussed our plans for the compiler (which was to be completed within about six months [!]; this was to remain the interval to completion whenever we were asked, until it actually was completed over two years later, in April 1957). In addition to informing customers about our plans, another purpose of these talks was to assemble a list of their objections and further requirements. In this we were disappointed; our listeners were mostly skeptical; I believe they had heard too many glowing descriptions of what turned out to be clumsy systems to take us seriously. In those days, one was accustomed to finding lots of peculiar, but significant restrictions in a system when it finally arrived that had not been mentioned in its original description. Most of all, our claims that we would produce efficient object programs were disbelieved. Whatever the reasons, we received almost no suggestions or feedback; our listeners had done almost no thinking about the problems we faced and had almost no suggestions or criticisms. Thus, we felt that our trips to Washington, D.C., Albuquerque, Pittsburgh, Los Angeles, and one or two other places were not very helpful.

One trip to give our talk, probably in January 1955, had an excellent payoff. This talk, at United Aircraft Corp., resulted in an agreement between our group and Walter Ramshaw at United Aircraft that Nutt would become a regular part of our effort (although remaining an employee of United Aircraft) to contribute his expertise on input-output and assembly routines. With a few breaks due to his involvement in writing various SHARE programs, he would thenceforth come to New York two or three times a week until early 1957.

It is difficult to assess the influence the early work of the Fortran group had on other projects. Certainly the discussion of Laning and Zierler's algebraic compiler at the ONR symposium in May 1954 would have been more likely to persuade someone to undertake a similar line of effort than would the brief discussion of the merits of using "a fairly natural mathematical language" that appeared there in the paper by Herrick and myself.[11] But it was our impression that our discussions with various groups after that time, their access to the Preliminary Report, and their awareness of the extent and seriousness of our efforts, that these factors either gave the initial stimulus to some other projects or at least caused them to be more active than they might have been otherwise. It was our impression, for example, that the "IT" project[33] at Purdue University and later at Carnegie-Mellon University began shortly after the distribution of our Preliminary Report, as did the "Math-Matic" project[4] at Sperry Rand.

> ## I don't know what the language of the year 2000 will look like, but I know it will be called Fortran.
>
> Tony Hoare

It is not clear what influence, if any, our Los Angeles talk and earlier contacts with members of their group had on the PACT I effort,[13] which I believe was already in its formative stages when we got to Los Angeles. It is clear that whatever influence the specifications for Fortran may have had on other projects in 1954–1956, our plans were well-advanced and quite firm by the end of 1954, before we had contact or knowledge of those other projects. Our specifications were not affected by them in any significant way, as far as I am aware, even though some were operating before Fortran (since they were primarily interested in providing an input language rather than an optimization, their task was considerably simpler than ours).

The Construction of the Compiler

The Fortran compiler (or "translator," as we called it then) was begun in early 1955, although a lot of work on various schemes that would be used in it had been done in 1954. Herrick had done a lot of trial programming to test our language, and we had worked out the basic sort of machine programs that we wanted the compiler to generate for various source language phrases. Ziller and I had worked out a basic scheme for translating arithmetic expressions.

But the real work on the compiler got under way in our third location on the fifth floor of 15 East 56th Street in New York. By the middle of February, three separate efforts were under way. The first two of these concerned sections 1 and 2 of the compiler, and the third concerned the input, output, and assembly programs we were going to need (see below). We believed back then that these efforts would produce most of the compiler.

(The entire project was carried out by a loose cooperation between autonomous, separate groups of one, two, or three people; each group was responsible for a "section" of the compiler; each group gradually developed and agreed on its own input and output specifications with the groups for neighboring sections; each group invented and programmed the necessary techniques for doing its assigned job.)

Section 1 was to read the entire source program, compile what instructions it could, and file all the rest of the information from the source program in appropriate tables. Thus, the compiler was "one pass," in the sense that it "saw" the source program only once. Herrick was responsible for creating most of the tables, Peter Sheridan (who had recently joined us) compiled all the arithmetic expressions, and Nutt compiled and/or filed the I/O statements. Herrick, Sheridan, and Nutt got some help later on from R.J. Beeber and H. Stern, but they were the architects of section 1 and wrote most of its code. Sheridan devised and implemented a number of optimizing transformations on expressions[39] that sometimes radically altered them (of course, without changing their meaning). Nutt transformed the I/O "lists of quantities" into nests of DO statements, which were then treated by the regular mechanisms of the compiler. The rest of the I/O information he filed for later treatment in section 6, the assembler section. (For further details about how the various sections of the compiler worked, see the 1957 paper by Backus et al.[12])

Using the information that was filed in section 1, section 2 faced a completely new kind of problem; it was required to analyze the entire structure of the program in order to generate optimal code from DO statements and references to subscripted variables. The simplest way to effect a reference to A(I, J) is to evaluate an expression involving the address of A(1, 1), I, and $K \times J$, where K is the length of a column (when A is stored columnwise). But this calculation, with its multiplication, is much less efficient than the way most hand-coded programs effect a reference to A(I, J), namely, by adding an appropriate constant to the address of the preceding reference to the array A whenever I and J are changing linearly. To employ this far-more-efficient method, section 2 had to determine when the surrounding program was changing I and J linearly.

Thus, one problem was that of distinguishing between, on the one hand, references to an array element that the translator might treat by incrementing the address used for a previous reference and those array references, on the other hand, that would require an address calculation starting from scratch with the current values of the subscripts.

It was decided that it was not practical to track down and identify linear changes in subscripts resulting from assignment statements. Thus, the sole criterion for linear changes, and hence for efficient handling of array references, was to be that the subscripts involved were being controlled by DO statements. Despite this simplifying assumption, the number of cases that section 2 had to analyze in order to produce optimal or near-optimal code was very large. (The number of such cases increased exponentially with the number of subscripts; this was a prime factor in our decision to limit them to three; the fact that the 704 had only three index registers was not a factor.)

It is beyond the scope of this paper to go into the details of the analysis that section 2 carried out. It will suffice to say that it produced code of such efficiency that its output would startle the programmers who studied it. It moved code out of loops where that was possible; it took advantage of the differences between row-wise and column-wise scans; it took note of special cases to optimize even the exits from loops. The degree of optimization performed by section 2 in its treatment of indexing, array references, and loops was not equaled until optimizing compilers began to appear in the middle and late 1960s.

The architecture and all the techniques employed in section 2 were invented by Nelson and Ziller. They planned and programmed the entire section. Originally, it was their intention to produce the complete code for their area, including the choice of the index register to be used (the 704 had three index registers). When they started looking at the problem, it rapidly became clear that it was not going to be easy to treat it optimally. At that point, I proposed that they should produce a program for a 704 with an unlimited number of index registers and that later sections would analyze the frequency of execution of various parts of the program (by a Monte Carlo simulation of its execution) and then make index register assignments so as to minimize the transfers of items between the store and the index registers.

Fortran is a language to avoid—unless you want some answers.

Anon.

This proposal gave rise to two new sections of the compiler that we had not anticipated, sections 4 and 5 (section 3 was added to convert the output of sections 1 and 2 to the form required for sections 4, 5, and 6). In the fall of 1955, Lois Mitchell Haibt joined our group to plan and program section 4:

- to analyze the flow of a program produced by sections 1 and 2;
- to divide the program into "basic blocks" (which contained no branching);
- to do a Monte Carlo (statistical) analysis of the expected frequency of execution of basic blocks—by simulating the behavior of the program and keeping counts of the use of each block—using information from DO statements and FREQUENCY statements; and
- to collect information about index register usage (for more details, see the paper by Backus et al.[12] and the one by John Cocke and J.T. Schwartz[19,p.511]).

Section 5 would then do the actual transformation of the program from one having an unlimited number of index registers to one having only three. Again, the section was entirely planned and programmed by Haibt.

Section 5 was planned and programmed by Sheldon Best, who was loaned to our group by agreement with his employer, Charles W. Adams at the Digital Computer Laboratory at MIT. During his stay with us, Best was a temporary IBM employee. Starting in the early fall of 1955, he designed what turned out to be, along with section 2, one of the most intricate and complex sections of the compiler, one that had perhaps more influence on the methods used in later compilers than any other part of the Fortran compiler. (For a discussion of his techniques, see the paper by Cocke and Schwartz.[19,pp.510-515]) It is impossible to describe his register allocation method here; it suffices to say that it was to become the basis for much subsequent work and produced code very difficult to improve.

Although I believe that no provably optimal register allocation algorithm is known for general programs with loops etc., empirically, Best's 1955–1956 procedure appeared to be optimal. For straight-line code, Best's replacement policy was the same as that used in L.A. Belady's MIN algorithm, which Belady proved to be optimal.[14] Although Best did not publish a formal proof, he had convincing arguments for the optimality of his policy in 1955.

Late in 1955, it was recognized that yet another section, section 3, was needed. This section merged the outputs of the preceding sections into a single uniform 704 program that could refer to any number of index registers. It was planned and programmed by Richard Goldberg, a mathematician who joined us in November 1955. Also, late in 1956, after Best had returned to MIT and during the debugging of the system, section 5 was taken over by Goldberg and David Sayre (see below), who diagrammed it carefully and took charge of its final debugging.

The final section of the compiler, section 6, assembled the final program into a relocatable binary program (it could also produce a symbolic program in SAP, the SHARE Assembly Program for the 704). It produced a storage map of the program and the data that was a compact summary of the Fortran output. Of course, it also obtained the necessary library programs for inclusion in the object program, including those required to interpret FORMAT statements and perform input-output operations. Taking advantage of the special features of the programs it assembled, this assembler was about 10 times faster than SAP. It was designed and programmed by Nutt, who also wrote all the I/O programs and the relocating binary loader for loading object programs.

By the summer of 1956, large parts of the system were working. Sections 1, 2, and 3 could produce workable code, provided no more than three index registers were needed. A number of test programs were compiled and run at this time. Nutt took part of the system to United Aircraft (sections 1, 2, and 3 and the part of section 6 that produced SAP output). This part of the system was productive there from the summer of 1956 until the complete system was available in early 1957.

From late spring of 1956 to early 1957, the pace of debugging was intense; often we would rent rooms in the Langdon Hotel (which disappeared long ago) on 56th Street, sleep there a little during the day, and then stay up all night to get as much use of the computer (in the headquarters annex on 57th Street) as possible.

It was an exciting period; when we later began to get fragments of compiled programs out of the system, we were often astonished at the surprising transformations in the indexing operations and in the arrangement of the computation that the compiler made, changes that made the object program efficient but that we would not have thought to make as programmers ourselves (even though, of course, Nelson or Ziller could figure out how the indexing worked, Sheridan could explain how an expression had been optimized beyond recognition, and Goldberg or Sayre could tell us how section 5 had generated additional indexing operations). Transfers of control appeared that corresponded to no source statement, expressions were radically rearranged, and the same DO statement might produce no instructions in the object program in one context, and in another it would produce many instructions in different places in the program.

By the summer of 1956, what appeared to be the imminent completion of the project started us worrying (for perhaps the first time) about documentation. Sayre, a crystallographer who had joined us in the spring (he had earlier consulted with Best on the design of section 5 and had later begun serving as second-in-command of what was now the "Programming Research Department"), took up the task of writing the *Programmer's Reference*

Manual.[24] It appeared in a glossy cover, handsomely printed, with the date 15 October 1956. It stood for some time as a unique example of a manual for a programming language (perhaps it still does): It had wide margins, yet was only 51 pages long. Its description of the Fortran language, exclusive of input-output statements, was 21 pages; the I/O description occupied another 11 pages; the rest of it was examples and details about arithmetic, tables, etc. It gave an elegant recursive definition of expressions (as given by Sheridan) and concise, clear descriptions, with examples, of each statement type, of which there were 32, mostly machine-dependent items like SENSE LIGHT, IF DIVIDE CHECK, PUNCH, READ DRUM, and so on.

One feature of Fortran I is missing from the *Programmer's Reference Manual,* not from an oversight of Sayre's, but because it was added to the system after the manual was distributed. This feature was the ability to define a function by a "function statement." These statements had to precede the rest of the program. They looked like assignment statements, with the defined function and dummy arguments on the left and an expression involving those arguments on the right. They are described in the addenda to the *Programmer's Reference Manual,*[2] which we sent on 8 February 1957 to John Greenstadt, who was in charge of IBM's facility for distributing information to SHARE. They are also described in all subsequent material on Fortran I.

In the good old days, physicists repeated each other's experiments, just to be sure. Today, they stick to Fortran so they can share each others' programs, bugs included.

Edsger Dijkstra

The next documentation task we set ourselves was to write a paper describing the Fortran language and the translator program. The result was a paper entitled, "The Fortran Automatic Coding System,"[12] which we presented at the Western Joint Computer Conference in Los Angeles in February 1957. I have mentioned all of the 13 authors of that paper in the preceding narrative except one: Robert A. Hughes. He was employed by the Livermore Radiation Laboratory; by arrangement with Sidney Fernbach, he visited us for two or three months in the summer of 1956 to help us document the system.

At about the time of the Western Joint Computer Conference, we spent some time in Los Angeles still frantically debugging the system. North American Aviation gave us time at night on their 704 to help us in our mad rush to distribute the system. Up to this point, there had been relatively little interest from 704 installations (with the exception of Ramshaw's United Aircraft shop, Harry Cantrell's GE installation in Schenectady, New York, and Fernbach's Livermore operation), but now that the full system was beginning to generate object programs, interest picked up in a number of places.

Sometime in early April 1957, we felt the system was sufficiently bug-free to distribute to all 704 installations. Sayre and Grace E. Mitchell (see below) started to punch out the binary decks of the system, each of about 2,000 cards, with the intention

to make 30 or 40 decks for distribution. This process was so error-prone that they had to give up after spending an entire night in producing only one or two decks. Apparently one of those decks was sent, without any identification or directions, to the Westing-house-Bettis installation, where a puzzled group headed by Herbert S. Bright, suspecting that it might be the long-awaited Fortran deck, proceeded, entirely by guesswork, to get it to compile a test program—after a diagnostic printout noted that a comma was missing in a specific statement! This program then printed 28 pages of correct results—with a few FORMAT errors. The date: 20 April 1957. Bright wrote an amusing account of this incident in *Computers and Automation.*[17] [*Editor's note: This story is also told in Annals, vol. 1, no. 1, pp. 72–74.*]

After failing to produce binary decks, Sayre devised and programmed the simple editor and loader that made it possible to distribute and update the system from magnetic tapes; this arrangement served as the mechanism for creating new system tapes from a master tape and the binary correction cards that our group would generate in large numbers during the long field debugging and maintenance period that followed distribution.

With the distribution of the system tapes went a *Preliminary Operator's Manual*[31] dated 8 April 1957. It describes how to use the tape editor and how to maintain the library of functions. Five pages of such general instructions are followed by 32 pages of error stops, many of these say, "source program error, get off machine, correct formula in question and restart problem" and then, for example, (stop 3,624) "non-zero level reduction due to insufficient or redundant parentheses in arithmetic or IF-type formula." Shortly after the distribution of the system, we distributed—one copy per installation—what was fondly known as the "Tome," the complete symbolic listing of the entire compiler plus other system and diagnostic information, an 11 × 15 inch volume about four or five inches thick.

The proprietors of the six sections were kept busy tracking down bugs elicited by our customers' use of Fortran until the late summer of 1957. Hal Stern served as the coordinator of the field debugging and maintenance effort; he received a stream of telegrams, mail, and phone calls from all over the country and distributed the incoming problems to the appropriate members of our group to track down the errors and generate correction cards, which he then distributed to every installation.

In the spring of 1957, Mitchell joined our group to write the *Programmer's Primer* for Fortran. The primer was divided into three sections; each described successively larger subsets of the language, accompanied by many example programs. The first edition of the primer was issued in the late fall or winter of 1957; a slightly revised edition appeared in March 1958. Mitchell planned and wrote the 64-page primer with some consultation with the rest of the group; she later programmed most of the extensive changes in the system that resulted in Fortran II (see below).

The primer had an important influence on the subsequent growth in the use of the system. I believe it was the only available simplified instruction manual (other than reference manuals) until the later appearance of books such as those by Daniel McCracken[28] (1961), Elliot Organick[32] (1963), and many others.

A report on Fortran usage in November 1958[7] says that "a survey in April [1958] of twenty-six 704 installations indicates that over half of them use Fortran [I] for more than half of their problems. Many use it for 80% or more of their work ... and almost all use it for some of their work." By the fall of 1958, there were some 60 installations with about 66 704s and "more than half the machine instructions for these machines are being produced by Fortran. SHARE recently designated Fortran as the second official medium for transmittal of programs [SAP was the first]."

Fortran II

During the field debugging period, some shortcomings of the system design, which we had been aware of earlier but had no time to correct, were constantly coming to our attention. In the early fall of 1957, we started to plan ways of correcting these shortcomings; a document dated 25 September 1957[35] characterizes them as:

1) the need for better diagnostics (clearer comments about the nature of source program errors) and
2) the need for subroutine definition capabilities.

(Although one Fortran I diagnostic would pinpoint, in a printout, a missing comma in a particular statement, others could be very cryptic.) This document is titled, "Proposed Specifications for Fortran II for the 704"; it sketches a more general diagnostic system and describes the new "subroutine definition" and END statements, plus some others that were not implemented. It describes how symbolic information is retained in the relocatable binary form of a subroutine so that the "binary symbolic subroutine [BSS] loader" can implement references to separately compiled subroutines. It describes new prologues for these subroutines and points out that mixtures of Fortran-coded and assembly-coded relocatable binary programs could be loaded and run together. It does not discuss the FUNCTION statement that was also available in Fortran II. Fortran II was designed mostly by Nelson, Ziller, and myself. Mitchell programmed the majority of new code for Fortran II (with the most unusual feature that she delivered it ahead of schedule). She was aided in this by Bernyce Brady and LeRoy May. Sheridan planned and made the necessary changes in his part of section 1; Nutt did the same for section 6. Fortran II was distributed in the spring of 1958.

Fortran III

While Fortran II was being developed, Ziller was designing an even more advanced system that he called Fortran III. It allowed one to write intermixed symbolic instructions and Fortran statements. The symbolic (704) instructions could have Fortran variables (with or without subscripts) as "addresses." In addition to this machine-dependent feature (which assured the demise of Fortran III along with that of the 704), it contained early versions of a number of improvements that were later to appear in Fortran IV. It had "Boolean" expressions, function and subroutine names could be passed as arguments, and it had facilities for handling alphanumeric data, including a new FORMAT code "A" similar to codes "I" and "E." This system was planned and programmed by Ziller with some help from Nelson and Nutt. Ziller maintained it and made it available to about 20 (mostly IBM) installations. It was never distributed generally. It was accompanied by a brief descriptive document.[3] It became available on this limited scale in the winter of 1958–1959 and was in operation until the early 1960s, in part on the 709 using the compatibility feature (which made the 709 order code the same as that of the 704).

Fortran After 1958, Comments

By the end of 1958 or early 1959, the Fortran group (the Programming Research Department), while still helping with an occasional debugging problem with Fortran II, was primarily occupied with other research. Another IBM department had long since taken responsibility for the Fortran system and was revising it in the course of producing a translator for the 709 that used the same procedures as the 704 Fortran II translator. Since my friends and I no longer had responsibility for Fortran and were busy thinking about other things by the end of 1958, that seems like a good point to break off this account. There remain only a few comments to be made about the subsequent development of Fortran.

The most obvious defect in Fortran II for many of its users was the time spent in compiling. Even though the facilities of Fortran II permitted separate compilation of subroutines and, hence, eliminated the need to recompile an entire program at each step in debugging it, nevertheless, compile times were long and, during debugging, the considerable time spent in optimizing was wasted. I repeatedly suggested to those who were in charge of Fortran that they should now develop a fast compiler and/or interpreter without any optimizing at all for use during debugging and for short-run jobs. Unfortunately, the developers of Fortran IV thought they could have the best of both worlds in a single compiler—one that was both fast and produced optimized code. I was unsuccessful in convincing them that two compilers would have been far better than the compromise that became the original Fortran IV compiler. The latter was not nearly as fast as later compilers like WATFOR[20] and did not produce as good code as Fortran II. (For more discussion of later developments with Fortran, see the 1964 paper by Backus and W.P. Heising.[10])

My own opinion as to the effect of Fortran on later languages and the collective impact of such languages on programming generally is not a popular opinion. That viewpoint is the subject of a long paper.[9] I now regard all conventional languages (e.g., the Fortrans, the Algols, and their successors and derivatives) as increasingly complex elaborations of the style of programming dictated by the von Neumann computer. These "von Neumann languages" create enormous, unnecessary intellectual roadblocks in thinking about programs and in creating the higher-level combining forms required in a powerful programming methodology. The von Neumann languages constantly keep our noses pressed in the dirt of address computation and the separate computation of single words, whereas we should be focusing on the form and content of the overall result we are trying to produce. We have come to regard the DO, FOR, and WHILE statements and the like as powerful tools, whereas they are, in fact, weak palliatives that are necessary to make the primitive von Neumann style of programming viable at all.

By splitting programming into a world of expressions, on the one hand, and a world of statements, on the other, von Neumann languages prevent the effective use of higher-level combining forms; the lack of the latter makes the definitional capabilities of von Neumann languages so weak that most of their important features cannot be defined, starting with a small, elegant framework—but must be built into the framework of the language at the outset. The gargantuan size of recent von Neumann languages is eloquent proof of their inability to define new constructs: No one would build in so many complex features if they could be defined and would fit into the existing framework later.

The world of expressions has some elegant and useful mathematical properties, whereas the world of statements is a disorderly one without useful mathematical properties. Structured programming can be viewed as a modest effort to introduce a small amount of order into the chaotic world of statements. The work of C.A.R. Hoare[23] (1969), Edsger Dijkstra[21] (1976), and others to axiomatize the properties of the statement world can be viewed as a valiant and effective effort to be precise about those properties, ungainly as they may be.

This is not the place for me to elaborate any further my views about von Neumann languages. My point is this: While it was perhaps natural and inevitable that languages like Fortran and its successors should have developed out of the concept of the von Neumann computer as they did, the fact that such languages have dominated our thinking for 20 years is unfortunate. It is unfortunate because their long-standing familiarity will make it hard for us to understand and adopt new programming styles that one day will offer far greater intellectual and computational power.

Acknowledgments

My greatest debt in connection with this paper is to my old friends and colleagues whose creativity, hard work, and invention made Fortran possible. It is a pleasure to acknowledge my gratitude to them for their contributions to the project, for making our work together so long ago such a congenial and memorable experience, and, more recently, for providing me with a great amount of information and helpful material in preparing this paper and for their careful reviews of an earlier draft. For all this, I thank all those who were associated with the Fortran project but who are too numerous to list here. In particular, I want to thank those who were the principal movers in making Fortran a reality: Sheldon Best, Richard Goldberg, Lois Haibt, Harlan Herrick, Grace Mitchell, Robert Nelson, Roy Nutt, David Sayre, Peter Sheridan, and Irving Ziller. I also wish to thank Bernard Galler, J.A.N. Lee, and Henry Tropp for their amiable, extensive, and invaluable suggestions for improving the first draft of this paper. I am grateful, too, for all the work of the Program Committee in preparing helpful questions that suggested a number of topics in the paper.

References

[Editor's note: Most of the items listed below have dates in the 1950s, thus many that appeared in the open literature will be obtainable only in the largest and oldest collections. The items with an asterisk were either not published or were of such a nature as to make their availability even less likely than that of the other items.]

[1] Adams, Charles W., and Laning, J.H., Jr., "The MIT Systems of Automatic Coding: Comprehensive, Summer Session, and Algebraic," Proc. Symp. Automatic Programming for Digital Computers. Washington, D.C.: Office of Naval Research, May 1954.

[2] *Addenda to the Fortran Programmer's Reference Manual, 8 February 1957. (Transmitted to Dr. John Greenstadt, Special Programs Group, Applied Science Division, IBM, for distribution to SHARE members, by letter from John W. Backus, Programming Research Dept. IBM. 5 pages.)

[3] *Additions to Fortran II, Description of Source Language Additions to the Fortran 11 System. New York: Programming Research, IBM Corp., 1958. (Distributed to users of Fortran III. 12 pages.)

[4] *Ash, R., Broadwin, E., Della Valle, V., Katz, C., Green, M., Jenny, A., and Yu, L., Preliminary Manual for MATH-MATIC and ARITH-MATIC Systems (for Algebraic Translations and Compilation for UNIVAC I and II). Philadelphia: Remington Rand Univac, 1957.

[5] Backus, J.W., "The IBM 701 Speedcoding System," J. ACM, vol. 1, no. 1, pp. 4-6, Jan. 1954.

[6] * Backus, John, Letter to J.H. Laning, Jr., 21 May 1954.

[7] Backus, J.W., "Automatic Programming : Properties and Performance of FORTRAN Systems I and II," Proc. Symp. Mechanisation of Thought Processes. Teddington, Middlesex, England, National Physical Laboratory, Nov. 1958.

[8] Backus, John, "Programming in America in the Nineteen Fifties—Some Personal Impressions," N. Metropolis, J. Howlett, and Gian-Carlo Rota, eds., A History of Computing in the Twentieth Century (Proc. Int'l Conf. History of Computing, Los Alamos, N.M., 1978). New York: Academic Press, in press.

[9] Backus, John, "Can Programming Be Liberated From the von Neumann Style? A Functional Style and Its Algebra of Programs," Comm. ACM, vol. 21, no. 8, pp. 613-641, Aug. 1978.

[10] Backus, J.W., and Heising, W.P., "Fortran," IEEE Trans. Electronic Computers, vol. 13, no. 4, pp. 382-385, Aug. 1964.

[11] Backus, John W., and Herrick, Harlan, "IBM 701 Speedcoding and Other Automatic Programming Systems," Proc. Symp. Automatic Programming for Digital Computers. Washington, D.C.: Office of Naval Research, May 1954.

[12] Backus, J.W., Beeber, R.J., Best, S., Goldberg, R., Haibt, L.M., Herrick, H.L., Nelson, R.A., Sayre, D., Sheridan, P.B, Stern, H., Ziller, I., Hughes, R.A., and Nutt, R., "The Fortran Automatic Coding System," Proc. Western Joint Computer Conf., Los Angeles, Feb. 1957.

[13] Baker, Charles L., "The PACT I Coding System for the IBM Type 701," J. ACM, vol. 3, no. 4, pp. 272-278, Oct. 1956.

[14] Belady, L.A., Measurements on Programs: One Level Store Simulation. Yorktown Heights, N.Y.: IBM Thomas J. Watson Research Center, Tech. Rep. RC 1420, 15 June 1965.

[15] Böhm, Corrado, "Calculatrices digitales: Du déchiffrage de formules logico-mathématiques par la machine même dans la conception du programme," Ann. di Mat. Pura ed Applicata, vol. 37, no. 4, pp. 175-217, 1954.

[16] Bouricius, Willard G., "Operating Experience With the Los Alamos 701," Proc. Eastern Joint Computer Conf., Washington, D.C., Dec. 1953.

[17] Bright, Herbert S.,. "Fortran Comes to Westinghouse-Bettis," Computers and Automation, Nov. 1971. Also in Annals of the History of Computing, July 1979.

[18] Brown, J.H. and Carr, John W., III, "Automatic Programming and Its Development on MIDAC," Proc. Symp. Automatic Programming for Digital Computers. Washington, D.C.: Office of Naval Research, May 1954.

[19] Cocke, John, and Schwartz, J.T., Programming Languages and Their Compilers. New York: New York Univ., Courant Institute of Mathematical Sciences, Apr. 1970.

[20] Cress, Paul, Dirksen, Paul, and Graham, J. Wesley, Fortran IV With WATFOR and WATFIV. Englewood Cliffs, N.J.: Prentice Hall, 1970.

[21] Dijkstra, Edsger W., A Discipline of Programming. Englewood Cliffs, N.J.: Prentice Hall, 1976.

[22] Grems, Mandalay, and Porter, R.E., "A Truly Automatic Programming System," Proc. Western Joint Computer Conf., 1956.

[23] Hoare, C.A.R., "An Axiomatic Basis for Computer Programming," Comm. ACM, vol. 12, pp. 576-580, 583, Oct. 1969.

[24] *IBM, Programmer's Reference Manual, the Fortran Automatic Coding System for the IBM 704 EDPM. New York: IBM Corp., 15 Oct. 1956 (Applied Science Division and Programming Research Dept., Working Committee: J.W. Backus, R.J. Beeber, S. Best, R. Goldberg, H.L. Herrick, R.A. Hughes [Univ. of Calif. Radiation Lab., Livermore, Calif.], L.B. Mitchell, R.A. Nelson, R. Nutt [United Aircraft Corp., East Hartford, Conn.] D. Sayre, P.B. Sheridan, H. Stern, I. Ziller).

[25] * IBM, Programmer's Primer for Fortran Automatic Coding System for the IBM 704. New York: IBM Corp., form no. 32-0306, 1957.

[26] Knuth, Donald E., and Pardo, Luis Trabb, "Early Development of Programming Languages," Encyclopedia of Computer Science and Technology, vol. 7, p. 419. New York: Marcel Dekker, 1977.

[27] *Laning, J.H., and Zierler, N., A Program for Translation of Mathematical Equations for Whirlwind 1. Cambridge, Mass.: MIT Instrumentation Lab., Engineering Memorandum E-364, Jan. 1954.

The History of Fortran I, II, and III

[28] McCracken, Daniel D., *A Guide to Fortran Programming.* New York: John Wiley, 1961.

[29] Moser, Nora B., "Compiler Method of Automatic Programming," *Proc. Symp. Automatic Programming for Digital Computers.* Washington, D.C.: Office of Naval Research, May 1954.

[30] Muller, David E., "Interpretive Routines in the ILLIAC Library," *Proc. Symp. Automatic Programming for Digital Computers.* Washington, D.C.: Office of Naval Research, May 1954.

[31] *Preliminary Operator's Manual for the Fortran Automatic Coding System for the IBM 704 EDPM.* New York: IBM Corp., Programming Research Dept., 8 Apr. 1957.

[32] Organick, Elliot I., *A Fortran Primer.* Reading, Mass.: Addison-Wesley, 1963.

[33] *Perlis, A.J., Smith, J.W., and Van Zoeren, H.R., *Internal Translator (IT): A Compiler for the 650.* Pittsburgh, Pa.: Carnegie Institute of Technology, Mar. 1957.

[34] * "Preliminary Report," *Specifications for the IBM Mathematical FORmula TRANslating System, Fortran.* New York: IBM Corp., 10 Nov. 1954 (report by Programming Research Group, Applied Science Division, IBM. Distributed to prospective 704 customers and other interested parties. 29 pp.).

[35] * "Proposed Specifications," *Proposed Specifications for Fortran II for the 704,* 25 Sept. 1957. (Unpublished memorandum, Programming Research Dept., IBM.)

[36] *Remington Rand, Inc., *The A-2 Compiler System Operations Manual.* Prepared by Richard K. Ridgway and Margaret H. Harper under the direction of Grace M. Hopper, 15 Nov. 1953.

[37] Rutishauser, Heinz, "Automatische Rechenplanfertigung bei programmgesteuerten Rechenmaschinen," *Mitteilungen aus dem Inst. fir angew. Math. an der E. T. H. Zunch.,* nr. 3. Basel: Birkhauser, 1952.

[38] Sammet, Jean E., *Programming Languages: History and Fundamentals.* Englewood Cliffs, N.J.: Prentice Hall, 1969.

[39] Sheridan, Peter B., "The Arithmetic Translator-Compiler of the IBM Fortran Automatic Coding System," *Comm. ACM,* vol. 2, no. 2, pp. 9-21, Feb. 1959.

[40] *Schlesinger, S.I., *Dual Coding System.* Los Alamos, N.M.: Los Alamos Science Lab., Rep. LA1573, July 1953.

[41] Zuse, K., "Uber den Plankalkül," *Electron Rechenanl.,* vol. 1, pp. 68-71, 1959.

[42] Zuse, K., "Der Plankalkül," *Benchte der Cesellschaft für Mathematik und Datenverarbeitung,* vol. 63, part 3. Bonn, 1972. (Manuscript prepared in 1945.)

John Backus led the development of Fortran and participated in designing the IBM 704 and Algol, he proposed "BNF" for syntax description. He received the National Medal of Science in 1975, the Turing Award (ACM) in 1977, the IEEE Computer Society Pioneer Award in 1980, and the Charles Stark Draper Award from the National Academy of Engineering in 1993. He is a member of the National Academy of Sciences and the National Academy of Engineering. He is currently retired from his job at the IBM Research Laboratory, San Jose, California, but continues to consult with IBM from time to time.

The author can be contacted at
91 St. Germain Ave.
San Francisco, CA 94114

System/360:
A Retrospective View

System/360:
A Retrospective View

BOB O. EVANS

Editor's Note: In January 1983 (Vol. 5, No. 1) the Annals *published the* SPREAD *report, the 1961 IBM task group recommendations for IBM's future processor products that led to the System/360. Bob O. Evans was among the participants in a 1982 discussion of the* SPREAD *report, also published in that issue, and he wrote an introduction for us.*

In the current article, adapted from a lecture he gave at the Computer Museum on November 10, 1983, Evans summarizes the events, organizations, product lines, and motivations that led to the System/360, IBM's major shift to compatible processors, peripherals, and software for both business and scientific applications. A version of this article was published in the Computer Museum Report *(Number 9, Summer 1984). Some of this IBM history has been detailed in the* Annals *previously; see special issues on the 701 (Vol. 5, No. 2) and 650 (Vol. 8, No. 1) and articles by Bashe, Hurd, McPherson et al., Phelps, etc.; also see the recent volume by Bashe et al.,* IBM's Early Computers *(MIT Press, 1985). We are pleased to have the author's personal view of the principles involved in the System/360, the environment during its development, some of the problems encountered, and the consequences of the 360, both for IBM and for the information processing industry.*

Prologue

This personal review of events that led to one of the most significant decisions in modern business, IBM's undertaking of the product line that became the System/360, begins with a few preludes. Small steps themselves, each added force to the conditions that eventually led to the decision to produce a completely new, unified IBM product line that portended substantial potential, but also put the corporation at high risk.

Categories and Subject Descriptors: C.0 [**General**]; K.1 [**The Computer Industry**]; K.2 [**History of Computing**]—*hardware, IBM System/360, people, software, systems. General Terms:* Design, Management. *Additional Key Words and Phrases:* compatibility.
Author's Address: Hambrecht & Quist, 235 Montgomery Street, San Francisco, CA 94104.
© 1986 AFIPS 0164-1239/86/020155-179$01.00/00

The Early Years (1911–1945)

Formed in 1911 from three tiny companies, the Computing-Tabulating-Recording Company (CTR) was still a small enterprise when, in 1914, Thomas J. Watson became its leader. Through the 1920s and early 1930s the company's products were electric clocks, electric scoreboards, attendance recorders, nurse-call systems, equipment to weigh and slice meat, and punched-card products. Watson was intrigued with the inventions of Herman Hollerith who, in the previous century, had conceived the use of paper cards with punched holes to store, retrieve, and manipulate information. Hollerith's Tabulating Machine Company was one of the forerunners of CTR, renamed International Business Machines in 1924 by the imaginative Watson when the company's annual sales were less than $20 million.

How IBM withdrew from or divested itself of its primary product lines and moved into the age of information processing based on the punched card is a fascinating story in itself. Bolstered by the calculating, record-keeping, and reporting requirements of the Social Security Act of 1931, demand for punched-card processing equipment rose steadily. IBM became the leader in products that included card readers, punches, printers, and calculating equipment. Through the 1930s and into the 1940s, IBM's sales growth was steady but not spectacular; however, Watson and his management team's ability was clearly demonstrated in that net profit was always strong (Figure 1a).

IBM continued to expand its punched-card line through the 1940s. World War II diverted almost all of the company's development away from its main product line as Watson, a staunch patriot, directed IBM's engineering and production facilities to the war effort. IBM's two manufacturing plants, at Endicott and Poughkeepsie, New York, turned to production for national needs, incuding fire-control equipment and navigation and bombing systems. These wartime products had little technological relationship to IBM's commercial products, but they became a foundation for IBM's future national-interest efforts, which continue today as the Federal Systems Division.

Electronic Data Processing—A New Direction (1946–1957)

IBM emerged from World War II in a strong position in terms of finance, plant, personnel, and potential. As the economy returned to peacetime conditions, IBM had substantial opportunities in punched-card products as user demand increased. Investors were solid in their support, and the company was financially very healthy (Figure 1b). While IBM remained the electric accounting machine (EAM) product leader, its managers understood that prewar electromechanical technology could be greatly improved.

A new voice was calling. Small groups of researchers at IBM's two laboratories were evaluating the application of vacuum-tube electronics to company products. A few prototypes were designed, mostly by a direct translation of electronics to existing EAM structures. In 1946 IBM produced the 603, an electromechanical calculator, and in 1948 IBM announced the 604 electronic calculator, which became very popular, with more than 5000 eventually produced.

Commencing with some work just prior to the U.S. entry into World War II, J. P. Eckert and J. W. Mauchly at the Moore School of the University of Pennsylvania and J. V. Atanasoff at Iowa State College were experimenting with pioneering devices that ultimately led to the "stored-program" concept, which would profoundly affect computing. Other research and development efforts sprang from research at the Institute for Advanced Study at Princeton, New Jersey, where John von Neumann and his colleagues built an electronic computer; at Cambridge University un-

der M. V. Wilkes; and later, at Los Alamos, the National Bureau of Standards, U.S. Army laboratories, MIT, and the Rand Corporation.

In 1950 at IBM an unusual event triggered a major corporate change. At the start of the Korean War, Thomas J. Watson, Sr., offered President Truman the resources of IBM to aid the national need. As a result of this offer, two IBM executives, Cuthbert C. Hurd and Ralph L. Palmer, toured several national laboratories to ascertain how IBM could best contribute. Their analysis concluded that the United States urgently needed new computational capabilities for such problems as ballistic table computations, two-dimensional hydrodynamic calculations, nuclear weapon and reactor design, and aircraft design. Palmer and Hurd recommended that IBM produce electronic computers similar to von Neumann's Institute for Advanced Study design. The corporation affirmed the recommendation; Jerrier A. Haddad and Nathaniel Rochester, leading young development managers, assumed overall direction of the project. Cost estimates and demand forecasts resulted in an estimate that the system rental would have to be approximately $20,000 per month, an unheard-of price. A program was nevertheless established to manufacture 18 systems, which were quickly sold—eventually 19 were produced. Internally called the IBM 701 EDPM (Electronic Data Processing Machine) Defense Calculator, the first sys-

Bob O. Evans was born in Nebraska, served in the U.S. Navy, received a B.S.E.E. from Iowa State University in 1949, and studied mathematics and electrical engineering at Syracuse University. He joined IBM in 1951 as a junior engineer working on the 701, and he had various responsibilities in the company through 1962, when he was appointed vice-president of development for the Data Systems Division, developing the System/360. He was president of the Federal Systems Division (1965), the Systems Development Division (1969), and Systems Communications Division (1975), and was elected an IBM vice-president in 1972. In 1984, as vice-president for engineering, programming, and technology, he retired from IBM and joined Hambrecht & Quist Venture Partners as a general partner.

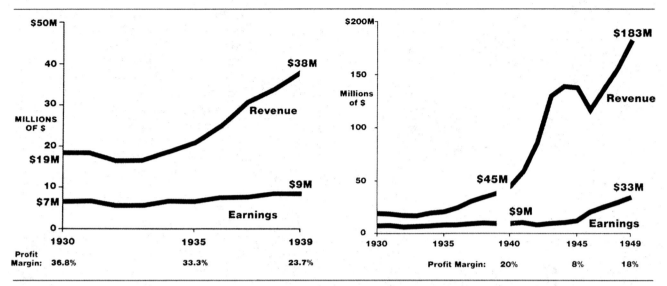

Figure 1a. IBM growth, 1930 to 1939.

Figure 1b. IBM growth, 1940 to 1949.

tem was installed as the IBM 701 EDPM at IBM's world headquarters in December 1952. The renters of the 18 other 701s included the Atomic Energy Commission laboratories, the Rand Corporation, the National Security Agency, and several aircraft companies. The electronic revolution was under way in IBM, even though the forecasts were that only a few of the largest companies and major government agencies would need and be able to afford electronic data processing systems. In retrospect, it is remarkable that the management of a company with EAM product-line leadership, EAM customer loyalty, and strong demand for new EAM features and functions, but with esti-

Editor's Note: The form of the illustrations for this article is of historical interest. They are reproductions of the viewfoils used by the author at his 1983 lecture at the Computer Museum and are typical of the graphics used in the 1960s, the System/360 era.

At the start of the century, lectures were illustrated with figures projected from 3″ × 3″ glass slides. Just after World War II, the slides were replaced by single frames of 35mm film, which permitted many individual slides to be carried in a carousel and handled automatically. This technique is still in use today.

In the mid-1960s, with the development of higher-intensity projection lamps and plastic lenses, the viewgraph arrangement became popular. Here 8″ × 10″ plastic sheets, made by photocopying machines from typed or drawn copy, were mounted in cardboard carriers. The projector was no longer at the rear of the auditorium but was at the front, where the speaker could handle the slides.

The graphic capability of computers, even personal ones, is already making this type of lecture illustration archaic. We can expect that at first viewgraphs will be made on computers and projected in the usual way, but before the end of the century, lectures will be illustrated with material created by a computer, stored in digital form, and presented to the audience on the equivalent of giant television screens.   —Eric A. Weiss

mates of only limited EDPM potential, would turn such a sharp corner to a wholly different world. In a sense management's willingness to abandon a successful past and strike out in new directions had been the story of IBM's success. Watson's act of patriotism triggered IBM's first stored-program computer-product efforts, and his son, Thomas J. Watson, Jr., completed the turn from electric accounting machines to electronic data processing.

At this time, business use of electronic computers loomed as the major prospect, since scientific computing, while important, did not promise the same high volume. IBM's 701 Defense Calculator, designed for scientific computing, was followed by a new business computer, the IBM 702, which was in production in 1953. The IBM laboratories now quickly converted almost all of their development efforts to electronic computer systems, and several vacuum-tube editions emerged: the 702, followed by the 705 Model 1, which later evolved to the 705 Model 3.

One of IBM's most successful vacuum-tube systems was the 650, a serial, decimal, fixed-word-length machine. Using a magnetic drum as its principal memory, the 650 far outsold its forecast and was used in both business and scientific applications. The 650 became the first electronic computer to have more than 1000 systems installed.

Capitalizing on IBM's invention of disk storage, the 305 RAMAC was developed in a new laboratory in San Jose, California. The 701's capacity for scientific applications was improved: the costly, primitive Williams cathode-ray-tube main memory was replaced by

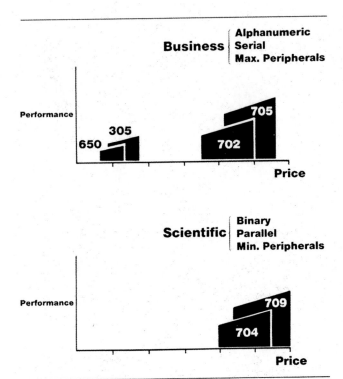

Figure 2. IBM vacuum-tube computer families, 1952–1956.

new ferrite core technology. Gene M. Amdahl, fresh from the University of Wisconsin, led the team that designed the 704. It had substantial improvements in its architecture, including being the first commercially produced computer to include indexing and floating-point arithmetic as standard operations. The 704 was followed later by the 709; both were highly successful.

Business machines of the 700 series operated in decimal and serially by character, and thus were relatively slow. The larger business systems had variable data-record lengths to accommodate the many data formats required. These systems also had many peripheral devices—card readers, card punches, magnetic tapes, and printers—to process the voluminous data of business problems. The scientific computers of the 700 series, however, operated in binary and in parallel for speed, and usually did not have extensive peripheral equipment. Their handling of variable field lengths and alphanumeric characters was cumbersome.

Programming provided by IBM and other systems manufacturers was primitive, and load, dump, sort, print, and control utilities were simple. The codes were usually written in a processor's native language, and thus were not transportable to other architectures. FORTRAN and other high-level languages were conceived in this era, but did not gain widespread use because of both inertia and the learning required.

Thus in the period 1953–1957 IBM produced a number of new electronic computer products, for both scientific and business applications (Figure 2).

Design of business systems had taken one direction, scientific applications another. Within user organizations, specialties were increasing in each area, and all were competing for funds and personnel. The various computer families were incompatible; that is, programs for the 704 could not run on a 702 or 650 or even its predecessor, the 701. The IBM metamorphosis to electronic computing was nonetheless under way: a few hundreds of the 704, 709, 702, and 705 systems were produced; approximately fifteen hundred 650s were installed; and more than a thousand 305s were produced. IBM's revenues and profits grew steadily through the 1950s, exceeding $1 billion in 1957 (Figure 3).

The Transistor Age Begins (1958–1960)

The transistor, invented in Bell Telephone Laboratories in the late 1940s, brought great potential to the growing computer industry. The transistor offered substantial improvements in computer size, power consumption, speed, and reliability. A small group of IBM researchers developed transistors optimized for IBM needs, and soon pilot manufacturing lines produced customized IBM transistors used in early production. IBM purchased the higher production quantities of transistors tailored to its specifications from semiconductor manufacturers, often assisting them in establishing the production and test processes. On occasion, IBM even provided company-designed process and test equipment to expedite production of IBM-specification transistors.

The scientific area, with less volume promise and thus fewer engineering resources allocated, elected to produce a transistorized, higher-performance version of the successful vacuum-tube 709 system. It became the popular 7090 system, and more than 500 were sold.

Since business applications were perceived as having the highest volume potential, most of the engineering resources focused on the business sector. Competition grew as Sperry-Rand, Bendix, General Electric, General Precision, National Cash Register, and many other companies offered new computers. During this period RCA, which had commenced its business entry with the BIZMAC system, announced a new product for business, the RCA 501. The 501 appeared to be the first new technology entrant for the major business applications area. The marketing and management pressure was thus on IBM's laboratories to produce an expeditious and competitive product. To compete, IBM needed a new computer architecture, so a principal effort was established to design and produce the 7070 system, which was first installed in 1960. It is important to the 360 story to relate one part of the 7070 history.

In 1957, Ralph Palmer, IBM's incisive director of engineering, wanted the best system possible in the to-be-designed new business computer. He established a design competition between the Endicott and Poughkeepsie laboratories. The Poughkeepsie laboratory had more extensive large-electronic-computer design experience with the 701, 702, 705, and 709 products, all of which were reasonably successful. The Endicott laboratory was still heavily involved with electric accounting machines, but under the direction of Frank E. Hamilton had produced the SSEC and later the 650, the smaller but highly successful computer system which, by 1958, had achieved the largest volume of IBM's vacuum-tube computers. The interlaboratory competition to win responsibility for the new business computer design was vigorous. Poughkeepsie advocated a new architecture based on a stored-program version of a special extension of the 604–607 designed for Northrop Aircraft by William Woodbury, Gregory J. Toben, and Truman Wheelock, while Endicott started from the 650 structure. The Endicott design group was more aggressive, however, adding new features and functions to the original proposed design, and won the competition to Poughkeepsie's dismay. Endicott's resulting 7070 was a very complex architecture. The system had a number of new capabilities, but the development program ran into difficulty, as Poughkeepsie had predicted. Additional engineering and programming resources were added to the Endicott project.

Then in 1959, as discussed later, a major organization change was made. In the shifting of responsibilities, ironically the 7070 responsibility was transferred to Poughkeepsie just before first customer shipment. With its prior recommendations for an alternate direction, Poughkeepsie did not want the 7070 and its problems. Elements of the Poughkeepsie engineering organization set out to terminate the program through initiation of a project internally dubbed the 70AB, which had very simple goals: build a system that had twice the performance and half the cost of the 7070. Even though the goals were noble, the proposal was not practically achievable in the light of time and the existing 7070 customer commitments. Palmer interceded with senior vice-president T. Vincent Learson, who ordered Poughkeepsie to produce the 7070. The group complied, but the 7070 events added fuel to the fires of interlaboratory competition that was to promulgate future divergent plans.

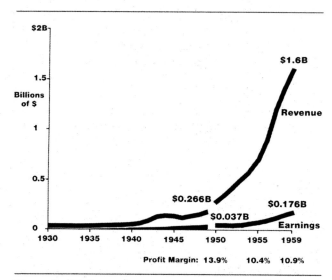

Figure 3. IBM growth, 1950 to 1959.

Another element in the 360 prelude was the "transistorization" of the punched-card area. The electromechanical parts in use had continual wear and were increasingly costly to produce and service, yet a large number of users, worldwide, were expanding their use of punched-card accounting. IBM urgently required new punched-card products, preferably not mechanical. The search for transistorized replacements for the electric accounting machines was under way in the 1950s. An approach dubbed The Accounting Machine in the Endicott laboratory failed, as costs were too high. An international effort commenced with the Endicott laboratory working with the recently formed French development laboratory on the proposed Worldwide Accounting Machine project. This failed, when the direct substitution of transistors for electromechanical and mechanical devices proved too costly. Then an Endicott laboratory engineer, Francis O. Underwood, conceived an entirely different approach. Instead of directly mapping transistors onto the existing structures, Underwood proposed an architecture to bring the stored-program principle to calculating equipment. The project, led by Charles E. Branscomb, was called SPACE (Stored Program Accounting and Calculating Equipment). The processing electronics were combined with a new IBM printing technology utilizing a revolving chain of alphabetic and numeric characters; the system was announced as the IBM 1401. First shipped to customers in 1959, renting for $2495 per month for a basic system, the 1401 was the Model-T Ford of the computer industry. More than 12,000 were produced; this new business system far exceeded IBM's original estimates.

In 1960 the San Jose laboratory started delivery of the 1620, a small scientific computer. Renting for $1600 per month, more than 1000 were eventually produced. Curiously, unlike its contemporaries, which were binary, the 1620 architecture was to have a decimal structure. That fact was later to play a role on the route to System/360.

Customers liked and ordered Poughkeepsie's 7090 scientific system, but the 7070 reception was weak. Customers with vacuum-tube 702, 705, 650, and 305 business computers were not converting as expected to the new 7070 architecture. Poughkeepsie found it necessary to produce the 7080, a transistorized version of the 705, to satisfy immediate growth needs of the large-business customer set. The seeds of program compatibility were beginning to sprout.

One other IBM project affected the System/360 story—the Stretch or 7030 computer, which was begun in 1955. Intended to stretch both technologies and performance with improvement goals of two orders of magnitude over the 704, its history is fascinating. Suffice it to say here that when it was first delivered in 1961, it failed to meet a performance claim of being eight times faster than the 7090. Conceivably, IBM might have avoided taking action on user-performance issues, since performance measures were vague in those times. After hearing a complaint from the Atomic Energy Commission's Livermore Laboratory, however, Thomas J. Watson, Jr., engaged an independent consultant. The consultant, examining a variety of applications, deduced that most customers would use the 7030 system in 7090-type applications, and concluded that without substantial reprogramming, Stretch would produce an average of 5.4, not 8 times the 7090 performance. Thus IBM reduced the price by 5.4/8, from $13.5 million to $8.8 million—an example of Watson Jr.'s keen sense of fairness.

Stretch had been significant in the recruiting of bright young engineers and programmers, many of whom played key roles in the 360 engineering and programming effort. Programming, still not an established science, remained rudimentary. Some progress had been made in developing compilers, but lack of standards, differences in compiler implementations, and performance problems dampened code portability to negligible proportions. Systems manufacturers' programming support was growing, but was generally limited to load, sort, unload, and peripheral unit utilities, such as programs for tape to printer, card to tape, etc. For the 7090 an input/output control system was produced, which was an important step toward modern operating systems. The 1401 had a powerful report generator, which among other functions, more automatically organized and formatted the computer's printouts.

Vendor-furnished programming remained sparse and elemental, as evidenced by IBM's programming development budget of less than 5 percent of the research and development budget in 1961, at the very beginning of volume shipment of the new transistorized products—the 1401, 1620, 7070, and 7090 systems.

As of 1960, therefore, the IBM transistorized computer products consisted of two classes—business and scientific—with more than one noncompatible family within each class: 1401, 7070, and 7080 for business; 1620, 7090, and 7030 for scientific applications; limited programming was provided with each family.

People

To put the 360 story in perspective, we should briefly discuss people and organization. Thousands of people across the world worked to make the System/360 happen; hundreds had important management roles in all functions: development, manufacturing, marketing, service, and administration. A few who were deeply involved in its management and engineering are most important to the System/360 history. Their abilities and 1960 positions in the IBM organization structure had substantial influence on what transpired.

T. Vincent Learson. Senior vice-president for the data processing group. Learson, a Harvard-educated marketing professional, had risen rapidly in the IBM ranks. In the 1950s, he had been a principal, together with Watson Jr., in leading IBM into electronic computers. Learson was tough, decisive, forceful, and, like Watson, intolerant of mediocrity.

Orland M. Scott. President of the successful General Products Division. A University of Missouri graduate and marketing trained, Scott was a decisive and respected leader.

Jerrier A. Haddad. General manager of the Advanced Systems Development Division. A Cornell University graduate in electrical engineering, Haddad held a number of engineering management positions and was a respected technical leader.

John W. Haanstra. Vice-president of development, General Products Division. A University of California M.S.S.E., Haanstra was the first IBM development professional named a division vice-president. Brilliant, respected, and strong-willed, Haanstra had significant influence and was admired by both senior corporate management and other divisions.

Donald T. Spaulding. Director of systems development and planning in the General Products Division. Harvard-educated, he joined IBM as a sales trainee, and was selected early in his career for higher management preparation. As of January 1960, Spaulding managed all of GPD's product areas and was demonstrating his foresight in strategic planning.

Bob O. Evans. Systems manager, processing systems, in the Endicott, New York, laboratory of the General Products Division. An Iowa State University electrical engineer previously assigned to the Poughkeepsie laboratory, I had responsibility for most of GPD's computer product development.

Gene M. Amdahl. From the University of Wisconsin and employed by IBM from 1952 until 1956, and from 1960 until 1970, Amdahl was recognized for his work on the WISC at Wisconsin and on the IBM 704 and 709.

Erich Bloch. An electrical engineer from the Federal Polytechnic Institute of Zurich and the University of Buffalo, Bloch had risen rapidly in engineering ranks, managing several advanced technology programs. In 1960, he managed the Stretch engineering program and the Harvest program, which was a special project for the National Security Agency with advanced magnetic tapes and special electronics integrated into a Stretch processor base.

Frederick P. Brooks, Jr. Systems manager for the 8000 series in the Data Systems Division. Educated at Duke and Harvard universities, Brooks, a brilliant, eloquent, and natural leader, was rapidly assuming leadership of the Data Systems Division's product plans.

Maxwell O. Paley. Special project manager for the 7070 in the Data Systems Division. A Penn State electrical engineer, Paley had managed development of the 608, IBM's first transistorized computer, and later was a development principal in a number of IBM systems projects.

Organizational Considerations

As of 1955 IBM was organized functionally with vice-presidents for engineering, manufacturing, and sales. The vice-president for sales was also responsible for service. Small headquarters staffs for finance, legal, contracts, etc., supported the principals. Each vice-president had diverse responsibilities because the functional areas of each one covered electric accounting machines, electronic computers, typewriters, and supplies (such as cards and forms), as well as IBM's continued national-interest contracts.

Thomas J. Watson, Jr., led a major restructuring of IBM that established smaller functional groups and delegated more of the decision making. The first of the new organizations appeared in 1955 when the national-interest engineering, manufacturing, and sales organizations formed a new, independent division called the Military Products Division, later renamed the Federal Systems Division.

The Military Products Division was followed by the formation of an Electric Typewriter Division; later a

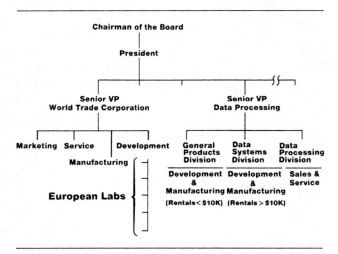

Figure 4. Organization of IBM in 1960.

Supplies Division was established. Overall the reorganization took almost four years, concluding in 1959 with the formulation of three new divisions to forge the electronic computer future (Figure 4). The Data Processing Division (DPD), headed by Gilbert E. Jones, was responsible for sales and service; the General Products Division (GPD), headed by Scott, was responsible for development and manufacture of small systems; and the Data Systems Division (DSD), headed by W. B. McWhirter, was responsible for development and manufacture of larger electronic computer systems.

Learson was the executive in charge of the two product-development–manufacturing divisions. The two product divisions had responsibility for the "books"—that is, forecasting, cost estimating, pricing, revenue allocations, etc. DPD, the sales and service division, was financed by an allocation from revenues.

A line of demarcation separated the product divisions' missions. GPD was responsible for products of very low price up to systems renting for $10,000 per month, while DSD was responsible for products renting for $10,000 and higher. DSD was centered in the Poughkeepsie laboratory and plant; GPD was at the Endicott and San Jose laboratories and plants. A few products were shifted to conform to the new organization: the 1620, designed in Poughkeepsie, was moved to San Jose for development completion and manufacture, and the 7070 was moved to Poughkeepsie from Endicott, as previously mentioned.

Relevant to the 360 story, IBM senior management in 1959, literally at the very beginning of the 1400, 1600, and 7000 series, assigned the Poughkeepsie laboratory the task of planning the next generation of

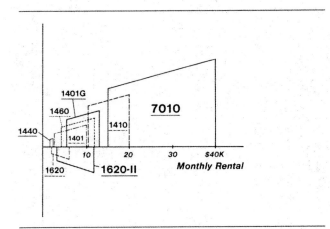

Figure 5. Plan of IBM General Products Division, 1961.

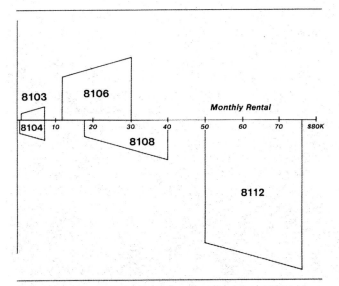

Figure 6. Plan of IBM Data Systems Division, 1961.

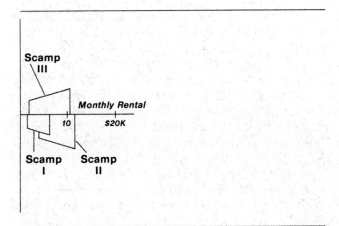

Figure 7. Plan of IBM World Trade Corporation, 1961.

computer systems. Two of the leading 7030 designers, Frederick P. Brooks and Gerrit A. Blaauw, joined the future systems development effort, which began on the base of the project previously described as the 70AB that had been launched as a 7070 replacement, but had been set aside on Learson's order in favor of the 7070. Poughkeepsie, with its mission to design the next generation, needed complementing small computers to complete its plan. GPD, however, with Endicott's very successful 1401 system, preferred not to replace the 1401 with Poughkeepsie's exotic new architecture. Instead, they planned compatible extensions of the 1401 to meet their customers' projected growth requirements. A 1410 was planned to rent for $8000 to $20,000, and an even larger system, the 7010, was under consideration (Figure 5). DSD thus proceeded to define its own small systems: one for business applications and another for small scientific applications.

As Brooks assumed leadership, in Poughkeepsie, a family of systems was defined. Internally called the 8000 series, a midrange 8106 was proposed for business computing with a scientific attachment, the 8108, the 8103 would be a small business system, and the 8104 a small scientific system; the 8112 was to be a large scientific system (Figure 6). The first system of the family, the 8106, was scheduled for announcement in the second quarter of 1961. In net, the GPD product plan was in conflict with DSD.

Meanwhile, the World Trade Corporation's (WTC) U.K. laboratory was active. For more than two years the marketing organizations, especially in Europe, had called for a small binary computer, because they found the decimal-structured 1620 scientific computer unsatisfactory for certain types of scientific applications. A U.K.-Hursley laboratory project led by John W. Fairclough responded with the design of a 48-bit, small scientific computer code-named SCAMP, and aimed for a 1961 announcement. The SCAMP design incorporated novel read-only memory controls. (Previous IBM systems had controls consisting of standard logic circuitry. Because control was literally intertwined with all of the arithmetic and logic elements, control electronics were complex. When engineering changes were necessary, changes proliferated throughout many areas of the central electronics, much like unraveling a knitted sweater. Hursley's approach, adapted from concepts invented by Maurice V. Wilkes's group at Cambridge University, used small wired transformers that, when combined with timing pulses, emitted streams of pulses in sequence that served as the control electronics.) Control costs were reduced, and engineering changes and functional extensions were substantially simplified by changing the "1" and "0" patterns of the control memory instead of altering contemporary control electronics. This "microcode" ultimately became a way of life in the computer industry.

In mid-1961 the SCAMP project was in difficulty, as the forecasted demand for SCAMP was insufficient to justify its production. The Hursley laboratory promptly proposed a second version, SCAMP II, expecting to capitalize on the original design and expand the volume to improve the justification. The anticipated demand for the additional model was still insufficient, however, so Hursley began to consider SCAMP III, a business application version of the original design that Hursley hoped would acquire greater volume by being capable in business applications (Figure 7).

The stage for confrontation among divisions was now set. As of 1960, GPD had its successful product line centered on the 1401, with plans for expanding that base upward, even into the DSD mission area. DSD had some successful products and others that were less successful. Armed with the corporate mission to plan the next generation of computers, however, DSD was busy with its proposed 8000 series which was being extended into GPD's domain. WTC, in its quest for a small scientific product, was touting SCAMP, which was being expanded in both business and scientific performance to obtain volume.

Formation of the Integrated Product Family Concept (1961)

The IBM organization changes continually, as is the case with most dynamic enterprises. A change that affected many of the individuals mentioned was that as of January 1961, Spaulding had been promoted from GPD to lead Learson's Group Staff, a group of only a half-dozen highly capable professionals, but quite influential in future product matters.

As the three organizations pursued overlapping and competing programs (Figure 8), Spaulding, as Learson's aide, understood the undesirable features of this competition and convinced Learson of possible difficulties. Spaulding recommended a first step of bringing me from GPD to head systems development and planning in DSD. Learson agreed, and in January 1961 Learson told me of the assignment. Learson's instructions were simple: "Go to DSD, evaluate their 8000 series. If it's right, produce it as quickly as possible. If it's not right, do what's right!"

As of January 1961 the relevant organization had thus changed again. Now viewed as an opponent by the DSD development force, I spent two months evaluating the 8000 series. In April I took the position that the 8000 was a mistake (see the appendix). At

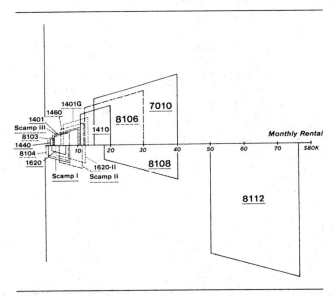

Figure 8. IBM's overlapping product line in 1961.

the same time Haddad, who had led the 701, IBM's first computer development, became the DSD vice-president of development. Haddad agreed with me, and in May 1961, the decision to terminate the 8000 and commence a new program "that was right" was affirmed.

Earlier in 1960 with the 1401 success ensured, Spaulding and I had teamed in Endicott to terminate a proposed unique architecture called ARS (Advanced Retrieval System). Palmer had earlier moved the project from the San Jose Laboratory to Endicott, hoping for synergism with the 1401. The Endicott engineers started design of a structure quite different from the 1401, however. Spaulding and I stepped in to make ARS compatible with the 1401, and the 1410 was born.

I pressed the principle that data and instruction repertoire compatibility was essential as I reassembled the DSD development plans. An eventful reorganization meeting was held in May 1961 at the Gideon Putnam Hotel in Saratoga Springs, New York. Two plans were required: a short-term tactical set of current product-line improvements, plus a major effort on the new strategic product family plan. Between mid-1961 and mid-1963, what I dubbed "temporizers" were produced to respond to increasing customer demand. Thus, GPD proceeded with a 1620-II and the 1410, while DSD joined the "1401 family" by producing the larger 7010. DSD also had extended the 7070 with two more powerful models, the 7072 and 7074, completed the 7080 and 7030, and added two models to the 7090—the 7094 and the 7094-II. For the mid-

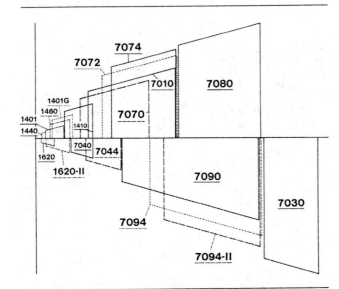

Figure 9. IBM's immediate products to strengthen the product line, 1961–1963.

range DSD added two new scientific systems, the 7040 and 7044 (Figure 9). I named Brooks to lead the development of the new product line and Amdahl to be its principal architect. Amdahl had returned to IBM in 1960 and was working in the research organization on the structure of an advanced high-performance system. Emanuel R. Piore, IBM's vice-president for research, had agreed to my request for Amdahl on the condition that DSD would develop a new superperformance processor, an area that had been dormant following the performance problems and reduction in price of the Stretch computer in 1961. I agreed, and a high-performance processor project was established in both technology and systems design.

The establishment of Brooks and Amdahl on the project brought two of IBM's best systems architects into the undertaking. A certain amount of rivalry and debate ensued between the two, but their leadership and intellectual contributions proved to be extremely important to what became System/360.

The Need to Change the Systems' Structure

The seven noncompatible families that emerged in the period 1952–1962 had a number of serious problems, from the standpoint of both the users and IBM.

1. With so many types of architectures, IBM was spending most of its development resources propagating the wide variety of central processors. Little development effort was devoted to either peripherals or programming (see Figure 23 later). A user could move

from one processor in a family to one twice as fast, but only achieve 10 percent improvement in throughput (problem-solving ability), since the existing disk or tape peripheral devices and programming could not keep pace with the central processors.

2. The differing architectures of the families made it impossible to develop optimized peripheral equipment—disks, magnetic tape units, etc. The volume of any single system or family was usually too small to justify a disk or tape optimized to that particular architecture. Thus new peripheral devices, if available at all, were suboptimized across differing architectures—business systems with their serial-by-character, variable-field-length characteristics, and the scientific units with their binary, highly parallel characteristics. Expensive electronic adapters had to be designed to attach the available peripheral devices to the different systems (Figure 10). Some systems had to live with older peripherals when new developments could not be justified, so throughput was too often constrained.

3. When transistors came into service, IBM strove to take fullest advantage of the new capability through standardization of circuits and centralization of circuit design groups. In 1955 a new circuit-packaging technology was developed for IBM's future transistorized products. Called the standard modular system (SMS), a comprehensive assemblage of printed circuit cards and circuit boards were designed with insertion equipment, automatic soldering equipment, automatic circuit wire wrapping equipment, etc. SMS was created over a weekend by Edward J. Garvey, then laboratory manager for Endicott. The system provided a standard set of building blocks on fixed-size printed circuit

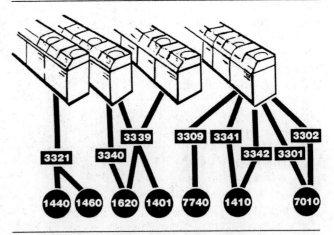

Figure 10. Before System/360, many adapters were required to attach disks to existing IBM systems.

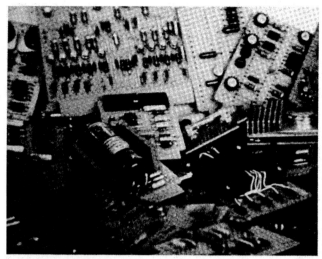

Figure 11. Hundreds of types of circuit cards were used before System/360.

cards and was the predecessor of the solid logic technology (SLT) family. The SMS family was used throughout the 1400 and 7000 product lines. Palmer and Haddad, leaders of the circuit standardization plan, hoped that approximately 100 types of printed circuit cards with a range of AND/OR logic circuits, inverters, amplifiers, flip-flops, etc., would suffice for the to-be-designed 7000, 1400, and 1600 families. The demands of the varying architectures and the rapid invention and innovation taking place in transistors, however, thwarted the aspirations of the standardization plan (Figure 11). By 1963 there were more than 2500 types of circuit cards, causing new levels of problems in the logistics of manufacture, test, inventory control, spare parts stocking in the field, and customer engineer training, as well as limiting engineering's ability to improve the designs.

4. In the early 1960s IBM learned that functional capability, performance, and reliability of programming were key to volume sales. With seven different families, programming not yet an established science, and a relatively small group of programmers assigned to individual systems, IBM had increasing programming problems and demands. Each system type needed its array of compilers for a variety of languages—COBOL and FORTRAN, for example—usually designed separately for magnetic tape input/output and disk input/output. Each system type needed utility programming, such as loaders, memory dump, sort, and peripheral control (Figure 12). Users were generally unable to move across system boundaries and sometimes had difficulty moving from one processor of a family to another. In net, migration was difficult,

conversion was expensive, often prohibitive, and available resources had to be spread across a wide range of processor and peripheral equipment products.

5. The scientific–business products split limited the users because, in addition to the internal competition for resources and mission, increasingly the scientific areas needed the alphanumeric and peripheral powers of the business systems, and the business systems needed the logical and computational powers of the scientific machines.

6. Main memory was chronically too small in each IBM system. As early as 1955, John von Neumann, then a consultant to IBM, estimated that 10,000 binary words of memory should be sufficient for any problem he could foresee, and, allowing for inefficient programming, 20,000 would be ample. In the addressing structure of the vacuum-tube scientific computers, IBM had generously allowed for 32,768 words. On successive designs IBM repeatedly increased the memory-addressing structure and the amount of memory available. In each case—7070, 7094, 7080, 1620, and 1401—the memory capacity nonetheless proved to be far less than users eventually required. Clearly, orders of magnitude of improvement in main memory addressing and capacity would be needed, thus requiring a substantial change in system architecture.

7. As of 1961 the internal coding of most systems used four bits to represent a single decimal digit and six bits to represent an alphabetic character; this system allowed only 64 combinations of numbers, characters, and symbols, and was clearly restrictive. A new character structure was needed that allowed substantially more combinations for upper- and lowercase alphabets, special symbols, superscripts, and subscripts.

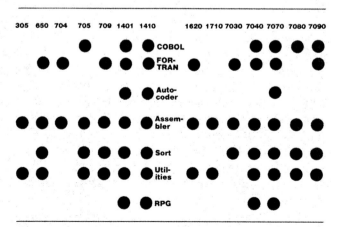

Figure 12. Before System/360, IBM computers had too many programming systems.

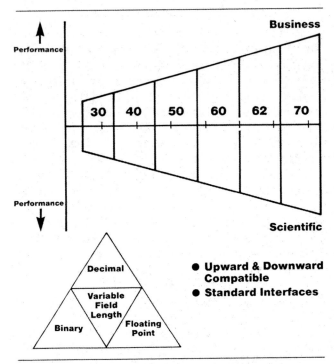

Figure 13. IBM's new plan, patterned on the SPREAD report in 1961.

For many reasons a wholly new system architecture structure was required. In May 1961 the Data Systems Division set out to produce one.

In August 1961 the World Trade Corporation (WTC) continued to argue for the SCAMP series. A small binary scientific system was certainly needed, but much of the pressure for SCAMP had to do with WTC management's view of the need to make the European laboratories more viable; thus it was reluctant to give up a development program that was well along. Thomas J. Watson, Jr.'s brother, Arthur K. Watson, was in charge of WTC. He had lived through an earlier attempt by the WTC laboratories to develop unique punched-card equipment that had failed, so he had an open mind about the advantages of the WTC laboratories joining the international plan. A. K. Watson met with me in Poughkeepsie in August 1961, when the pros and cons of the emerging new product line (NPL) were discussed. Watson elected to terminate the SCAMP plan and have the WTC laboratories join the international plan. The WTC laboratories were assured appropriate roles in the NPL development. With this decision, the relevant IBM organizations were in agreement.

The Poughkeepsie design team coalesced quickly under Brooks. By October 1961 the scope of the NPL undertaking was being detailed. There was increasing apprehension in Poughkeepsie, however, that the General Products Division and its strong development leader, Haanstra, would not join the NPL effort but would opt to enhance the 1401 further, for two reasons:

1. The 1401 architecture was clearly inadequate for the foreseen spectrum of new applications.

2. Haanstra's demonstrated tendency to keep his operations independent worried DSD that GPD's withdrawal from the NPL would damage the new family by reducing the volume of planned new technologies, thus increasing costs.

In October 1961, Spaulding, still Learson's aide, proposed an international task force to put the master systems plan in place. Spaulding conceived the approach of having Haanstra lead the task force. Spaulding's scheme was to get Haanstra personally involved in setting the plan and to have the plan locked in by placing Haanstra in the position of being personally committed to corporate management. The task force was launched in the beginning of November 1961; it built on DSD's work since May 1961. Named SPREAD, meaning Systems Programming Research and Development, internally the study was affectionately dubbed, "Spaulding's Plan to Reorganize Each and All Divisions." Among the 13 participants were Haanstra, the chairman; Evans, the vice-chairman; Brooks; and a number of other professionals representing development, marketing, the Federal Systems Division, and the World Trade Corporation. To allow concentration, the group was deliberately convened offsite in the Sheraton New Englander Motel in Greenwich, Connecticut. We worked diligently on detailing a joint plan.

In December 1961, Scott, president of the General Products Division, was promoted to IBM vice-president and group executive for the Data Processing Division and the Federal Systems Division. Haanstra was promoted to president of the General Products Division. He assumed his new post, but periodically returned to the SPREAD task force throughout December, while I assumed the chairmanship. By the end of December 1961 the study was complete and the plan documented. Early in January 1962, Haanstra presented the report to Watson Jr., Learson, and other involved corporate and division officers. The plan was approved and became the ruling guide for the development groups. Remarkably, the SPREAD report was followed essentially without change.

The New Product Line Plan—New Solutions

The joint-product plan was bold and strived to resolve the major problems that had arisen in the contemporary systems.

1. SPREAD planned a family of central processing units, each of which was to be proficient at both scientific and business applications as well as having facilities for the foreseen communications processing (teleprocessing) and event-driven (real-time) applications areas. The plan called for the data formats, instruction repertoires, and principal interfaces within each processor to be identical. Each system would have the capability of processing both decimal and binary formatted information, and have variable-field-length capability and floating-point arithmetic capabilities (Figure 13). The SPREAD proposal was for each system to be compatible both upward and downward; that is, given the main memory capacity and the number of peripheral devices called for by a program, any processor could run any other's program.

Previously within the product lines of IBM and other computer vendors, systems had been upwardly compatible; that is, a program from a smaller system could operate on a larger system, and the larger system's program could run on a still larger system. Usually, however, the small processor had a very simple instruction repertoire, the larger machine had the instruction repertoire of the smaller machine plus additional computational capabilities for increased performance, and a still larger processor had the instruction repertoire of the smaller two plus additional instruction and processing capabilities. There was no downward compatibility. A program prepared for a larger system could not run on a smaller unit, which meant the NPL undertaking of both upward and downward compatibility was extremely ambitious. IBM faced major technical questions as to whether the smallest processor's instruction repertoire and data flow would be so rich as to thwart the cost objectives and whether the largest processors, constrained to an instruction repertoire limited by the low-cost family members, could be powerful enough to be competitive. If successful, however, within a few years a declining percentage of IBM's development resources could administer processor evolution, with increasing resources allocated to programming and peripheral device development.

2. To solve the throughput problems brought about by the suboptimal and limited peripheral devices, the NPL design called on a 7030 invention to have standard peripheral-device interfaces across each of the processors in the family. Because all of the interfaces were identical, peripheral devices such as disks could be designed for the entire family, and their manufacture could thus enjoy the fullest volume potential. Electronics on the peripheral-device side of the interface would adapt the differing devices to the standard processor interface, which meant that when new tech-nologies permitted a new peripheral device, it could be attached with relative ease; reprogramming for the new devices would be simplified.

3. IBM had been investigating several areas with respect to transistor technologies. By 1961 integrated circuits were increasingly discussed; however, IBM's most advanced research was in a project called COMPAC, a hybrid microminiaturization technology with potential for automatic production processes. COMPAC promised substantial reductions in size (Figure 14) and marked improvement in cost. In the summer of 1961, Emanuel Piore called for a review of the potential technologies to make certain the NPL technology choice was the best. John W. Gibson, Bloch, and I reviewed the technology alternatives and concluded that COMPAC hybrid microminiaturization was a major advance and as far as IBM could go for the new product line, since integrated circuits were thought to be still some years away.

Renamed solid logic technology (SLT), the research effort on the new circuit and package technology was moved into full-scale development. Gibson later became president of IBM's first Components Division, and Bloch became the principal manager in charge of developing SLT. With the unified SLT technology across the NPL, the potential was substantially improved for standardization, use of automatic process and testing equipment, reduced field stock, simplified training for service, and a narrower range of circuit candidates for engineering refinement.

4. With the plan for compatible families, programming could be developed independent of individual

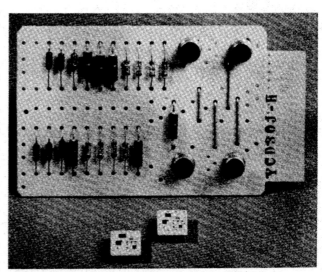

Figure 14. Two COMPAC modules (*bottom*) were equivalent to the standard modular system card (*top*) in 1961.

processors. A control program, for example, was planned for three different processors and could be used on all members in the family, given the required memory and peripheral devices. Language compilers and utility programs such as loaders could be developed to serve the entire family. Software's new freedom from specific hardware promised substantial gains in programmer productivity. More important, hardware independence signified that a customer would have to change little or no programming to move to higher-performance processors or to move from a tape-oriented to a disk-oriented system. Similarly, if economics were adverse or a business decision was made to decentralize, an installation could move down in computing capacity without reprogramming. Programming independence was perhaps the single most important advantage of the NPL structure.

5. With the plan for integration of scientific and business capabilities into single processors, businesses no longer needed to split computing facilities. Considerable efficiency and productivity could accrue, and the scientific applications would have the alphanumeric and variable-field-length capabilities; business applications would have scientific capabilities. Simultaneously, IBM undertook the specification and development of a single high-level language, eventually called PL/I, to serve not only the scientific applications where FORTRAN was then the most widely used language, but business applications as well where COBOL had become the most widely accepted language in the United States.

With compatible processor architectures, programming independence from specific hardware implementations could be achieved; with a single high-level language, unification of the scientific and business applications could be achieved.

6. The SPREAD plan was to increase main memory by two to three orders of magnitude. In previous systems, addressing had been straightforward; that is, within a computer's instruction a number of bits were reserved for the memory address. One bit will define two memory positions (1 or 0), two bits four positions (00, 01, 10, 11), 15 bits will address 32,768 positions, etc. Sixteen million positions require address lengths of 24 bits, however, which is expensive in terms of both storage occupied by long addresses in each instruction and performance losses, as the processor has to analyze the address in most instructions. The architects concluded that the millions of addresses necessary could not efficiently be addressed by a direct structure.

The architects developed an approach called "base register offset" where the system would operate within only a small portion of the main memory around a designated point, with each instruction having 12 bits for addressing, thus allowing conservation of address length but requiring extra action whenever the offset point needed to be moved outside this memory area. For much of computing the instruction sequence does operate within such a contiguous memory area. The architects' analyses were that the base-register-offset approach was best. The final design allowed the NPL processors to address 16 million characters, with the capability added later of expanding to 2 billion characters.

In net, more than two orders of magnitude increase in main memory capacity was designed into the NPL.

7. An 8-bit character named the "byte" was selected for the basic alphanumeric structure. This allowed 256 different combinations, and thus prepared the NPL for most application areas and most countries in the world with their differing alphabets and symbols.

The NPL had definitive plans to improve substantially each of the important shortcomings of the contemporary product lines.

From the beginning of the NPL in 1961, engineering management recognized that a line of new processors alone would not be enough, because the peripheral needs must also be planned. In the second quarter of 1962, Haddad led another task force called STORE. Haddad's group examined emerging and promising technologies, user needs, potential product configurations, and system bottlenecks, and made recommendations for future peripheral-unit research and development. The most important STORE study recommendation had to do with future disk-file direction. The disk file was rapidly proving to be the most important member of storage hierarchy of the computer systems. The San Jose laboratory had the disk-file mission, and plans began to take shape for new disk products to serve the NPL.

NPL Implementation (1962–1964)

The Data Systems Division was given responsibility for worldwide development coordination. The SPREAD plan specified five initial processors in the family. The smallest system was assigned to the General Products Division laboratory in Endicott. The next larger system was assigned to the WTC laboratory in Hursley. The three largest units were assigned to DSD's Poughkeepsie laboratory. Programming for smaller machines was assigned to Endicott, and programming for midrange and larger machines was assigned to Poughkeepsie. Poughkeepsie, which also had responsibility for magnetic-tape development, was stretched to its resource limits with the extensions to the contemporary systems and NPL stewardship. As a result, only minimal extensions of magnetic-tape products were planned at that time.

The worldwide development of both solid logic technology and the new product line gathered speed throughout 1962. For security, code names were given to the processor development projects. Endicott's small system was named the 101, Hursley's the 250, Poughkeepsie's the 315, 400, and 501. That the code names corresponded to certain competitive products in each system's performance area was no coincidence.

DSD organized a small project to plan an alternative should the new product plan not succeed. The "catastrophe alternative" generally examined applying the new SLT to existing processors; however, no substantive development was conducted, only paper analyses. Additionally, at Piore's insistence and as a condition to transfer Amdahl from research to the NPL project, DSD started work on a very high-performance version of the new architecture. Dubbed the 604, it was not planned that the high-performance products would be ready for announcement at the same time the basic five CPUs in the product line would be announced, because improvements on the technology were required to meet the performance goals. Eventually, the higher-performance CPUs were announced as the System/360 Model 90 series.

The most serious problem in 1962 was the inability of the architects and processor developers to achieve an acceptable plan for the desired upward and downward compatibility, as costs and performance had to balance from the smallest to the largest. One major attempt pursued for nine months failed. Then Brooks brought in a larger group of participants and established a design competition. Thirteen teams submitted design approaches. From this work came a solution with agreement that full upward and downward compatibility could be achieved. During this period memory addressing and the 8-bit byte were established. The architecture's detailed functional specifications were then quickly drawn, and the detailed design accelerated.

The project moved through IBM's methodical evaluations of cost, forecast, and business analysis. Across the corporation hundreds of development and manufacturing tasks were aimed at matching component production to development and test schedules, and production schedules to the forecasted requirement. We had the usual problems: the availability of personnel with the right experience, SLT parts availability, coordinating subassembly and test schedules, resolution of architecture anomalies, and programming plans. By early 1963 the project was progressing rapidly, and thoughts turned more seriously to announcement strategy. The engineering group pressed for all

five systems to be announced simultaneously. The announcement target was March 1964, with first customer shipment of the smaller systems in March 1965 and the larger systems targeted for the third and fourth quarters of 1965. GPD was reluctant because it did not want to impact the successful 1401 family so soon. Thus GPD proposed that the rest of the family announce and ship when ready, but GPD was thinking of 1965, perhaps even 1966 before announcing the smallest system. Other views held that sequential announcement might be less risky, for if the users did not show enthusiasm for the new structure, IBM could minimize its losses and change direction before total commitment. Supporting this approach was the fact that IBM had never undertaken such a massive program, made more complex by such radical new technology. Sequential announcement would, it was argued, show the supply-line flaws so the company could better prepare for the volume that was hoped to follow. The sequential alternative was examined in enough detail to consider early 1964 announcement of a limited version of the next-to-smallest system, the 250.

Pacing all of the plans was programming, which had been late in staffing and was facing a bold reach with new operating systems and a full range of supporting utility programs plus the hoped-to-be omnipotent universal language later dubbed Programming Language One (PL/I).

One of the most difficult obstacles to hurdle was the question of users' investment in applications and control programming for their contemporary products. While the NPL architecture was viewed as much more pervasive and powerful, it was incompatible with all previous systems. Programs written for existing systems would therefore not run on the NPL systems unless the application had been coded in a high-level language and could be recompiled. At that time few users coded in high-level languages, however, so recompilation was viewed as an asset in a small percentage of cases but not a solution. Throughout 1962 and 1963, DSD pursued approaches to application program conversion. Substantial research was expended on program translation, the concept being that specially developed software would "process" users' programs and automatically translate them to run efficiently on the new architecture. Progress was slow because the problems to be solved were very complex. Automatic translation gave way to "semiautomatic," wherein translation software would do much of the translation and highlight anomalies to expedite manual rewriting.

IBM also analyzed having the NPL programming simulate the contemporary products' architectures. Because simulation is usually 10 to 100 times slower than native operation, however, DSD concluded that performance would be unacceptable.

By mid-1963 the translation approach was not proving a satisfactory solution, and the pressure was on the engineering forces, for they fully recognized that without a program conversion solution, widespread customer acceptance of the NPL would be questionable. Necessity breeds invention, as the maxim goes, and so it was with the NPL engineering group. A very capable professional, Stewart Tucker, contributed significantly to the eventual solution. Tucker noted that the NPL had registers and data paths sufficient to encompass those of each of the contemporary products. Even though the instruction repertoires were completely different, Tucker concluded that with microcoding made possible by the new read-only memories used for control, it would be relatively inexpensive to add the full instruction sets of an existing architecture. In effect, the user could "throw a switch" and have the NPL system take the form of a contemporary system and run contemporary programs efficiently and economically—the process of emulation.

Refinement of the emulator concept took place swiftly. By late 1963 enough was understood to know a solution for the critical problems of migration, and conversion was in hand.

Eleventh-Hour Opposition

As the new product line moved closer to announcement, a number of contrary viewpoints arose. Some were financial and some were technical. One of the opposition was the Strategic Planning Group, which argued that the compatible line was "all the eggs in one basket" and IBM would be faced with double jeopardy—failure of customer acceptance that would, of course, be sweeping, and also, even if the users accepted the architecture and the full line went into production, a superior competitive approach would adversely affect IBM's entire systems products. On the other hand, they argued, a successful attack on any of the existing seven families would not be disastrous. The perceived user appeal of compatibility, standard interfaces, programming independence, and the application power of the new architecture was too persuasive, however. IBM senior management never seriously considered the "continue several architectures" philosophy.

A variation of the preceding viewpoint came from a senior IBM programmer. He worried that the performance span of the family was too broad, and suggested that two or even three families be produced, each optimized for their respective areas. This suggestion, too, fell on deaf ears, since by late 1963 the NPL

development had confirmed achievability of the performance range.

One opposition to the NPL came from some programmers and engineers who specialized in scientific applications. The successful 7090 had a 36-bit parallel "word" as its basic structure. Double-precision arithmetic used double word lengths, or 72 bits. The memory-addressing structure of contemporary systems was direct; that is, a number of bits in each instruction determined the maximum memory size. The NPL architecture distressed the scientific group because its basic byte (or character) was eight bits, and since four bytes made up a word, NPL words had only 32 bits; double precision used 64. The programmers fretted that mapping the 36 bits of 7090 information into the NPL would be inefficient, requiring two NPL words for each 36 bits. They also worried that the NPL's base-register-offset memory-addressing architecture would be cumbersome and inefficient in contrast to the homogeneity of direct addressing. The debates lasted several months and came to the attention of senior management. In the end, however, the NPL designs prevailed.

Because such a significant percentage of IBM's engineering resources were working on the NPL, the usual flow of new products and improvements for existing products slowed to a trickle. Meanwhile, competitors were steadily improving their products, and new competitors were entering the electronic data processing industry at a quickening pace. New requirements and complaints from the marketing forces thus brought great pressure on the engineering groups, despite the fact that through 1962 and 1963 the tactical "temporizers" were announced and shipped on or very close to their internally estimated schedules. The 7094 and 7094-II were very successful; the 7040, 7044, 1410, and 1620-II were well accepted; but the 7072, 7074, and 7010 achieved somewhat less acceptance than originally estimated. IBM's "temporizers" were nonetheless not a complete answer to the flood of enhanced and new competitive products. Important sales were lost as IBM paid a price for forgoing immediate product improvements. Senior management pressed for new studies and alternatives to help the situation. By mid-1963, however, no time was left to start alternative solutions, and, in all cases, the NPL would be the earliest.

In December 1963 all the debates on announcement alternatives were terminated after Honeywell's announcement of the H200—the first competitive announcement of a system that was architecturally almost identical to a leading IBM system. Honeywell's new system was touted to be four or more times faster than IBM's 1401. It had some architectural differ-

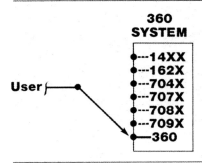

360 SYSTEM

- ---14XX
- ---162X
- ---704X
- ---707X
- ---708X
- ---709X
- —360

User

Figure 15. Emulation was the key to user conversion to System/360.

ences, for which Honeywell announced a software product called the Liberator; this was advertised as enabling 1401 users to modify the 1401 applications programs quickly so as to run efficiently on the H200.

Through most of December 1963, the plan was to proceed with the NPL. GPD had also been developing an alternative in case the NPL failed to materialize— a new 1401 version in contemporary technology, called the 1401S. It was approximately six times faster than the existing 1401 central processing unit, and was estimated to be approximately 15 percent faster than the Honeywell 200. Late in December 1963, Haanstra and GPD reversed field, recommending that GPD proceed with the 1401S and defer its NPL version, the 101. A senior management review of GPD's plan was held in January 1964, but DSD representatives did not participate. The report finally came back that the 1401S would proceed; Watson Jr. was reported to have said that the 1401S was "the finest 50th birthday present a man could ever have." The NPL advocates were dejected, for to proceed with the 1401S meant that GPD's 101 would be deferred or killed. The 101 was the NPL's smallest and thus highest-volume member, and its deferral would take substantial volume away from the new SLT, thus increasing costs and destroying the business case of the rest of the NPL. Further, the rest of the NPL systems would be without the small system deemed essential for support and peripheral applications.

Brooks argued for the NPL with the marketing and corporate constituencies; I met with Watson and A. L. Williams, then IBM president. Both Brooks and I argued that Honeywell's 200 and the 1401S would appear negligibly different, and only production availability would determine which manufacturer's system would be accepted; when the two suppliers' production capacity exceeded demand, a price war would inevitably result. Watson and Williams rebutted that user program conversion to the NPL would be slow, thus giving Honeywell an advantage as IBM manufacturing resources were consumed with the new line. Watson

and Williams had not heard of the emulation solution, however; emulation became the key to the senior management decision to proceed with the 101 (Figure 15).

By late January 1964 the tide of corporate thinking had turned to the NPL, and in February the final management meeting was held to review the NPL test status, compare it to contemporary products, and review the financial projections. That meeting culminated in the decision to proceed with simultaneous NPL announcement as soon as the systems were ready. A late March 1964 announcement date was desired, but since Easter fell late in March that year, announcement was set for April 7.

In March, Haanstra was replaced by Clarence E. Frizzell as president of the General Products Division. Frizzell was a manufacturing specialist and brought important experience to GPD as that division prepared for the NPL.

The announcement took place in Poughkeepsie on April 7, 1964. Watson Jr. led the IBM professionals who presented the System/360 family to a large group of invited press. Six machines were announced; GPD's 101 became the 360 Model 30, Hursley's 250 became Model 40, and Poughkeepsie's 315, 400, and 501 became Models 50, 60, 62, and 70. The die was cast!

IBM held its breath as customers evaluated the new offering. For a brief period there was concern, but gradually user acceptance was clear and sales soared.

A Controversial "Gap" in System/360?

A serious concern arose in the third quarter of 1964. The Massachusetts Institute of Technology (MIT) had a highly respected computer research reputation. An MIT team had conducted pioneering research into time-sharing—multiple remote users using terminals operating into a computer with the computer's control programming responding to each user's input, automatically moving users' data and programs back and forth between disk storage and main memory. With dozens of users independently operating from terminals, an extremely complex control program was required to manage the availability of programs and data in real time so as to provide no more delay than a few seconds between the time a user inquired of a computer and the time the response returned. To ease this complex task, MIT's Jack Dennis concluded that an essential addition was required in the computer's architecture, called dynamic address translation. Such a capability relieves the programmer of much of the difficulty and tedium of keeping track of data and instructions throughout the memory and storage systems. Watson Jr. had instructed me to make certain

IBM stayed close to MIT's research. I regularly sent professionals, such as Amdahl and Brooks, to MIT to discuss philosophy of design and architecture. The NPL team did not feel that changing the NPL architecture to MIT's time-sharing philosophy would be justified because of the added cost and schedule consequences. Dynamic address translation was thus not a part of System/360's architecture.

After the announcement of System/360, one of IBM's senior researchers, John Cocke, learned of MIT's negative view of IBM's new line. He pressed me to understand MIT's viewpoint personally. In June 1964, Cocke and I therefore conferred with Robert Fano and Fernando Corbató at Cambridge. MIT's conclusion was that without dynamic address translation, System/360 was unsuitable for time-sharing environments. The Data Systems Division immediately started a specific time-sharing programming project for System/360. At this time, however, General Electric announced a new family of processors with integral dynamic address capability, which was exactly the feature MIT considered essential. MIT rejected System/360 for its use and opted for GE's systems; some leading users followed MIT's lead. Concerns were amplified within IBM as some IBM planners forecasted that time-sharing would be essential in 75 percent of all systems installed within the next three years. With the MIT negative viewpoint of System/360's time-sharing capability, there was fear that System/360 would be judged inadequate by most users.

IBM management reacted to the time-sharing marketing perception with a special project that was independent of the 360 engineering group. Under Watts S. Humphrey, the project set out to add dynamic address translation to the Model 62 and to develop a new time-sharing operating system to be called TSS. Development of the System/360 project's own time-sharing option (TSO) continued in parallel. In time, both systems were produced and offered to customers. TSO, available to the full System/360 product family, commenced delivery in 1970 and eventually became the time-sharing workhorse of the System/360 and System/370, its successor. The special project TSS and its processor, the 360/67, took longer and cost more than originally estimated, but were delivered to several customers. In the early 1970s TSS and the special model 360/67 were withdrawn as IBM offerings.

Other Problems After Announcement

IBM had many problems, large and small, as the development groups pressed to finalize the engineering, as component manufacturing tooled for volume SLT production, and as manufacturing prepared for the NPL volume that was anticipated. Programming problems were most serious as reality overtook the earlier concepts. Increasing concern pervaded corporate headquarters. Learson held meetings with the principal programming management. Brooks reassigned himself to concentrate on the programming, and other professionals were assigned to programming to help meet the commitment.

An executive conference had been held in Colorado in September 1963. Harwood Kolsky, an experienced IBM programmer who had previously worked for the Atomic Energy Commission (AEC) at Los Alamos, wrote Watson Jr. just before the conference to express his concern that IBM products were not being selected by the AEC. The Control Data Corporation 6600 enjoyed widespread AEC acceptance. Kolsky worried that AEC requirements were a signal of requirements that would emerge more broadly. Much of the executive conference was devoted to the subject, and action was taken to establish a "czar" for high-performance systems, with Charles R. DeCarlo becoming the executive responsible for this area. At first DeCarlo rejected the System/360 high-performance project and conducted meetings with large scientific users to ascertain what they desired. Quickly, however, the euphoria of a new design gave way to the capability and potential availability of the 604 project. DeCarlo's effort thus turned to pressing DSD to accelerate the announcement of the 604, hoping for a simultaneous announcement with the rest of the series. In fact, a statement was included in the April 7, 1964, System/360 announcement to the effect that IBM was also developing a higher-performance system. With DeCarlo's special task relating to high performance and Humphrey's relating to time-sharing, however, the development structure was affected because no single voice spoke to corporate management. This fact, coupled with increasing difficulties in 360 programming and manufacturing, led Watson Jr. to have an assessment made of IBM product competitiveness in late 1964. Charles J. Bashe, an experienced engineering manager, conducted the analysis, and reported that IBM led in processors, programming, and disk storage, but that the competition had equal or better price performance in magnetic tapes, printers, card input/output equipment, optical character-recognition equipment, and other areas as well.

In reality, the gigantic task of producing System/360 had consumed all of IBM's development resources. The culmination of studying the several problems came in January 1965, when a major reorganization was announced. Of necessity, IBM reorganized to a unified structure to meet the demands of its new unified product line. An integrated engineering divi-

Table 1. System/360 Shipment Schedules

360 Processor Model	April 1964, Announced First Customer Shipment (FCS)	April 1964 Manufacturing Estimate for FCS	Actual Shipment Date	First Rental Start Date
2030		June 1965	June 1965	June 1965
2040	16–24 Months	May 1965	April 1965	May 1965
2050		September 1965	August 1965	August 1965
2060 and 2062		December 1965	November 1965[a]	December 1965
2070		January 1966	January 1966[a]	April 1966

[a] Models 2060, 2062, and 2070 were withdrawn and replaced by models 2065 and 2075, which were delivered on the dates shown.

sion was established to develop IBM's products worldwide. Haanstra returned from his special assignments to lead this division, the Systems Development Division. An integrated manufacturing division for U.S. production was established, with Frizzell named its president. I was headed for the "penalty box" over time-sharing, large scientific processors, and loss of IBM leadership in certain peripheral products, and was thus moved from the 360 area to what proved to be a great opportunity as president of the Federal Systems Division.

In net, while some of the more complex programming for System/360 was late, in some cases as much as a year late, the System/360 units announced on April 7, 1964, were generally shipped on schedule (Table 1). A number of systems were added to the 360 family. Before first customer shipment, Models 60 and 62 were superseded by Model 65, and Model 75

superseded Model 70. Each of these systems had a new, faster main memory and improved price performance. Smaller systems, the 360/20, 22, and 25, extended the line into smaller user domains. A system optimized for scientific applications, the 360/44, was produced. The system for the special time-sharing project, a model 360/67, was produced, and high-performance systems were added to extend the family upward, the 360/85 and Models 91, 92, and 95 (Figure 16).

IBM saw widespread user acceptance of all the main System/360 processors, Models 30, 40, 50, 65, and 75, and the main programming support, including the disk operating system and two more comprehensive operating systems, MFT and MVT, together with the supporting utility programs. Programming Language One did not meet its goals, however. Although the language is widely used and continues to be enhanced, PL/I did

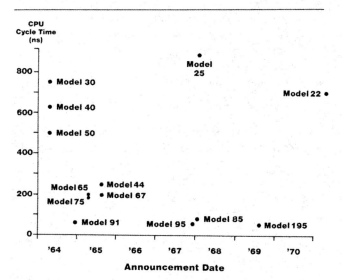

Figure 16. Growth of System/360 family from 1964 to 1970.

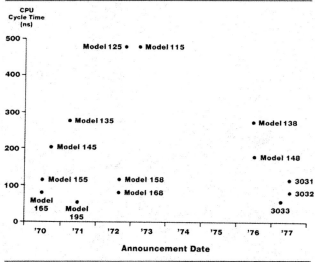

Figure 17. From 1970 to 1977, System/370 replaced System/360, and the 303X family began to replace System/370.

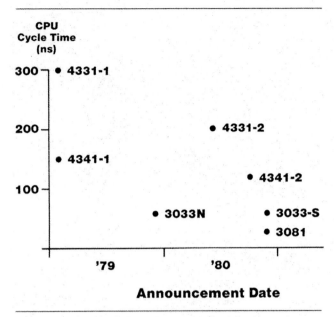

Figure 18. System/360 architecture continues into the 1980s.

not become the single unifying language that had been desired. FORTRAN and COBOL language extensions continue, and new languages, such as BASIC, Pascal, and APL, have been added to the repertoire of high-level languages offered by IBM.

After the 360

The unified 360 product line allowed redistribution of IBM's engineering resources (see Figure 23). By 1970 approximately one-third of these resources went to processor development, another third to new peripheral devices, especially disk files and printers, and the remaining third to programming.

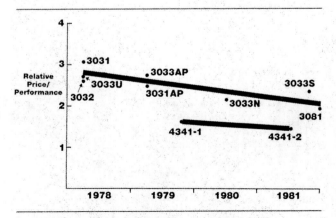

Figure 19. Price/performance scale of IBM CPUs.

In September 1969, I returned to be president of the unified Systems Development Division (SDD) established in 1965. In my Federal Systems Division (FSD) assignment, I had seen a number of leading-edge applications characteristic of some advanced government applications. Additionally, while some in IBM were still not persuaded, from my MIT and FSD experiences, I was convinced of the need for new architecture to enhance storage management. I returned to SDD to find the first 360 replacements imminent, but with no architecture or programming provided for dynamic address translation. Plans were quickly set in motion in 1969 to develop "virtual systems" capability, an extension of dynamic address translation. One dilemma was that the design and programming changes would require two years or more. System/360 had been marketed for six years; new price performance was ready, and users needed increased power. In mid-1970 IBM therefore commenced sequential announcements of System/370, starting with the 370/155 and the 370/165 systems, followed in October 1970 by the 145, in 1971 by the 135, and in 1972–1973 with the 125 and the 115. Hardware and programming additions and changes to provide dynamic address translation were developed throughout the period. In August 1972, IBM announced 370 advanced function, incorporating virtual systems capability. Later, the 370/158 and 168 replaced the 155 and 165, and the 138 and 148 replaced the 135 and 145. As the systems were announced, virtual systems capability was included in the 125 and 115, thus providing dynamic address translation across the 370 product line (Figure 17). Additionally, the core-memory technology of the 155 and 165 was replaced by new semiconductor technology using field-effect transistors that provided dramatic gains in size, speed, required power, and cost/price.

In 1977 the high end of the 370 series began to be replaced by the 303X family. In 1979 the midrange was replaced by the 43XX, and the higher-performance systems were further extended by improved price performance, attached processors, and multiprocessors (Figure 18). The price performance was steadily improved by using better technology (Figure 19). In 1981 the first of the new generation of high-performance processors were introduced: the 3081, later followed by the 3083 and 3084 systems—all with System/360 and 370 architecture.

As of 1986, it appears that the System/360 architecture, having already served over 20 years, is likely to continue as the IBM architectural base for midrange and high-performance systems for another decade or longer, which is a record for computer architecture durability by a wide margin!

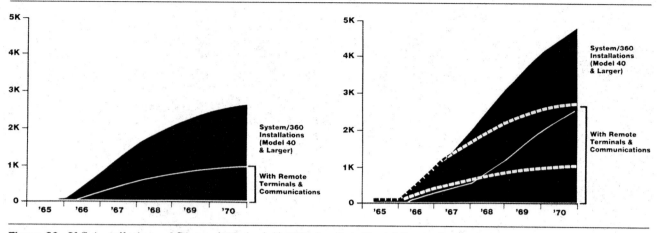

Figure 20. U.S. installations of System/360. (*a, left*) 1964 forecast; (*b, right*) actual.

One Special Result of 360 Standardization

Consolidation of IBM system product lines allowed the company to apply the systems in new directions not clearly foreseen when the 360 series was designed in 1962–1963. One application area anticipated was increasing use of remote terminals communicating to a central computer via telephone lines. This application could not be foreseen with clarity; thus 360's initial design included only the fundamental "hooks" for the communications hardware and programming to come. The forecast of communications attachments was strong (Figure 20a), estimating that approxi-

mately one-third of the Models 40 and larger would have remote terminal/communications applications by 1970. The 360 planners underestimated the demand, however (Figure 20b); the original 1970 estimate was reached in 1968. By 1970 almost as many systems were used in communications applications as had been estimated in 1964 to be installed totally. The "teleprocessing" era was well under way. IBM had been saturated with the basic 360 processor family task, however, and a consistent communications subsystem architecture did not exist, nor had sufficient communciations control programming developed. Users, impatient to expand their operations, moved

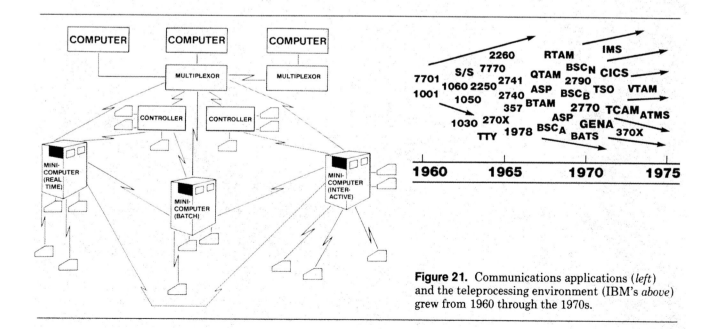

Figure 21. Communications applications (*left*) and the teleprocessing environment (IBM's *above*) grew from 1960 through the 1970s.

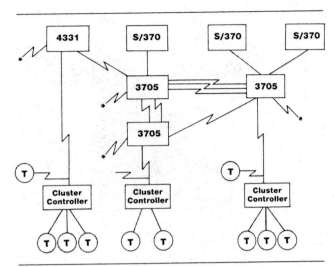

Figure 22. IBM system network architecture (SNA 4.2), November 1960.

on their own into communications applications with bits and pieces of communications control programming provided by their own programmers, by independent vendors, by local IBM systems engineers, or by IBM laboratories. The result was a deluge of dissimilar communications control programming, all serving particular purposes, but none coordinated into a coherent and comprehensive communications subsystem plan.

Rampant growth of communications applications came throughout the 1970s (Figure 21). Users connected computers into networks and attached distant terminals by the hundreds. Moreover, rapid growth of minicomputers gave rise to attached remote terminals used in many applications across the spectrum of what is called batch processing (payroll, accounts receivable, inventory control, sales statistics), interactive computing (airline reservations, on-line banking terminals, retail point-of-sale applications), and real-time computing (refinery control, for example). Then, inexorably, large computer applications needed access to databases gathering in minicomputer applications, or minicomputers needed access to central databases, and minicomputers communicated across networks of minicomputers. Communications applications thus quickly became a large and fast-growing segment of the computer industry. IBM responded to the need for standardization of the communications subsystem in 1972 with its system network architecture (SNA, which has been steadily extended. By 1986 it had substantial capabilities in terms of networking, a wide variety of them using central processors and terminal types (Figure 22).

In effect, the standardization of processor architecture freed resources and gave increased impetus to a major new communications subsystem unification, SNA, that now proliferates across other manufacturers' equipment as well as other IBM product lines.

The disbursement of development resources had changed by 1980 (Figure 23). An increasing percentage of resources was allocated to central processors, primarily due to investment in much more advanced semiconductor circuit and packaging technologies as the era of very large-scale semiconductor integration (VLSI) began to move into production. Peripheral development remained approximately constant, programming contracted, and resources were being allocated to development of a wide variety of communications products and terminals.

Was System/360 Worth It?

The standardization of processors allowed IBM to direct substantial resources to areas of the full system previously neglected—peripherals, communications, and new applications. System/360's value is best measured by IBM's financial performance, however (Figure 24). In the five years from January 1, 1966, until January 1, 1971, IBM's gross income increased 2.3 times from $3.6 billion to $8.3 billion, and net earnings after taxes increased 2.3 times, from $477 million to $1.1 billion. In 1982 the descendants of System/360 accounted for more than half of IBM's gross income and an even greater share of its earnings (Figure 25); the statistics hold for 1986.

Perhaps most important, the standardization of the 360 permitted a focus on excellence not possible with multiple architectures. The standardization eventu-

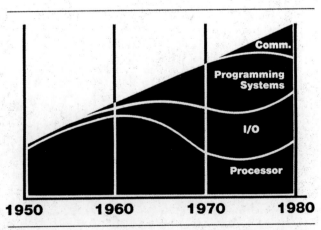

Figure 23. Change in proportion of IBM development resources from 1950 to 1980.

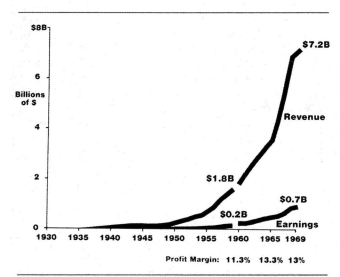

Figure 24. IBM growth, 1960 to 1969.

the fainthearted to renege. IBM senior management appreciated the potential of the 360, however, and was reluctant to compromise. In the process the company's future was risked; failure of System/360 would have seriously endangered and perhaps ruined IBM. It would have taken years and hundreds of millions of dollars to start over. To regain the leadership would not have been probable, even if capital formation had been possible. The rationale is, of course, that big risks go with giant gains. In System/360's case the gains paid off beyond expectations.

Negatives?

In the course of such a difficult undertaking, problems were numerous—financial stresses, personnel stresses, the saga of programming difficulties, and others. The most severe negative was litigation. All shook the foundations of IBM, but also toughened the company as the 360 experience gave IBM an invaluable education.

The high volumes resulting from the success of System/360 probably motivated a new form of competition that produced copies of IBM products, as given in the following list of typical competitors that produced System/360 plug-compatible equipment.

1960s
Tape: Telex
Disk: Telex, Memorex, Calcomp, Marshall, etc.
Multiplexors: Memorex, etc.
Main Memory: Cambridge, etc.

ally resulted in powerful new peripherals, terminals, high-volume applications, and diversification into areas such as satellite communications, plant-floor automation, and business services whose future can only be imagined.

In retrospect, what were the principal factors that led or drove IBM to risk its future and take such a bold step? What management lessons might be gathered from the 360 experience? From an insider's viewpoint, we can see five important factors.

1. A strategically minded senior management assigned responsibilities, freed resources, and regularly monitored progress.

2. Learning from the problems of incompatibilities that plagued all facets of users and IBM alike, we established a bold new direction with specific solutions for each problem area.

3. IBM's senior management did not make the mistake of trying to manage each detail. While complaints and divergent viewpoints were carefully considered, the detailed implementation was delegated to the professionals most capable of resolving and carrying out the designs.

4. At appropriate times senior management did not hesitate to reorganize the entire business to make 360 implementation more efficient. Senior management carefully monitored progress and problems along the way, moving resources and changing management when they determined that change was in order.

5. The most important attribute of IBM's senior management was tenacity. On many occasions and in many ways there were signals and opportunities for

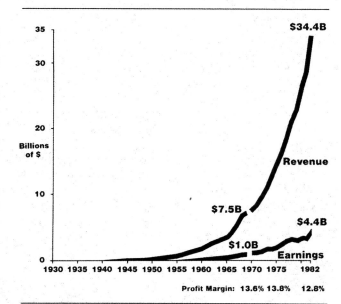

Figure 25. IBM growth, 1970 to 1982.

1970s
Terminals: Raytheon, AT&T, Sanders, etc.
Central Processors: Fujitsu (Amdahl), Hitachi, Magnuson, etc.
Programming: Fujitsu, Hitachi, etc.

A major industry grew as first magnetic tapes, then disk files, and eventually most parts of the IBM systems were functionally copied by a number of competitors. As IBM responded to this competition, an antitrust suit was filed by the Telex Corporation, which won a judgment in the federal district court in 1972. The Department of Justice filed an antitrust suit in the last business day of Lyndon B. Johnson's administraton. Several companies judged that they, too, had been aggrieved and filed similar lawsuits. By 1984, however, the Telex case was completely overturned in the appellate court, and six other cases had gone to trial, with IBM prevailing in each one. Sixteen federal judges ruled in IBM's behalf. The Department of Justice dropped its antitrust suit in January 1982 as "without merit." The litigation of the 1970s seemed at an end.

Epilogue

The 360 concept continues to propagate. An increasing number of companies, including Japanese manufacturers, have adopted the IBM architecture. Hundreds of companies provide plug-compatible or programming-compatible peripheral devices, and hundreds of programming companies offer both control and applications software for the IBM 360 successor products. Indeed, a number of large worldwide businesses have sprung from the 360 product line. The System/360 principals have taken a variety of directions.

T. Vincent Learson became IBM president and then chairman of the board following the 1971 retirement of Thomas J. Watson, Jr. Now retired, Learson is active in both government and business matters.

Frederick P. Brooks, Jr., left IBM in the mid-1960s to return to academia. A prestigious educator and computer architect, Brooks is head of the Department of Computer Science at the University of North Carolina. He continues as an IBM consultant and member of IBM's Science Advisory Committee.

John W. Haanstra resigned from IBM in 1968 and joined General Electric. He was killed in a private aircraft accident in 1969.

Jerrier A. Haddad retired from IBM in 1981 and now lends his experience to industry and national-interest matters.

Orland M. Scott retired from IBM in 1980 and continues to serve IBM in a consulting capacity.

Gene M. Amdahl resigned from IBM in 1970 and founded Amdahl Corporation. In collaboration with Japan's Fujitsu Corporation and others, it provided an IBM-compatible line of high-performance processors. Amdahl Corporation and Amdahl were very successful. In 1979, Amdahl resigned from Amdahl Corporation and founded Trilogy Corporation.

Donald T. Spaulding held a number of executive positions and retired in 1982.

Maxwell O. Paley resigned from IBM in 1971 to join Raytheon Corporation, and in 1973 established his own consulting and engineering firm, Palyn Associates, which he continues to serve as president. Palyn Associates was approached by a Japanese firm to acquire plans and designs of IBM's planned 308X series. Cooperating with the FBI, Paley was a principal in investigations that led to federal indictments against two Japanese firms as well as an IBM civil lawsuit that was settled out of court with terms quite favorable to IBM.

Erich Bloch held a number of executive positions, the most recent as IBM vice-president for technical personnel development. He retired from IBM in September 1984 to become director of the National Science Foundation.

Bob O. Evans held a number of executive positions, with the last seven years spent as IBM vice-president for engineering, programming, and technology. I retired from IBM in July 1984 to become a general partner in the investment firm of Hambrecht & Quist.

Thus ends this report on the 360 story. Whether the 360 architecture will still be evident 20 years hence remains to be seen, but it is likely. Whether IBM or the Japanese manufacturers or others become superior in the evolution of System/360 follow-on products also remains to be seen, and it will be an interesting and important set of events to observe and measure.

Clearly IBM's risk in the 1960s paid handsomely and rewarded not only IBM but also the industry at large and the users through the excellence of that unified product line.

APPENDIX

B. O. Evans Memorandum to W. B. McWhirter,
March 23, 1961

Memorandum to: Mr. W. B. McWhirter
Subject: DS Product Line

I have reviewed the proposed DS product line and conclude as follows:
1. The 8000 series as proposed should not be announced. My supporting reasons follow.
2. The 1410X development program should be implemented consistent with the results of market analyses conducted to establish the precise announcement/production strategy in terms of market need and current product displacement/replacement.

3. A maximum development program should be immediately inaugurated to evolve a scientific computer in the form of a 7090 derivative operating in the $7,500 to $35,000 range. The program would be charged to produce outstanding cost/performance over the present market gap consistent with the IBM market need. 1Q62 legal announcement is feasible, first pilot units 3Q62 and customer shipment commencing 1Q63. . . .

7. The 7090 provides an undeniable growth market. Therefore, a study program should be manned to establish the organization of a 7090X operating at 4 to 7 times the present performance. This program should be chartered to institute the necessary technology support programs immediately and a systems development program commencing in 1962. . . .

14. Recognizing the desirability of an "ultimate" IBM systems family, an interdivisional GPD/DSD/ASDD/FSD program should be staffed under the chairmanship of Dr. G. M. Amdahl with a charter to develop a total cohesive product line with a target of 1965 availability. The group should be comprised of eight select full-time representatives, two from each division, and should be established in a proper environment. Specific progress mileposts must be established. A *mandatory* monthly progress meeting with the division Presidents/General Managers must be established to insure that the objectives are met.

My reasons for concluding the 8000 series should not proceed are as follows:

1. *General*

A. New technology is essential to a new IBM machine family. Committing a new family's lot to current technology is opening IBM to a major competitive coup. The machine family needs the technology to optimize applicability and machine performance. Technology demands the family to achieve cost/performance.

B. Eight bit character representation has a profound implication on the future. Any such significant step should be an *IBM* rather than a divisional plan. GPD and DSD must reconcile a unified plan for data representation. . . .

D. I challenge the stated DSD market strategy on the basis that we will not be acceptable in the new application areas if we are not outstanding in the base line areas. This point is emphasized by the fact that 8000 series is a relatively complex machine which will be difficult to understand, optimally program, and sell to its true capability. If DPD cannot support this machine enthu-

siastically in the base line area it will not realize its potential in the new applications area.

E. NPN transistor speed is critical to the 8108 performance. The parallel unit requires information to move through a full 48-bit adder with true/complement controls, a left shift unit, a right shift unit, then into a register in one microsecond. Loss of NPN performance on conversion to PNP would delay 8108 speed probably linearly in relation to degradation of device performance. On the other hand, D7090 speeds were established on PNP NAND performance, now operating in 1410. . . .

2. *Scientific*

A. The 8000 series does not have outstanding price/performance *across* the critical intermediate scientific areas.

B. I am concerned that the base organization is not conducive to higher speeds. The 8108 approach is conducive to systems problems, cost, and general complexity. I am wary that this is a restrictive rather than general speed increase as the hardware attachment will be rather ineffective for nonfloating point operation.

C. I am concerned that the lack of pure binary will taint the effectiveness of this system in a scientific market. . . .

G. The 8104 is an incompatible anomaly in the proposed line. The proposed program level compatability is shaky.

3. *Commercial Data Processing*

A. The 8000 series opposes rather than capitalizes on the 1400 series.

B. There is an agreement that 1410X is inevitable. Agreement that we will produce a major competitor to our base line is a poor strategy. The result may be a split major product line, 6 and 8 bit. Each series will require the full support of IBM's software and sales complement. The resultant dilution of support and intramural competition can permit IBM's competition to continue its inroads. . . .

E. The 8103 is absolute duplication forced by failure to recognize the existing major product line. . . .

The above critiques are both general and philosophical. Some can be individually refuted or rationalized. However, in total, I believe they constitute an irrefutable argument against moving into the market with the 8000 series now. I fear that we will commit IBM to a major program of mediocrity.

B. O. Evans
Manager of Systems Planning and Development

Software Unbundling:
A Personal Perspective

Software Unbundling: A Personal Perspective

Watts S. Humphrey
Carnegie Mellon University

This article summarizes the author's invited talk at the Charles Babbage Institute conference on unbundling held in Palo Alto, California, on 23 September 2000. Humphrey, who worked at IBM for many years and was involved in many of the company's software unbundling decisions, was in a unique position to offer his perspectives on why, and how, IBM made its decisions.

This article recounts my personal experiences with unbundling at IBM. Before unbundling, IBM offered customers its programs and systems engineering services without a separate charge: IBM bundled the cost of these services with the hardware price. The bundled offering was very attractive to customers because it simplified their data processing acquisition decisions. It also provided seemingly free support for all aspects of the customer's data processing operations.

At the time of IBM's unbundling decision, IBM management worried that the Justice Department would view bundling as an anticompetitive practice. Because the separate parts of IBM's offering were not separately priced, competitors had to offer a similarly comprehensive bundle. Bundling, therefore, made it more difficult for small firms to compete with IBM in almost any part of the rapidly growing computer business. In writing this article, I must necessarily reflect my personal biases as an IBM employee and as a manager responsible for some of the work involved in the unbundling decision. While IBM's competitors frequently viewed the company as aggressive and predatory, that was not my perception. However, this article is neither a defense of IBM nor an attempt to discredit IBM's critics. It is a simple recitation of the facts as I recall them.

Background

I joined IBM in 1959 as a senior engineer in the Advanced Systems Development Division. Four years later, I was made IBM director of systems and application engineering on the corporate staff. My job was to oversee IBM's software development and systems engineering operations.

In 1964, IBM announced its new System/360 (S/360) line of computers to replace its then multiple, incompatible series of computers. The objective of the new compatible S/360 line was to let customers upgrade to larger systems without replacing or modifying their application programs. The S/360 series initially ranged from the low-end model 30 to the high-end model 75; it was soon enhanced with the larger 85, 91, and 95 models, and the smaller model 20 and 25 systems.

The RCA Spectra 70

Shortly after the IBM 360 announcement, RCA announced its new Spectra 70 system as compatible with the IBM 360. If the Spectra 70 series of computers really could run the S/360 programs, RCA's hardware prices would not have to include the large programming costs required to support a line of compatible systems. As we knew, these costs could be substantial. While it was not clear that RCA could produce an S/360-compatible computer line, we had to assume that they could.

As part of my corporate staff job, I reviewed the proposed RCA system to identify the problems such an offering would cause IBM and to recommend how to handle these concerns. Because management was concerned about the study's legal implications, the review was done under the IBM legal staff's guidance and was privileged information.

In the summer of 1964, when the lawyers and I made the final study report to IBM's Board of Directors, we did not use any charts or overhead transparencies, and we provided no written report. In making the presentation, I used a blackboard to show the key points as I discussed them. At the end of the meeting, I erased the blackboard.

Our study concluded that, if RCA could produce a truly S/360-compatible computing system, they could easily replace IBM's installed machines. While IBM would not have to install or service its software on RCA machines, we could not prevent RCA from marketing systems that used our software. Furthermore, we could not charge RCA's customers for the use of this software unless we also charged our own customers. In short, we told the IBM board that ultimately the only protection from a plug-compatible competitor was to unbundle IBM's software.

Even though the RCA Spectra 70 system was seen as a serious competitive threat, it never turned out to be a real problem. The RCA engineers did not understand the importance of full compatibility and could not resist making some architectural "improvements" to the S/360 design. As a result, the RCA machines could not run IBM's or the customer's S/360 programs without some modifications. Because the conversion was difficult, few customers bought the RCA systems.

The Figueroa task force

Following its product announcement of the S/360, IBM developed the required hardware and software and, by mid-1965, started delivering the hardware. I was then in charge of IBM's programming work, and we started delivering the 360 system software in March of 1966.

In December 1966, IBM established its first unbundling task force led by Howard Figueroa, the IBM director of policy development on the corporate staff. He was responsible for IBM's product, marketing, and pricing policies. The task force members were Howard, representing corporate policy; me, representing development; Jim Manning, from marketing; and I believe Ted Ross, from corporate legal. I do not remember who represented corporate finance.

The task force met for about a month starting in December 1966. Our charge was to recommend how to unbundle software, not whether it should be unbundled. We debated a family of asset protection alternatives, including patenting, trade secrets, and copyright. We quickly dismissed patenting. It was not clear that software could be patented, and the volume of software products and versions would quickly overwhelm the patent process. Trade secrets were also thought impractical because, once secrecy was breached, the trade secret would be lost. Also, because many people would necessarily be involved with every software release, we felt that the required level of secrecy would be impractical.

That left copyright as the only viable alternative. While we viewed copyright as a weak form of protection, it was all that we had. To improve the level of protection, we coupled the copyright with a license and counted on the license to provide the real protection.

The copyright-license strategy

Our proposed approach was that IBM offer its software products only under a license. The customers would sign an agreement that permitted them to copy and use specified programs. Because a seller cannot generally impose product usage restrictions on a purchaser, we felt that a paid-up license might not be enforceable as a lease. The concern was that such a license might look too much like a sale. Therefore, because we wanted IBM to retain the title to its programs, our plan was to offer programs only on an open-ended lease with no paid-up provisions.

In addition to copyright and license protection, we felt that physical security measures were also needed. Our worry was that unethical people could copy and use programs without paying for them and that IBM would have no easy way to identify these people or prevent them from using the programs. While we thought that cryptography might be technically feasible, particularly with special hardware assists, every approach we could think of would have made it difficult for reputable customers to use our programs. Large businesses often needed backup copies, programs were frequently moved among machines, and IBM encouraged upgrading to larger systems. With cryptography, these activities would all require IBM permission. We felt that this would be impractical and inconvenient for users and expensive for IBM. We also concluded that any single-machine locks and keys, or special time-out and self-destruct programs, would be onerous to our best customers and not effective against clever thieves.

Because we could not devise practical physical security measures, we had to rely on the inherent honesty of our customers. Our hope was that legal protection and criminal prosecution would limit the piracy problem. In the end, we recommended that security measures be studied in hopes that better methods could be devised. No one has since devised a suitable security system, so the problem is still with us.

While trusting our customers might seem like a naive strategy, particularly for developing countries, it is not as bad as one might imagine. Software is an attractive technology for developing countries because it requires little capital investment, uses highly trained and talented people, pays attractive wages, and can be marketed and delivered worldwide over the Internet. However, for any country to seriously pursue an indigenous software industry, it must provide copyright-license protection for this industry. Otherwise, the product economics would not support anything but a marginal business. Therefore, if software is to become a robust industry in any country, that country must enforce copyright-license protection for everyone. While this self-limiting mechanism could take time to develop, ultimately, the software copyright and license strategy should be enforceable throughout the world.

AFIP 1968

In the summer of 1968, I was asked to participate in a panel discussion on unbundling at the AFIP (Association for Information Processing) conference in Edinburgh, Scotland. IBM had not yet announced any unbundling plans, and there were many rumors and misconceptions. Many customers felt that unbundling would mean hardware price reductions of at least 25 percent. As far as I knew, the IBM corporate management committee had not yet decided to unbundle, and many of us thought it was a bad idea. I was therefore anxious to make a statement that would counter the growing customer pressure for unbundling. I discussed this invitation and what I planned to say with the corporate director of policy development who agreed with my planned statement.

When the question of unbundling came up at the AFIP conference, I explained that the common view of software unbundling was unrealistic, and that any reduction would almost certainly result in much less than a 25 percent hardware price reduction. While IBM had no official position on this matter, I told the audience that, by considering a few facts, they could judge for themselves how big a price cut was likely. At the time, IBM had about 130,000 employees, about 4,000 (or 3 percent) of whom worked on programming. Because the price of IBM's products must reflect the company's total costs and because its costs were proportional to the number of people in each area, this suggested that any price reductions would be closer to 3 percent than 25 percent.

This brief comment created quite a stir. When the press asked IBM headquarters about my remarks, the senior executives were very upset. However, because I had cleared my comments with the policy director, I got off with a slap on the wrist. In the end, my comments were prophetic. When IBM unbundled, the hardware price reduction was exactly 3 percent.

The IBM unbundling plan

In late 1968, Spike Beitzel, an IBM senior vice president, led a second, corporate unbundling task force. Management had decided that unbundling was needed for competitive reasons as well as to prevent an antitrust lawsuit. The job of Spike's task force was to define precisely how to unbundle and to devise a plan for it. The final software unbundling plan almost precisely followed the earlier recommendations of the Figueroa task force, except that it also unbundled systems engineering.

Almost immediately after the unbundling announcement in June 1969, the task force plan required several adjustments. The unbundling plan had been developed by large-systems people, and we had not adequately considered how to handle hundreds of thousands of small customers. It was impractical to dun every one of these customers every month for their relatively modest bills. Therefore, single-use charges were added, both to reduce billing costs and to ensure that IBM got the customer's money. IBM soon adopted paid-up licenses, not only for small systems but also for most of its application programs.

While we were concerned about the potential legal problems of one-time charges, the company had no alternative. In fact, the paid-up license issue was subsequently tested in court and the license concept upheld. Therefore, even with a paid-up one-time license, IBM has been able to retain title to its programs and to enforce the license. Lower priced programs are now generally offered for a one-time charge.

The second major change to the task force's unbundling recommendations concerned tying program licenses to specific computers. Because large customers needed more flexibility than the original strategy permitted, IBM introduced site licenses to let customers use programs on any computer in its facility. It also offered multiple licenses for multiple users on distributed systems. In general, however, the copyright-license approach worked pretty much as we had hoped. Customers accepted it as reasonable and the courts have enforced the contracts.

The product transition

The GUIDE organization was an association of IBM's largest commercial users. Because it represented our most-valued customers, we treated its views seriously, and I often met with the GUIDE Executive Board. In one such meeting in late 1968, the board members said that their members desperately needed functions added to IBM's large-system Cobol compiler. GUIDE had polled its membership and produced a long list of needed additions. I told the Executive Board that we would evaluate their request and include everything we could afford to include. To ensure that we included their most important items, I asked them to put their list in priority order. GUIDE agreed, and sent us the list.

While IBM had not yet announced unbundling, we concluded that this Cobol program would be an ideal first priced product. Because a committee of our largest users had said these new functions were essential, there should be a ready market for the product. After some months of work and after IBM had publicly implemented unbundling, we announced the new Cobol as IBM's first priced systems program. Even though we had included all the requested critical functions and had set a relatively low price, very few customers ordered the new Cobol. In spite of all their rhetoric, when faced with the choice of the current free Cobol program or paying for the new features, most customers stuck with the free program. While the new Cobol program ultimately sold reasonably well, it took a long time to wean customers from the free program version.

IBM had a large inventory of available systems programs that customers could continue to use without charge. However, the basic control programs had special hardware-dependent features required for system installation, hardware and software service, and hardware diagnostics. Many systems also had time-critical or I/O management and control programs that were unique to specific machines. Therefore, when we introduced new hardware, we could price the operating system software required to support that hardware.

The move to priced systems programs took several years, but the transition was smooth and completed with no serious problems. While use of the older operating systems versions would decline as the older machines were replaced, use of the compilers, utilities, and application programs would not. Therefore, the biggest issue was how to handle the continuing maintenance for these free programs. We had to limit this support because otherwise many installed customers would continue to use these free programs indefinitely. Once a replacement priced program was available, we announced that the free program would be maintained for a limited time. While the specific limits varied, we made them quite long so as not to create customer resistance. The important point was to establish the principle that the free programs would not be supported indefinitely.

The IBM lawsuits

On the last day of the Johnson administration in January 1969, the US Department of Justice filed an antitrust lawsuit against IBM. Soon thereafter, IBM was deluged with corporate lawsuits alleging damage from IBM's monopolistic practices. IBM fought and won every lawsuit. The fact that IBM had unbundled its software and systems engineering undoubtedly contributed to this success.

The lessons of unbundling

In retrospect, several conclusions can be drawn from these experiences.

- First, the original trigger for unbundling was IBM's 1956 consent decree with the US Department of Justice. This decree forced IBM to offer its rented hardware products for sale and to separately price its hardware maintenance and spare parts. IBM was also required to provide the information needed for competitive maintainers to service IBM machines.
- Second, once IBM's hardware was available for purchase, competitors could purchase rental machines and lease them back to the original customers. Leasing companies were soon purchasing installed IBM systems and leasing them to the same customers at lower monthly charges than IBM's rental price. Previously, long product life had been an IBM advantage. Now, with the purchase option, leasing company profitability increased with the life of IBM's products. This forced IBM to introduce new machines at an increasing rate, which, in turn, made its rental business less profitable.
- Third, once maintenance information was publicly available, the IBM system interfaces were visible, and competitors could compete in any potentially profitable product areas. This enabled companies such as RCA, Amdahl, and Fujitsu to offer plug-compatible computers. It also enabled a host of companies to offer plug-compatible displays, disk drives, tape drives, and printers.
- Fourth, once companies could compete with parts of IBM's systems, it made the bundling of software and systems engineering uneconomic. The competitors' customers could continue to use at least some of IBM's "free" offerings without paying for them. This forced IBM to establish a host of restrictive practices to limit such services to pure IBM systems. By unbundling, the IBM hardware would no longer have to bear costs that the competitive machines did not have.
- Fifth, unbundling changed the software and systems engineering businesses. Once the hardware had to compete on its own, software and systems engineering also had to be

competitive. While it took IBM many years and a complete change of management to recognize the implications of this change, once they did, IBM Global Services became the largest and most profitable part of the company. IBM Global Services now offers essentially the support we used to call systems engineering, only it is now provided for a price and for any system, even for those manufactured by IBM's competitors.

- Sixth, application programs were clearly a separate and viable business from the computer hardware. Compatibility was important to users as they moved application programs among systems, so natural forces tended to make the application program interface (API) stable. Further, as user application needs expanded, unbundling would provide an economic incentive for competitors to meet any unfulfilled application needs. Therefore, unbundling application programs made both technical and economic sense.

- Seventh, the best economic approach for the systems programs was not as clear. One school of thought argued that operating systems were software and that all software should be priced separately from the hardware. The other view was that the dividing line between the hardware and the system software was essentially arbitrary and would likely alter with changes in hardware and software technology. For example, even in the original S/360 computer family, identical functions were implemented in microcode in some machines and with physical logic in others. Technically speaking, microcode is software, but it is typically treated as part of the hardware because it is included in the hardware product description and price.

This arbitrary division between software and hardware raises the question of what is in the system software. At the time of unbundling, IBM's OS/360 programming system was very large and growing. We had to slow the rate of growth because the development and support costs were proliferating. However, many of IBM's systems offerings were built on top of the API and could have been priced along with the applications, which would have substantially alleviated IBM's economic concerns with systems programs. Furthermore, hardware and system control programs were—and still are—generally procured and used together. Because there is no clear technical dividing line between them, unbundling these programs was not economically or technically sound.

Conclusion

Throughout my career as a computer architect, system designer, and software development manager, our system design decisions have steadily moved system control functions from the software into the hardware. As the cost and performance of hardware has improved, these hardware-software tradeoff decisions have changed. With unbundling, such tradeoffs are potentially more difficult. By unbundling systems programs, we have imposed an artificial barrier to the advancement of technology.

As long as the same organization offers the hardware and system software, and as long as the two are procured and used together, unbundling will not likely cause technical problems. However, the purpose of unbundling is to create separable markets and thereby inject economic and competitive considerations into the suppliers' and users' engineering and business decisions. If this was not the intent, then unbundling was unnecessary and should not have been done. While this separation was almost certainly IBM's intent at the time of unbundling, in retrospect, I do not believe that the implications were clearly understood.

It will likely take some time for the full consequences of this unbundling decision to become evident. When they are, I believe that the decisions to unbundle application programs and systems engineering will be seen as positive but that unbundling systems programs will ultimately be recognized as a mistake.

Watts S. Humphrey joined Carnegie Mellon University's Software Engineering Institute after retiring from IBM in 1986. Humphrey holds graduate degrees in physics and business administration, is an SEI Fellow, a member of the ACM, an IEEE Fellow, and a past member of the Malcolm Baldrige National Quality Award Board of Examiners. Honors include the 1993 Aerospace Software Engineering Award, an honorary PhD in software engineering in 1998, a software quality institute in Chennai, India, named for him in 2000, and an award for innovation and leadership in software process improvement from Boeing. He holds five US patents.

Readers may contact Watts Humphrey at watts@sei.cmu.edu.

For further information on this or any other computing topic, please visit our Digital Library at http://computer.org/publications/dlib.

The Information Management System (IMS) Program Product

The Information Management System (IMS) Program Product

William C. McGee

The Information Management System (IMS) was one of the first program products offered by IBM. From its inception in a North American Rockwell and IBM joint study in the 1960s, the product has evolved into the preeminent transaction processing database management system (DBMS). Throughout its history, IMS has remained the leader in DBMS technology.

A few years after the introduction of the System/360 in 1964, IBM found itself with an overabundance of a certain kind of software for its new system. To attract customers to the System/360, almost all 15 industry development groups in IBM's marketing division had developed or were developing more than two dozen Type II and Type III programs[1] that were intended to ease customer development of applications for the query and update of databases from remote terminals. Such applications were called Data Base/Data Communication (DB/DC) applications and were made feasible for the first time through System/360 direct-access storage devices (DASDs) and terminals. The programs being offered to ease the development of these applications were called DB/DC systems.

The large number of DB/DC systems being offered understandably created confusion among IBM customers. To clarify IBM's position, the Jamison task force was convened in the summer of 1968 at the IBM Los Angeles Scientific Center to do a detailed survey of these systems. The task force identified three classes of DB/DC systems: Class I systems provided a framework in which users places their application programs to implement their DB/DC applications; Class II systems were conceptually Class I systems for which IBM supplied a set of application programs and/or specific file designs for specific classes of applications, such as inventory control and airline reservations; and Class III systems provided general-purpose data structuring and manipulation facilities that were invoked through high-level executive languages. Class I systems soon became known in IBM parlance as supervisory systems, and Class III systems as executive systems.

One of the supervisory systems being developed at that time was the Information Management System. IMS had its origins in a joint project between IBM and the North American Rockwell Space Division in Downey, California, to manage the manufacturing information produced by Rockwell's Apollo mission contract. (Robert Patrick's article in this special issue gives an account of this project.) The joint project ended in early 1968. Rockwell Space continued implementing its copy of the program, and IBM's Manufacturing Industry Development group in Los Angeles continued to develop its copy as a Type II program. IBM announced the program as IMS/360 Version 1 in April 1968.

In late 1968, IBM convened another task force to address the increasing pressure to unbundle its computer offerings—that is, to separate charges for software and other services from hardware charges. The task force identified a new kind of software offering, the program product, to replace its bundled Type II and Type III offerings. In June 1969, IBM announced 17 program products,[2] including three identified by the Jamison task force as DB/DC systems: the Generalized Information System (GIS), an executive system developed by the Scientific Development industry group; the Customer Information Control System (CICS), a supervisory system developed by the Public Utilities industry group; and the Information Management System (IMS).

As a result of the June 1969 announcement, GIS, CICS, and IMS became the foundation of IBM's strategy for DB/DC support. GIS provided generalized file-processing capability and a high-level language for invoking file-processing operations from terminals. The product was later withdrawn for lack of a continuing business case. CICS provided transaction processing for installations with relatively simple database structures, and went on to achieve more than 10,000 user installations. IMS provided batch and transaction processing for medium-to-large installations with complex data structures, and became a major factor in the DB/DC market.

IMS/360 Version 1 was released as a program product in September 1969, with a monthly license fee of $600. The initial marketing effort was focused on manufacturing applications. It was shipped to approximately 30 customers, including North American Rockwell, Caterpillar, Hughes Aircraft, Douglas Aircraft, and Boeing Aircraft. Customers who had previously committed to using IMS/360 were given gratis licenses.

IMS/360 Version 1 consisted of two major parts: a DB part for database management and a DC part for data communication. In IMS/360 Version 2, the DC part of the product was split off as a separately priced feature, recognizing that some customers required only the DB part. The monthly license fees then became $550 for the base DB product and $625 for the DC feature.

Initial capabilities

The initial IMS release ran on the IBM System/360 as a subsystem under the OS/360 operating system. IMS exploited the OS/360's multiprogramming capability by running in multiple regions or address spaces provided by the operating system. In particular, one or more IMS batch executions could run concurrently with a single online execution of IMS.

A batch execution was a normal operating system job. It was initiated by the system operator through a job request that specified the IMS region controller module as the program to be executed and allocated to the job the IMS databases to be accessed. The job request also specified the name of a user-written program to be run in this system execution.

An online execution used one or more operating system regions. One of these regions, the control region, held the IMS control program. The remaining regions were called dependent regions and were used for the user's application programs. By using separate regions, IMS was able to exploit operating system inter-region protection to prevent interference among application programs and the control program.

In an online execution, terminal inputs consisted of commands to be executed by the control program, transaction messages to be processed in dependent regions, and switched messages to be routed to another terminal. Communication facilities supported by the initial release included non-switched single and multidrop lines, switched lines, and local terminal-channel connections. Terminals supported included the IBM 1050 typewriter, the IBM 2740 printer/keyboard, and the 2260 display terminal. The operating system Basic Telecommunication Access Method was used.

Incoming transaction messages caused application programs to be scheduled into dependent regions. These programs could concurrently access the same databases with full data integrity.

The data model provided by the initial release of IMS was Data Language/1 (DL/1). In this model, databases consisted of records, records were hierarchic structures of segments, and segments were sets of fields stored in consecutive bytes. One field in a record root segment could be designated the record key. The program's interface to IMS provided calls to access records sequentially or by key; to navigate to segments within the record; and to insert, replace, and delete records. Databases were created by user-written load programs issuing insert calls.

Databases were implemented by IMS-provided access methods. The hierarchic sequential access method (HSAM) placed database records in consecutive records of a single operating system SAM data set, which was appropriate for sequentially retrieving database records. The hierarchic indexed sequential access method (HISAM) stored database records in two data sets, an operating system ISAM data set to hold the root segments and dependent segments up to the capacity of the ISAM record, and an IMS-developed overflow sequential access method (OSAM) data set to hold dependent segments that didn't fit in the ISAM data record. HISAM provided the direct retrieval of records through a key field in the root segment, as well as sequential retrieval. Operating system data sets were stored on IBM 2311 and 2314 direct-access storage devices.

User involvement

One of the main reasons for IMS's longevity has been IBM's responsiveness to customer requirements. The major forums for the formulation of requirements have been the

Share and Guide IBM users organizations. Share was organized about the same time that IBM started marketing large-scale computers, and its members were mostly concerned with technical and scientific application of computers. Guide came later, and its members concentrated on business applications. The two organizations merged in the 1960s, but the combined organization only lasted in Europe, where it is now known as Guide Share Europe. Guide was disbanded in North America in the 1990s, but Share remains active.

Both Share and Guide Share Europe have committees working on IMS requirements. William Grafton, who worked on the joint development of the IMS forerunner at North American Rockwell[3] and was one of the founders of the Share IMS committee, has provided a valuable and interesting account of early IMS committee activity in Share. According to Grafton, the chair of this committee, TRW's Joan Heinonen, established a closed committee meeting policy, in which committee meetings during the first three days of Share sessions were limited to committee members, and in some cases to committee members who had signed nondisclosure agreements with IBM. This permitted the free exchange of product information between IMS developers and committee members, many of whom came from IMS beta test sites. Many of the eventual external design features of IMS/360 Version 2 and IMS/VS ware hammered out at Share IMS meetings and presented to IBM as resolutions. The closed working sessions were not popular at the beginning, and for her efforts, Heinonen earned the sobriquet "Dragon Lady." Closed working sessions are no longer held at Share.

Enhancements

The IMS program product has undergone extensive enhancement since its introduction in 1969. The product has remained basically a supervisory system, meaning that the user must still write application programs. An interactive query facility was added in IMS/360 Version 2 that let online users enter queries expressed in a high-level language, thus giving the product an aspect of an executive system, but the facility was withdrawn in 1978 for lack of a continuing business case.

The product underwent a major packaging change in 1989, when it was split into two program products: IMS Database Manager (IMS DB), which contained the IMS database facilities, and the IMS Transaction Manager (IMS TM), which contained its communication facilities. These products could be ordered separately, so that customers requiring only IMS database facilities need not pay for IMS communication facilities, and vice versa. The combination of the two could be ordered, giving a single IMS DB/DC product with the capability of the original IMS product. The split created a problem in servicing code common to both products, so shortly thereafter IMS DB and IMS TM were recombined back into a single IMS product and became separately orderable features.

Enhancements to IMS have been introduced through some 30 product releases, which have occurred approximately every 18 months. Table I identifies these releases by name, followed by a suffix to denote the principal new environment in which the release was intended to operate, followed by a version identifier consisting of a version number, a release-within-version number, and a modification level. Version identifiers were assigned consecutively through name changes, except at the first name change (IMS/VS), when version identifiers were restarted at 1.0.

Throughput

Throughput of IMS installations has benefited enormously from the increase in hardware speed and memory capacity that has occurred in the last 40 years as well as from more efficient hardware and operating system architecture. Important contributions made by IMS developers are as follows:

- HIDAM and HDAM access methods were introduced in IMS/360 2.0 to provide substantially improved performance on database insertions and deletions.
- Logical relationships were added in IMS/360 2.0 databases to provide more efficient handling of many-to-many relationships.
- In the original IMS release, application programs were scheduled only if they did not access databases currently being used. The IMS/VS 1.0 program isolation feature introduced locking architecture which permitted application programs accessing the same data to run concurrently without loss of data integrity.
- The original IMS release limited terminal access to programs running on a single CPU. The IMS/VS 1.1.2 multiple system coupling feature provided for the

Table 1. IMS program product releases.

Name and version ID	GA year	Hardware environment	Software environment	Major enhancements
IMS/360				
1.0	1969	System/360	OS/360	
1.1	1970			
1.2	1971			
2.0	1971			Logical relationships, logical databases, HIDAM and HDAM access methods
2.1	1971			
2.2	1972			Interactive query facility feature
2.3	1972			
2.4	1973			Message format service
IMS/VS				
1.0, 1.0.1	1974	System/370	OS/VS1	Program isolation
			OS/VS2	Secondary indexing
1.1, 1.1.1	1975		MVS	GSAM access method
1.1.2, 1.1.3	1976			Multiple systems coupling feature
1.1.4	1977			Fast path feature
1.1.5	1978			Database recovery control feature
1.1.6	1980			Intersystem communication
1.2	1981			Two-system data sharing, internal resource lock manager
1.3	1983			DB2 attach, DASD logging
2.1	1985			Improved I/O error handling
2.2	1987			Extended recovery facility
IMS/ESA				
3	1989	ESA/370	MVS/ESA	Database manager subsystem
4	1993			Transaction manager subsystem
				Advanced Program to Program Communication Protocol
				Extended terminal option
5	1995	System/390	OS/390	N-system data sharing
6	1998			Parallel sysplex support and shared queues
IMS				
7	2000			High availability large databases, Java program support
8	2002			Common service layer, IMSplexes.
9	2004	z servers	z/OS System Product	HALDB online reorganization, XML support
10	2007			Dynamic resource definition
11	2009			Open database

communication of transaction messages and program responses between online IMS executions running on different CPUs. This permitted the transaction processing load presented by a given terminal configuration to be shared by two or more CPUs.

- The original IMS release of was unable to meet the stringent throughput and response time requirements of critical banking applications. The IMS/VS 1.1.4 fast path feature enabled IMS to meet these requirements by trading off generality for specialized application program scheduling and data storage techniques and by "fast tracking" time-consuming operating system services. The fast path feature provided new fast path database structures, and existing databases came to be known as full-function databases.

- The two-system data sharing feature of IMS/VS 1.2 for full-function databases, and of IMS/VS 1.3 for fast path databases, let application programs running in one CPU directly access databases in a second CPU. This brought the processing power of two CPUs to bear on a common set of databases. By exploiting the parallel sysplex architecture of the IBM z series mainframes, data sharing was extended in IMS/ESA 5 for full-function databases and in IMS/ESA 6 for fast path databases to the sharing of databases in up to 32 CPUs.

Storage capacity

IMS has exploited improvements in DASDs and access methods to increase database capacity—notably, the increased sizes of the data sets that are used to implement IMS databases. Further growth in database storage capacity was achieved through database partitioning—that is, by using multiple data sets to implement a database. Partitioning examples include:

- *Data set groups.* IMS/360 provided for partitioning HISAM database record types into subtrees of segment types and storing instances of each subtree in a separate pair of ISAM/OSAM data sets referred to as a data set group.
- *High availability large databases* (HALDBs). IMS 7 provided for dividing HIDAM and HDAM databases into up to 1,001 partitions, each having the capacity of a single unpartitioned database.
- *Fast path database areas.* A similar capacity increase was provided in IMS 8 for fast path data entry databases, where the maximum number partitions or areas was increased from 240 to 2,048.

Such increases have effectively removed any constraints on IMS database size.

Availability

System availability is impacted by system hardware and software failures. The procedures followed in the early releases of IMS for recovering from system failure typically required shutting the system down and restarting it, which was quite time-consuming due to the large number of data sets that had to be closed and reopened. Measures to provide faster restart have included:

- The IMS/VS 2.2 extended recovery facility (XRF) (sometimes called hot standby) provided the ability to run a second or standby IMS execution on a separate channel-connected CPU in parallel with the primary IMS execution. Because the standby execution was primed, switching to it when the primary execution failed was relatively simple and typically required a minute or less.
- The IMS/ESA 5 remote site recovery facility was intended as a safeguard against physical damage to an IMS installation. It provided for the activity of one or more active IMS executions to be tracked by a single IMS execution at a remote site. The active executions sent log data to the tracking execution, which recorded as much data as required to take over for a failing active execution. Takeovers required operator intervention and the rebuilding of damaged databases, and hence were more time-consuming than with XRF.

System availability is also impacted by the need to repair broken databases and message queues; to reorganize databases; and to make changes in data, application, and network definitions, because these activities also generally require quiescing the system. Improvements in this area include:

- The IMS/VS 1.1.5 database recovery control facility systematized and automated much of the work required in database repair.
- A data entry database (DEDB) reorganization utility was provided in the first fast path release, and an enhanced version, the high-speed DEDB direct reorganization utility, was provided in IMS/ESA 5.
- A fast path DEDB online change function in IMS 6 enabled the addition, change, or deletion of fast path DEDBs at the database or area level without shutting down and restarting IMS.
- The IMS 9 HALDB online reorganization function allowed all partitions of a database to remain online and available during a database reorganization.

Accessibility

The data integrity and transaction processing facilities of IMS have generated strong requirements from other products to access these facilities. Some examples include:

- The rapid acceptance of CICS/OS generated a strong requirement for a database facility providing data integrity and recoverability. To meet this requirement, the DL/I part of IMS was repackaged in the IMS/360 Version 2 time frame and made available to CICS licensees.

- IMS/VS 1.1.6 introduced an intersystem communication (ISC) facility, which allowed IMS and other subsystems to exchange messages. This capability could be used, for example, by CICS/OS to route transaction messages directly to and receive responses from IMS executions, thereby giving CICS transactions access to IMS databases.

- The IMS DB feature of the reconfigured IMS product had no transaction processing ability. If this was required, it could be provided by a coresident transaction management subsystem which connected to and issued requests to the IMS DB control program. For example, instead of issuing transaction messages to access IMS databases via the ISC facility, CICS could issue DL/I calls directly.

- Similarly, the IMS TM feature had no database processing capability. If this was required, it could be provided by a coresident database management subsystem to which the IMS TM control program could issue data requests. For example, IMS application programs could access DB2 databases through the DB2 attach facility introduced in IMS/VS 1.3. This was generalized through the external subsystem attach facility in IMS/ESA 6 to allow access to any database system. Access to IMS TM executions has been broadened to permit access from application programs running in many different environments, including Web servers.

Usability

IMS has provided numerous enhancements to improve its usability by application programmers, system administrators, and operators. Some examples include:

- A message format service (MFS) introduced in IMS/360 2.4 significantly simplified the application programmer's view of terminals and communication facilities. MFS converted input streams into conventional message formats before handing them to application programs, and converted outgoing messages into data streams acceptable by terminals.

- Logical databases were introduced in IMS/ 360 2.0 to preserve the programmer's

---

The IMS project has been fortunate in attracting and keeping a large number of talented developers and planners.

---

hierarchic view of data, even in the presence of logical relationships. Like a physical database, a logical database consists of a set or records of a single tree-structured record type, with segments that are materialized as required from underlying physical segments using logical relationships.

- The IMS/VS 1.3 DB2 attach facility let IMS application programmers use the DB2 relational technology to rapidly and conveniently create and access DB2 databases. This facility was also key to meeting a common requirement for using the same data in both IMS transaction processing and DB2 data analysis applications. In IMS/ESA 3, the facility was extended to permit changes to IMS full-function databases to be synchronously propagated to attached DB2 databases. An asynchronous propagation capability was provided in IMS/ESA 4 by logging IMS data changes and processing the log at a later time to update the DB2 data.

- In IMS 7, Java was added to the growing number of programming languages that can be used to write IMS application programs. The IMS Java function provided the discipline of object-oriented programming and the use of industry-standard Java database connectivity for accessing relational data in general and DB2 data in particular. In IMS 9, the Java function was extended to support Extended Markup Language (XML) data. With this support, programmers could write programs to compose XML documents from existing IMS database data and to receive XML documents and store them in IMS databases.

- IMS 8 introduced the concept of an IMSplex, a set of IMS executions that work together as a unit. To counter the increased complexity of system operation brought about by IMSplexes, an operations manager component was introduced. This component provided an application programming interface through which commands could be issued and responses received. The interface could be used to route IMS commands to IMSplex members, and consolidate command responses from individual IMSplex members and provide that response to the command originator.

Development environment

The initial release of the IMS program product was carried out under the aegis of IBM's Data Processing Division (DPD), which was responsible for marketing IBM products and developing Type II programs. Responsibility for hardware and operating systems (Type I programs) lay with the System Development Division (SDD), located in Poughkeepsie and Endicott, New York, and in Raleigh, North Carolina. This division of effort was the source of considerable angst among IMS and system house personnel as they competed for development resources (typically measured in headcount) and vied for leadership in technology breakthroughs. At the same time, they depended on one another, with IMS depending on key hardware and operating system extensions to meet its own product objectives, and the system houses depending on IMS to attract new customers to IBM mainframes (IMS licenses were said to "drag iron"). The symbiotic relationship has served both groups well and continues to the present day.

In 1970, IMS development was moved to the Palo Alto Development Center in California. In September 1972, responsibility for IMS development was shifted from DPD to SDD, possibly to improve communications between the two divisions. This "shotgun wedding" did not last long, however. In September 1975, IMS development was again shifted, this time to the newly formed General Products Division (GPD) in San Jose, California, the main responsibility of which was the development of storage devices and printers. In February 1977, IMS development was physically moved from Palo Alto to a new Santa Teresa Laboratory (STL) south of the main IBM plant in San Jose. STL has been renamed Silicon Valley Laboratory (SVL), a more *a courant* name to attract new hires. IMS today is still located at SVL and is part of the Information Management Division of the IBM Software Group. IBM hardware and operating system operations are now part of the IBM Systems Technology Group. So the division of effort lives on.

At some point in its journey through the IBM organization, IMS adopted a product release methodology used elsewhere in the corporation as well as in many other companies. In this methodology, each product release is carried out in a series of phases in which the output of one phase becomes the input to the next. When depicted graphically, the methodology has the appearance of a waterfall, and is often referred to as the "waterfall method" of development. For IMS, Phase 0 consisted of documenting requirements for the release, writing release objectives, and forecasting the number of licenses to be added by the release. Phase 1 involved writing initial specifications, Phase 2 the final specifications, and so on to a final phase when the release was announced by a "blue letter" distributed to branch offices. Exiting each phase was conditioned on satisfying several dozen criteria, which ranged from the esoteric (Kanji enabling) to the sublime (reliability, availability, and serviceability). The total elapsed calendar time required to complete this cycle for a major release was on the order of two years. Customers were often frustrated at having their requirements accepted and then having to wait so long for solutions to appear in the product. However, the deliberate pace has proved highly effective in maintaining product quality. Also, the confidential nature of release content up to announcement time has been essential to preserving good customer relations.

IMS continues to use the phased development of releases. The major phases are now called concept, plan, and availability, the latter consisting of "quality partner" program testing followed by general availability. Involving customers in the testing process has been key to IMS's success. An early support program was inaugurated in IMS/VS 1.2 to address the complexity of testing the new data sharing facility. A similar program called managed availability provided for the early release of IMS/VS 1.3 to customers who could demonstrate the ability and readiness to test the new extended recovery facility.

The IMS project has been fortunate in attracting and keeping a large number of talented developers and planners. IBM staff who contributed to the first IMS release included Uri Berman, Darwin Busa, John Calvert, Carl Chamberlin, Carol Damerval, Bill Frantz,

Herb Ganske, Dan Gilbert, Joni Gutierrez, Pete Hill, Don Hyde, Howard Keller, Sid Kornelis, Homer Leonard, Bud Lowe, George Mackay, Ted Messinger, Larry Morgan, Ron Obermarck, Herb Pereyra, Vern Watts, and Tom Work. Calvert played as especially important role in the project; it was his responsibility to travel to corporate headquarters and obtain the final sign-off for each release. His phone calls were eagerly awaited at STL, and good news was received with the same kind of enthusiasm as a successful moon landing.

Foremost among the original IMS group was Uri Berman, the inventor of DL/I, whose insight and drive were instrumental in creating the joint IBM/North American Rockwell effort leading to the IMS product. His invention of DL/I resulted from noticing the redundancy inherent in traditional punched-card records and listings of manufacturing parts data and devising a hierarchic segmented-record design that eliminated this redundancy. This design was also being used contemporaneously in other software products, but it was Berman's initiative and access to IBM resources that resulted in DL/I becoming the exemplar hierarchic data model. In recognition of his contribution to IBM business, the company in 1981 presented Berman with an Outstanding Contribution Award of $100,000.

Vern Watts was an IBM systems engineer on the Hughes Aircraft account at the time that DL/I was being developed for the IBM System/360 at Rockwell. Watts provided copies of the DL/I routines to Hughes, which used them in some early database applications. Other major aerospace companies such as TRW and General Dynamics also received copies of these DL/I routines in the same time frame and were beginning to do production work with the code. Watts joined the IMS development team at its inception and made major contributions to the product, especially in the areas of extended recovery and high availability large databases. For these contributions, he was awarded the title of IBM IMS Distinguished Engineer.

Another key figure in the early days of IMS was Pete Hill. According to Grafton, Hill's charisma, leadership, energy, and commitment were of incalculable value to the success of IMS. Hill was a powerful salesman for the product. He was excellent with customers and probably had a lot to do with IMS being referred to figuratively as a

> **The richness of IMS has resulted from the product's response to diverse requirements over a long period of time.**

Fortune 500 company. From a developer and product planner perspective, Hill was a tough manager because he was not afraid to go out on a limb to promise enhancements to customers. He followed IMS as it moved around California and the IBM organization and finished his illustrious IBM career at STL.

Key contributions to IMS were made by individuals joining the project after the initial release. These included Dieter Gawlick who identified IMS's performance problems in banking applications while working for IBM Germany and led the design of the fast path architecture that overcame these problems; Ed Lassettre, who acted as IMS's point man to IBM Poughkeepsie and negotiated crucial departures from operating system architecture to meet fast path and other IMS objectives; Ron Obermarck, who identified a weakness in the logging procedure during system failures and invented a log tape write ahead scheme to resolve the problem; and Kent Treiber, who along with Obermarck, represented IBM Research in an ad tech partnership with IMS and originated the design for the remote system recovery facility.

Contributions to database technology

When viewed in the broader context of database technology, IMS has made numerous original contributions, both in its initial release and subsequent enhancements. The following are the most significant:

- *Data consistency.* While the concepts of transaction atomicity and data consistency in the presence of multiple concurrent updaters were being published in research papers in the 1970s, the program isolation facility in IMS/VS 1.0 was the first generally available implementation of these concepts. The scalability of program isolation to data sharing across systems was demonstrated by the IMS/VS 1.2 internal resource lock manager (IRLM) facility, and by the adoption of the IRLM architecture by IBM mainframe designers in the cross system coupling facility for mainframe sysplexes.

- *Data integrity through failure.* IMS was the first product to recognize the reality of hardware and program failures and provide remedies for protecting data from these failures, including the checkpointing of data, logging of data changes, and backing out uncommitted changes from failing transactions.

- *Continuous availability.* IMS originated the architecture for the takeover of a failing system by a standby system. This architecture was first used in Tandem nonstop systems and implemented shortly after as the extended recovery facility of IMS/VS 2. The disaster recovery facility in IMS/ESA 5 is believed to be original to IMS.

- *Queued transaction processing.* Early online systems used the interactive entry and response mode of operation. IMS was the first system to interpose queues between users and responders. This architecture has proved to be robust, capable of adequate performance (as demonstrated by the fast path feature) and gracefully scaling up to transaction processing across systems (as demonstrated by the multiple system coupling and intersystem communication facilities).

Current status

On IMS's 20th birthday in 1988, IMS was being used in 7,000 installations throughout the world. Customer investment in IMS application had grown to an estimated 10 to 12 billion lines of code. Bank of America was processing three million transaction a day with IMS.

On IMS's 30th birthday in 1998, more than 90% of major worldwide companies in the areas of manufacturing, finance, banking, retailing, aerospace, communication, government, insurance, high technology, and healthcare were using IMS to run their daily operations.[4] IMS was processing more than 50 billion transactions from 200 million end users per day, with transaction rates at single installations of 100 million or more transactions per day.[5]

IMS's contribution to IBM revenue has consistently grown over the years and is currently estimated to be in the area of $1 billion per year.

In an age when software projects tend to have short lifetimes, it is instructive to consider why IMS has remained so successful for 40 years. An informal poll of a few IBM pioneers has elicited the following reasons for IMS's longevity:

- *Application program interface stability.* There are numerous examples of application programs written 30 or more years ago that still run on today's system.

- *Product service and support.* This is a "given" for IBM products. IMS has continued the tradition and gained a reputation for openness to customers and customer involvement.

- *Data integrity and recoverability.* The original goals have been maintained and strengthened.

- *Innovation.* IMS pioneered a number of significant advances in database technology. IMS developers had a cowboy mentality—that is, the talent and willingness to push the envelope, often to the dismay of their more conservative colleagues in the operating system houses, whose typical reaction to some IMS requirements, such as XRF having the same data set open for update by two (trusted) users at the same time, was "you're crazy."

An evolutionist might conclude that IMS has survived because it has no viable competitors. There are have been numerous successful database management products coexisting with IMS, but none that has combined database management with robust transaction management in the same manner. The only real competitor to IMS is the recurring emergence of decentralization trends, which threatens not only products like IMS but large mainframes as well. Still, it is difficult to imagine today's global economies working without large, centralized databases.

IMS is a functionally rich product. This richness has resulted from the product's response to diverse requirements over a long period of time. Although this richness offers flexibility, it makes the product hard to describe coherently. For example, someone not familiar with product's history might wonder why IMS has two database flavors (full-function and fast path) instead of one. These flavors provide a useful tradeoff between function and performance, but they might have been integrated more elegantly had the product been born 10 years later when the importance of performance to banking applications was better understood. One might also struggle to understand the number and variety of other products with which IMS is required to interoperate. It takes books to describe IMS's offerings in this area, and it is reasonable to ask whether IMS will be able to maintain its current level of support. Notwithstanding, IMS literature goes to great lengths to point out the strategic position of the product in IBM's business, and if this assertion is valid, we can expect to see the product celebrating many happy returns of its 40th birthday.

Acknowledgments

I gratefully acknowledge the assistance of IBM staffers Carl Chamberlin, Jeff Horton, Barbara Klein, Rich Lewis, Rick Long, Dean Meltz, Geoff Nichols, Frank Ricchio, and Suzie Wendler as well as retired IBM staffers Dieter Gawlick, Ron Obermarck, Kent Treiber, and Vern Watts in preparing this article.

References and notes

1. IBM had four categories of programs in the 1960s. Type I programs were operating systems, languages, and utilities produced by the product divisions. Type II programs were developed and supported by the marketing division. Type III programs were developed by IBM system engineers. Type IV programs were developed by customers, who contributed them to IBM libraries for distribution. These programs were bundled with IBM computers, i.e., available at no extra cost to IBM hardware users.
2. B. Grad, "A Personal Recollection: IBM's Unbundling of Software and Services," *IEEE Annals of the History of Computing,* vol. 24, no. 1, 2002, pp. 64–71.
3. W.P. Grafton, "IMS: Past, Present, Future," *Datamation,* Sept. 1983.
4. From SHARE Session 1226 presentation, 26 Feb. 1998.
5. D. Meltz et al., *An Introduction to IMS,* IBM Press, 2005.

 **William (Bill) C. McGee** joined IBM in 1964 at the Palo Alto Scientific Center, where he worked on physics and graphics applications. In 1970, he transferred to the IBM DB/DC Systems Department in Palo Alto, and later relocated to the Santa Teresa Laboratory in San Jose, where he participated in DB/DC requirements and strategy, DB/DC product architecture, and the planning and development of IMS, DB2, and Data Dictionary program products. McGee has an MA in physics from Columbia University. Contact him at wcmcgee@aol.com.

IBM Timeline

1886

- Herman Hollerith uses his newly invented electromechanical punch card tabulation machine technology for its first application—processing vital statistics for the Maryland Department of Health.

1889

- Herman Hollerith is awarded his first set of patents for his electromechanical tabulating machine.

1890

- US Census Bureau holds competition to find better technology to calculate the US Census—Hollerith wins and receives contract for machines to process data for the 1890 US Census.

1896

- Herman Hollerith officially launches the Tabulating Machine Company in Washington, DC.

1905

- The Tabulating Machine Company is incorporated in New Jersey.

1906

- Herman Hollerith introduces the first automatic feed tabulator.

1907

- The US Census Bureau contracts with Hollerith tabulating machine competitor James Powers—marking the end of Hollerith's exclusive hold of US Census information processing applications.

1911

- Computing-Tabulating-Recording Company (C-T-R), the precursor to IBM, is formed by Charles Flint after acquiring and combining Hollerith's Tabulating Machine Company and two other firms: Computing Scale Company and International Time Recording Company.
- James Powers forms the Powers Accounting Machine Company, the primary competitor to C-T-R/IBM in the teens and twenties.

1914

- Thomas J. Watson, Sr., is hired as general manager of C-T-R.

1915

- Thomas J. Watson, Sr., is promoted to president of C-T-R.

1916

- Thomas J. Watson, Sr., establishes an education program for C-T-R's sales force.

1920

- C-T-R introduces its first printing tabulating machine.

1923

- C-T-R introduces its first electric key punch.

1924

- Computing-Tabulating-Recording Company changes its name to International Business Machines (IBM) to reflect its rapidly growing business around the world. It had operated under this name in Canada since 1917.

1925

- IBM completes plant in Vincennes, France.

1927

- IBM introduces first automatic gang punch.
- IBM tabulating machine competitor, Powers Accounting Machine Company, merges with Remington Typewriter and Rand Kardex to form the Remington Rand Corporation.

1928

- IBM initiates its first engineering training course for its customers.
- IBM introduces famed 80-column card that would become standard for decades.

1929

- IBM introduces first card counting printing sorter.

1930

- IBM, in contrast to its office machine competitors, increases its number of employees at the start of the Great Depression.

1931

- IBM introduces a number of new product lines, including the IBM 400 series of accounting machines, the IBM 600 series of calculating machines, and its first automatic multiplying punch.

1932

- IBM introduces Alphabetical Duplicating Punch.

1933

- IBM enters typewriter business with its acquisition of Electromatic Typewriters, Inc.

1934

- IBM introduces its IBM 801 Bank Proof machine (for clearing bank checks).

1935

- IBM publishes its first issue of *Think* magazine—at that time a broad-based news, education, science, and arts publication.
- IBM markets its first electric typewriter.
- IBM completes new plant in Milan, Italy.
- IBM's German subsidiary, Dehomag, comes out with the Dehomag D11 Tabulator—the first IBM production machine with serious scientific calculating potential.
- President Franklin Delano Roosevelt forms the Social Security Administration with the US Social Security Act.

1936

- IBM punch card tabulating equipment is first used for the Social Security Administration's information processing.
- US Justice Department antitrust case (first against IBM) results in IBM needing to relinquish its exclusive control of the punch card market for IBM machines.

1937

- IBM introduces its IBM Type 805 International Test Scoring Machine, the first of its kind.
- IBM introduces IBM 007 Collator.
- Small-scale partnership is formed between IBM and Columbia University to create Thomas J. Watson Astronomical Computing Bureau.

1938

- IBM dedicates its new IBM World Headquarters Building on Madison Avenue in Manhattan.

1941

- IBM transfers some of its resources toward war production as US enters World War II—Munitions Manufacturing Corporation is incorporated.

1942

- IBM builds plant in Poughkeepsie, New York—initially focused on munitions work, it will became one of the company's core facilities for information processing technology after the war.

1943

- IBM launches its first West Coast facility, a card manufacturing plant in San Jose, California.

1944

- Dedication of Automatic Sequence Control Calculator (ASCC)/ Harvard Mark I—IBM's first electromechanical computer.

1945

- IBM partners with Columbia University to form Watson Scientific Computing Laboratory— seen as the start of IBM Research.

1946

- First significant electronic digital computer in the US is completed: Electronic Numerical Integrator and Computer (ENIAC)—the US Army-funded machine was designed and built at the University of Pennsylvania's Moore School of Electrical Engineering.
- First two computer companies in the US are formed: Electronic Control Company (soon to be renamed Eckert-Mauchly Computer Corporation) in Philadelphia, Pennsylvania, and Engineering Research Associates in St. Paul, Minnesota.

1947

- Research scientists at Bell Laboratories invent the transistor, which becomes the dominant component for computer memory and processing in the second half of the 1950s.

1948

- IBM introduces Selective Sequence Electronic Calculator, its first independently designed electromechanical digital scientific computer—housed behind glass on the ground floor of its headquarters in Manhattan, it becomes an early symbol of the computer age.

1949

- Thomas J. Watson, Sr., becomes Chair of the IBM Board.
- World Trade Corporation is formed as an IBM subsidiary for all overseas operations.

1950

- IBM begins operations at new facility in Tel Aviv, Israel.
- IBM redirects facilities toward war work to aid the US Government during Korean War.

1951

- IBM forms IBM United Kingdom.
- Remington Rand's Universal Automatic Computer (UNIVAC) hits the market—it is the first significant commercial digital mainframe computer, and for years the name UNIVAC is used synonymously with computers.

1952

- IBM introduces Defense Calculator/IBM 701—its first fully electronic digital computer and a machine marking IBM's entrance into the computer industry.
- UNIVAC is used in high-profile national television broadcast predicting results of 1952 US Presidential Election.
- Thomas J. Watson, Sr.'s, son Thomas J. Watson, Jr., becomes the president of IBM.
- IBM launches research laboratory in San Jose, California.

1953

- IBM announces IBM 650 Magnetic Drum Calculator; the first computer to achieve more than a thousand installations, it marks the beginning of mass production in computing.
- IBM gets the primary computer contract for the Semi-Automatic Ground Environment radar and computer air defense system—to build 52 AN/FSQ-7 computers (physically largest computers ever built).

1954

- IBM 650 on the market and is adopted for both business data processing and for scientific computation.
- IBM introduces IBM 704, a scientific computer successor to the IBM 701.

1955

- Remington Rand and Sperry Corporation merge to form the Sperry Rand Corporation; the computer division of the firm is called Sperry Univac.
- IBM introduces IBM 608, a small-scale transistorized computer.
- IBM loses contract bidding for LARC—a powerful computer for Livermore Scientific Laboratory—to Remington Rand.
- IBM receives contract to build IBM Stretch (IBM 7030) for Los Alamos Scientific Laboratory.

1956

- Thomas J. Watson, Sr., transfers IBM Chief Executive Officer title to Thomas J. Watson, Jr.
- Thomas J. Watson, Sr., dies at age 82, weeks after relinquishing CEO role.
- Newly available IBM 305 RAMAC (Random Access Method of Accounting) and IBM 650 RAMAC—both of which used magnetic disk storage technology pioneered at IBM San Jose's research laboratory—mark the origin of disk drive technology and the disk drive industry.
- Consent decree results from US Justice Department antitrust suit for IBM's anti-competitive practices to maintain its dominance in the punch card tabulator industry.

1957

- Control Data Corporation is launched and becomes the leading supercomputing firm in the 1960s.
- Digital Equipment Corporation is launched and becomes the leading minicomputing firm in the 1960s.
- IBM makes its programming language, FORTRAN, available to customers—it becomes the leading programming language for scientific computing.

1958

- IBM 7090 is introduced.
- Texas Instrument's Jack Kilby and Fairchild Semiconductor's Robert Noyce independently develop the integrated circuit.

1959

- IBM introduces IBM 1620, primarily a scientific computer.
- IBM introduces the IBM 1401, the first computer to have more than 10,000 installations.
- IBM develops the first automatic assembly line for producing transistors.

1960

- IBM delivers Stretch to Los Alamos Scientific Laboratory.

1961

- Thomas J. Watson Research Center opens in Yorktown Heights, New York.
- Systems Programming, Research, Engineering and Development (SPREAD) task force launched to rationalize IBM's incompatible lines of computers (results in IBM System/360).
- IBM launches a development laboratory at its Rochester, Minnesota manufacturing plant.

1962

- IBM completes early iteration of Semi-Automatic Business Research Environment (SABRE) for American Airlines; the system is further refined by IBM and becomes fully operational later in the 1960s.

1963

- IBM greatly expands its laboratories internationally—adding laboratories in Zurich, Switzerland; La Gaude, France; and Vienna, Austria.

1964

- IBM System/360 series announced—a highly influential line of compatible computers that extends IBM's success in the 1960s and early 1970s.

1966

- New IBM plant and development facility launched in Austin, Texas.

1967

- IBM produces its first monolithic integrated circuits.

1968

- IBM launches Customer Information Control System (CICS), a highly influential and profitable database and data communication system.
- IBM announces it will unbundle its software—price it separately from hardware.

1969

- IBM systems used in the Apollo mission that puts a man on the moon.
- IBM introduces System/3, the first in its midrange series of computers.
- IBM begins to price some of its software—implementing unbundling.
- IBM rationalizes its disparate database/datacommunications software offerings around three primary products: CICS, IMS, and GIS.

1970

- IBM San Jose researcher Edgar Codd publishes landmark article inventing relational databases, the dominant database model for the succeeding three decades.
- IBM introduces the IBM System/370 series.

1971

- T. Vincent Learson succeeds Thomas J. Watson, Jr., as IBM's Board Chair.

1972

- Frank Cary succeeds T. Vincent Learson as IBM's Board Chair.
- IBM completes management facilities in West Germany and Mexico.

1973

- IBM scientist Leo Esaki receives Nobel Prize in physics for his discovery of electron tunneling.

1975

- IBM scientist Benoit Mandelbrot develops field of fractal geometry.
- IBM announces IBM System/32 as its new midrange series.

1976

- IBM introduces IBM 3800 laser printer.

1977

- IBM's Data Encryption Standard (DES) is established as standard in cryptography by the US National Bureau of Standards.
- IBM announces IBM System/34 as its new midrange series.

1978

- IBM announces IBM System/38 as its new midrange series.

1980

- IBM develops IBM 801 using its Reduced Instruction Set Computer (RISC) architecture.
- IBM makes the decision to enter personal computing.

1981

- IBM sets up an independent business unit at its Boca Raton, Florida, laboratory to quickly develop its IBM PC personal computer—the software and much of the hardware is outsourced.

1983

- IBM announces IBM System/36 as its new midrange series.

1985

- President Ronald Reagan awards National Medal of Honor to mainframe digital computer pioneer and IBM Fellow Herman Goldstine and National Technology Medals to IBM's retired employees Erich Bloch, Frederick Brooks, and Bob Evans.

1986

- IBM Zurich scientists Heinrich Rohrer and Gerd Binnig win the Nobel Prize for physics for scanning tunneling microscopy.
- John Akers becomes IBM Board Chair.
- IBM Alamaden Research Center in San Jose, California, is dedicated.

1987

- IBM Zurich scientists J. Georg Bednorz and Alex Mueller receive Nobel Prize for physics for their work on high-temperature superconductivity.
- IBM Personal System/2 (PS/2) is introduced, a powerful new addition to IBM's personal computer offerings.

1988

- IBM begins to deliver AS/400 series models, its highly successful midrange series.

1989

- IBM signs contract to run a major Eastman Kodak data center—it is IBM's first data center management services contract and marked the beginning of the company's heightened concentration on computer services as a business.

1990

- IBM introduces comprehensive System/390 series, ranging from midrange computers to supercomputers.

1991

- For the first time ever, IBM loses money—the first of three consecutive years of negative net earnings.
- President George Bush awards National Medal of Technology to IBM's John Cocke for inventing Reduced Instruction Set Computing system.

1992

- IBM's financial troubles worsen as the shift to personal computers and the client-server model results in further erosion of IBM's profits.
- IBM launches successful new line of IBM ThinkPad laptop computers.

1993

- For the first time, IBM looks outside the company for its leader and hires former RJR Nabisco Chief Executive Officer Louis Gerstner as the new IBM Chief Executive Officer and Board Chair.
- CEO Gerstner sees the services business as the key to integrating the disparate resources and capabilities of the corporation to return IBM to profitability.

1994

- IBM launches its IBM Global Network, a massive high-speed voice and data network to take advantage of increasing opportunities in the client-server environment.

1995

- IBM acquires the Lotus Development Corporation, extending IBM's software business and making it one of the largest in the world.

1996

- IBM announces DB2 Universal Database, the first fully scalable web-based database management system.

1997

- CEO Gerstner launches major "e-business" initiative.
- IBM's Deep Blue computer beats chess grandmaster Garry Kasparov.

1998

- IBM sells its Global Network to AT&T for $5 billion.

1999

- IBM announces plans to develop Blue Gene supercomputer, a machine designed to be 500 times more powerful than any existing supercomputers.

2000

- IBM launches a new generation of powerful, reliable servers—IBM eServer series.
- Samuel Palmisano becomes the president and chief operating officer of IBM.

2002

- Samuel Palmisano is named IBM Chief Executive Officer and Board Chair.
- IBM buys PricewaterhouseCoopers (PwC) for $3.5 billion, further extending its fast-growing IT consulting services business.

2003

- IBM receives more than 3,400 patents, breaking the annual record for any corporation.

2004

- IBM sells its Personal Computer Division to Chinese personal computer manufacturer Lenovo Corporation.

2005

- IBM introduces the IBM System z9.
- IBM Blue Gene/L is certified as the world's most powerful computer.

2006

- IBM introduces the IBM System p5 595, the world's most powerful server.

2008

- IBM launches powerful IBM System z10 mainframe enterprise server, showing a continuing commitment to certain strategic hardware markets as it focuses much of its resources on software and services.

2009

- IBM introduces its "Smarter Planet" advertising campaign—focusing on green computing and more efficient and effective computer controlled systems.

2010

- IBM sets another annual record for most patents by a corporation at 5,896.

IBM History:
An Annotated Bibliography

The following annotated bibliography contains more than 170 secondary and primary sources documenting, tracing, and interpreting the history of IBM. Books and articles were chosen for their depth and quality of analysis as well as accuracy of information. The articles in the bibliography are limited to history articles, and the bibliography does not include technical articles by IBM scientists, engineers, and managers writing on contemporary developments and reporting research findings. The *IEEE Annals of the History of Computing* articles that were re-published in this volume are listed, but they are not annotated in the bibliography. Many archival collections at the Charles Babbage Institute, the Computer History Museum, and other repositories have miscellaneous documents pertaining to IBM's history—the bibliography below contains only archival collections with a substantial volume of significant documents on IBM. Likewise, IBM, as the longtime computer industry leader, is discussed in countless oral histories. The oral histories below are fundamentally on IBM's history and in most cases are career-spanning interviews with longtime IBM engineers, scientists, managers, and executives. In a small number of cases early users of IBM systems or competitors provide unique and valuable discussion of IBM, and thus their oral histories are included. IBM sponsored a major oral history initiative as part of the IBM Technical History Project in the 1980s that resulted in several large published book volumes of oral histories. Because these oral history volumes were published as books, they are listed in the "books" section, and a list of all the interviewees in the volumes is included in the annotation. A portion of these are long, detailed oral histories, while many others are shorter and relate to specific information sought for a particular IBM history book project. For a small number of sources, I was unable to secure a copy for review or I do not have a reading knowledge of the language of the publication. In these instances, there is a listing of the source without an annotation.

Books

Akera, A., *Calculating a Natural World: Scientists, Engineers, and Computers During the Rise of US Cold War Research*, MIT Press, 2007.

> This is the best study of the early history of scientific computing, including discussion and analysis of scientific computing at IBM. With regard to IBM, Akera writes on the work of scientific computing pioneers Wallace Eckert and Cuthbert Hurd. He also has an excellent chapter on the history of the IBM user group, Share.

Austrian, G., *Herman Hollerith, Forgotten Giant of Information Processing*, Columbia University Press, 1982.

> This thorough and well-researched biography of Herman Hollerith is the top study of the person behind early IBM punch card tabulation machine technology. It provides great insight into his invention of punch card tabulation machines, his contract for processing the 1890 US Census, other business of Hollerith's Tabulating Machine Company, his selling the Tabulating Machine Company to allow it to become part of Charles Flint's C-T-R, and Hollerith's role with C-T-R prior to retiring in 1914.

Balance, R.S., and W. Buchholz, *Planning a Computer System: Project Stretch*, McGraw-Hill, 1962.

> This short book is the most detailed study specifically on IBM Stretch. It was published shortly after IBM delivered Stretch to Los Alamos Scientific Laboratory.

Baldwin, C.Y., and K.B. Clark, *Design Rules*, MIT Press, 2000.

> These two management scholars examine the origins of modularity in computing technology with the IBM/System 360 family of computers. They explore the evolution of the computer industry as modularity spread beyond IBM in the 1970s and 1980s, and led to what they term a "modular cluster" in the industry by the 1990s.

Bashe, C.J., L.R. Johnson, J.H. Palmer, and E.W. Pugh, *IBM's Early Computers*, MIT Press, 1986.

> This was produced as part of IBM's Technical History Project and is the most thorough historical survey of IBM computers between the early 1950s and the early 1960s. The authors provide extensive technical detail on the IBM 650, IBM 704, IBM 1401, IBM 1620, IBM Stretch, and other systems prior to IBM System/360. They also provide extensive discussion of memory and storage (with chapters on magnetic tape, ferrite-core, and disk storage), as well as on programming (Speedcoding, FORTRAN, and Share).

Bashe, C.J., L.R. Johnson, J.H. Palmer, and E.W. Pugh, *Interviews and Discussions for IBM's Early Computers, Volumes 1–4*, Thomas J. Watson Research Center, 1987.

As part of IBM's Technical History Project, C.J. Bashe, L.R. Johnson, J.H. Palmer, and E.W. Pugh conducted a total of 125 interviews (many by phone) with (primarily) IBM employees in researching the book, *IBM's Early Computers* (see above). Most of the interviews were done by one of the four researchers, while a few were conducted by multiple members of this four-man research team. Transcripts and notes of these interviews were bound into four volumes and published by IBM's Thomas J. Watson Research Center in 1987. The transcripts vary considerably in length, ranging from 5 pages to 70 pages. Some target very specific information, while others are broader in scope. Very few are career oral histories—they are targeted toward the book project on particular IBM systems. Only a few public repositories have these volumes—Burndy Library (part of the Huntington Library in San Marino, California) and the Charles Babbage Institute, University of Minnesota-Minneapolis. An alphabetical list of the interviewees follows: C.W. Allen, G.M. Amdahl, A. G. Anderson, R.B. Arndt, A.J. Atrubin, E.W. Bauer, F.S. Beckman, J.W. Birkenstock, L.W. Blenderman, R.E. Blue, W.G. Bouricius, C.E. Branscomb, A.W. Brooke, G. Bruce, W. Buchholz, P.W. Case, J. P. Cedarholm, C.L. Christiansen, E.P. Clarke, A.M. Clayton, R. I. Cline, D.J. Crawford, P.O. Crawford, G.F. Daly, E.S. Drake, K.E. Drangeid, S.W. Dunwell, J.P. Eckert, N.P. Edwards, B.O. Evans, M.A. Every, H. Fleisher, J.W. Forester, K.D. Foulger, P.E. Fox, E.L. Fritz, R.M. Furman, C.H. Gaudette, J.W. Gibson, J.A. Goetz, H.H. Goldstine, W.A. Gross, G.R. Gunther-Mohr, J.A. Haddad, A. Hamburgen, J.F. Hanifin, W.E. Harding, J.M. Harker, J.T. Harrison, G.V. Hawkins, W.P. Heising, L. Hellerman, R.A. Henle, A.S. Hoagland, A.J. Hoffman, P.H. Howard, E.S. Hughes, Jr., L.P. Hunter, C.C. Hurd, J.J. Ingram, P.W. Jackson, R.C. Jackson, A.H. Johnson, S.P. Keller, G.F. Kennard, R.W. Landauer, T.J. Leach, J.J. Lentz, J.B. Little, J.C. Logue, W.F. McClelland, J.A. Mc-Donnell, W.W. McDowell, J.C. McPherson, R.G. Mork, J.H. Morrissey, R.W. Murphy, W.E. Mutter, H.W. Nordyke, Jr., L. Nowakowski, B.E. Phelps, E.R. Piore, D.A. Quarles, Jr., E.J. Rabenda, N. Rochester, W.S. Rohland, J.P. Roth, R.F. Rutz, D. Sayre, E.M. Schaefer, H.P. Schaleppi, B.N. Slade, B.R. Smith, P.P. Sorokin, P.K. Spatz, D.T. Spaulding, A.P. Speiser, L.D. Stevens, J.B. Tait, S. Triebwasser, J.J. Troy, T.J. Watson, Jr., J.A. Weidenhammer, J.H. Wilburn, W.D. Winger, V.R. Witt, L.M. Wood, D.R. Young, and H.S. Yourke.

Bassett, R.K., *To the Digital Age: Research Labs, Start-up Companies, and the Rise of MOS Technology*, Johns Hopkins University Press, 2002.

Bassett provides an important and well-researched history of Metal-Oxide-Semiconductor (MOS) technology. He tells of how AT&T's Bell Laboratories invented but then ignored this technology as a small group of other companies launched major MOS research and development efforts, including IBM, RCA, Fairchild Semiconductor, and Intel. Bassett emphasizes that the successful evolution of MOS technology resulted not just from the work by these individual firms, but through knowledge exchanges between them. The book offers great insight into IBM's semiconductor research and development efforts and the emergence of IBM's MOS program, and it is the best overall book on the history of IBM semiconductor technology.

Bauer, R.A., E. Collar, V. Tang, J. Wind, and P. Houston, *The Silverlake Project: Transformation of IBM*, Oxford University Press, 1992.

> Written by a team including three technical and managerial leaders at IBM, a management scholar, and a freelance journalist, this book explores the origins of IBM Rochester's Silverlake project to develop its AS/400 series of midrange systems. The book, a cross between narrative history and a "lessons learned" and "best practices" management case study, provides important insight into a pivotal project for IBM that led to a much-needed success with AS/400. The AS/400 family of machines also set up the firm—and the IBM Rochester facility—to become a major player in producing powerful servers.

Brennan, J.F., *The IBM Watson Laboratory at Columbia University: A History*, International Business Machines, 1971.

> This is an informative short history book produced by IBM. This source briefly outlines the history of IBM's supplying tabulation machines in 1928 to the Columbia University Statistical Computing Bureau, the firm's development of the "Ben Wood Calculator" for this statistical bureau, and the origins and work of the Thomas J. Watson Astronomical Computing Bureau (also at Columbia University). After establishing this important pre-history of IBM's early scientific computing work, the book focuses on the origin and work of Watson Scientific Computing Laboratory through three periods or missions: Mission I, "Applied Mathematics and Computational Theory," 1945-1952; Mission II, "Solid State Physics and Advanced Electronics," 1952-1970; and Mission III, "The Life Sciences," 1964–1970. An often overlooked resource, this is a wonderful book on the early history of scientific computing and on IBM's path breaking role in this area.

Campbell-Kelly, M., and W. Aspray, *Computer: A History of the Information Machine*, Basic Books, 1996.

> This is the best overall survey of the history of computer technology. The book begins by outlining different information processing technologies through the ages, before "Babbage's dream" came true with the advent of electronic digital computers in the mid 1940s. It is a highly readable book that does a strong job of making the technological evolution of the computer broadly accessible, as well as the dynamics of the computer industry. It describes many key developments at IBM and traces the company's technical and business history relative to its competitors.

Campbell-Kelly, M., *From Airline Reservations to Sonic the Hedgehog: A History of the Software Industry*, MIT Press, 2003.

> By far the best book on the history of the emergence and growth of the software products industry, the book surveys the early firms that transitioned from software services to launch the software products field, and this industry's dynamics from the late 1960s into the 1990s. With regard to IBM, it provides important perspective on IBM's deci-

sion to "unbundle" its software at the end of the 1960s, as well as some attention to key IBM database/data communications products including CICS and IMS.

Campbell-Kelly, M., *ICL: A Business and Technical History*, Clarendon Press, 1989.

This excellent business history of International Computers Limited (ICL) is really a history of the entire British punch card tabulation and computing industries, as ICL was the national champion spawned by the merger of the British Tabulating Machine Company (BTM) and Powers-Samas Accounting Machine Company (to become ICT), and later, English Electric (to become ICL). Tabulator Limited, which formed in 1902, secured rights to sell Hollerith tabulation machines and evolved to become the British Tabulating Machine Company. Throughout the first half of the twentieth century there was a licensing agreement between IBM and BTM that gave BTM rights to IBM technology in exchange for a substantial royalty on sales. In 1949 IBM severed this relationship, and IBM and BTM became competitors in the British and European markets. The book does a great job of analyzing this changing relationship and the competition between IBM and BTM both in the pre-computer era and throughout the computer era into the 1980s.

Carroll, P., *Big Blues: The Unmaking of IBM*, Crown Publishers, 1994.

Written by a *Wall Street Journal* journalist during IBM's late 1980s and early 1990s decline, the book stands as testament to the position of IBM at its deepest depths. It outlines some important problems and mistakes by IBM leaders in the personal computer era but lacks understanding of underlying capabilities at the corporation and how these capabilities were beginning to be profitably redirected toward the services business. The book contains no citations or bibliography.

Ceruzzi, P.E., *A History of Modern Computing*, MIT Press, 2003.

This is a strong survey of the history of computing technology and the evolving computing industry. It includes a chapter on IBM System/360 and more substantial coverage of semiconductor technology and personal computing than other surveys.

Clarke, S., N. Lamoreaux, and S. Usselman, eds., *The Challenge of Remaining Innovative: Insights from Twentieth-Century American Business*, Stanford Business School Books, 2009.

Steven W. Usselman's "Unbundling IBM: Antitrust and the Incentives to Innovation in American Computing" (Chapter 8) is by far the best analysis of the history of IBM and antitrust. The rest of the book provides useful context for understanding twentieth century antitrust issues and strategy.

Chposky, J., and T. Leonsis, *Blue Magic: The People, Power, and Politics Behind the IBM Personal Computer*, Facts on File, 1988.

This book was written by journalists and is primarily based on their access to some former IBM employees. It provides the only book-length treatment of the history of this project and its aftermath. It does not contain citations or a bibliography.

Cohen, B., *Howard Aiken: Portrait of a Computer Pioneer*, MIT Press, 1999.

Written by a leading historian of science, this is an excellent biography of computer pioneer Howard Aiken. Given his focus on Aiken, the role of IBM engineers in the design and development of the ASCC/Harvard Mark I is somewhat underemphasized.

Cohen, B., G.W. Welch, and R.V.D. Campbell, eds., *Makin' Numbers: Howard Aiken and the Computer*, MIT Press, 1999.

Like Cohen's biography of Aiken, the focus of this edited volume is also on the work of Aiken rather than IBM engineers. However, Robert Campbell's chapter "Constructing the ASCC" and Charles Bashe's chapter "Programming Mark I" offer useful insights into the role that IBM engineers played with the ASCC/Mark I.

Connolly, J., *History of Computing in Europe*, IBM World Trade Corporation, 1967.

This rare and important book provides the earliest survey examining IBM international operations. It was produced upon the request of top leaders of the IBM World Trade Corporation. In addition to the 62-page text that examines IBM's European history, there is also an excellent 51-page timeline for developments on or related to IBM's European operations.

Cortada, J.W., *Before the Computer: IBM, NCR, Burroughs, and Remington Rand and the Industry They Created, 1865–1956*, Princeton University Press, 1993.

Easily the best book on the pre-computing US office machine industry and its four leading firms that all entered the computing business in the first half of the 1950s, this book is a must for understanding the origins of the US computer trade. Along with excellent analysis of the evolution of the office machine industry and the capabilities that would later prove critical to computing, this book brings together a plethora of important and previously scattered company and industry statistics.

Cortada, J.W., T.S. Hargraves, and E. Wakin, *Into the Networked Age: How IBM and Other Firms are Getting There Now*, Oxford University Press, 1999.

The authors of this book offer one of the few secondary sources that discuss IBM's strategy in networking in the 1990s. Initially IBM was hurt by the rapid growth of the client-server model—this source outlines IBM's strong response to develop and execute a strategy to take advantage of the increasingly ubiquitous internet and World Wide Web. While primarily a management study, the book makes use of historical cases.

Dell, D.A., and J.G. Purdy, *ThinkPad: A Different Shade of Blue*, Sams, 2000.

Original ThinkPad team member Deborah Dell and mobile products consultant J. Gerry Purdy provide a unique study of the development of IBM's successful brand of laptop computers. They detail the challenges and corporate politics involved in navigating this project to successful completion and creating a brand that had a degree of pricing power—a rarity in personal computers and laptops (other exceptions were Apple, which had a closed system, and Sony's successful Vaio laptop line). As the ThinkPad project was after IBM's major Technical History Project, this is the single best source on ThinkPad's history.

DeLamarter, R.T., *Big Blue: IBM's Use and Abuse of Power*, Dodd, Mead & Company, 1986.

This book, by a US Department of Justice economist who worked on government antitrust efforts against IBM, definitely takes an anti-IBM stance. Nevertheless, it is a useful source text on perspectives within the Justice Department during antitrust efforts, especially those in the case filed in 1969 that was dismissed in 1982.

Elsasser, P., H.A. Bauer, and H. Heger, *IBM: 75 Jahre IBM Deutschalnd: 75 Jahre Informationsverabeitung*, IBM Deutschland, 1985 (in German).

Engelbourg, S., *International Business Machines: A Business History*, Arno Press, 1976.

This republication of the author's PhD dissertation for the Department of Political Science at Columbia University in 1954 provides one of the earliest histories of IBM, detailing developments from its origins through World War II. It has particularly useful chapters on labor policy, government relations, foreign operations, and wartime production. Its careful and extensive citations make this source all the more valuable as a reference resource.

Flamm, K., *Creating the Computer: Government, Industry, and High Technology*, Brookings Institution, 1988.

This is a strong contribution to the literature on the computer industry. It is particularly insightful in its analysis of the role of government in the industry's development, both domestically and overseas.

Fisher, F.M., J.W. McKie, and R.B. Mancke, *IBM and the US Data Processing Industry: An Economic History*, Praeger, 1983.

Based primarily on the testimony of these three individuals as industry experts in the US Department of Justice antitrust case against IBM that was filed in 1969 and dismissed in 1982, this lengthy book is full of useful data. Though it contains chapters and narrative discussion, it serves primarily as a reference resource. It frequently provides quotes of testimony and various documents, and it contains extensive financial statistics on IBM and other computer firms as well as industry-wide data.

Foy, N., *The IBM World*, Eyre Methuen, 1974.

> This short book explores IBM's history during its first six decades and its place in the evolving computer industry.

Gerstner, L.V., *Who Says Elephants Can't Dance: Inside IBM's Historic Turnaround*, HarperBusiness, 2002.

> Presenting perspectives from the CEO who helped push IBM to become increasingly focused on services as its core business, this "management lessons" book offers certain insights into how even the largest corporations can change. While informative on the view from the top of IBM during the 1990s, it at times lacks a cogent understanding of the history of organizational capabilities IBM possessed that made such a rapid business re-orientation possible.

Hausner-Stollhofen, E., and G. Reisenfelder, *50 Jahre IBM im Osterreich*, IBM Osterreich, 1978 (in German).

Heide, L., *Punched-Card Systems and the Early Information Explosion 1880–1945*, Johns Hopkins University Press, 2009.

> This is an excellent study of the history of punched card tabulation technology from its origins through the end of World War II. The book includes chapters on the 1890 US Census that used Hollerith machines, as well as a chapter on the rise of IBM. Overall, the book traces IBM's history throughout the punch card tabulation machine era and provides technical, business, social, and cultural context to this transformative information technology firm.

Heller, R., *The Fate of IBM*, Little, Brown and Company, 1994.

> This is another trade press volume published at the depth of IBM's decline in the early to mid 1990s. It seeks to examine the various factors leading to IBM's decline, tracing developments back to the 1970s and 1980s and examining IBM's history with mainframes, midrange-systems/minicomputers, and personal computers. It argues that technological change with the personal computer was the principal reason for IBM's fall.

Horan, S.J., *35 Years: 1956–1991*, IBM Kingston, 1991.

> This documents the history of the site where many of IBM's SAGE computers were built and surveys the subsequent work of the facility over the succeeding three decades. Shortly after this source was published, IBM deactivated the facility.

Hsu, F.-H., *Behind Deep Blue: Building the Computer that Defeated the World Chess Champion*, Princeton University Press, 2002.

Hsu led a team at IBM to develop and program a computer, Deep Blue, which beat world chess champion Gary Kasparov in 1997. This book insightfully recounts how the origins of Deep Blue lay in Hsu's work in graduate school in the computer science department at Carnegie Mellon University. Long among the leading schools in artificial intelligence, Hsu's computer science education shaped his thinking on chess computers and helped structure the project that was later carried out by Hsu's team at IBM. Ultimately Hsu's book is not only a highly engaging read, but also a fundamental contribution to the history of computer science, supercomputing, and artificial intelligence.

IBM United Kingdom, *IBM in Scotland*, IBM United Kingdom, Limited, 1987.

This provides a survey of IBM's roughly first three decades in Scotland following the company's first leased facility in Battery Park in Greenock in late 1951.

International Business Machines Corporation, *IBM at Hursley: The First Twenty-Five Years: A Technical History*, IBM, 1983.

This is a highly useful company-produced short book that documents major scientific and engineering accomplishments of IBM's Hursley laboratory during its first quarter century. Toward the end of this span, the facility gained full responsibility for refining CIS, and the laboratory has evolved fundamentally to be a critical facility for IBM's software development business.

International Business Machines, *Pages from the Past*, International Business Machines, 1976.

A company-produced short book, this presents highlights of the 35-year history of IBM Poughkeepsie. The book starts with a short section entitled "do you remember" on some very early IBM Poughkeepsie-produced technologies, before the body of the work focuses on a 35-year well-illustrated timeline with one to two pages per year. These highlight the facilities, the production technologies, the product technologies, the recreational activities, and the people of IBM Poughkeepsie. Descriptions range from a sentence to several paragraphs. Among the IBM Poughkeepsie products discussed are the IBM 024 Punch, IBM 026 Card Punch, IBM 704, IBM 705, IBM Stretch, IBM 7070, SABRE, IBM System/360, and IBM System/370.

International Data Corporation, *IBM and the Courts: A Six Year Journal*, International Data Corporation, 1975.

Produced by a market research firm, this rare resource was republished from an earlier IDC *EDP Industry Report*. It is an excellent source for analysis, context, and summary of court testimony on various antitrust cases against IBM between 1967 and 1973.

Kaisha, N.A.B.E.K., *Konpyuta Hattatsushi: IBM o Chushin Ni Shite*, IBM, 1988 (in Japanese).

Kean, D.W., *IBM San Jose: A Quarter Century of Innovation*, International Business Machines, 1977.

An important company-produced history of the first 25 years of the IBM San Jose Laboratory (launched in 1952), this short book provides insight into the management of this innovative facility and the many important technologies it produced. Among other topics, it discusses the laboratory's first leader, Reynold Johnson, recruiting engineers for the facility, the history of RAMAC, the lab's contributions to IBM Stretch, and the work of the Advanced Systems Development Division.

Malik, R., *And Tomorrow...The World? Inside IBM*, Millington, 1976.

One of the earliest trade press histories of IBM, this book explores some topics in greater depth than most other works, including IBM management practices and individual court cases, such as *Telex v. IBM*. It also provides more attention on IBM World Trade than other sources and emphasizes that power from the US headquarters largely dictated IBM's policies and actions worldwide.

Maney, K., S. Hamm, and J. O'Brien, *Making the World Work Better*, IBM Press, 2011.

This was not yet out at the time my introductory essay and this annotated bibliography were sent to the publishers.

Maney, K., *The Maverick and His Machine: Thomas Watson, Sr., and the Making of IBM*, J. Wiley & Sons, 2003.

Business journalist Kevin Maney provides a well-written and well-researched study of the longtime leader of IBM that also serves as a broader history of the first half-century of the company. Gaining access to more primary source material than most authors who have written on Thomas Watson, Sr., this is a unique, balanced, and important biography.

Norberg, A.L., *Computers and Commerce: A Study of Technology and Management at Eckert-Mauchly Computer Company, Engineering Research Associates, and Remington Rand, 1946–1957*, MIT Press, 2005.

This is an important book on the first two firms in the computer industry—Eckert-Mauchly Computer Company and Engineering Research Associates. Both were taken over in the first half of the 1950s by Remington Rand. Remington Rand and Sperry Corporation merged in 1955 to become Sperry Rand, and the computer division of the former Remington Rand became Sperry Univac. Sperry Univac was one of IBM's main competitors in the 1950s and 1960s in the computer field. This book does an excellent job of surveying the history of these early computer companies that competed against IBM and their strategy as IBM became increasingly dominant in the industry.

Norberg, A.L., and J.R. Yost, *IBM Rochester: A Half Century of Innovation*, IBM, 2005.

This provides a brief introduction to IBM's broader history as context to IBM leaders' decision to select Rochester, Minnesota for its new manufacturing facility in the second half of the 1950s. It details the important changes with the addition of a development laboratory at the facility in 1961 and the critical role IBM Rochester played in developing and manufacturing a midrange series (outside of System/360 and System/370) of computers. The authors introduce each new midrange series from the late 1960s into the 1980s, leading up to the phenomenally successful, award-winning AS/400 series. Other manufacturing and development work, including IBM Rochester's role in disk drive production, IBM Power PC, and IBM Blue Gene development, is also discussed.

Pugh, E.W., *Building IBM: Shaping an Industry and Its Technology*, MIT Press, 1995.

This is by far the leading survey published on the history of IBM. It explores both the technology and the managerial decisions that led to C-T-R/IBM's success in the early punch card tabulation business as well as the company's entrance into and long-term dominance of the computer industry. Although the book discusses IBM's development of the IBM PC, developments in the 1980s and early 1990s are not analyzed with the same depth as earlier events. The book contains appendices compiling financial, employee, and other statistics on the company.

Pugh, E.W., *Memories that Shaped an Industry: Decisions Leading to IBM System/360*, MIT Press, 1984.

This study concentrates on the important area of computer memory and traces technical development and managerial decisions on computer memory both within and outside of IBM. Pugh argues that IBM's leadership in reliable, ferrite core memory was critical to making the IBM System/360 series of compatible machines possible.

Pugh, E.W., L.R. Johnson, and J.H. Palmer, *IBM's 360 and Early 370 Systems*, MIT Press, 1991.

This is a well-researched history of the computing systems that extended IBM's lead in the computer industry. The book does an excellent job of providing the technical context to the industry-changing System/360 family of compatible computers, as well as the follow-up System/370 series. The book's strength is the detail and explanation of the evolution of the underlying technologies of these fundamentally important computer systems.

Pugh, E.W., L.R. Johnson, and J.H. Palmer, *Interviews and Discussions for IBM's 360 and Early 370 Systems*, Thomas J. Watson Research Center, 1991.

As part of IBM's Technical History Project, Pugh, Johnson, and Palmer conducted 85 interviews (many by phone) with IBM employees in researching their book, *IBM's 360 and Early 370 Systems* (see above). Most of the interviews were done by one of the three, while a few were done by either two or all three of the researchers. Transcripts of these interviews were bound and published by IBM's Thomas J. Watson Research Center in 1991. Most of the interviews are 5 to 25 pages in length. Some interviews resulted in just a page or two of notes rather than a transcript. Most target very specific information, while others are broader in scope. Very few are career oral histories—they are targeted toward the book project on the IBM System/360 and System370 series. Only a few public repositories have these volumes—Burndy Library (part of the Huntington Library in San Marino, California) and the Charles Babbage Institute, University of Minnesota-Minneapolis. An alphabetical list of the interviewees follows: B.J. Agusta, I. Ames, R.F. Arnold, J.I. Aweida, C.J. Bashe, M.A. Belsky, R.J. Black, L.J. Boland, W.D. Bolton, F.P. Brooks, R.H. Brooks, J.D. Carothers, R.P. Case, C.L. Christiansen, H.E. Cooley, C.M. Davis, E.M. Davis, J.T. Engh, A.H. Eschenfelder, B.O. Evans, P. Fagg, E.B. Fichelberger, J.H. Frame, C.V. Freiman, E.L. Fritz, J.W. Gibson, G.A. Grover, J.A. Haddad, J.J. Hagopian, W.E. Harding, J.M. Harker, K.E. Haughton, R.A. Henle, G.G. Henry, J.M. Hewitt, L.O. Hill, J.A. Hipp, A.J. Hoffman, A.H. Johnson, R.B. Johnson, G.F. Kennard, B.W. Landeck, A.B. Lindquist, O.S. Locken, A.U. Marcotte, H.T. Marcy, J.C. Marinace, R.E. Matick, C.A. Meller, G.F. Nielson, R.E. Pattison, W.A. Pliskin, J.H. Pomerene, G. Radin, C.H. Reynolds, J. Riseman, M. de V. Roberts, D. Sayre, E.S. Schlig, P.R. Schneider, E. Shapiro, B.N. Slade, F.J. Sparacio, C.J. Spector, H.C. Stephens, R.B. Stryker, E.H. Sussenguth, H. Tashjian, P.A. Totta, S.G. Tucker, J.L. Walsh, J. Wells, W.D. Winger, R.E. Woody, K.K. Womack, and H.J. Zentgraf.

Rogers, F.G., with R.L. Shook, *The IBM Way: Insights Into the World's Most Successful Marketing Organization*, Harper & Row, Publishers, 1986.

This was the first book to focus primarily on the marketing side of IBM. Different in style and less engaging a read than Simmons' memoir, this book is similar in exploring IBM as a powerful marketing organization and the role of marketing in IBM's success. Rogers joined IBM in 1950 and moved up the ranks of the corporation—becoming the leader of the Data Processing Division by 1967 and later an IBM director and vice president of marketing. Rogers uses the history of IBM's marketing organization to make a case for the existence of an "IBM Way" and provides best practices for other firms' marketing structures and efforts.

Simmons, W.W., with R.B. Elsberry, *Inside IBM: The Watson Years, A Personal Memoir*, Dorrance & Company, Inc., 1988.

This memoir provides a valuable look inside IBM, which, like Rogers' *The IBM Way*, complements the books growing out of the IBM Technical History Project by focusing on IBM as a marketing organization. Simmons established product planning and market planning functions for IBM in the 1950s and a strategic planning system for the company in the 1960s. In addition to detailing these important contributions, Simmons paints vivid portraits of the personalities and interactions within IBM's executive circle—from the Watsons to a range of important managers. While many books focus primarily on IBM's technology, this book covers the important work of the marketing managers who played a critical role in the corporation's success.

Sobel, R., *I.B.M., Colossus in Transition*, Times Books, 1981.

This well-written trade press volume did much to popularize IBM's rich history. Written by a well-known professional historian, this engaging book is generally accurate and balanced, but frustrating to future researchers. Much research obviously went into the book (he mentions he interviewed more than 50 current and former IBM engineers and managers), but it does not include footnotes, and its "select bibliography" is particularly short and does not connect sources to chapters. Published at a time before personal computing had become dominant, it does not cover the crisis and transition brought by this technological and industry change.

Sobel, R., *IBM vs. Japan: The Struggle for the Future*, Stein and Day Publishers, 1986.

Written at the height of fear over Japanese ascendancy in technology—following the success of the Japanese auto industry at the expense of Detroit automakers in the second half of the 1970s and first half of the 1980s—this book examines IBM and the Japanese challenge in computing. The book is divided into two parts: "at home," and "abroad." The first half focuses on IBM's achievement of its dominant position in computing, while the second addresses competition from the European and Japanese computer industries. Despite the fact this book was written at an extreme period of "Japan watching," it is relatively balanced in analyzing IBM's past, present, and future overseas competition.

Tedlow, R.S., *The Watson Dynasty: The Fiery Reign and Troubled Legacy of IBM's Founding Father and Son*, HarperBusiness, 2003.

A well-written double biography—of both Thomas Watson, Sr., and Thomas Watson, Jr. — this explores the personality, achievements, and shortcomings of these two talented and charismatic leaders of IBM through the company's first six decades.

Watson, T.J., and P. Petre, *Father, Son & Co.: My Life at IBM and Beyond*, Bantam Books, 1990.

This is a highly engaging memoir that provides perspective on the personalities and leadership qualities of Thomas J. Watson, Sr., and Thomas J. Watson, Jr. While it offers a general survey of IBM's history, its strength is Thomas J. Watson, Jr.'s, introspective analysis of his at times difficult interactions with his father, as well as how he made challenging decisions that helped IBM achieve and maintain dominance in the computer industry.

Yost, J.R., *The Computer Industry*, Greenwood Press, 2005.

This provides a survey of the computer and software industries. It analyzes how many of IBM's decisions and organizational capabilities in the pre-computer punch card tabulation era served it well as it entered the computer industry. The book highlights how IBM's primary competition from Sperry Univac in the first decade of the industry gave way to more powerful threats at the low end of the price spectrum from minicomputer giant Digital Equipment Corporation and at the high-end from supercomputer leader Control Data. Despite these challenges IBM persevered until industry revenue dispersed in the personal computer era—to many different personal computer manufactures, and especially to the leading suppliers of microprocessors (Intel) and software (Microsoft).

Articles

Akera, A., "Voluntarism and the Fruits of Collaboration: IBM User Group, Share," *Technology and Culture*, vol. 42, no. 4, 2001, pp. 710–736.

In this well-researched article, the author documents and analyzes the first half decade of IBM user organization Share. He explores the rationale behind the formation of the organization, its founding members, its early growth, what it achieved for the young computer industry, and what it meant for computer professionals who participated. He also places Share within the historic context of other types of technical intermediaries.

Armer, P., "SHARE—A Eulogy to Cooperative Effort," *Annals of the History of Computing*, vol. 2, no. 2, 1980, pp. 122–129.

One of the founding members of Share reflects on the history of the organization and the broader context of cooperative efforts in computing in general and scientific computing in particular.

Aron, J.D., et al., "Discussion of the SPREAD Report, June 23, 1982," *Annals of the History of Computing*, vol. 5, no. 1, 1983, pp. 27–44.

Annals Editor-in-Chief Bernie Galler and historian Nancy Stern moderate this discussion of a group of IBM pioneers recounting the work of the SPREAD committee and the completion of the final report. The SPREAD final report was the underlying basis for moving forward with the IBM System/360 family of computers. In addition to Galler and Stern, the panel included F.P. Brooks, B.O. Evans, J.W. Fairclough, A. Finerman, W.P. Heising, and W.H. Johnson.

Astrahan, M.M., and J.F. Jacobs, "History of the Design of the SAGE Computer—The AN/FSQ-7," *Annals of the History of Computing*, vol. 5, no. 4, 1983, pp. 340–349.

This important article, from two principal architects of the IBM AN/FSQ-7 SAGE computers, documents the partnership between MIT's Lincoln Laboratory, which created a rough precursor to the SAGE machine in their path-breaking Whirlwind computer, and IBM engineers who came to lead the development project and deliver the machines. The article discusses Project Whirlwind, the Cape Cod System, Whirlwind II, the selection of IBM as the primary computer contractor, the contract, work on the project, development and production of the systems, and the technical innovations it possessed.

Backus, J., "The History of FORTRAN I, II, III," *Annals of the History of Computing*, vol. 1, no. 1, 1979, pp. 21–37.

Article is republished in this volume.

Bashe, C.J., "The SSEC in Historical Perspective," *Annals of the History of Computing*, vol. 4, no. 4, 1982, pp. 296–312.

This article outlines precursors to the SSEC before highlighting the innovative contributions of this early computer—the first computer to combine electronic computation and stored program capability. The SSEC was the fastest scientific computer at the time of its dedication in 1948—and IBM donated time on the machine to advance scientific projects and understanding.

Bastian, M., et al., "IBM France La Gaude Laboratory Contributions to Telecommunications: Part I," *IEEE Annals of the History of Computing*, vol. 31, no. 2, 2009, pp. 4–17.

This article begins with a brief history of the IBM La Gaude Laboratory, from its origin in 1959 into the 1980s. The body of the article surveys technical contributions of the laboratory in error control, modems, digital networks, communication controllers, digital speech processing, and European public data networks.

Bastian, M., et al., "IBM France La Gaude Laboratory Contributions to Telecommunications: Part II," *IEEE Annals of the History of Computing*, vol. 31, no. 2, 2009, pp. 18–30.

This article concentrates on specific technical contributions of the IBM La Gaude Laboratory in computing and telecommunication. The first part of the article concentrates on the IBM Private Automatic Branch Exchange—a network switching system. The article goes on to outline the laboratory's innovations with signal processing architectures and algorithms in the 1960s and 1970s, and data transmission in the 1980s.

Birkenstock, J.W., "Pioneering: On the Frontier of Electronic Data Processing, a Personal Memoir," *IEEE Annals of the History of Computing*, vol. 22, no. 1, 2000, pp. 4–47.

Article is republished in this volume.

Brosveet, J., "IBM Salesman Meets Norwegian Tax Collector: Computer Entrepreneurs in the Making," *IEEE Annals of the History of Computing*, vol. 21, no. 2, 1999, pp. 5–19.

A fascinating examination of IBM European sales operations and interactions with users, this article explores IBM's effort to sell computers in Norway in the 1950s. Specifically it looks at both IBM's efforts, and those of key Norwegian actors, to try to facilitate the creation of computer automated tax collector offices in Norway. It also demonstrates the balance IBM had to strike between providing expertise and capacity at its service bureau operations and efforts to place its machines within government bureaus.

Buck, G., and S. Hunka, "Development of the IBM 1500 Computer-Assisted Instructional System," *IEEE Annals of the History of Computing*, vol. 17, no. 1, 1995, pp. 19–31.

> An important contribution to early computer education efforts, this article examines the IBM 1500 Instructional System. The article provides brief discussion of experimental and production efforts IBM had with developing computer educational systems on the IBM 650, IBM 1401, and other computers prior to its IBM 1500 project. In the mid 1960s IBM began working with Stanford University, efforts that evolved into the IBM 1500 Instructional System. The article includes tables listing the 13 known institutions with installed IBM 1400 series instructional systems as well as the 35 known installations of IBM 1500 systems.

Evans, B.O., "System/360: A Retrospective View," *IEEE Annals of the History of Computing*, vol. 8, no. 4, 1986, pp. 155–179.

> Article is republished in this volume.

Endres, A., "IBM Boeblingen's Early Software Contributions," *IEEE Annals of the History of Computing*, vol. 26, no. 3, 2004, pp. 31–41.

> Industrial software development efforts in the 1960s and 1970s posed some unique challenges, as well as ones that continue to this day. In this engaging article, Endres uses three cases at IBM Boeblingen Laboratory to explore software development: software for System 360 Model 20, software for low-end PL/I compilers, and software for the DOS/VS operating system. He also explores the issue of what practical contributions academics have made to industrial software engineering efforts.

Ganzhorn, K.E., "IBM Boeblingen Laboratory: Product Development," *IEEE Annals of the History of Computing*, vol. 26, no. 3, 2004, pp. 20–30.

> IBM Boeblingen started full product development work at the beginning of the 1960s. This article details the development of data processing systems, semiconductor components, peripherals, and software at IBM Boeblingen. The article provides insights into how this laboratory operated in a multinational environment and its relationship to the larger corporation.

Ganzhorn, K.E., "The Buildup of the IBM Boeblingen Laboratory," *IEEE Annals of the History of Computing*, vol. 26, no. 3, 2004, pp. 4–19.

> This important article details the origins (in 1953) and early work of IBM Boeblingen Laboratory, which initially focused on research and exploratory development, but shifted to also include product development in the 1960s. This article focuses primarily on the pre-1960 period, and a second one in this same issue—see above—concentrates on the post-1960 product development era.

Goetz, M., "Memoirs of a Software Pioneer: Part I," *IEEE Annals of the History of Computing*, vol. 24, no. 1, 2002, pp. 43–56.

> Martin Goetz, the leader of ADR Software Products Division discusses ADR and the emerging software products industry. A section of the article is devoted to ADR's suit against IBM.

Grad, B., "A Personal Recollection: IBM's Unbundling of Software and Services," *IEEE Annals of the History of Computing*, vol. 24, no. 1, 2002, pp. 64–71.

> In this engaging and significant article, Grad, who was a manager within IBM's Data Processing Division in the late 1960s, recalls the organization and work of the IBM Unbundling Task Force, their decision to unbundle some of the company's software, the public announcement of this new policy, customer and market reaction, and how this unbundling impacted both IBM and the emerging software products industry.

Haanstra, J.W., et al., "Processor Products—Final Report of Spread Task Group, December 28, 1961," *Annals of the History of Computing*, vol. 5, no. 1, 1983, pp. 6–26.

> This famous report from the end of 1961 was republished in its entirety in the *Annals*. It details the evaluation and recommendation of this important IBM task group that came up with the basic underlying conclusions in support of a compatible family of computers and the characteristics of such a system. The SPREAD task group final report was the ultimate basis for the highly influential and successful IBM System/360 series of computers.

Haigh, T., "Computing the American Way: Contextualizing the Early US Computer Industry," *IEEE Annals of the History of Computing*, vol. 32, no. 2, 2010, pp. 8–20.

> This important article focuses on the broad political and economic context of the US computer industry—drawing from business, labor, and social history. Haigh characterizes the early US computer industry as devoted to government applications, liberal political leanings, and paternalistic corporate culture. IBM figures prominently in this analysis and is the fundamental case demonstrating such industry attributes.

Head, R.V., "Getting Sabre off the Ground," *IEEE Annals of the History of Computing*, vol. 24, no. 4, 2002, pp. 32–39.

> Article is republished in this volume.

Heide, L., "Shaping a Technology: American Punched Card Systems 1880-1914," *IEEE Annals of the History of Computing*, vol. 19, no. 4, 1997, pp. 28–41.

> This well-researched article is largely on the history of Herman Hollerith, his first punch card tabulation machines, the applications of this technology in processing the 1890 US Census, first standardization of the technology in 1907, punch card tabulation applications in the railroad and life insurance industries, and the emergence of

competitors to Hollerith's firm.

Hellerman, H., et al., "The SPREAD Discussion Continued," *Annals of the History of Computing*, vol. 6, no. 2, 1984, pp. 144–151.

>This article contains comments from H. Hellerman, R.W. O'Neill, G.M. Amdahl, and J. Svigals on IBM's SPREAD task group. Readers are also encouraged to see the article in this bibliography on SPREAD discussion by J.D. Aron, et al.

Hensch, K., "IBM History of Far Eastern Languages in Computing, Part 1: Requirements and Initial Phonetic Product Solutions in the 1960s," *IEEE Annals of the History of Computing*, vol. 27, no. 1, 2005, pp. 17–26.

>Hensch joined IBM in 1957 and was assigned to IBM World Trade in 1961—where he worked on Far Eastern language processing issues. The article is the first in a three-part series (see other Hensch, et al., articles) and examines the early history of IBM's work to foster versatility in handling Far Eastern languages with IBM computer systems. Specifically, it surveys Far Eastern language processing challenges given characteristics of the Japanese, Korean, Chinese, and Thai languages.

Hensch, K., T Igi, M. Iwao, A. Oda, and T. Takeshita, "IBM History of Far Eastern Languages in Computing, Part 3: IBM Japan Taking the Lead, Accomplishments Through the 1990s," *IEEE Annals of the History of Computing*, vol. 27, no. 1, 2005, pp. 38–55.

>Third article in a three-part series by IBM engineers and managers who worked on language processing issues (see other Hensch articles), this concentrates primarily on IBM's efforts between the 1970s and the 1990s to ensure Japanese and other Far Eastern language processing with IBM systems.

Hensch, K., T Igi, M. Iwao, and T. Takeshita, "IBM History of Far Eastern Languages in Computing, Part 2: Initial Efforts for Full Kanji Solutions, Early 1970s," *IEEE Annals of the History of Computing*, vol. 27, no. 1, 2005, pp. 27–37.

>Second article in a three-part series by IBM engineers and managers who worked on language processing issues (see other Hensch, et al., articles). This article examines IBM's work to foster versatility in handling Far Eastern language with IBM computer systems in the 1970s. Specifically, the article concentrates on character encoding, processing, and printing on the first commercial Kanji IBM system.

Humphrey, W., "Software Unbundling: A Personal Perspective," *IEEE Annals of the History of Computing*, vol. 24, no. 1, 2002, pp. 59–63.

>Article is republished in this volume.

Hurd, C.C., "About this Issue," *Annals of the History of Computing*, vol. 5, no. 2, 1983, p. 107.

Brief description of a special issue of the *Annals* devoted to the history of the IBM 701 and guest edited by Hurd. The issue contains many very short articles, accounts, and anecdotes on the hardware, software, and early customers of the IBM 701. While many of these short articles (some less than a page) are interesting and informative, they do not warrant individual listing in this bibliography. Interested readers are encouraged to look at the issue. It contains short pieces from IBM 701 chief architect Nathaniel Richards, accounts by a handful of programmers for the IBM 701, pieces by several on the marketing side, and more than a dozen customer reflections.

Hurd, C.C., "About this Issue," *Annals of the History of Computing*, vol. 8, no.1, 1986, pp. 3.

Brief description of a special issue of the *Annals* devoted to the history of the IBM 650 and guest edited by Hurd. The issue contains many very short articles, accounts, and anecdotes on the engineering, programming, and use of the IBM 650. While many of these short articles are interesting and informative, they do not justify individual listing in this bibliography. Readers and researchers interested in the IBM 650 are encouraged to look at the whole issue. Authors of the short articles and pieces include: E.S. Hughes, F.E. Hamilton, E.C. Kubie, G.R. Trimble, E.L. Glaser, B.A. Galler, G.L. Bach, A.J. Perlis, H.A. Simon, A. Newell, D.E. Knuth, B. Arden, J.G. Herriot, R.W. Bemer, D. Hemmes, B. Gordon, R.R. Haefner, and G.T. Hunter.

Hurd, C.C., "Early Computers at IBM," *Annals of the History of Computing*, vol. 3, no. 2, 1981, pp. 163–182.

Article is republished in this volume.

Johansson, M., "Big Blue Gets Beaten: The Technological and Political Controversy of the First Large Swedish Computerization Project in a Rhetoric of Technology Perspective," *IEEE Annals of the History of Computing*, vol. 21, no. 2, 1999, pp. 14–30.

An important article on early computer history in Scandinavia, this article analyzes the history and rhetorical strategies of a political controversy over the first major Swedish computerization project—for a computerized national register and taxation system. By examining internal memos, IBM and Sweden computer producer Datasaab's advertisements and public relations materials, photos, journalistic accounts, and interviews, Johansson careful evaluates each phase of this computerization effort in the early 1960s. He shows that what on its surface appeared to be a purely technological debate, actually rested on rhetoric having economic, political, nationalistic, ideological and other dimensions.

Jones, W.D., (D. Black, ed.), "Watson and Me: Life at IBM," *IEEE Annals of the History of Computing*, vol. 24, no. 1, 2002, pp. 4–18.

Article is republished in this volume.

Kistermann, F., "The Way to the First Automatic Sequence-Controlled Calculator: The Dehomag D

11 Tabulator," *IEEE Annals of the History of Computing*, vol. 17, no. 2, 1995, pp. 33–49.

Important article on IBM's German subsidiary Dehomag's D11 Tabulator—a pioneering 1930s machine with significant scientific calculating potential.

Lee, J.A.N., and H.S. Tropp, "About this Issue," *Annals of the History of Computing*, vol. 6, no. 1, 1984, p. 3.

This piece, from guest editors of this FORTRAN history special issue of the *Annals*, introduces the issue. Individual articles are short recollections and anecdotes and not individually listed or annotated in this bibliography. Readers interested in the history of FORTRAN are encouraged to look at the whole issue. It includes articles and pieces by J.C. McPherson, R.W. Bemer, R. Goldberg, R. Nutt, F.E. Allen, J. Backus, H.S. Bright, R.A. Hughes, W.P. Heising, M.N. Greenfield, D.D. McCracken, C. Davidson, J.M. Sakoda, B. Rosenblatt, D.N. Leeson, and H.S. Tropp. The issue also has a bibliography on FORTRAN compiled by J.A.N. Lee.

McGee, W., "The Information Management System (IMS) Program Product," *IEEE Annals of the History of Computing*, vol. 31, no. 4, 2009, pp. 66–75.

Article is republished in this volume.

McPherson, J.C., F.E. Hamilton, and R.R. Seeber, Jr., "A Large-Scale General Purpose Electronic Digital Calculator—The SSEC," *IEEE Annals of the History of Computing*, vol. 4, no. 4, 1982, pp. 313–326.

Article is republished in this volume.

Medina, E., "Big Blue in the Bottomless Pit: The Early Years of IBM Chile," *IEEE Annals of the History of Computing*, vol. 30, no. 4, 2008, pp. 26–41.

This is an excellent analysis of how IBM entered and came to dominate the computer market for a country in the developing world—Chile. The article studies IBM corporate strategy in Chile within the context of Chilean national history. Medina outlines how IBM sought to reproduce its corporate culture in Chile in light of rapidly evolving political and economic changes.

Meyers, G.E., "IBM Field Engineering Experiences: A Personal Memoir," *IEEE Annals of the History of Computing*, vol. 21, no. 4, 1999, pp. 72–76.

This short article provides a rare glimpse into an important activity at IBM's computer business from its beginnings—field engineering. IBM had superior sales and service infrastructure and its sales engineers provided critical service that made IBM hardware systems more attractive to customers. This article briefly details the experience of one IBM field engineer in the early digital computer era.

O'Neill, J.E., "'Prestige Luster' and 'Snow-Balling Effects': IBM's Development of Computer Time-Sharing," *IEEE Annals of the History of Computing*, vol. 17, no. 2, 1995, pp. 50–54.

As IBM began planning the IBM System/360, it was caught off guard by how rapidly computer time-sharing was taking off. Prestigious institutions such as MIT and Bell Laboratories chose General Electric time-sharing systems in the early to mid1960s, which hastened IBM leaders to quickly launch the development of a time-sharing product of its own. This article tells the story of IBM's motivation in time-sharing and its time-sharing development efforts.

Phelps, B.E., "Early Electronic Computer Developments at IBM," *Annals of the History of Computing*, vol. 2, no. 3, 1980, pp. 253–267.

Important personal account and technical article from engineer Byron Phelps, who joined IBM in 1935, this article details pre-electronic computers and electronic digital computers that he worked on, including the IBM 603, IBM 604, SSEC, and the IBM 701. The article is accompanied by a set of excellent photographs of these systems.

Schlombs, C., "Engineering International Expansion: IBM and Remington Rand in European Markets," *IEEE Annals of the History of Computing*, vol. 30, no. 4, 2008, pp. 42–58.

This strong work of scholarship compares and contrasts IBM's and Remington Rand's strategies in entering and expanding in Germany and other European markets. Schlombs explains how IBM made far stronger efforts than Remington Rand to adapt its European facilities to each country's business, governmental, and cultural contexts. She argues that this helped contribute to IBM's greater success in European markets.

Speiser, A.P., "IBM Research Laboratory Zurich: The Early Years," *IEEE Annals of the History of Computing*, vol. 20, no. 1, 1998, pp. 15–28.

This is an important and engaging first-person account of the history of the IBM Research Laboratory in Zurich by the founding director of the laboratory. Speiser provides a brief section on his educational and work background before joining the IBM Zurich laboratory in 1955. He left the laboratory in 1966 to become corporate research director of Brown Boveri, a multinational electrical company, and the account documents the laboratory only during its formative first dozen years. He discusses the establishment of physics research as a primary mission of the laboratory. Along with successes, including Nobel Prize winners, the laboratory had its share of difficulties and challenges in the early years, such as strained relations with public, business, and academic communities in Switzerland—often over hiring away top talent from companies or universities, employing resident aliens, and the stability of the laboratory (for years it was housed in rented facilities) and its jobs.

Spicer, D., "The IBM 1620 Restoration Project," *IEEE Annals of the History of Computing*, vol. 27, no. 3, 2005, pp. 33–43.

This is an excellent article examining theory and practice involved with a major computer system restoration project in a museum setting. Spicer, the senior curator at the Computer History Museum (CHM), outlines the organization, structure, theory, and work of a CHM restoration project of an IBM 1620 system. The project took advantage of the expertise and work of technically oriented volunteers, as well as the expertise of CHM staff.

Stierhoff, G.C., and A.G. Davis, "A History of the *IBM Systems Journal*," *IEEE Annals of the History of Computing*, vol. 20, no. 1, 1998, 29–35.

The authors document the origin and evolution of the *IBM Systems Journal*—a publication founded out of IBM's Systems Research Institute. In 1962, when the journal was launched, it was primarily to keep IBM employees informed on state-of-the-art systems research and applications programming. Over time it became a more traditional scholarly technical journal useful not only to IBM technical staff, but also to customers, suppliers, and the academic computer engineering and computer science communities.

Trimble, G.R., Jr., "A Brief History of Computing: Memoirs of Living on the Edge," *IEEE Annals of the History of Computing*, vol. 23, no. 3, 2001, pp. 44–59.

In these memoirs, Trimble documents his rich career in the field of computing. He joined IBM in 1952 and was one of the principal engineers working on the hardware and programming of the IBM 650. In addition to documenting work on this system, he also discusses his work on the IBM 608 and his work on the initial design specifications on what became IBM Stretch. The article also documents his career prior to joining IBM at Aberdeen Proving Ground and, after leaving, at computer services pioneering firm Computer Usage Company.

Trimble, G.R., Jr., "The IBM 650 Magnetic Drum Calculator," *Annals of the History of Computing*, vol. 8, no. 1, 1986, pp. 20–29.

Article is republished in this volume.

Usselman, S.W., "IBM and Its Imitators: Organizational Capabilities and the Emergence of the International Computer Industry," *Business and Economic History*, vol. 22, no. 2, 1993, pp. 1–35.

This is the finest scholarly, article-length examination of the history of IBM's computer business. It outlines how IBM's organizational capabilities allowed it to quickly secure the lead in the international computer industry in the 1950s and maintain and extend this lead in the 1960s. Unlike many studies that compare IBM to just its domestic competitors, Usselman also provides insights into its competition with major international competitors.

Vernay, J., "IBM France," *Annals of the History of Computing*, vol. 11, no. 4, 1989, pp. 299–311.

Vernay provides a survey of the 75-year history of IBM France. The article details early punch card tabulation customers, the management structure, visits and involvement by Thomas Watson, Sr., the origins of the computer market, and technical, business, and governmental challenges in the 1960s and 1970s.

Weiss, E., "Eloge: Cuthbert Corwin Hurd (1911-1996)," *IEEE Annals of the History of Computing*, vol. 19, no.1, 1997, pp. 65–73.

While most obituaries do not warrant inclusion in this bibliography, this one does. Hurd was a founding member of the *Annals* editorial board, in addition to his highly important contributions to the management of IBM. This is a longer obituary that addresses Hurd's life before IBM, his critical roles with the IBM Card Program Calculator, the IBM Applied Science Department (in which he was founding director), the IBM 701, IBM 650, FORTRAN, SAGE, IBM Stretch, and his life after IBM.

Yost, J.R., "Manufacturing Mainframes: Component Fabrication and Component Procurement at IBM and Sperry Univac, 1960-1975," *History and Technology*, vol. 25, no. 3, 2009, pp. 219–235.

This article compares the semiconductor strategies of IBM and one of its primary competitors in the early computer industry, Sperry Univac. It discusses the origins of IBM's Components Division, which increasingly brought semiconductor design and development in-house, and IBM's relatively early commitment to use integrated circuits for main memory. It contrasts IBM's vertically integrated path with that of Sperry Univac, which looked to extend capabilities for effectively outsourcing semiconductor components.

Serials

IBM Journal of Research and Development [1957–]

This has long been a technical journal on research and engineering work at IBM on computer systems, software engineering, and other fields. In 2009 *IBM Systems Journal* was merged into the *IBM Journal of Research and Development*.

IBM Systems Journal [1962–2008]

Launched out of IBM's Systems Research Institute in 1962 primarily to inform and educate IBM technical staff, this evolved into a broader-based peer-reviewed journal publishing scholarship on hardware systems, software, and services. As such its audience extended beyond just IBM staff to customers, suppliers, and the academic computer engineering and computer science communities. At the start of 2009 it was merged into *IBM Journal of Research and Development*.

Think [1935–]

This magazine evolved from a public affairs and literary-style publication, somewhat similar to *The Atlantic* in its early years, to a company magazine to communicate to its workforce in recent decades.

Archival Collections (Alphabetical by repository)

American Philosophical Society

Emanuel Ruben Piore Papers

> This collection contains 22.5 feet of records on Piore's life and career. He worked as chief scientist at the Office of Naval Research and in several other positions before coming to IBM as the first IBM Director of Research. He later served as IBM Chief Scientist and a vice president and director of IBM. This collection contains significant materials on the latter portion of his tenure at IBM and provides insights into the organizational structure and management of IBM Research.

Charles Babbage Institute, University of Minnesota (CBI, UMN)

> More than 100 of the Charles Babbage Institute's 200-plus collections contain some material on or relevant to IBM history. Below are a small number of collections with extensive material on or relevant to IBM history. CBI also has an extensive collection of photographs on IBM—primarily of IBM mainframe systems.

Applied Data Research, Software Product Division Records

> Applied Data Research was the first company to produce and sell a software product and the first company to patent a software product. It was also the first software company to sue IBM. The emergence of the software products business, and likely ADR's suit, was a factor in IBM's decision to unbundle. These records have significant material on the ADR antitrust suit against IBM.

James W. Cortada Papers

> James Cortada has held various sales, research, and executive positions with IBM for more than three decades. This large collection includes some IBM publications, IBM reports, and other documentation on the company and its history. It also contains extensive material on uses of computers within different industries.

James W. Birkenstock Papers

James Birkenstock joined IBM as a salesman in 1935. He became a sales manager and then a senior executive with the company. This very small collection has some important documentation on IBM and its British licensee, British Tabulating Machine Company (BTM), the severing of their partnership in 1949, as well as histories of BTM.

Wallace J. Eckert Papers

Wallace Eckert was a scientific computing pioneer at Columbia University who partnered with IBM to form Columbia University's Thomas J. Watson Astronomical Computing Bureau in the 1930s. These records contain correspondence with IBM regarding scientific calculators.

GUIDE International Corporation Records

Guidance of Users of Integrated Data-Processing Equipment (GUIDE) is an IBM user group that formed a year after IBM user group Share. GUIDE was limited to large-scale users. The collection contains materials from GUIDE conferences, GUIDE quarterly and annual reports, and organizational reports.

Robert V. Head Papers

Robert Head joined IBM in 1959 and supervised aspects of the programming for the IBM project to develop SABRE for American Airlines. The collection contains records on American Airlines standards, SABRE project planning records, and records from the SABRE programming committee.

Cuthbert C. Hurd Papers

Cuthburt Hurd joined IBM in 1949 and formed and led the IBM's Applied Science Department. The collection includes correspondence and reports on this department, as well as customer reports from field visits for the IBM Defense Calculator.

Market and Product Reports Collection

This large collection contains a number of industry reports on various IBM products and systems.

Share, Inc. Records

Share was the first software user group—formed in 1955 by IBM 701 users in the Los Angeles-area aerospace industry. The organization quickly grew nationally. This substantial collection contains correspondence, technical reports, manuals, meeting agendas, meeting proceedings, Share publications, and administrative records.

US National Bureau of Standards Collection of Computer Literature

This large collection of published and unpublished reports, manuals, white papers, and gray literature contains a number of documents related to IBM.

Computer History Museum

The Computer History Museum in Mountain View, California is the premier museum in the world for computer history and has by far the best collection of IBM physical artifacts (systems, peripherals, etc.) from both the punch card tabulator and digital computer eras. It also has substantial photograph collections on IBM. CHM has extensive primary documents detailing the history of IBM Stretch and likely has other strong archival collections on IBM.

IBM Corporate Archives

This is by far the largest and most extensive set of archival materials on the corporation and its history. As with nearly all corporate-owned, corporate-managed collections, it is a collection that serves as a resource for the corporation and is not a public archive.

Library of Congress

Herman Hollerith Papers

This substantial collection of 30 boxes contains more than 10,000 items on Hollerith's life, the Tabulating Machine Company, C-T-R, and IBM. The bulk of the collection is from between 1910 and 1927. The collection includes blueprints of machines, scrapbooks, newspaper clippings, and business papers.

Oral Histories

ADAPSO Reunion Workshop: IBM Relations (oral history panel), interview by M. Campbell-Kelly, P. Ceruzzi, L. Johnson, O. Schactner, and B. Grad, 4 May 2002, Computer History Museum (CHM).

A group of ADAPSO members—Martin Goetz, Bernie Goldstein, John Gracza, Burt Grad, Luanne Johnson, Kim Jones, and Lee Keet—explore the relationship between IBM and the emerging software industry of the second half of the 1960s. Among the topics discussed are antitrust and IBM unbundling of software, ADAPSO and its view of problematic IBM policies, and the overall impact of the computer giant on the software industry.

Advanced Ferrite Disk Heads Oral History Panel, interview by I. Croll, 3 Nov. 2005, CHM.

Three panelists, Paul Frank, Erik Solyst, and Michael Warner, discuss IBM's use of different types of magnetic recording heads on the firm's disk drives—from ferrite core heads to thin film heads. They relate technological developments in magnetic recording heads both inside and outside of IBM.

G.M. Amdahl Oral History, interview by A.L. Norberg, 16 Apr. 1986 and 5 Apr. 1989, Charles Babbage Institute (CBI), University of Minnesota (UMN).

Interview includes Amdahl's discussion of his technical work at IBM—helping to design the IBM 701, IBM 701A, IBM 704, and IBM Stretch.

J. Backus Oral History, interview by G. Booch, 9 Sep. 2006, CHM.

IBM programming language pioneer discusses his early career before joining IBM and his work with IBM in leading the project to create FORTRAN. He also discusses his work on functional programming.

J.W. Birkenstock Oral History, interview by E. Tomash and R.H. Stuewer, 12 Aug. 1980, CBI, UMN.

Birkenstock joined IBM and moved from salesman to sales manager to upper executive posts with the corporation. He was a close advisor to IBM president Thomas J. Watson, Jr., and served as Director of Product Planning and Market Analysis. Among other topics, he discusses the development of the IBM Defense Calculator, magnetic core memory development, and IBM's move into the commercial computing business.

C. Branscomb Oral History, interview by R. Garner, 10 Nov. 2009, CHM.

Branscomb discusses his nearly four-decade-long career at IBM, including his work on the IBM 1401, IBM System/360, and various IBM midrange series systems—this work included development responsibilities of the IBM 1401. In 1974 Branscomb was named IBM VP Development and Manufacturing for the General Systems Division.

M. Campbell Oral History, interview by D. Spicer, 8 Sep. 2005, CHM.

Campbell was one of the lead technical employees on IBM's Deep Blue development project. He discusses his work and that of other members of the Deep Blue team to develop the hardware and software of the system that beat the world chess champion in matches during the second half of 1990s.

R.V.D. Campbell Oral History, interview by W. Aspray, 22 Feb. 1984, CBI, UMN.

Campbell worked at the Harvard Computational Laboratory and subsequently at IBM's research facility in Endicott, New York. He was involved in the latter stages of the ASCC/Harvard Mark I project and discusses the relative contributions of IBM and

Harvard.

D. Chamberlin Oral History, interview by P. McJones, 21 July 2009, CHM.

This interview covers Chamberlin's education, his lengthy career at IBM in the database field, and his activities since retiring from IBM. Chamberlin, co-developer of the SQUARE and SEQUEL languages, discusses his work with Ray Boyce in creating these influential languages. Other software technologies discussed include DB2, XQuery, and IMS.

D.D. Chamberlin Oral History, interview by P.L. Frana, 12 Nov. 2001, CBI, UMN.

Chamberlin, a leading database software pioneer at IBM Almaden Research Center in San Jose, California, discusses his work at the Almaden laboratory. Specifically, he details his work on relational database technology and his work with Ray Boyce in codeveloping the highly influential database language SQL.

J. Clemens Oral History, interview by J.N. Porter, 9 July 2007, CHM.

Clemens discusses his work on IBM disk storage technology from his arrival at the firm in 1957 until he left in 1970. In particular, he relates his work on early production engineering on RAMAC. Clemens also discusses his post-IBM work for other firms and as a consultant in the data storage industry.

W. Crooks Oral History, interview by T. Gardner, 13 Nov. 2008, CHM.

Crooks was one of the early engineers hired by Rey Johnson at the IBM San Jose Laboratory. In this interview he discusses his work on RAMAC, including his duties to select the material for coating RAMAC disks.

C.J. Date Oral History, interview by T. Haigh, 13 June 2007, CHM.

Trained as a programmer at IBM Hursley, Date relates his background, education, career at IBM, and post-IBM work. He worked on database management with PL/I and later was involved with Edgar Codd on relational database systems. He also discusses the business he and Codd created after leaving IBM, as well as his scholarship and database textbook writing efforts.

S.W. Dunwell Oral History, interview by W. Aspray, 13 Feb. 1989, CBI, UMN.

Dunwell became the leader of IBM Stretch, a project to build the firm's first supercomputer. He discusses this project as well as other projects he worked on at IBM.

G. Durbin Oral History, interview by P.L. Frana, 7 May 2004, CBI, UMN.

Software pioneer Durbin never worked for IBM, but programmed on some of the earliest IBM electronic digital computers, including the IBM 650. With regard to IBM history, this oral history is noteworthy for his discussion of the hegemony of the IBM database system IMS. He also relates the impact the IBM "unbundling" decision had on the software industry.

R.L. Garmin Oral History, interview by F. Aaserud, 23 Oct. 1986, American Institute of Physics (AIP), Neils Bohr Library and Archives (NBLA).

Garmin, a physicist who received his PhD from the University of Chicago under famed atomic scientist Enrico Fermi, joined IBM Watson Laboratory in 1952 and worked at the laboratory as a research scientist until 1970. This interview documents the scientific work of Garmin during his 18 years at IBM, as well as before and after his tenure at IBM.

R. Gentry Oral History, interview by B. Grad, 24 May 2006, CHM.

Gentry discusses his education and service in the Air Force before joining IBM and his work at IBM—where he worked on programming IBM 1401 and IBM 1620 systems. He relates his invention of what came to be known as the Gentry Monitor, which evolved into the FASTER Type II Program. He also recounts co-founding, with his wife Grace Gentry, Gentry, Inc., a computer services independent contractor brokerage company.

M. Goetz Oral History, interview by J.R. Yost, 3 May 2002, CBI, UMN.

Goetz, a software pioneer, headed Applied Data Research's Software Products Division. This firm produced the first software product, inaugurating the software products industry. He was awarded the first software patent. Among other topics in this interview, he discusses his and ADR's role in litigation against IBM, competition with IBM, IBM's "unbundling" decision, and the impact of IBM's unbundling of software on the young software products industry.

B. Grad Oral History, interview by E. LaHay, 28 Nov. 2007, CHM.

Grad, who worked on the pioneering business application for GE's UNIVAC system at the GE Louisville Appliance Park facility in the second half of the 1950s, joined IBM in 1960. In this interview (one specifically on his IBM work), he relates his early work on IBM's Study Organization Plan and Decision Tables, operations research, simulation, and other areas. Grad was part of the IBM unbundling task force and discusses the work of this group that led the effort to unbundle IBM's software at the end of the 1960s. He became the Development Director in the Data Processing Division and discusses key early software products such as CICS. He also relates IBM's failure to develop successful application software products for customers of its large systems.

J. Harker and C.D. Mee Oral History, interview by C. Bajorek and T. Gardner, 30 May 2007 and 10 July 2007, CHM.

Two longtime IBM San Jose Laboratory engineers discuss the work of the laboratory over multiple decades. Harker joined the laboratory shortly after its formation. He became the laboratory director in 1972. Among other work, he discusses his leadership on removable disk storage and the Image Storage System. Mee started at Yorktown Heights as an IBM research engineer before joining the IBM San Jose laboratory in 1965. He founded IBM's Magnetic Recording Institute and authored and edited multiple books on magnetic recording.

R.L. Hawkins Oral History, interview by W. Aspray, 20 Feb. 1984, CBI, UMN.

Hawkins worked as a technician at Harvard University and in 1950 joined the IBM ASCC/Harvard Mark I computer development project. He discusses the work on that project, including project leader Howard Aiken's dissatisfaction with off-the-shelf IBM components.

D. Hedger Oral History, interview by P.L. Frana, 17 May 2001, CBI, UMN.

Hedger joined IBM Rochester to work in its optical character recognition group, but switched to focus on software development. He discusses his software and programming services work on the IBM System/3, IBM System/360, IBM System/32, IBM System/38, and IBM AS/400. More broadly, he discusses common IBM programming techniques and practices.

F.-H. Hsu Oral Hisotry, interview by Dag Spicer, 14 Feb. 2005, CHM.

Hsu relates his graduate studies on artificial intelligence and computer chess at Carnegie-Mellon before joining IBM. He then discusses his work leading the effort to build IBM Deep Blue, the supercomputer that defeated a chess champion in the second half of the 1990s.

W. Humphrey Oral History, interview by G. Booch, June 2009, CHM.

In this lengthy oral history Humphrey relates his work as an executive at IBM and his early leadership role in managing software efforts for the company. Humphrey made major contributions to the study and practice of software engineering at IBM, and after leaving IBM as an academic and academic administrator.

A.L.C. Humphreys Oral History, interview by E. Tomash, 28 Feb. 1981, CBI, UMN.

Humphreys served as an upper executive and became managing director of ICL. He discusses his years with the British Tabulating Machine Company (BTM) and its mergers to become ICT and then ICL—including the severing of IBM's longtime licensing agreement to BTM and subsequent competition with IBM.

C.C. Hurd Oral History, interview by C.R. Fillerup, 28 Aug. 1995, CBI, UMN.

Hurd came to IBM in 1949 and founded its Applied Science Department. In this interview he discusses his work at IBM as well as his subsequent leadership role at computer services firm Computer Usage Corporation.

C.C. Hurd Oral History, interview by R.W. Seidel, 18 Nov. 1994, CBI, UMN.

Hurd relates his work at Oak Ridge National Laboratory prior to joining IBM and provides detailed discussion of his first years at IBM.

C.C. Hurd Oral History, interview by N.B. Stern, 20 Jan. 1981, CBI, UMN.

Hurd discusses IBM's early research on computer technology and the development and launch of some of its earliest computers, including the IBM 701, the IBM 704, and the IBM 705.

IBM 5.25 and 3.5 Inch Floppy Drives Oral History Panel, interview by J. Porter, 13 Jan. 2005, CHM.

A panel of IBM technical employees who helped establish the 5.25-inch and 3.5-inch standards—Warren Dalziel, Don Massaro, and George Sollman—discuss the technical and business aspects of the transition from 8-inch to 5.25-inch, and subsequently, to 3.5-inch disk drives.

IBM 8 Inch Floppy Disk Drives Oral History Panel, interview by J. Porter, 17 May 2005, CHM.

A panel of IBM engineers who helped establish the 8-inch standard disk drive—James Adkinson, Warren Dalziel, and Herbert Thompson—explore the technical and business issues involved with developing the technology and establishing the 8-inch standard disk drive.

IBM 1311 and 2311 Disk Drives Oral History Panel, interview by J. Porter, 22 Feb. 2005, CHM.

This panel consisted of three IBM technical employees—James Carothers, John Harker, and Erik Solyst—who had major roles in the design and development of the IBM 1311 and IBM 2311 disk drives.

IBM 2314 and 3330 Disk Drives Oral History Panel, interview by I. Croll, 16 June 2004, CHM.

This panel is made up of IBM employees who had major roles in the design and development of the IBM 2314 and IBM 3330 14-inch disk drives—including the recording heads, disks, and controllers of these systems. The panel was made up of Paul Frank, Erik Solyst, and Michael Warner. They also discuss plug-compatible drives from competitors to IBM.

IBM 3340 and 3350 Disk Drives Oral History Panel, interview by J. Porter, 6 Apr. 2004, CHM.

The IBM 3340 disk drive used technology designed and developed by panel members—Chris Coolures, Robert Friesen, John Harker, and Michael Warner. Certain new attributes of the IBM 3340, including low mass heads and lubricated disks, defined the drive which was codenamed "Winchester." The so-called "Winchester" method influenced future drives, including the IBM 3350. The panelists discuss the design and development of these important technological innovations of the early to mid 1970s.

IBM 3380 Disk Drive Oral History Panel, interview by J. Porter, 3 Jan. 2006, CHM.

This drive, developed by members of the panel—Chris Coolures, Jack Grogan, Jim Lucke, Mike Warner, and Dick Whitney—encountered a number of technical challenges but was ultimately a highly successful product for IBM in the early 1980s. The panel relates both the difficulties and how they were overcome to perfect this drive—including discussion of the recording heads, disks, and motors.

IBM Data Cell Drive Oral History Panel, interview by J. Porter, 8 Dec. 2004, CHM.

A panel from the IBM team that developed the firm's Data Cell System—David Bennet, Clarke Carey, Harold Hester, and Herbert Thompson—discuss the development effort and business and technical context of this work. They relate the many problems with manufacturing the magnetic strips, reliability problems in the field, and efforts to overcome these challenges.

IBM RAMAC Follow-on Oral History Panel, interview by J. Porter, 29 Oct. 2004, CHM.

A panel of key personnel who helped develop the famed IBM RAMAC 350, pioneering disk drive technology and the disk drive industry, discuss the technical issues involved with this path-breaking effort. The panel included John Harker, Kenneth Haughton, Albert Hoagland, and Lou Stevens.

R.W. Landauer Oral History, interview by J. Bromberg, 17 Oct. 1984, AIP, NBLA.

Landauer discusses the early years of his work and the research agenda and management at IBM T.J. Watson Research Center.

W.W. Lang Oral History, interview by R.J. Peppin, 12 July 2004, AIP, NBLA.

Physicist William Lang discusses his research at IBM.

R.G. Lareau Oral History, interview by M. Price, 16 Apr. 1982, CBI, UMN.

Lareau describes the court case of Control Data versus IBM—particularly the preparation of Control Data for the trial.

R.B. Lazarus Oral History, interview by A. Fitzpatrick, 10 Oct. 1995, CBI, UMN.

Lazarus joined Los Alamos Scientific Laboratory in 1951, working in its Theoretical Division. He developed an expertise with digital computer applications for nuclear weapons research and development. He discusses early systems he used at the laboratory, including IBM 701, IBM 704, and IBM Stretch. A valuable oral history on early scientific computing in high energy physics, Lazarus relates both the science and politics of obtaining and using these machines in the laboratory.

J. McCormack Oral History, interview by W. Aspray, 23 Feb. 1984, CBI, UMN.

McCormack worked at IBM as a marketing representative, before leaving to co-found software products company McCormack and Dodge (with Frank Dodge, an IBM engineer and manager). He discusses his work both at IBM and at McCormack and Dodge.

W. McGee Oral History, interview by P.L. Frana, 12 Nov. 2001, CBI, UMN.

McGee joined IBM in 1964. He went on to make fundamental contributions to IBM's database and data communication systems (DB/DC), including IMS. The interview offers unique insight into IBM's DB/DC development efforts.

A. McGill Oral History, interview by L. Johnson and B. Grad, 10 Dec. 1985, CHM.

McGill provides a fascinating discussion of the difficulty establishing a software business at IBM at the end of the 1960s and early 1970s due to the hardware orientation of top executives of the corporation. He discusses how falling down on software led IBM to lose touch with customers and was responsible for some of the stagnation that occurred during the 1970s. He relates the detrimental impact of software unbundling at IBM on the the firm's systems engineering operation.

M. Maples Oral History, interview by N. Ensmenger, 7 May 2004, CBI, UMN.

Mike Maples discusses his role in working on display products at IBM and, later, with the IBM PC. He subsequently joined Microsoft to manage its applications products and discusses differences in the management philosophies and cultures of the two corporate IT giants.

M.I. Nathan Oral History, interview by J. Bromberg, 17 Oct. 1984, AIP, NBLA.

This oral history focuses on the invention of the semiconductor laser at IBM in the early 1960s.

PC Software Workshop Oral History, interview by L. Johnson, 6 May 2004, CHM.

A group of PC software pioneers—Ben Dyer, Bill Goodhew, Gary Harpst, Douglas Jerger, and Mitch Russo—discuss critical accounting issues in the early PC software era. They relate how the entry of IBM into the personal computing market was critical to legitimizing the personal computer software industry by establishing a dominant standard platform.

B. Persons and H. Pelnar Oral History, interview by P.L. Frana, 17 July 2001, CBI, UMN.

Person and Pelnar, central figures at the IBM Rochester development lab who worked on the influential IBM AS/400 series midrange system, discuss this system as well as predecessor midrange systems, IBM System/38, and IBM System/32.

RDBMS Plenary Session: Early Years Oral History, interview by B. Grad, L. Johnson, and D. Jerger, 12 June 2007, CHM.

A large panel of relational database management systems pioneers discuss database management systems before moving on to relational database management systems (RDBMS) made possible by the pioneering work of IBM San Jose research scientist Edgar Codd. Among the RDBMS systems discussed are IBM products System R, SQL/DS, and DB2, as well as systems outside the company such as Ingres, Oracle, Sybase, and Informix. The panel included the following individuals: Greg Batti, Michael Blasgen, Marilyn Bohl, Don Chamberlin, Sharon Codd, Chris Date, Martin Goetz, Don Haderle, Roy Harrington, Jerry Held, Mark Hoffman, Mike Humphries, Ken Jacobs, Bruce Lidsay, Robert MacDonald, Jan Phillips, Stu Schuster, Roger Sippl, Jim Strickland, and Moshe Zloof.

RDBMS Workshop: IBM Oral History, interview by B. Grad, 12 June 2007, CHM.

IBM Research, behind the work of Edgar Codd, Don Chamberlin, and many others, was the inventor and a key developer of relational database management system technology. This panel of relational database researchers, engineers, programmers, and managers explore many critical issues with the history of IBM's work in developing relational database management systems. The discussion explores IBM Research's development of SQL and System R, and the development and delivery of RDBMS products SQL/DS and DB2. They explore the dominance of IBM's IMS and concern with erosion of revenue by other products. The panel also explores the challenges of communications and collaboration in an organization as large and geographically dispersed as IBM. The panel included: Michael Blasgen, Marilyn Bohl, Peter Capek, Don Chamberlin, Sharon Codd, Chris Date, Don Haderle, Bruce Lidsay, Jan Philllips, Jim Strickland, and Moshe Zloof.

D.L. Schleicher Oral History, interview by A.L. Norberg, 24 Jan. 2006, CBI, UMN.

Longtime IBM Rochester programmer and manager David Schleicher relates his work on integrated database software programming for IBM System/38 and IBM AS/400. He also discusses the style of development laboratory managers at IBM Rochester.

R.B. Smith Oral History, interview by R. Mapstone, May 1980, CBI, UMN.

IBM Salesman R. Blair Smith discusses selling early IBM systems, his role in the founding of IBM user group Share, and his encounter with American Airline's leader C.R. Smith that led to the massive SABRE contract to build a real-time reservation system for American Airlines.

J. Svigals Oral History, interview by D. Spicer, 19 June 2007, CHM.

> Longtime IBM executive Jerome Svigals discusses his work on some pioneering systems outside IBM, including the Moore School's ENIAC and RCA's BIZMAC, before joining IBM. He relates the technical and managerial issues with major developments at IBM including the SPREAD task force and the creation of the IBM System/360. He also discusses his work at IBM international facilities, as well as IBM's efforts to develop a magnetic strip standard for electronic transactions.

E.B. Trousdale Oral History, interview by D. Norris, circa 1977, CBI, UMN.

> Trousdale was a lawyer at the firm used by Control Data Corporation (CDC) in its famous suit against IBM. He provides insight into this litigation against IBM that resulted in a favorable settlement for CDC.

T.J. Watson, Jr., and J.W. Birkenstock Oral History, interview by A.L.C. Humphreys, 25 Apr. 1985, CBI, UMN.

> The principal topic in this short interview is the pivotal decision by IBM and BTM to end their licensing agreement in 1949.

Index

B

C

Teyro, George, 94
Thomas, Gordon, 94
Thomas J. Watson Astronomical Computing Bureau, 7, 90
Toban, Gregory J., 177
Tordella, Louis, 86
Toshiba, 123
Transistors, 16, 176, 182
Trimble, George, 12, 80, 138–147
Truman, Harry S., 74–75, 174
TX-0, 146
Typewriter, 2, 179

U

Underwood, Francis O., 177
United Aircraft, 14, 77, 166
United States Air Force, 87
United States Census, 3–7, 16
United States National Bureau of Standards (NBS), 128, 174
United States Patent Commission, 129
United States Steel Corporation, 5, 8, 39
Universal Automatic Computer (UNIVAC), 7–8, 16, 106
University of California-Berkeley, 77
University of California-Los Angeles, 90
University of Wisconsin, 176

V

Vacuum Oil Company, 40
Valley, George, 82
Vance, Cyrus, 120
Von Neumann Architecture, 14, 15, 72, 168, 174
Von Neumann, John, 14, 75, 85, 113, 168, 174, 183

W

Wagner, Frank, 77
Wang Laboratories, 116
Watson, Arthur, 121–122, 183
Watson, Jr., Thomas J., 8–9, 16–120, 73–76, 79, 82, 88, 104, 106–107, 110, 114–115, 117–120, 122, 128–130, 152, 175, 178, 183, 189–190
Watson Scientific Computing Laboratory, 6, 56, 75, 90, 96, 128
Watson, Sr., Thomas J., 6–8, 24, 29–30, 40–41, 46–50, 73–82, 100–104, 106, 109–110, 173–175
Watts, Vern, 215
Webb, Cecil, 154–155
Weidenhammer, James, 78

Welch, Gregory, 6
West, Charles, 71
Western Electric, 82
Westinghouse Corporation, 8
Wheeler, D.J., 160
Wheelock, Truman, 177
Whirlwind, 72, 112
Wiesner, Jerome, 82
Wiley, Claud, 121
Wilkes, Maurice, 174, 180
Williams, A.L., 50, 73, 75, 79, 82, 119
Williams, Theodore, 71
Williams Tubes, 9, 85
Wilson, Joseph, 42
WINTEL, 27
Woodbury, William, 71, 177
Work, Tom, 215
World War II, 5, 49, 73, 99–101, 121, 138, 174

X

Xerox Corporation, 106

Z

Zierler, N., 160–161, 165
Ziller, Herrick, 164, 166
Ziller, Irving, 14
Zollinger, Ed, 102, 112
Zuse, Konrad, 16